Heavy

# Heavy

## THE OBESITY CRISIS IN CULTURAL CONTEXT

HELENE A. SHUGART

OXFORD
UNIVERSITY PRESS

Oxford University Press is a department of the University of Oxford. It furthers
the University's objective of excellence in research, scholarship, and education
by publishing worldwide. Oxford is a registered trade mark of Oxford University
Press in the UK and certain other countries.

Published in the United States of America by Oxford University Press
198 Madison Avenue, New York, NY 10016, United States of America.

© Oxford University Press 2016

Library of Congress Cataloging-in-Publication Data
Names: Shugart, Helene A., 1966–
Title: Heavy : the obesity crisis in cultural context / Helene A. Shugart.
Description: Oxford : Oxford University Press, [2016] | Includes bibliographical
references and index.
Identifiers: LCCN 2015041902| ISBN 9780190210625 (hardcover : alk. paper) |
ISBN 9780190210632 (ebook (updf)) | ISBN 9780190210649 (ebook (epub)) |
ISBN 9780190210656 (online content)
Subjects: LCSH: Obesity—Social aspects. | Body image—Social aspects. |
Weight loss. | Group identity.
Classification: LCC RC628 .S494 2016 | DDC 362.1963/98—dc23 LC record
available at http://lccn.loc.gov/2015041902

9 8 7 6 5 4 3 2 1

Printed by Edwards Brothers Malloy, United States of America

# Contents

*Acknowledgments*   vii

1. Introduction   1

2. Calorie Laden: The Official Story of Obesity   19

3. Circumstantial Case: The Environmental Story of Obesity   34

4. Destiny Obesity: The Fatalistic Story of Obesity   51

5. Heavy Legacies: The Cultural Story of Obesity   66

6. Heavy Heart: The Story of Emotional/Spiritual Dysfunction   88

7. Fighting Weight: Stories of Resistance   106

8. Feeling Fat: The Story of Disgrace   127

9. Conclusion: Getting Real   143

*Notes*   155
*References*   191
*Index*   217

# Acknowledgments

Many thanks to the Oxford University Press editorial, production, and marketing staff who guided this manuscript to its final form, especially to Hallie Stebbins, for her supervision, advice, and support throughout the process; and Jamie Chu, for her apt assistance and patience. Thanks also to two anonymous reviewers, who offered valuable feedback and direction at different points of development.

While the argument and analysis in this book are new, portions of some chapters were published in the scholarly journals *Health Communication*—Shifting the Balance: The Contemporary Narrative of Obesity 26(1): 37–47 (2011); Heavy Viewing: Emergent Frames in Contemporary News Coverage of Obesity 26(7): 635–648 (2011)—and *Obesity Reviews*: Weight of Tradition: Culture as an Explanatory Device for Obesity in Contemporary US News Coverage 14(9): 736–744 (2013). Early versions of some of this work were also presented to conferences of the National Communication Association and the European Association of American Studies; and as invited talks at Wittenberg University, the University of New Mexico, and the University of Denver.

Many thanks to good friends who patiently listened to and sometimes argued with several of my ideas as I was sorting through them, especially Dennis Owens, Deborah Elton, Catherine Egley Waggoner, Werner Gellerman, Philip Jeffs, Lynn O'Brien Hallstein, Shannon Jones, Lynn Markert, Theresa Del Casale-Merino, and Kody Partridge. My mother, Anni Shugart, has my eternal gratitude for her unconditional and enthusiastic support of my work; her regular mailings of news clippings about obesity always arrived at just the right time, and not only due to their content. I am so grateful for my partner, Edward Bennett, who not only encourages but facilitates my desires and ambitions, and this project was no exception: he, even more than I, was vigilant about ensuring that I had the time and space to work and write. Finally, I am indebted to Plug, whose steady, loyal presence and companionship was the backdrop against which this project unfolded and made working on it—like every occasion that he graced—a pleasure.

Heavy

# 1

# Introduction

By now, we are all acutely aware that national and, increasingly, global obesity rates are at an all-time high and continue to escalate.[1] The current and anticipated costs incurred by this phenomenon are also familiar to us, most sensationally apparent in reports that health expenditures related to obesity are poised to ruin the national economy, both in terms of direct medical costs as well as, less directly, worker (un)productivity.[2] In addition, other reports describe the national security threat posed by obesity, citing the lack of a physically qualified fighting force.[3] Perhaps the most scandalous assertion among a truly impressive number is that, due to alarming rates of childhood obesity and continuing trends across the general population, this generation of children is the first whose lifespan is expected to be shorter than those of their parents.[4]

For these reasons, experts and officials have characterized the situation a "crisis," "epidemic" in proportion, and in light of even the small sampling of claims mentioned above, it is difficult to refute those designations. They are grave, provocative, and thus demand action; over the last decade, a number of public campaigns and initiatives have been designed and implemented to redress the issue, and myriad proposed remedies have emerged to that end, ranging from self-help literature to weight-loss programs to drugs to surgery. But although these proposals all purport to solve the problem of obesity—with variable success and controversy—perhaps the most important issue to address is what causes it. Everyone "knows" the answer to that question, of course: calories in versus calories out. But that is a deceptively simple answer: science aside, which incidentally rejects that explanation, how people actually think and talk about obesity belies it. In this book, I identify and assess the culturally predominant ways in which people in the United States currently understand, make sense of, and engage the issue of obesity "on the ground." In other words, this book asks: What are the various stories of obesity that are being told today? Why? And what are their implications?

To be clear, this is not a medical treatise that addresses the biology and physiology of fat or the actual causes of obesity: I am not a medical doctor. Rather, I am a cultural critic whose interest and expertise lies in identifying and assessing cultural trends and patterns, and furthermore making sense of what they mean in light of broader cultural, political, and economic contexts. As both a critic and a member of the culture, I am struck by the fact that, despite the ostensibly obvious answer to the question "What causes obesity?"—the one on which scores of campaigns, advice, programs, and interventions are founded—it is only nominally reflected in the ways obesity is taken up in the broader culture: something that may explain, in part, why obesity rates continue to rise despite the considerable collective attention, energy, and resources devoted to addressing the current crisis. In fact, a number of stories about obesity are in circulation today, some complementary to and some in competition with each other. This book is about identifying those cultural stories and evaluating them against the contemporary context in which they occur. Without an awareness and appreciation of how obesity is actually framed and understood by people—and why—attempts of redress are academic, at best.

## What It Means to Be Fat

Fat has always been more than material. While it is certainly a physical property, one that can be touched, seen, measured, and modified, it carries significant weight, in every age and culture. What fat means—indeed, whether and when it means anything at all—is at least as important as (if not more important, than) its existence because how we respond to it, or whether we respond at all, has everything to do with its perceived significance. A very basic example of this is how we define overweight or obesity: Is it 10 pounds over ideal body weight? Thirty percent over it? And how do we determine what ideal weight is in the first place? As drawn against the average size of comparable bodies at a given point in time? As a proportion of body fat, which can furthermore be measured in various ways, often with different results depending on the method? Which way is superior, in that case—body mass index, or BMI, the prevalent method at the time of this writing? Is all fat the same: is there good fat and bad fat? Each of these issues is highly contentious, even today, and even (especially) among medical researchers. Fundamentally, what we decide fat is and means has everything to do with whether, what, and how we do anything about it.

The designation of obesity as an epidemic or crisis reflects our current cultural evaluation of fat—and especially extreme fat—as not only problematic but ominous. And there appear to be grounds for this characterization: the plethora of debilitating, chronic, or even fatal health issues correlated with obesity, such as heart disease, high blood pressure, and diabetes,[5] not to mention the associated economic costs to affected individuals and their families, corporations, medical institutions and agencies, and taxpayers.[6] As I discuss in the next chapter, these premises are actually not so straightforward or uniformly accepted; for now, however, suffice it to say that fat—including obesity, in some instances—has been and still is understood as a positive, even ideal condition in some contexts. This is true even as regards health benefits: some studies suggest that excess weight and even some degree of technical (by current measures) obesity has no significant impact on overall health and, moreover, appears to be correlated with better bone health and greater longevity—the so-called obesity paradox.[7] But it is especially true as regards the social and moral significance, or meanings, of fat.

A number of anthropologists, social scientists, and cultural critics have documented cultures and epochs in which fat has been celebrated and encouraged and why. For instance, in many cultures historically and still today, especially where resources are limited, fat is associated with success and wealth insofar as one's weight is a directly proportionate index of one's resources: a plump, well-nourished body is a visible symbol of one's ability to access and consume.[8] It can also serve as a symbol of physical power, in ways that are often gendered: obese male bodies signify strength and potency in many Pacific Island cultures; Japanese sumo wrestlers also are venerated for their massive size, as are socially high-ranking men of some African tribes, where obesity signifies tribal prosperity and legitimizes political power. In contemporary developed nations, significant physical size, whether by dint of muscle or fat, is desirable among men of disenfranchised communities, especially men of color, for whom an historical legacy of physical subjugation may be salient: it is a means by which a powerful presence can be established in the absence of economic or social capital.[9] Overweight and/or obesity in women has been culturally prized for its aesthetic and/or reproductive value, and these features may implicate each other evolutionarily: excess weight in women is generally perceived as a guarantor of fertility, thereby enhancing attractiveness, in the same ways in which excess size in men is perceived as a guarantor of virility. The Venus of Willendorf figurine is an ancient symbol of this concept, which persists in contemporary cultures as well, for example in Mauritania, Tunisia, and Polynesia, as well as among subcultures in more developed nations, especially those of Latin, Caribbean, or African descent, who valorize "thickness," or fat, in women.[10] In many cultures historically and in some cases today, select members of a given community have been or are "fattened" in order to increase or secure or establish political, cultural, aesthetic, or moral status.[11]

It is important to note that these positive meanings of fat and, more to the point, obesity, make sense—in fact, only make sense—when examined in context: specifically, in political, social, and economic contexts. That is, against the backdrop of scarcity or deprivation, abundance in general, including and sometimes especially as manifested bodily, is an obvious asset. That scarcity may be material, as in lack of food or other resources; or it may be political, as in lack of power to change or influence one's circumstances. But when I write that the valorization of fat only makes sense in this context, I do not mean to imply that this is not reasonable or sensible otherwise. Rather, I mean that fat has meaning, whatever that meaning may be, *only* in context; moreover, those meanings have practical consequences. In other words, negative perceptions of and attitudes about fat and obesity, similarly, only make sense and have particular practical consequences in light of the political, economic, and social conditions in which they occur.

Certainly, obesity is perceived negatively throughout most of the world today, a handful of exceptions, including those already mentioned, notwithstanding. Its ostensibly epidemic and critical proportions, both current and projected, are reported as global, and many nations and international agencies have accordingly launched campaigns addressing the matter, for the reasons cited earlier: significant costs to individual physical health and welfare, as well as economic costs sustained by institutional and corporate entities and, ultimately, the broader citizenry. But these reasons, dismal as they are, don't paint the whole picture of how fat in general and obesity in particular are generally understood negatively today: as with positive cultural perceptions, at least as significant are their social and moral meanings and the contexts that prompt them.

Overwhelmingly, obesity is understood as a failure of character: specifically, a lack of self-control and/or discipline. People who are overweight or obese are perceived as literally materializing their inability to control their excessive appetites, their physical sloth, or both.[12] In a zero-sum sort of way, overweight or obesity can be and has been associated with selfishness, as well, to the extent that one individual's excessive consumption is understood as predicated on denying another. This is especially true in small communities that encounter sudden and extreme deprivation, such as experienced across Europe and the Soviet Union during World War II, and in concentration camps, as an extreme example.[13] There are important gendered, raced, and classed dimensions to contemporary negative perceptions of fat as well, which draw upon pervasive and abiding cultural inequities on these counts. Fat is frequently perceived as feminine or feminizing, for instance, whether apparent on male or female bodies. It is seen as "soft," signifying weakness, passivity, and impotence—as in lack of power or agency, including as relevant to sexuality.[14] Paradoxically, obese women are often perceived as unfeminine—the antithesis of diminutive or dainty, as our contemporary culture prefers women to be. Moreover, obese women suggest voracious female appetites and they literally take up more space, both specters that are especially threatening to the traditional gender order.[15] Similarly, raced connotations are often implicitly or explicitly invoked in relation to obesity rates in ways that correlate obesity among people of color with lack of refinement or consciousness, especially to the extent that race and poverty or working class intersect.[16] Certainly, the correlation between obesity and lower socioeconomic status has been well documented and is common knowledge by now;[17] cultural interpretation of this knowledge often translates into a perception of obesity as déclassé in general, which may take on particular connotations in relation to race.

As with positive perceptions of obesity, however, these negative evaluations only make sense in context. Perhaps not surprising, given that positive connotations emerge in contexts of scarcity, negative ones tend to occur in contexts of abundance.[18] The basic logic here is that when resources are plentiful and easily accessible, virtue is demonstrated by self-restraint. Schwarz documents this initial shift—from positive to negative connotations of fat and obesity—in the United States in the late 19th century, in the wake of the Industrial Revolution, which resulted in national prosperity and abundance, due to the mass production and distribution of many resources, including foods.[19] Farrell makes a complementary case that increasing national prosperity at the time prompted a commensurate valorization of the slender body as a marker of civility, thus distancing US Americans from relatively less developed cultures and populations typically characterized by scarcity—a premise rife with racial and ethnic implications, as Farrell argues.[20] Moral anxieties regarding heretofore unparalleled excess and consumption came to a head in this context, and the fat body became an obvious and readily available scapegoat: public figures, most notably President William Taft, came under significant fire and ridicule for their portliness, despite the fact that stout, even obese public figures proliferate the annals of US history prior to that time.[21] This era, perhaps inevitably, also gave rise to the concept and practice of dieting; E. F. Graham, an early, vocal, and popular diet guru who championed extreme restriction of food intake, created the Graham cracker as one of the first diet foods during this time.[22]

## Obesity Today

Clearly, a context of material and economic abundance goes a long way toward explaining our contemporary vilification of fat. But as critics and historians have established, this context is not new. Why the current alarm about an obesity crisis or epidemic? One answer could well be that current rates of overweight and obesity are at an historic high and increasing. However, that fact is itself contested, including among obesity experts: some suggest that our standards of fitness have shifted, such that people who would have been considered normal weight or slightly overweight in the past now qualify as overweight or obese.[23] Everyone is probably familiar with the frequently cited example of 1950s sex symbol Marilyn Monroe, for instance—specifically, that she would be considered overweight by today's standards. Others point out that our metrics for obesity, such as BMI, do not adequately take into account such things as bone density, fat distribution, fitness level, and other biometrics, so that a BMI over 30 might read very differently on different bodies.[24] Nonetheless, clinically, a BMI of 30 or above currently constitutes obesity and is recorded as such, which could artificially inflate the statistics. And still others argue that rates for overweight and obesity have not increased significantly over the last several decades.[25]

Acknowledging the apparent arbitrariness of current designation of obesity as epidemic or critical in proportion, a number of critics have identified it as a specific instance of a moral panic, characterized by widespread alarm and attendant extreme responses, that occur in particular historical moments and focus on a particular phenomenon, to the point of fetishization, that is perceived to threaten the social order. The exact focus of a moral panic is generally informed by broader, more abstract anxieties or concerns that characterize that point in time. Past examples of moral panics in the United States include, for example, the "Red Scare" of communism in the 1950s, certainly prompted by fears around security and an uncertain future in the wake of World War II; and ritual day-care child sexual abuse in the 1980s, arguably fueled by a backlash against feminist gains as well as anxieties on the part of parents in a time when women working outside the home became a default phenomenon in order to maintain living standards.[26] Identifying current concerns about obesity as a "fat panic," some critics assert that current designations of obesity as critical and epidemic in nature function to (re)secure social control over bodies in an era where conventional strategies, such as force or overt discrimination, are less acceptable or effective.[27] Less abstractly, others place current anxieties over obesity directly at the feet of industries that profit greatly from that panic, what several scholars have identified and described as the "obeseconomy," which has emerged and grown phenomenally in the last decade in direct response and proportion to the identified obesity epidemic.[28] Specifically, the obeseconomy includes commerce around products such as weight-loss drugs, both over-the-counter and prescription; diet foods; weight-loss programs; and bariatric and other surgeries. Although it has less to do with projected sin than with the promise of redemption, the obeseconomy, too, turns on—literally, capitalizes on—the moral dimensions of fat as culturally defined. Another prong of this market features products and services designed to accommodate obese individuals, such as extra-large ambulances, hospital beds, and coffins; cars and furniture; and a host of mobility aids for those too large to walk comfortably, if at all—phenomena that are frequently featured as spectacle in the mainstream, in ways that implicitly chastise those who require them. The entities that profit from obesity of course have a vested interest in a cultural apprehension of obesity as a significant problem, and if they do not function in the same way as broad anxieties about security or consumption do in shaping that apprehension, they have at their disposal considerable resources, primarily in the form of lobbying (hospitals and physicians, for example) and advertising to help ensure that those anxieties remain prominent and profound.[29] Another factor contributing to current perceptions of obesity as critical in proportion, some critics assert, is its manifestation in policies and sanctioned practices—for example discrimination, misdiagnosis, and bullying—that both sediment and fuel fetishistic focus on and panic about fat.[30] Individually and collectively, these observations regarding the fact, dimensions, and consequences of current anxieties regarding obesity are each compelling and actually complementary to this project. My interest is in determining more specifically the exigent anxieties informing current panic about obesity in the United States in particular; and tracing how those concerns manifest and are navigated across various emergent cultural accounts of obesity.

One factor contributing to contemporary concerns about obesity is assuredly fears around national security: specifically, fears of attack or infiltration as well as of vulnerability to those things. If diffuse and for the most part indirect, the line between 9/11 and contemporary alarm regarding obesity is not difficult to trace; certainly, the timeline coincides, for even if concerns about a possible looming obesity epidemic were first identified in 1999,[31] it was not until 2003 that then-Surgeon General Richard Carmona presented testimony to Congress regarding the obesity crisis in the United States and officially placed it on the national agenda.[32] The timing could have been purely coincidental. However, it is notable that obesity has been regularly called out explicitly as a national security threat by government and health officials since January 2003, when Carmona addressed the inaugural California Childhood Obesity Conference. Echoing the gendered features described earlier regarding how we perceive obesity today, specific concerns are that the nation in general and recruits in particular have been rendered too "soft" and "impotent" by fat to defend the nation.[33] Moreover, concerns about "tightening" and "controlling" national security and borders are mirrored and materialized in exhortations, as well as practices, directed to controlling our bodies to keep them lean and vigilant.[34] My point here is not that current anxieties about national security have fabricated or even prompted an obesity epidemic; rather, because these anxieties were and continue to be so exigent, they inevitably shape and even direct our perceptions and understandings of social issues and trends, especially those that feature symmetrical cultural anxieties—about control, vulnerability, and impotence, in the case of obesity. Moreover, the body is an imminently obvious, available, and tangible field on which to project profound and abstract fears that are fueled in the absence of inaccessible, intangible targets: put another way, a war on obesity, which mobilizes several of the same anxieties, appears more promising and productive than a war on terror.

A case can be made, then, that obesity gained purchase and visibility as a critical issue in the mainstream at least in part because of the affective symmetry of concerns regarding control, discipline, monitoring, and strength relevant to both actual bodies and the national body. And this may likewise explain why widely acknowledged and similarly officially designated epidemic levels of heart disease, cancer, or diabetes have not generated the same degree of concern and efforts of redress: none of these are characterized by qualities congruent to the same extent with a national cultural climate of fear. Yet another contextual factor has secured if not intensified the designated crisis proportions of obesity, however: the 2008 financial crisis, whose effects continue to be very much felt. As with concerns about national security, profound and pervasive economic concerns do not create or prompt concerns about obesity and attendant responses to it, but they inevitably inform them and lend them shape and depth. And also as with fears about national security, obesity presents an ideal site of projection for economic anxieties: whereas cultural concerns regarding security and fat converge on weakness, concerns regarding the economic collapse converge with fat on the enmeshed issues of consumption, greed, and excess. This is directly traceable to cultural anxieties about abundance that emerged in the late, post–Industrial Revolution 19th century that effectively turned the moral tide against fat in most Western cultures, as noted earlier; but of course, in the case of the financial crisis, abstract worst-fears regarding the evils of abundance that turned on moral excesses and lapses were concretized to an extreme degree.[35] The well-established (by the time of the collapse) and accepted obesity epidemic provided excellent fodder to further materialize and, more to the point, moralize these anxieties in the same way that it provided material traction for anxieties regarding security: that is, in light of prevailing cultural attitudes, fat and obesity functioned as literal manifestations of the greed, overconsumption, and lack of discipline and control that were universally identified and understood as the causes of the 2008 economic crisis. In other words, profound and exigent economic fears were handily, even logically, projected onto obesity, thereby reinforcing and augmenting its own established crisis status.

Related to that economic context in ways I shall describe momentarily, fueling our contemporary cultural definition of obesity even more broadly and fundamentally is an ideology of individualism. This is hardly surprising, for the United States is thoroughly founded upon individualist principles, both formally—as established in the Constitution—and informally, as reflected in cultural beliefs in and valorization of self-reliance, independence, and autonomy. As described earlier, obesity is consistently and arguably inevitably engaged in the United States in terms of broader cultural and political notions of individualism: fat, much less obesity, is assumed to be an individual phenomenon, specifically indicative of individual character failure(s): lack of self-discipline and self-control, gluttony, and/or sloth. Indeed, the individualist bias in our culture inevitably endows the issue with its moral dimension: that is, one is fat or obese because one is either unable or unwilling to control one's actions, which are both moral transgressions. By the same token, overcoming obesity—or simply having and maintaining physical fitness—signals strength of character. Because individualism is so deeply ingrained in our culture and our psyches to the point that it is accepted as natural fact, it can be difficult to imagine how morality might be other than an individual matter, especially as relevant to our bodies and what we put into them. Complicating the matter of obesity as an exclusively individual issue, however, is the question of financial and physical access to healthy foods, increasingly a subject of discussion, and it inevitably raises the question of whether healthy food should be provided. Is it a right or a privilege; if so, who is responsible for providing it; and how? In different ways, these are all moral questions, but ones that complicate the role or, at least, the extent of responsibility of the individual.

The general specter raised by this scenario, in fact—of structural intervention, regulation, or oversight—is and long has been a sticky wicket in light of the culture's powerful individualist moorings: such things are perceived as diametrically opposed to individual liberties, a relationship traceable, again, to the nation's founding principles and text. So profound and poignant is this configuration in the foundational precepts of the country that individual autonomy is effectively conflated with democracy: many US citizens do not recognize forms of democracy based on different principles, such as socialism or communism. Accordingly, government regulation in the United States is inevitably and inherently suspect by default: any mitigation of individual autonomy is reflexively construed as at least potentially antidemocratic by most citizens. As if this imagined dialectic were not sufficiently intractable, it is further complicated by the powerful presence of the market in the contemporary national landscape, which introduces the matter of consumption into the mix: specifically, individual rights have, over time, become imbricated in the right to access and consume goods and services. The matter of oversight and regulation of the market, or the businesses and corporations that furnish those goods and services, is accordingly often taken up in the terms of individual rights and autonomy—for example, in the case of obesity, restricting the sale of certain foods, like trans fats or Big Gulps, as New York City (then) mayor Michael Bloomberg attempted; or restricting the establishment of fast-food franchises in certain neighborhoods, as the city of Los Angeles has done. Other practices could conceivably entail regulating or even determining ingredients in mass-produced foods; banning the use of hormones, pesticides, genetically modified organisms (GMOs), or antibiotics insofar as any or all of these things are increasingly implicated in obesity; or mandating that businesses provide exercise facilities and/or fresh, whole foods for their employees—and these are but a few examples. Real or hypothetical, these scenarios engender heated controversy and debate regarding cultural, political, and economic priorities and ideals: specifically, as relevant to the appropriate rights, roles, and responsibilities of the market; the government; and citizens-cum-consumers. Indeed, in the wake of the recent financial crisis, these three entities and the relationships among them have been and remain a—arguably, *the*—focal point of contemporary politics in the United States.[36]

While perspectives and policies regarding the appropriate balance among the trifecta of government, market, and citizen vary widely, several scholars have identified the political economy that has held presumption in the United States over the last several decades in terms of configuring these interests as *neoliberalism*. Despite its presumption, and perhaps surprisingly in light of the prominence and significance of the debates around these issues currently, this term remains unfamiliar to most US citizens. This lack of familiarity is in part due to the fact that most political economic philosophies, which posit in various ways a particular relationship between the government and market in social context, are not familiar by name to the general populace. Most citizens would probably be unable to define *utilitarianism* or *libertarianism* if prompted, for example, even if they would probably recognize their principles. But in the case of neoliberalism, it may also be because its basic tenets entail configuring the relationships among market, government, and the citizenry in such a way as to clearly privilege the market to a point that some critics describe as exploitative, and thus it is more profitably (literally and figuratively) left obscure.[37] Operationally, neoliberalism ascribes virtually all responsibility for personal and social welfare to the individual, which is further articulated as crucial to individual liberty under the auspices of choice—a very powerful warrant, given the formative and constitutive nature of individualism to the US cultural identity. Importantly, this individual choice is tightly linked with consumption to the extent that individuals are expected to choose with their dollars and thus customize the priorities (and goods and services to the end of realizing them) that matter to them—in this way, exercising their individual choice is articulated as tantamount to democracy. The theoretical role of government within a neoliberal framework is to ensure that individual choices and desires, which are satisfied by the market in the form of goods and services, as well as advice and expertise, may be sought out, procured, and implemented by the individual at his or her discretion. Thus, under this framework, the practical role of government is to facilitate the market; moreover, government intervention at any level—in the form of social services, for instance, or with respect to regulation of industry—is represented as cultivating or enabling dependence and, more to the point, undemocratic, thus hampering if not denying individual liberties and aspirations.

Political economies are inevitably funded by but not interchangeable with political and economic philosophies, respectively; political economies can be feasibly understood as mobilizations of governing respective political and economic philosophies. Perhaps obviously, then, although it is not the only available mobilization of those philosophies, neoliberalism as it plays out in the United States is founded upon the intersection of the economic philosophy of capitalism and the political philosophy of democracy, which, again, is historically and culturally predicated on—to the point of conflation with—individual liberty. Scholars offer a plethora of examples that illustrate the deployment of neoliberalism, ranging from the massive deregulation of industry that began in the 1980s and continues today, resulting in the rise and domination of large, transnational corporations, to the gutting and, in some cases, eradication (euphemistically, "privatization") of a host of social services, including health and medical facilities and services, unemployment benefits, job training, and education programs, to name but a few.[38] If it remains unnamed in the mainstream, neoliberalism has been central to every national debate about universal health care, for instance. For defenders of the private model, individual responsibility for one's own health care, even at potentially great cost to oneself, is framed as an individual right, and proposed government intervention as an abrogation of that right—a relatively easy impression to secure, in light of founding national precepts that position the government as suspect.

But neoliberalism's presumption as the nation's governing political economy was dealt a powerful blow with the recent economic crisis. As noted, one of neoliberalism's key tenets is the role of government to facilitate and accommodate the market, ostensibly to the end of facilitating the rights, liberties, and self-fulfillment of citizens, a logic that became difficult to sustain in the wake of the 2008 financial crisis, which was by all accounts attributable largely to unfettered—that is to say, unregulated—corporate greed and unethical practices. This has prompted a reevaluation of the proper role of government: significant and abiding questions on the national table since the crisis are whether, and if so to what extent, government regulation and oversight of industry on behalf of the citizenry are warranted. If the financial crisis constitutes the most obvious and visible challenge to the precepts of neoliberalism, they are also being threatened by other notable contemporary social issues, including (but not limited to) gun control and, as noted earlier, health care. These issues, too, turn fundamentally on the contested appropriate relationships among and respective roles and responsibilities of government, the market, and the individual.

As crucial as these matters are, with nothing less than the economic welfare and future of the nation at stake, I suggest that the most profound cultural impact of the recent financial crisis has been relevant to the concept of individualism itself—more specifically, who and what the individual is in the cultural imaginary. Within neoliberalism, which has held presumption for decades, the individual is posited as a rational, self-determined agent, whose identity is secured by autonomy and choice: she or he is the quintessential citizen consumer whose citizenship is secured by consumption. But the financial crisis gave the lie to that imaginary, or at least ruptured it: in the wake of that crisis, in highly visible and public ways, emerged people—not concepts, but people—who challenged the neoliberal version of the individual on every count. Individual rationality was troubled, for instance, by accounts of people who had made unwise choices, whether out of desire, greed, or ignorance; individual self-determination and agency were troubled by incontrovertible evidence that businesses and corporations intentionally misled, manipulated, and exploited people. Moreover and crucially, the neoliberal tenet of consumption as the path to realizing individual liberty and, thus, democracy was deeply troubled. These real people, damaged rather than fulfilled by consumption, proliferated in mainstream screens, pages, and spaces ranging from news reports that chronicled the real, material impacts of the crisis to the nationwide social movement Occupy Wall Street. The

"99 percenters," who comprised Occupy, in fact constituted an explicit pushback against the neoliberal mythology of consumption by exposing the elite privilege and corruption that funds it.

I contend that the recent financial crisis forced a rift between conventionally presumed notions of individualism, as predicated on rationality, self-determination, agency, and (implicitly) privilege; and authenticity, understood as "real" lived, material, embodied, and subjective experience. Authenticity is not a new or unfamiliar concept, even in the mainstream; to the contrary, it is proliferate and resonant. While authenticity can be and is taken up in troubling ways around racial, ethnic, or national "otherness"—for instance, as relevant to establishing "real" Black identity or procuring "authentic" Thai food[39]—the concept certainly has broad cultural traction as an ideal to which all individuals can and should aspire. "Being real" or "getting real," for instance, implying truthfulness and sincerity, have long been culturally valued and are part of the everyday lexicon. Authenticity is likewise contrasted with superficiality and artificiality, including and especially as relevant to the self: people who reveal or embrace their "true," unique selves are celebrated for "being themselves," contrasted with those who are insincere—"fake" or "phony."[40] What authenticity is—or, for that matter, whether there even is such a thing—is notoriously slippery; where and how to draw a line between cultural notions and expectations of self and a self separate from those things is a challenging if not categorically impossible task. But that is beside the point, in general and with respect to current contestations: the fact is that the *idea* of authenticity is powerfully compelling and widely resonant in our culture currently.[41]

The current relevance and resonance of authenticity, ironically, can at least in part be feasibly attributed to the very neoliberalism that is currently deeply troubled by its failure to account for authenticity. A primary—arguably, *the* primary—warrant for the imaginary of the rational, self-determined neoliberal individual is self-actualization. That is, market products and services are promoted under neoliberalism as facilitative of the full realization or at least substantial improvement of the self; thus, individuals must have unfettered access to the full range of what the market can offer in order to make the choices necessary to realize that goal.[42] While self-actualization is not interchangeable with authenticity, the concepts are not unrelated, insofar as each is predicated on a notion of the individual and the primacy thereof. Importantly, although authenticity is not inherently incommensurate with individualism per se—obviously, the self is the crux of each of these concepts—the financial crisis brought these concepts into poignant tension and onto the national stage, thereby forcing a disconnect between broader circulating discourses of authenticity as embodied and felt (for instance, as prompted by what some critics have described as a "therapy" culture, predicated on the primacy of the unique, feeling subject),[43] and individualism as an abstract, homogenizing political concept entirely lacking animus. Individualism as construed, operationalized, and culturally presumed per entrenched neoliberal imperatives—specifically, as predicated on rationality, self-determination, and agency—was rendered in the wake of the crisis as contradictory to and, more to the point, *contraindicative of* authenticity, or "real," embodied, felt human experience. Because, as I have described, exigent social and cultural issues, especially to the extent that they entail questions of regulation, are inevitably informed and often shaped by the broader cultural contexts in which they occur, current contestations around social issues—again, like gun control and health care—reflect this tension around how to appropriately imagine ideals of liberty and choice in relation to "real," lived experience of particularized human bodies.

Obesity is no exception, but it is distinctive as an especially ideal field for this tension for two reasons: first, it is a literally embodied, felt condition; and second, it is inextricably bound up with consumption, a central motif of the presumptive, neoliberal imaginary of individualism. In other words, the current culturally salient tension between authenticity and individualism is specifically, pointedly, and directly brought to bear on the obese body. Moreover, obesity is explicitly located at the very nexus of political economic debates regarding the proper configuration of the individual, the government, and the market. As I describe in the next chapter, obesity's official designation as an epidemic and thus a national priority, together with the official characterization of its causes and redress, are a precise mobilization of neoliberal imperatives. And, like neoliberalism itself, that official story of obesity is in crisis. Consequently, a host of alternative stories of obesity have emerged across the broader culture, each of which turns in different ways, I argue, on authenticity—more specifically, navigating the authentic self in relation to presumptive neoliberal notions of individualism. Assessing these stories not only can offer theoretical and practical insight into the cultural significance of obesity, but also can serve more broadly as a roadmap for evolving contemporary cultural principles, priorities, and politics. Notably, some critics have assessed earlier cultural texts, such as *The Oprah Winfrey Show*,[44] *Queer Eye for the Straight Guy*,[45] and "makeover" reality television shows, such as *What Not to Wear, The Dog Whisperer,* and *The Biggest Loser*,[46] in terms of how they manifested and legitimized neoliberal precepts and sensibilities. A similar impulse drives this project, but I seek to assess how stories of obesity that are told across media fare are informed by and, in turn, shape responses to neoliberalism *in crisis*—or more precisely, responses to the fallout of that crisis, namely the tension that it forced between presumptive individualism and authenticity.

## Taking Measure

I am approaching this task as a cultural critic, which is a rather vague and potentially general designation, so I want to clarify it as relevant to this endeavor. My own approach is interdisciplinary to the extent that it draws on the fields of cultural studies, media studies, and communication studies. Each of these disciplines is vast in its own right, but they converge in my work to the extent that I am interested in how cultural perceptions and practices are produced, circulated, influenced, shaped, challenged, and negotiated. In the broadest sense, then, I am interested in *meaning*—what things mean, why, and how—and I incorporate media studies to the extent that I examine and evaluate mediated messages to answer that question: I believe that media are both a reflection and purveyor of culture. That is, they serve as an index for what is culturally important at a given time, and how and what it means; and they also shape our cultural perceptions, attitudes, and practices. The relative proportions of these functions can vary, although most cultural critics, including myself, are inclined to think that these days, the balance lies heavily in favor of media's function as a purveyor of culture.[47] In fact, cultural studies as a field often dovetails with media studies because this is a key assumption of the field, although media studies more broadly encompasses exclusively descriptive scholarship as well; cultural studies goes beyond this to take an evaluative stance, specifically with respect to the role of power. That is, cultural critics seek to understand what prompts certain issues to become salient in the first place; how they are represented; who benefits from those articulations; who or what is being left out, and why; and/or how are challenges or changes posed and negotiated. To address these issues, cultural critics typically examine phenomena and issues in political, economic, and social context: that is, what other things are going on that engage the issue at hand, explicitly or implicitly? How do these things affect our understanding? With respect to media in particular, cultural critics ask how the political economy of media—that is, their agenda, and who or what drives it—affects what (and whether) we see, hear, come to "know," and do about issues. The concept of media dependency, which asserts that we depend extensively if not primarily on the media for our understanding of the world around us, people, and events, has been long and well established, tracing back to the advent of television as a mass medium, and it is truer today than ever.[48]

By way of example, consider the issue of gay rights in the United States; generally speaking, mainstream tolerance and, to some extent, even acceptance of lesbian, gay, bisexual, transgender, and queer (LGBTQ) individuals and issues have advanced significantly in the last decade or so. Given the extreme and pervasive homophobia that characterized the mainstream not so long ago (and that persists in some contexts), and even if heterosexual presumption remains secure, this is quite remarkable. What might account for this change in attitude and even practice, for instance in terms of legal and policy changes? It's quite a stretch to imagine that it could be a purely coincidental widespread change of heart. To answer that question, a cultural critic could reference the trajectory of relatively recent human rights-based social movements over the last several decades and

increasing mainstream intolerance for discrimination; as well as the AIDS epidemic in the United States, which created greater and inevitably tragic visibility of
the gay men who were disproportionately affected at the time; and extreme, shock-
ing, reprehensible acts of homophobic violence, such as the murder of Matthew
Shepherd. Note that media are implicated here at every turn, which behooves the
incorporation of a media studies angle. Certainly, news media reported on social
movements, the AIDS epidemic, and egregious instances of homophobia, thus
establishing greater visibility. But neither historical trajectory nor simple visibility can explain the turning of the tide: many cultural critics also point to the role
of groundbreaking mainstream entertainment fare in the 1990s and continuing
today—television shows like *Ellen, Will and Grace,* and *Modern Family*; friendly
gay sidekicks (at first) and heroic gay protagonists (later) in mainstream films
like *As Good as It Gets* and *My Best Friend's Wedding* (the former) and *Milk* and
*Brokeback Mountain* (the latter), irrespective of motives, which may have ranged
from an attempt to draw greater audiences with novel or sensationalist fare to
altruism; as well as the significant number of celebrities, musicians, athletes, and
public figures who have come out in the last two decades, like Ellen DeGeneres,
Neil Patrick Harris, Melissa Etheridge, Ricky Martin, Greg Louganis, Elton John,
Wanda Sykes, Anderson Cooper, and Jason Collins. Although these representations and personas are not uncontroversial, as reflected in persistent if increasingly minority homophobic responses as well as concerns of some members of
LGBTQ communities that they may promote assimilation rather than change
(not to mention a distinct privileging of a particular gay white male identity), they
were positively perceived by mainstream audiences. These mediated representations, set in historical, political, and social context, probably did a great deal to
foster mainstream acceptance of sexual identities other than heterosexual.

As noted, the questions about meaning that shape my approach at the broadest
level are communication questions, which I've operationalized in tandem with
cultural and media studies perspectives. More specifically, my communication
training and approach is steeped in rhetoric, which is the study of influence, or
how meanings are shaped, challenged, resisted, negotiated, and/or changed.
Perhaps obviously, this is an ideal theoretical base camp for my work in light of
my interests in culture and media; it also furnishes me with an effective meth-
odological approach and tools to realize those interests. Studies of influence are
accomplished via rhetorical analysis, which, upon repeated viewing and reading
and careful scrutiny of selected texts (which might include television programs,
films, news reports, websites, blogs, magazines, etc.), identifies specific patterns,
themes, techniques, and strategies that assemble symbols and their meanings in
particular ways. While rhetorical analysis can be undertaken in various ways,
I take a critical rhetorical approach, which is especially congruent with my cultural studies commitments: that is, it makes power a central consideration of
analysis. Critical rhetoricians examine not only conventional power—that is,

the rhetoric of official entities, such as government agencies, corporations, and designated experts and authorities—but also myriad other unconventional, resistive, or hybrid forms of it practiced by various factions in various forums. They also don't assume an either/or scenario wherein there are powerful entities and oppressed entities, with a hard line drawn between them.[49] Further, their interest is not simply in identifying and describing rhetorical maneuvers but also investigating how and why those maneuvers influence. Finally, critical rhetoricians are self-reflexive insofar as they recognize that by selecting what (and what features) to analyze and making claims, they are themselves creating rhetoric that seeks to influence and shape understandings about the very thing that they are assessing.[50]

For this project, I am bringing to bear my interests in studying how prevalent cultural meanings around obesity are produced and negotiated in context and with a particular eye toward power—that is, how vested political, economic, and social interests are implicitly or explicitly, consciously or unconsciously, mobilized or challenged in those negotiations. To do so, I examine contemporary mainstream media fare across a range of venues—print, broadcast, digital; as well as genres—news, entertainment, blogs. I am especially interested in assessing the themes and patterns within and across these texts and how they coalesce in distinctive accounts, or stories, of obesity. In so doing, I am myself inevitably engaged in the production of rhetoric about obesity: on the basis of my observations and speculations about what obesity variously means as a member of this culture, I have made strategic choices regarding what to examine, what features to privilege, and how to interpret them. The subjective features of this approach do not inherently qualify the validity of my approach, any more than they do when a medical researcher generates a hypothesis based on impressions; determines what microorganism to study; selects specific aspects or behaviors thereof at the expense of others; and interprets those features, assigning meaning to resultant findings. Furthermore, even though I am studying intangible phenomena, the merits of my findings are still obligated to criteria of accurate, substantial, and representative data—in this case, data gathered from the mediated texts that I assessed for this project—as well as valid and sound reasoning in interpreting that data.

## Intake Assessment

In light of my interests and expertise, the issue of obesity as it is currently engaged is ideal subject matter. As I hope I've established, it's very much a cultural issue: how we define fat in general and obesity in particular is significantly influenced by political, economic, and social contexts and considerations and how, in turn, we interpret them. In other words, absent of those considerations, fat doesn't mean anything beyond its material properties, any more than does a femur or a fingernail. This brings up a very important theoretical issue, however, regarding the relationship between reality and its representation. I am not suggesting that material things in the world are irrelevant and that only our interpretations and representations—that is, only our symbolic exchanges about those things, like words and images—matter. I am suggesting, however, that how we understand these material things and what we do about them are culturally negotiated in highly complex ways. At the same time, the *materiality*, or "reality," of the thing or event and its role in how we construct meaning about it constrains or enables this cultural negotiation to varying degrees: depending on our perspectives, interests, and agendas, we might construct the same collision between two cars as, variously, minor; traumatic; accidental; intentional; one person's fault, or another's. The collision remains a material fact, but how we interpret and/or represent it is relatively variable. On the other hand, interpretation of an event like 9/11 is more constrained—while it can be (and has been) interpreted and represented in various ways, it is virtually impossible to characterize it as insignificant or accidental, for instance.

The body is an especially intriguing field of enquiry in this regard because its indisputable material fact and cultural interpretations of it are so closely entertwined: in other words, because we are products of our cultures and understand ourselves through culture, whether and where we draw the line between our bodily experiences of the world and how to understand them is extremely complicated. The state of illness, for instance, illustrates this very effectively. It is, on the one hand, an undeniable and extremely individual felt physical experience that may be prediscursive or beyond discourse; that is, unable to be effectively (re)constructed by language or other symbols. But it is also discursive, in various ways; consider how some illnesses carry significant cultural stigma, such as AIDS or schizophrenia. Consider further how and where we culturally determine what constitutes illness as opposed to "difference" or even identity: until 1973, homosexuality was understood as a mental illness, and only in 1986 was that designation fully rescinded by the medical establishment. Whether or not a physical condition is identified as illness or health at all is itself culturally determined, either in ways that reflect or complement medical research, and it is also influenced by cultural priorities and perceptions. For instance, consider the differences between how erectile "dysfunction" is perceived and treated in aging men as compared to menopause, which is perceived and treated as natural and inevitable in aging women. Finally, many illnesses intersect with cultural contexts in very much the same ways that obesity has and does; for example, certain strains of influenza, like avian or swine flu, merged with salient contemporaneous political or economic concerns regarding invasion or overtaking, literal or figurative, by foreign "others" to prompt extensive attention, anxiety, and action regarding these "epidemics."[51]

In the case of fat, as well, there is no denying its material existence; moreover, fat, to a greater or lesser material extent, is literally an integral part of *who we are* and inevitably part of our experience of ourselves. But it is also a highly fraught cultural concept, so what it is, what it means, and what to do about it are nearly impossible to distinguish. In the case of obesity—materially, a proportionately excessive (itself a variable designation) accumulation of fat on a particular body— these tensions are brought to commensurate extremes. One of my interests in examining the competing contemporary discourses of obesity is to identify and assess where that line—between fat as material and fat as cultural—is variously drawn in each case; and moreover, where the self is located in that relationship. The body's intersection and engagement of the world, in general terms, inevitably invites consideration of what is apprehended currently as authenticity, the liminal borderland between the self and culture that refuses the primacy of either mate- riality or symbolicity but acknowledges the profound significance of both. In this particular historical moment, the fat body is thus an ideal field for current tension and navigation thereof between the competing imaginaries of rational individual- ism and lived, felt authenticity, particularly around the matter of consumption.

The fact that obesity is such a contentious, even volatile issue today makes it especially intriguing to study in this regard. Even medically, what obesity is and what causes it are highly contested issues, such that the "reality" of fat itself is con- troversial. To cite just a few examples, there are authoritative studies that variously identify genetic predisposition; dismiss genetic predisposition; establish obesity as a threat to health; establish that obesity appears to have no bearing on overall health; assert that all fat is problematic; distinguish between good (brown) and bad (white) fat; establish sedentariness as a key contributor to obesity; establish that exercise or lack thereof has nothing whatsoever to do with obesity. Culturally, as I hope I have established, obesity can serve as field for the projection of anxiet- ies of a particular Zeitgeist; but how those are negotiated and operationalized in any given account, or story, in turn shapes our culture. In other words, stories of obesity are not simply ciphers for or reflections of broader cultural contexts; they "speak back" to those cultural contexts in specific ways, as well, furnishing us with principles and priorities that are relevant not merely to obesity but to and for the broader culture, as well. Thus, although I'm interested in what these stories reveal about obesity, I am also interested in what it reveals about and for broader cultural, political, and even economic negotiations.

Each of the stories of obesity that I assess will very likely be familiar to read- ers already—each has substantial cultural traction and resonance in the main- stream. Notably, each features distinctive, often highly divergent assumptions and implications, particularly around perceptions and practices of consumption. As I will argue, however, each turns on an imaginary of authenticity that is implic- itly drawn against presumptive neoliberal logics of individualism. As such, these stories are productively understood as an index of our culture and, more precisely, contemporary exigent negotiations of our cultural identity.

# 2

# Calorie Laden

*The Official Story of Obesity*

Government and industry response to the identified obesity epidemic has been substantial and varied in terms of energy and resources devoted to the matter; it has come in the form of myriad campaigns, initiatives, literature, programs, products, and services. Irrespective of form or motive, however, these endeavors are predicated on a singular, prevailing theory of obesity, familiar to all: calories in, calories out. That is, the favored explanation for obesity—and its resolution—is that fat is a function of the relationship between calories consumed and those expended, such that excess intake relative to output results in fat. Conversely, caloric expenditure that exceeds intake results in weight loss, or less fat; and a perfect balance between the two results in weight maintenance.

This story of obesity has extensive traction, to the point of being presumed as fact; it is at least as prevalent as the obesity epidemic is visible and notorious. Most people, when asked what causes obesity or how to overcome it, will cite caloric imbalance, and it is reflected everywhere in the mainstream: in aforementioned campaigns and initiatives as well as news, diet books and magazines, weight-loss programs, and advertising for, for instance, everything ranging from appetite suppressants to gym memberships. However, despite the aggressive promotion and wide propagation over the last decade of a plethora of information, goods, and services predicated on this account, rates of obesity have held steady and even increased among some populations.[1] Put bluntly, these efforts appear to constitute a collective failure. This raises the obvious question: How can this be? How can such a broad, multifaceted, and fervent effort fail so dramatically? No other public health campaign, official or unofficial, has experienced the same results, at least to the same spectacular degree, despite the fact that none have featured the breadth or depth of resources elicited in response to obesity: contemporary examples include acquired immune deficiency syndrome (AIDS), smoking, skin cancer, and influenza, all of which have achieved levels of success ranging from at least slight to significant.[2] So what is different in the case of obesity?

There are a few explanations, and many of them dovetail with some of the stories of obesity that I present in the following chapters: fundamentally and functionally, those stories are alternative and often competing accounts of what obesity is, what causes it, and how to prevent or eliminate it, in large part prompted by the fact that the official version simply doesn't wash. The most logical and obvious answer to the question of the ineffectiveness of official efforts, however, is by far the most prevalent, simply because that account does have presumption: that people are failing to practice prescribed actions and behaviors. Specifically, they are not sufficiently disciplined to control their intake and/or ensure adequate output. A secondary explanation for the same outcome that upholds the caloric imbalance story is more lenient: that is, circumstances and/or environmental factors conspire to prevent appropriate individual practices, a perspective that I discuss in detail in the next chapter. But perhaps the most compelling answer to why current mainstream measures and efforts have failed is simply that the theory on which they're predicated—and thus, the story—is wrong.

This assertion is neither novel nor radical among obesity specialists; to the contrary, obesity researchers long ago summarily rejected the caloric imbalance model due, quite simply, to lack of evidence: not room for doubt, not margin of error, but lack of evidence.[3] Rather, extensive research over the last decade commensurate with increasing public concerns regarding obesity strongly suggests that obesity is a consequence of hormonal and endocrinal disruption prompted by a variety of triggers, either in isolation or in concert with each other, including but not limited to (and variously attributed to, across studies) refined and processed foods; food additives; antibiotics; pesticides; plastics; drugs; stress; and lack of sleep. When these triggers are controlled for, simple quantity of calories consumed versus calories expended has been conclusively found to be relatively inconsequential to fat or to weight.[4] For many, this may be a radical revelation, given the entrenchment of the caloric imbalance model. At the same time, it may not be entirely surprising to anyone insofar as it confirms the exceedingly common experience or observation—dismissed as exceptional, ironically—that some people can eat significant quantities of food and/or rarely or never exercise without gaining weight, while others eat modest if not miniscule amounts of food and exercise faithfully but either gain weight or cannot lose it.

My point in noting this is not to assert the actual cause of obesity or its redress; as noted in the last chapter, I do not have the medical or scientific expertise to make any such claim, and moreover, obesity research continues. Although significant current research supports the hormonal/endocrinal disruption theory of obesity, those are each complex systems in their own rights, much less in tandem, so the nature and function of said disruption doubtless warrants further examination. Moreover, there may be other relevant physiological or environmental factors yet to be identified. Rather, my aim is relevant to the substantial gap that exists between obesity as experienced or observed and its official characterization in the mainstream, as represented by government and industry; that gap, I argue, is filled with a host of alternative accounts, or stories, of obesity, each of which function practically the same way: to make sense of the matter. But as described in the first chapter, what obesity is, what is means, and what to do about it in a particular time or place only ever make sense in context: cultural, political, and economic. I am interested in the stories of obesity that have emerged in *this* particular time, place, and context, in light of the failure of extensive and concerted efforts to address the ostensible crisis of obesity.

Prior to embarking on this project—in fact, a necessary precursor to doing so—it is important to examine this prevailing, official account of obesity in more detail because it constitutes a story as well, one every bit as driven and shaped by context as the others to come. A good springboard for that assessment is provided by the questions that are inevitably generated by the mismatch between the science of obesity and that official account, which include: Why is the science of obesity not common knowledge? Why don't authorized official and/or cultural entities address obesity in a way that implements that science effectively? Put another way: why does the caloric imbalance account not only persist but have presumption despite the fact that it has been definitively rejected by science?

The shorthand answers to all of these questions inevitably boil down to context. The more specific answer in this case is that this story is a classic manifestation and mobilization of neoliberal tenets that are themselves currently in contention, as I described in the prior chapter. By centering the individual as rational consumer-citizen, both practically and morally, the "calories in, calories out" story features a particular configuration of government, market, and individual that benefits industry, absolves government of obligation and regulation, and privatizes the welfare of the individual. At least as important a factor in explaining the persistence of the inaccurate caloric imbalance model is that acknowledgment of and action regarding the current science on obesity poses a substantial threat to those imperatives. Aside from the fact that industries that currently profit from the prevailing model—the "obeseconomy"[5]—would be rendered superfluous, thus hampering the market by definition, the specter of structural oversight and regulation of industry more broadly is inevitably raised, for while some of the culprits identified in the litany of upsets to the hormonal and endocrine systems could conceivably be managed, to a greater or lesser extent, by the individual, many if not most cannot, especially in cases where individuals are unaware of the presence of those disruptors and/or have no choice but to consume or be exposed to them. This scenario conscripts and compromises the imaginary of the rational consumer-citizen that funds neoliberalism, which inevitably invites oversight and regulation, translating into a stronger role for government and a minimized one for industry.

I discuss that scenario and its implications in detail in the next chapter, which examines the environmental story of obesity. However, in this chapter I want to chronicle the official account first in order to demonstrate its narrative elements and how they mobilize classic neoliberal imperatives and sensibilities. The official story of obesity, precisely mobilizing neoliberal tenets, turns on a particularized imaginary of individual will and autonomy, which is realized by a responsive market and a benevolent and facilitative, laissez-faire government. That story has proven to lack resonance, however, in part because (like neoliberalism writ large) it fails in practice, but also because it lacks animus: specifically, via the conspicuous absence of authenticity, or the felt, lived experience—real or imagined—of obesity.

## Little Brother

The individual is centered and showcased in every official or culturally sanctioned directed redress to obesity—governmental, nonprofit, industry, and popular media—and each of those efforts tells the story of caloric imbalance. In most of these cases, so central is the individual to this story that the specters, much less the roles, of government and industry are minimized, implicit, or even absent. However, this is obviously impossible in government campaigns, which inherently constitute a form of intervention. Thus, they bear assessment on their own terms: the features and themes that characterize them are necessarily unique, if entirely complementary with other versions of the official story.

The overriding theme of government campaigns is a disclaiming of paternalism—in other words, centering and confirming the individual via the back door. A primary way in which this is accomplished is by focusing on child obesity: that way, even as paternalism is very clearly and consistently disavowed in these initiatives, any lingering whiff of it could be rationalized to the extent that the welfare of children, who are incapable of being fully self-directed, is justified. While directed efforts from nonprofits, industry, and popular media also address childhood obesity, this is not typically, primarily, or consistently the case, as it is with government initiatives.

The most well-known, developed, and organized government initiative regarding obesity is *Let's Move!*, launched in February 2010 and spearheaded by First Lady Michelle Obama. Subtitled "America's Move to Raise a Healthier Generation of Kids," the campaign is described as "a comprehensive initiative . . . dedicated to solving the challenge of childhood obesity within a generation, so that children born today will grow up healthier and able to pursue their dreams."[6] Similarly, the less well-known but thoroughly official National Institutes of Health (NIH) initiative *We Can!* (Ways to Enhance Children's Activity and Nutrition) focuses exclusively on childhood obesity,[7] and that program is also allied with the Department of Health and Human Services (DHHS) as part of a joint *Childhood Obesity Prevention* campaign.[8] Each of these campaigns, accessible primarily online,

features extensive information regarding childhood obesity: its current and projected rates, trends, causes (consistently, caloric imbalance), and solutions. While
*Let's Move!* furnishes a link to information and advice regarding adult obesity, it
is not at all prominent; in fact, it is relegated to the very bottom of the "Physical
Activity" page, one of six pages featured on the website.[9] Childhood obesity in all
of these campaigns is the clear and overriding, if not exclusive, focus.

Accordingly, each of these websites features child-friendly fare: pictures of
children enjoying various physical activities and cooking healthy meals; clickable
cartoon icons designed to appeal to children—large, simple, primary-colored
symbols of sports paraphernalia or vegetables; and promotional videos featuring
familiar childhood characters like *Sesame Street*'s Cookie Monster as well as several featuring sports figures or action heroes. These are clearly included in order to
entice children to access and engage targeted (to them) information on the website, and the tone adopted for that content confirms this: "Help Make Dinner!" and
"Do Jumping Jacks to Break Up TV Time!" and "Try New Fruits and Veggies . . .
there are a lot of sweet and delicious fruits that you can have fun tasting" appear
on the *Let's Move* site.[10] On the *We Can* site, each page features a cartoon drawing
of a character with a speech balloon that states such things as "Children should
get at least 60 minutes of physical activity each day!" and "Packing a healthy lunch
everyday vs. eating out can save you money and calories!"[11]

But the primary audience for government obesity campaigns is indisputably
parents. *We Can!* describes itself as a "national movement designed to give parents, caregivers, and entire communities a way to help children 8 to 13 years old
stay at a healthy weight . . . provid[ing] helpful information and dozens of valuable resources for your family, including tips, worksheets, and tools, all designed
to help your family stay healthy."[12] *Childhood Obesity Prevention*, the joint DHHS
and NIH initiative, is similarly "focused on helping parents and caregivers help
children maintain a healthy weight."[13] And *Let's Move!* notes that

> Parents and caregivers play a key role in not only making healthy
> choices for children and teaching children to make healthy choices for
> themselves. But in today's busy world, this isn't always easy. So *Let's
> Move!* offers parents and caregivers the tools, support and information
> they need to make healthier choices while instilling healthy eating
> habits in children that will last a lifetime.[14]

Some of the suggestions that *Let's Move!* offers parents is to "keep fresh fruit in
a bowl within your child's reach"; "plan a menu for the week. Get your children
involved in planning and cooking"; and "plant a kitchen garden."[15]

Targeting parents (and/or other caregivers, as relevant) for these childhood
obesity campaigns makes obvious sense because parents rather than children
are, by definition, in a position to make decisions for their children, who are

not or cannot be self-directed agents. It is parents who ostensibly have the ability to determine a child's diet and activity level, crucial elements in the caloric
imbalance story of obesity. It is at this point that the second level of disavowal
of paternalism, or "nanny statism," kicks in, however—the first being the choice
of government obesity initiatives to focus on child obesity, despite the fact that,
although that rate is high, it is not as high and does not pose as immediate a health
or economic threat as adult obesity. This second level is apparent in the great
pains taken across these campaigns to frame proffered suggestions, advice, and
resources as optional to parents. This ensures a perception of government as a
benevolent optional resource for citizens but one that is neither responsible for
nor obligated to redress, morally or materially, the obesity epidemic.

Across the board, the campaigns describe themselves as "enabling," "empow-
ering," "assisting," and "encouraging" parents in the fight against childhood obesity. For instance, *Childhood Obesity Prevention* notes that, "In order to reverse
the trend of childhood obesity in this country, it is crucial that parents have the
information they need to help them teach children the importance of healthy eating and being physically active." Thus, the campaign is designed to "encourage
parents and caregivers to challenge their kids to make healthy choices."[16] *We Can!*
predicates its campaign on

> Research [that] shows that parents and caregivers are the *primary influ-
> ence* [italics in original] on this age group. The *We Can!* national educa-
> tion program provides parents and caregivers with tools, fun activities,
> and more to help them encourage healthy eating, increased physical
> activity, and reduced time sitting in front of the screen (TV or com-
> puter) in their entire family.[17]

Likewise, *Let's Move!"* offers parents and caregivers the tools, support and information they need to make healthier choices while instilling healthy eating habits
in children that will last a lifetime."[18] But it is consistently "up to you to choose the
activities that are right for you and your family";[19] the point of these campaigns
is "giving parents helpful information and fostering environments that support
healthy choices."[20]

Although some of these campaigns acknowledge the relevance or roles of
schools, communities, and even industry for childhood obesity, these too are
articulated in terms of resources or venues for individual parental or caregiver
agency rather than responsibility or obligation on the part of those entities.
Parents are encouraged to "talk to the principal about organizing a school health
team" and, in general, "help schools create an environment that will encourage
a child's overall academic success by taking action to encourage healthy meal
options and physical activity programs."[21] In addition to making healthy choices
for their families, *We Can!* encourages parents to

just as important, . . . talk to your friends, co-workers, and others about the importance of eating better, being more physically active, and spending less time in front of the computer, TV, and other screens. Or, you can go even further by . . . convincing a local group (e.g., your employer, your child's school, your church/temple/mosque, your city's park and recreation department) to sign up to become a site that runs *We Can!* programs, or become a partner that contributes in some other way.[22]

These exhortations unequivocally locate responsibility for intervention into the obesity epidemic on individuals: effectively, in the language of neoliberalism, they privatize the matter. Moreover, that responsibility is implicitly laid at the feet of women, in particular: while gender is not specified in these campaigns (other than a page tailored to pregnant women on the website of *Let's Move!*), it is a fact that women remain overwhelmingly the parent or primary caregiver responsible for children's diets, day-to-day activities, and school matters. Thus, appeals to "parents" in this vein inevitably confer greater responsibility for childhood obesity upon women.

In fairness, the privatization of health, especially in the United States, is not new with obesity. A number of economists, political scientists, and social critics have chronicled this trend across the last several decades, and it is certainly highly concomitant with individualist principles foundational to the United States,[23] not to mention both philosophically and chronologically commensurate with (if not fueled by) the rise of a neoliberal political economy.[24] One of the first to describe this trend, Crawford introduced the idea of "healthism"—that the individual is, at base, morally responsible for his or her own health, and attendant practical and economic actions, articulated as a matter of personal choice, logically follow from that imperative. As discussed earlier, a caloric imbalance account of obesity, reliant as it is upon individual consumption and expenditure of calories, dovetails perfectly with this perspective, which does much to explain its tenacity and its proliferation in official attempts of redress despite the fact that it is, plainly stated, wrong.

Thus, an assessment of government campaigns designed to address the obesity epidemic confirms the centrality of the self-determined individual in the official story of obesity: specifically, obesity is a matter of individual responsibility and agency. Moreover, those campaigns secure an understanding of government as benevolently facilitative, if distant: willing and eager to provide information and resources, but only at the behest of the ultimately passive individual. Structural interventions are not proposed or addressed beyond their articulation as a possible scenario should individuals, singly or collectively, seek to create, initiate, and manage school, community, or school programs, which conveniently redefines structural intervention to a point that actually denies it. While industry is not engaged directly in any of these campaigns, the fact that the other two neces-sary premises of individual choice and facilitative government are so thoroughly established is, on the one hand, sufficient to set the stage for a neoliberal frame-work. Furthermore, industry is, in fact, inherent in these campaigns to the extent that the choices available to individuals—especially in the form of foodstuffs and health goods, and services—are implicitly understood to be furnished by the market—and sometimes explicitly, as when, for instance, *Let's Move!* notes that

> five of America's largest media companies have teamed up with Pinterest and the Partnership for a Healthier America on an effort to make it easier for their millions of online visitors to put nutritious meals on the table every day. Condé Nast, Hearst Magazines, Meredith, Food Network and Time, Inc. have identified thousands of nutritious recipes that meet the guidance that supports USDA's [United States Department of Agriculture] MyPlate, and are labeling, compiling and promoting these recipes on their most popular cooking websites. Check out a new Pinterest page for thousands of recipes, a site that pro-vides a one-stop- shop where parents, beginner home cooks and even the most experienced chefs can find and share healthier recipes.[25]

Similarly, *We Can!* is partnered with a number of organizations and corporations; in its invitation to become part of that alliance, the campaign notes that "Each *We Can!* partner brings something unique and valuable to the mix. That's why *We Can!* is thankful that you are considering using your experience and resources to help spread science-based messages about maintaining a healthy weight to even more American families."[26] If direct profit is not at issue here, the promotion of the marketplace as the ideal and most convenient supplier of the resources touted in the campaigns is notable. Furthermore, the articulation of government and industry as allied in the interest of self-determination of the individual consumer-citizen is significant: indeed, it is the basic plot of the story of neoliberalism.

## Trade Mark

The centrality of the individual to the caloric imbalance account of obesity is reflected and elaborated upon in the market in the form of diet books and maga-zines, weight-loss programs, and gyms, all of which are likewise founded upon the caloric imbalance theory of obesity. In these variations, however, the specter of government is entirely absent, and the market is explicitly and ardently advanced as the purveyor of resources necessary to the redress of excess weight.

As noted, the overriding focus of government campaigns is childhood obesity, feasibly understood as a defense against potential charges of paternalism, and the agent in question is the parent or caregiver. Market efforts, however, which constitute the other locus of the official account of obesity, overwhelmingly focus upon adult obesity; while childhood obesity is occasionally identified, it is peripheral. This makes sense for a number of reasons: first, while childhood obesity numbers are certainly high, adult obesity rates far outstrip them; second, because children do not have purchasing power, adults are the obvious target for the market; and/ or, third, the assumption may well be that goods and services of which adults avail themselves will "trickle down" to children, directly or indirectly.

Also logical is the fact that redress to obesity offered by in the market is highly specific, unlike the general, vague, or intangible advice and resources offered in government initiatives. To that end, the caloric imbalance account of obesity is mobilized in concrete ways in industry response, and the individual's agency and responsibility in relation to that theory similarly gain definition: that is, the actual number of calories consumed and expended, respectively, by an individual becomes paramount. The market's relevance comes in the form of providing tools and resources designed to monitor and/or regulate the ratio of calories, and the individual's agency and responsibility accordingly is directed to securing and utilizing those tools and resources to the end of monitoring and regulating his or her caloric intake and output.

Those tools and resources run the gamut and include (but are by no means limited to) tables and charts chronicling the number of calories of a given food or the number of calories burned while engaging in a certain activity; gauges that count the number of steps one takes a day; personal trainers; and prepared meals delivered to one's door. Jenny Craig and Medifast, for instance, two of the most prominent weight-loss programs in the United States, offer meals or "meal replacements" that are "low in calories and fat,"[27] "a model of balance, variety and moderation."[28] Although Weight Watchers, the most popular and well known of such programs, does not furnish prepared meals, it does offer a number of similarly "balanced" recipes, many furnished by corporate food sponsors like Welch's and Gorton's, as well as its "PointsPlus" plan, which assigns every food a value: "one easy-to-use number, based on protein, carbohydrates, fat and fiber content."[29] To assist members with their efforts, all of these programs offer counseling—either "in-centre" (at locations across the country) or with a "one-on-one coach" (Medifast) or "consultant" (Jenny Craig)—and access to "community," or support groups, also available either at designated sites or online. Moreover, each program features a host of "digital tools and mobile apps," such as planning and tracking software and databases as relevant to food and exercise. All of these features, and the programs more broadly, are predicated on the caloric imbalance model; meals, meal replacements, and tools are all relevant specifically to managing the ratio of calories consumed (primarily) to those expended.

Diet books and magazines—in the latter case, sometimes dedicated diet magazines but more often feature articles in health, fitness, or women's or men's magazines—are similarly predicated upon caloric imbalance. Magazines and magazine articles (and complementary websites) feature the same focus found in weight-loss programs, where emphasis is on appropriate foods—what kinds as well as when, where, and how to eat them—and increasing exercise. For instance, recent issues of *Health* magazine featured articles on "Weight Loss Tips that Work!" (March 2013) and "Surprising Foods that Fight Fat" (October 2012); recent fare on *Self* magazine's website similarly featured articles titled "How Many Cals in that Omelet?" and "Build Lean Muscle in 8 Moves."[30] Not surprisingly, gendered stereotypes proliferate in women's and men's magazines as relevant to weight management: proportionately greater emphasis is on food (counting calories, literally or figuratively) for women and on exercise for men: "Get Ripped!"; "Torch Fat Faster"; "Build a Badass Body" have all been feature articles (some linked with products) on *Men's Health*'s website,[31] and *FHM* similarly features articles regarding, for instance, "How to Understand Fitness Supplements and Get Ripped."[32] While the majority of diet books (and their accompanying websites) available in the mainstream subscribe to the caloric imbalance model in conventional ways by offering calorie-restricted plans, strategies, and advice, some popular diet "fads" feature some variation on it, or hook, to distinguish their approach in ways that sometimes even appear to reflect current science regarding the quality of food. These include low-fat diets (popular gurus include Dean Ornish as well as John and Mary McDougall); low-carbohydrate diets (e.g., the Atkins diet); high-protein diets (e.g., the Paleo Diet); "formula" diets, which advance a carefully calibrated balance between fat, carbohydrate, and protein (e.g., the Zone diet); juicing diets; single-food diets (e.g., the grapefruit diet); and blood-type diets, which suggest that people with particular blood types should consume or avoid corresponding particular foods in order to maximize weight loss. Although these books take very different tacks to the matter of overweight and obesity—and in some cases offer novel, even apparently radical theories about what causes excess fat—in fact they all can be said to operate under the auspices of the caloric imbalance model to the extent that they rely upon proportion and regulation of intake rather than the actual quality of food consumed. Most significantly, they all staunchly reflect and reinforce the personal responsibility motif that is, after all, the moral of the calories in/calories out story of obesity.

Gyms, of course, address the other side of the caloric imbalance equation: caloric expenditure. Fat-burning, muscle-building, and metabolism-boosting opportunities are furnished in the form of aerobic and anaerobic machines, free weights, fitness classes, and personal training. Many gyms also offer meal replacements and nutritional supplements designed to further foster these aims through caloric intake, even if the emphasis is primarily on managing weight through exercise, or caloric output. Weight-loss products and supplements, which range from diet foods, appetite suppressants, workout DVDs, activity monitors, and machines or "systems" are similarly predicated on the caloric imbalance model in obvious ways, as is the increasingly common gastric bypass surgical procedure, which dramatically reduces the size of the stomach, thereby commensurately limiting the quantity of food—hence, number of calories—that can be consumed.

## Self-Regulation

To the extent that industry response to the obesity epidemic concretizes tools and resources for the fight against obesity, it lends definition to the individual, specifically as relevant to agency. In government campaigns, agency is articulated explicitly and implicitly in terms of choice: one may choose to avail oneself of the information, opportunities, advice, suggestions, and resources presented in these campaigns. While goods and services promoted by the market do not obviate choice—it is inherent in the decision of the consumer to purchase or subscribe to a given resource, of course—they specifically define individual agency in terms of self-control precisely due to their tangibility. This is consistent with the caloric imbalance story of obesity, which defines excess weight as a physiological consequence of how many calories a particular individual consumes versus how many he or she expends. Because adult individuals, the target audience for the market, have control of their bodies and thus determine what goes into them and how they use them, it makes sense that exercising that control is the key to weight loss. More precisely, the specific tools furnished by the market define self-control in terms of monitoring and discipline.

Monitoring of the self is promoted, encouraged, and facilitated by the market at every turn. Weight-loss programs offer a host of "etools"—computer or mobile programs and applications—that help members to plan, track, and monitor caloric consumption and expenditure. Jenny Craig, for instance, offers members a "dashboard" that permits them to "plan a flexible menu of your own," "track your calories to stay on target," and "create a plan for your meals and activities";[33] Medifast offers a "5&1 Food Journal" to complement its program as well as a "Dining Out" guide, among many other planning and tracking tools;[34] and Weight Watchers is predicated primarily on its PointsPlus plan that members can consult in regulating their intake of food, complemented by a host of other "online tools to track your food and exercise, chart your progress, find recipes, workouts and more."[35] Popular diets, as well—available both in books and online—invariably offer charts and databases as well as, sometimes, planning and tracking tools or charts that subscribers can consult and utilize. These range from simple calorie charts to those that isolate for one nutritional variable, such as fat (e.g., the Ornish Diet), protein (e.g., the Paleo Diet and the Dukan Diet), carbohydrates (the Atkins Diet), or glycemic value (the Zone Diet). These charts are designed to be consulted by subscribers to the end of monitoring the appropriate value of calories or particular nutrients that they are consuming. Indeed, the FDA-required nutritional breakdown for packaged foods serves the same purpose: even if it is not promoted and is instead offered in a manner more consistent with the "choice" component of individual agency apparent in government initiatives, the breakdown offers consumers an opportunity to monitor their caloric intake.

A number of manufactured products similarly encourage self-monitoring as relevant to caloric expenditure, the other part of the equation. "Activity trackers" range from simple pedometers (which measure the number of steps one takes) to more personalizable sophisticated versions that more precisely gauge activity level, calories burned, metabolism—even sleep patterns, glucose level, blood pressure, and hydration.[36] Most cardiovascular machines available for individual purchase and widely available at gyms perform the same function, tracking distance "covered" (for instance, on a treadmill, stationary bicycle, stair machine, or rowing machine), calories burned, and heart rate during the time the machine is in use, either as measured against an average individual or personalized data. Most recently, a host of interactive products that turn on monitoring calories expended have appeared on the market, ranging from workout video games compatible with NintendoWii, PlayStation, and Xbox to applications like Fitocracy, which "gamifies" one's activities, assigning points based on kind of activity, activity level, age, weight, and gender; and Polar Beat Fitness Coach, which "will keep you paced [during your workout] by reminding you of how much time you have left . . . There's also a live map to show you where you've been, and displays for your distance, calories burned, pacing and heart rate."[37]

If monitoring of the self is a primary way in which the individual gains dimension in the market response to the obesity crisis, discipline of the self is the point of that monitoring. Awareness of one's caloric intake and output makes it incumbent upon the individual to strike an appropriate balance between the two as relevant to weight loss, in keeping with the story of obesity as caloric imbalance, and this is articulated as precise regulation and control of one's intake and output. Diets, of course, are explicitly predicated on this: whether, what, and/or how much one eats, in terms of calories and/or particular nutrients, constitute the basic premise of any diet, such that the extent to which one controls one's eating along directed lines determines how effective the diet will be—in other words, whether or not one will lose weight. Across diets, certain foods are generally deemed "bad" or "good," or at least better or worse, although which foods occupy which camps vary according to diet. Similarly, every diet is predicated on restriction, typically severe, if not elimination of certain foods—for instance, fats, carbohydrates, sugar, wheat, and so forth—depending on the nutrient deemed calorically suspect. Thus, discipline is demonstrated by eating "good" foods, however defined, despite inevitable and constant temptations. Conversely, people who eat "bad" foods—who "fall off the wagon" or "can't resist"—lack discipline, at least temporarily. While appetite suppressant drugs, another popular market offering for weight loss available via prescription as well as over the counter, are not predicated upon particular foods, they certainly turn on the caloric imbalance model as well, operating on the premise that less food—fewer calories—consumed is tantamount to weight loss. Gastric bypass surgeries represent a more extreme and permanent variation of the same logic.

Discipline is also apparent as regards caloric output, or exercise, although in less concrete ways. The very tangibility and modifiability of food—its ability to be weighed and measured and broken down in myriad ways—lends itself to categorization, however determined. But activity is primarily drawn against inactivity in the prevailing story of obesity, so that any exercise is good, potentially effective, and thus demonstrative of discipline, even if some forms are identified as more efficient than others: some high-intensity or targeted activities may be identified, for instance, as "fat blasters" or "butt sculptors." Because caloric expenditure is far more general and ephemeral than consumption in the caloric imbalance model, however, discipline is encouraged through motivation. Gyms offer motivation directly, in the form of personal training services and fitness classes, as well as indirectly: most gyms (and their websites) are decorated with inspirational posters, for instance, featuring renowned athletes or pithy quotes ("Winners Embrace Hard Work!";[38] "We Are All Athletes")[39] and success stories—members who have lost significant amounts of weight that they attribute to exercise. Health magazines regularly publish articles designed to encourage readers to exercise, ranging from explicit exhortations ("Get a Motivation Makeover")[40] to appeals to efficiency ("10 Fast Weight Loss Tips!")[41] to challenge ("Push Your Limits")[42] to incentives ("Bikini Body Workout")[43] to success stories, a staple feature of every major mainstream health magazine. And a host of fitness trends and exercise regimes available as DVD sets or classes—in the last decade, they have included spinning, yoga, Pilates, Tae Bo, boot camp, and Zumba—devote extensive resources to motivating potential consumers, as demonstrated in the 30 to 60 minute infomercials that proliferate broadcast stations and feature numerous testimonials, celebrity endorsements, and the promise of physical transformation. Although motivation is not interchangeable with discipline, the fact that so much attention and so many resources are devoted to motivation on the caloric expenditure side of the equation underscores the necessity of discipline in ensuring weight loss in this story.

## Project Obesity

The logic of the caloric imbalance story of obesity is highly compelling on a number of levels. Perhaps most appealing is its elegance and simplicity—obesity is rendered a mere matter of arithmetic, such that both cause and solution are obvious and straightforward. Culturally, it is compatible with the individualist moorings that have long defined the United States; autonomy infuses every telling of this story. At the political economic level, this account is furthermore highly congruent with neoliberal logics and imperatives, which privatize social and individual welfare and privilege industry, even (perhaps especially) in relation to public crises. Inconveniently, obesity research does not bear out this account, currently or historically, but as noted, this is a little known fact, and the caloric imbalance story continues to have broad and profound popular presumption, probably for the reasons cited above—a version of "if the facts don't fit the theory, change the facts." Nonetheless, if paradoxically, this story fails to resonate with the populace even as its members accept and recite it: they may know it, but they aren't feeling it. This is undeniably attributable in part to the simple fact that the caloric budgeting doesn't work; even if people don't know or believe that, they experience and/or observe it when they or others diet and exercise but cannot lose weight or, conversely, consume substantial amounts of "bad" foods and don't exercise but don't gain weight. But I contend that the chief reason that so many alternative accounts of obesity are in play is because the official one simply doesn't ring true.

The caloric imbalance story of obesity is highly appealing because of its rationality—and this is precisely where it falls apart. The promoted success story, so to speak, is entirely reliant on the individual, who is charged with managing the caloric budget, and to do so effectively, she or he must necessarily be rational. However, humans are not exclusively or even mostly rational: they are motivated by myriad things, among them rationality, but also emotions, desires, pleasures, obligations, aversions, and many, many other things. Thus, a basic reason for the failure of this story is that it mischaracterizes the individual as an exclusively rational agent, which furthermore entails disembodiment by making him or her an agent of his or her objectified body. Another narrative flaw in this account, similarly traceable to assumptions of the rational individual, is its failure to acknowledge the complex and multilayered significance of food. While it certainly is and can be understood as fuel or as quantifiable energy (i.e., calories), it is almost always profoundly more than that in practice. Rather, it is highly personal, rife with culture, identity, class, nostalgia, pleasure—or, as the inverse case may be, revulsion, fear, antipathy, and erasure of identity or culture. For example, the consumption of "comfort foods" or favored dishes of one's childhood and/or culture is extremely meaningful, at least as significant—and typically far more significant—a reason for its consumption as sustenance. Similarly, consuming unfamiliar foods or those one has historically perceived to be unappetizing engenders considerable disappointment and irritation, irrespective of their nutritional value and typically dramatically disproportionate with perceptions of taste of the foods per se. Moreover, consumption of food is a profoundly visceral, sensual, and intimate experience: as several theorists have noted, the taking of food into our bodies is perhaps the most fundamental (not to mention earliest and formative) experience of all, a primal and profoundly intimate way of connecting with the world—literally, taking the material world into ourselves—and thus collapsing material and symbolic, the real and the imagined. Layered upon that, of course, is how, where, why, and by whom it is prepared, which is inevitably infused with culture, including social and political relations such as power, gender, class, race/ethnicity, and nation: all of this, too, is literally taken in with food.[44] In other words, it is impossible to eat and not be a very specific, embodied subject.

The tack of the official story of obesity is to cling stubbornly and exclusively to individualism as defined (arguably coopted) under neoliberalism—specifically, the rational, entirely self-determined consumer-citizen. And that is its downfall: the mandated disembodiment of the rational agent in this account, in tandem with the requisite denial of the deeply intimate significance of food, expose a conspicuous, fatal absence in the caloric imbalance story of obesity: authenticity, especially insofar as it speaks to the experiences of and relationships among the material world, the self, and culture. Accordingly, when people are encouraged to monitor and discipline their bodies and their food and, moreover, engage them as not only generic but suspect objects, they are effectively being asked to distance themselves from and suppress, if not deny, their felt, subjective, *authentic* experience. The denial of authenticity necessitated by the official story of obesity is impossible to sustain simply because obesity and the consuming practices that are so tightly linked with it are inevitably, incorrigibly embodied and intimate. In tandem with the failure of formal efforts of obesity redress, the absence of authenticity inevitably gives rise to a wellspring of alternative stories that step into that breach, which I will discuss in the following chapters. To the extent that authenticity is, in this historical moment, drawn specifically against rational individualism, each of the competing stories of obesity that ensue can be productively read as navigations of broader tensions relevant to cultural identity in the United States: specifically, what individualism, the founding precept of that identity, means, especially as it relates to practices of consumption. How each story respectively narrates obesity offers insight into those broader negotiations; in turn, inevitably, how those tensions are resolved will likewise feature implications, symbolic as well as practical, for obesity.

# 3

# Circumstantial Case

*The Environmental Story of Obesity*

The most explicit and readily available story of obesity that counters the official, "calories in, calories out" account is environmental, which asserts that obesity is attributable to situational factors ranging from the particulars of one's circumstances to meta-level trade and commerce policies. This collective alternative story, and the fact that it is the most explicit in the mainstream, is arguably inevitable because it is diametrically oppositional to the "official" one—even if it is not necessarily the most resonant of competing stories of obesity. This is so, I argue, because the environmental story relies entirely upon the reactive decentering, sometimes to the point of erasure, of individual agency on which the official account of obesity turns. Commensurately, the role of government—significantly downplayed if not absent in the official account—assumes that central role in the collective environmental account of obesity: the consistent antidote to the obesity epidemic proposed across environmental accounts is strong and active government intervention, regulation, and/or oversight. The market is the wild card in this overarching narrative; depending on the version, it is either absent or the chief (or exclusive) culprit; in the latter case, the nature and degree of culpability varies across versions. Ultimately, however, the environmental story of obesity does not earn clear cultural sanction for the very same reason that the official account doesn't: because authenticity is not acknowledged, much less engaged, such that the felt experience of obesity—whether materially experienced or apparent in anxieties regarding it—is denied.

Three versions of the collective environmental narrative about the current obesity epidemic are readily and explicitly available in the mainstream, primarily in news coverage and acclaimed, best-selling books penned by recognized experts in obesity or closely related relevant fields, such as food journalism or policy: (1) lack of access on the part of individuals to information, resources, and/or opportunities for redress; (2) compromised food supply; and (3) corrupt industry. Of these, access is by far the most prominent in the mainstream, both in terms of its availability and its perceived credibility. This is largely so because the facts on which it is founded are rather irrefutable; controversy may inhere with respect to what (or whether) to do about them, but not with the facts themselves. Conversely, the environmental account variants relevant to food supply and industry corruption, respectively, are inherently contentious to the extent that not only the claims but the data on which they rest are often contested, on grounds ranging from empirical validity to political or ideological motive. The inherent controversy that characterizes these last two versions of the environmental story of obesity may well constitute another reason why the environmental story of access is considerably more proliferate in the mainstream.

## Access Denied

When the received, or official, story of obesity—caloric imbalance—is challenged or elaborated at all, uneven access to means of redress is typically the first counternarrative tendered. Although there are several loci for this variant of the environmental story, they each turn on lack of access on the part of at least some individuals to information, resources, and/or opportunities cited as critical in countering obesity. What is notable about this account—and likely a primary reason why it is has more traction than other environmental variants, as noted—is that it does not necessarily challenge the premises of the official story, which places primacy on individual agency and responsibility; rather, it describes obstacles to those things, or unevenness in opportunities to realize them.

Most of the conversation around access in relation to obesity is relevant to socioeconomic status: that is, working- and poverty-class individuals are at a marked disadvantage with respect to obesity. This fact is incontrovertible: scores of credible studies and reports from various quarters definitively establish that obesity is significantly more prevalent in these populations.[1] At least to the extent that people of color are more likely than whites to populate these lower socioeconomic ranks, race and ethnicity are relevant considerations, as well.[2] Perhaps obviously, then, the first premise of this narrative is the sheer cost of products, services, and practices endorsed as healthy in the official story, specifically as relevant to diet and exercise.

As widely noted in the mainstream and likely personally familiar to all, foods designated as healthy and wholesome are significantly more expensive than "obesogenic" ones, or those clearly identified as correlated with obesity. Mark Hyman describes the classic dilemma as relevant to a conversation overhead at a grocery store:

> "Oh, these avocados look good, let's get some." Then looking up at the price, they said, "Two for five dollars!" Dejected, they put the live avocado back and walked away from the vegetable aisle toward the aisles

full of dead, boxed, canned, packaged goods where they can buy thousands of calories of poor-quality, nutrient-poor, factory-made, processed foods filled with sugar, fat, and salt for the same five dollars. This is the scenario millions of Americans struggling to feed their families face every day.[3]

Moreover, and likewise widely reported in the mainstream, obesogenic foods are substantially more energy dense than healthy foods, making them extremely energy efficient in the short term: one bunch of broccoli, for instance, weighing in at about 608 grams, contains 207 calories, as compared to a 100-gram serving of potato chips, which contains 560 calories.[4] Although some journalists and writers have challenged this assessment, they are few and they generally invoke specific conditions: that is, comparing the cost of an average fast-food meal for an average family against whole foods prepared at home; or comparing the long-term costs of a healthy, whole foods diet versus a processed one.[5] In terms of simple and immediate economics—financial as well as physiological—"unhealthy" foods clearly trump "healthy" ones, and for individuals with limited means on both counts, healthy foods are simply not an option in any event.[6]

Less visible in this environmental account but also salient is the cost of exercise, the "calories out" tenet of the official discourse. Its relative lack of prominence may be due to the general amorphousness of exercise: that is, that any movement or activity is deemed valuable in the fight against obesity. A common refrain is that one can get exercise anywhere, for example by taking the stairs instead of the elevator; doing sit ups at home; or parking at the furthest end of the lot. However, those with proportionately greater income are more able to afford products, venues, and services—ranging from appropriate footwear to gym memberships to personal training—that substantially increase their odds of realizing and sustaining effective (per the conventional model) levels of exercise. Moreover, the impoverished diet associated with lower socioeconomic status described earlier may have an adverse effect on one's ability to exercise as well. Health complications other than obesity attributable to a poor diet and impoverished circumstances in general, such as heart disease, osteoporosis, joint inflammation, or risk of stroke, can make exercise painful or even dangerous for affected individuals.[7]

Literal access is also addressed in this particular variation of the environmental discourse, especially as relevant to working and poverty class populations. That is, most individuals within these demographics live in locations—urban and rural—that have been coined "food deserts" due to the dearth of healthy, whole foods, especially fresh fruits and vegetables, available to residents. The nearest market is often several miles away, itself offputting, and especially so in light of the fact that many with limited incomes do not own transportation, so they must factor in the time, energy, and money of walking and/or public transit (if available) to purchase these foods—which, again, are significantly more expensive than processed fare typically available in their immediate neighborhoods, in the form of fast-food franchises and convenience stores disproportionately prevalent in these areas. In the case of rural poor populations, due to challenges imposed by geographic distance as well as a dearth of *any* nearby food options, grocery shopping may be a once-a-month event or even rarer, in which case stockpiling packaged foods with a long shelf life makes considerably more economic and practical sense. Several reasons for this phenomenon exist, ranging from (in urban areas) limited space, which prohibits supermarket-size venues; increased vermin populations that are attracted by fruits and vegetables, prohibiting smaller markets and grocery stores; cheap property values that attract fast-food franchise and convenience store operations; and for both urban and rural impoverished populations, most significantly, limited demand of local consumers who cannot afford healthier options, complemented by greater demand for cheaper, highly processed fare—which has further been demonstrated to evolve into individual and even cultural preferences over time.[8]

Geographic access to exercise is also identified as an issue in this account, specifically as relevant to conducive or even, in some cases, safe spaces in which to do so. Urban poor communities, in particular, often live in locations that feature very busy streets or highways, no foot or bicycle paths, and no green spaces, such as parks, in their vicinity, severely circumscribing the forms of exercise available to them. Furthermore, most low-income urban neighborhoods feature substantially higher rates of crime, in general and including against persons, making the choice to exercise risky in terms of personal safety in addition to impractical. While rural poor populations do not face these same constraints, they may be limited or inhibited by exposure to elements and/or inhospitable or dangerous terrain.[9]

If less prominent in the access narrative than money and geography, time is also featured, to the extent that the working poor, in particular, are likelier to have far less of it available to exercise, shop for, and prepare healthy foods. Many hold more than one job in order to earn a living or even subsistence wage; moreover, as noted previously, many do not own their own transportation, so the time necessary to walk to and from, wait for, and take public transportation—which may feature multiple stops and transfers—is an added impingement. If children are involved, tending to their needs represents yet another demand on time. While time constraints relevant to healthy practices are not unique to the working poor, they typically number more and are more extreme than for other populations.[10]

Finally, access to medical care and even information is markedly less available to working and poverty classes than it is to more economically privileged populations, which constitutes another dimension of the access discourse of obesity. While not unique to obesity, individuals of lower socioeconomic status are likelier to have no or limited health insurance, so health advice and/or treatment regarding weight and obesity is less accessible. Even those who do have insurance may avoid seeking medical care except in the most dire of circumstances due to expenses incurred in the form of copays or deductibles, and individual obesity is generally not understood as dire. More abstractly in terms of access, even "free" public health campaigns and initiatives that feature advice and information about obesity implicitly target populations with relatively higher socioeconomic status, as described in the prior chapter, for example by assuming that one has money and time to procure and prepare "healthy" foods. The majority of these campaigns do not address or, often, even acknowledge the circumstances of less advantaged populations, much less the particular challenges relative to obesity confronting them. Moreover, these campaigns are rarely tailored to non English-speaking populations, who are likelier to be poor and may feature additional variables in relation to obesity, such as a strong cultural preference for "fat" babies and children.[11]

While this narrative of access, or lack thereof, troubles the locus of the official account of obesity—individual agency—it does not inherently challenge it. The caloric imbalance account of obesity retains presumption insofar as appropriate individual caloric consumption and expenditure remain articulated as key to obesity redress. The access narrative thus functions descriptively, to explain or perhaps elaborate upon higher rates of obesity in some populations by furnishing context, but the practical implications of this story are decidedly ambiguous, for no recourse is inherently demanded by it. Indeed, because individual *responsibility*, unlike agency, is not explicitly countered in the access narrative, one response could be that working and poverty class individuals must put in extra or innovative effort to eliminate or prevent obesity, a "pull yourself up by your bootstraps" directive. On the other hand, the access narrative is typically accompanied by vague suggestions of redress in the form of intervention, by (variously) individual, community, local, state, or federal entities, to, for instance, create community gardens or green spaces or to incentivize grocery stores in food deserts. If these directives are generally not coherent or specific even when they are forthcoming, the story of access does introduce at least the specter of a rethinking of government or other regulatory agents, such that a more active and interventionist role is warranted if not incumbent. Other environmental narratives, however, are considerably more precise on this count: if the story of access pushes back against presumptive neoliberal logics that inform the official account of obesity, the respective environmental accounts of compromised food supply and corrupt industry deal serious blows to them.

## Bigger Living through Chemistry

A second environmental account of obesity that is rapidly gaining mainstream traction—what I call the compromised food supply story—is based on the actual current science of obesity, briefly described in the last chapter. Again, that science establishes that obesity is the result of endocrinal and hormonal disruption, and increasing rates of obesity are directly attributable to and proportionate with the number of powerful disruptors present in the environment. Moreover and significantly, most of these disruptors are inherent to the contemporary US diet. Despite extensive, very well-established, and virtually uncontested evidence for this assertion among scientists for decades, its entrée into the mainstream has been remarkably slow and continues to encounter considerable controversy. This is so for at least two reasons: first, the official account of obesity as a matter of caloric imbalance has such powerful and long-held presumption that any challenge to it would inevitably be controversial, dismissed as radical or "weird" science or as perhaps prompted by questionable motives, especially given that the conventional model is entirely scrapped in this discourse: it sounds like a radical and thus inevitably suspect assertion. Second, as I will discuss further later in this chapter, this "alternative" (to the official) account inherently troubles current policies and, more broadly, political economic tenets to the extent that it almost entirely shifts the burden of responsibility for the obesity epidemic away from the individual and to the market. This is so because this variant of the environmental story of obesity specifically indicts processed, refined, and/or mass-produced foods; if different studies identify different biochemical culprits, as reflected variously in this accounting, they converge upon that point without exception.

Perversion of food as relevant to production, refinement, or both is the focus of this narrative in the mainstream, and sugar, in its various incarnations, far and away leads the pack. This does not simply refer to table and baking sugars, labeled clearly as such, although it certainly includes them. But "sugars," per both the science and attendant mainstream account, encompass all simple carbohydrates, including high-fructose corn syrup (HFCS), an ingredient in an extraordinarily high number of packaged foods, as well as carbohydrate-rich foods that have been stripped, via "refinement" or processing, of features that render them complex, such as whole grains; or of features that otherwise mitigate their insulin-spiking properties, in the case of natural simple carbohydrates, such as the skin and fiber of whole fruits and vegetables. The body reads these "stripped" foods as sugar during metabolism, spiking insulin levels (and/or possibly activating other hormonal processes, according to various studies) to the end of triggering fat storage. In the past few years, these findings have been published in books targeting popular audiences by authors such as science writer Gary Taubes and pediatric endocrinologist Robert Lustig,[12] who themselves have become something of emissaries (if controversial, especially in Taubes' case) of the discourse in mainstream news outlets, popular magazines, and talk shows such as *Dr. Oz, Good Morning America*, and NPR's *Diane Rehm Show* and *Science Friday*.[13]

Notably, this account of obesity, whether hewing closely or loosely to the scientific studies that fund it, has been apparent in the mainstream prior to its advent as a coherent discourse, most obviously in the form of "low-carb" popular diets, such as Atkins, Zone, Sugarbusters, and Paleo. These have not posed the challenge that the discourse does, however, for a few reasons: first, in some of these diets, "sugar" has been characterized and often understood literally, in ways that don't necessarily upset the caloric imbalance model, given that sugar and sugary foods are generally highly caloric and thus their problematic nature could be attributed (by authors or readers) to calories rather than biochemistry. Second, these diets occur in a vast landscape of fad diets, most of which are characterized by extremes, founded upon outlandish premises, and invoke truly sketchy "science," such as the grapefruit diet, the Twinkie diet, and the cigarette diet. Thus, any revelations potentially provided by "low-carb" diets were and are arguably less credible simply by virtue of the genre. Third, along these lines, most of these diets draw unwarranted conclusions from the science or feature directives that fly directly in the face of other established medical evidence, for example urging unlimited and indiscriminate consumption of fats and proteins to promote ketosis, wherein the body utilizes fatty acids rather than glucose (derived from carbohydrates) for energy. The health implications of this scenario remain hotly contested among scientists and medical researchers, as does the quality of fats and proteins typically consumed in these diets; most feature significant amounts of saturated animal fats and meats, which have been correlated with a host of other health problems. Finally, in part related to their inclusion in the genre of diet plans writ large, these diets do not inherently challenge the cultural and official narrative premise of individual agency and responsibility as related to obesity. That is, diet plans inform and direct people regarding "right" and "wrong" dietary choices—choices that are entirely up to them. At most, the offerings of the market are indirectly or implicitly identified as problematic, but not to the extent that individual agency is compromised or even challenged: to the contrary, it is a key feature of the diet genre. That is, the now enlightened individual is empowered to make superior dietary choices. Indeed, perhaps a primary reason that the findings of obesity research are only now gaining traction in the mainstream outside of the popular diet genre and coalescing into a coherent narrative is that those findings are now being explicitly articulated as a direct challenge to the official account: Taubes has been unambiguous in his contention that "the authority figures in obesity and nutrition are so fixed on the simplistic calorie-balance idea that they're willing to ignore virtually any science to hold on to it";[14] likewise, Lustig has written that "'a calorie is a calorie' continues to be promulgated [by government and industry] . . . But it is as dishonest as a three-dollar bill."[15]

If the sugar tack does not inherently unsettle the individual responsibility premise of the official account and is only recently making the case for the roles and responsibilities of industry and government in the obesity epidemic, other angles in the food perversion discourse drawn from obesity science are more pointed due to their focus on practices of food production, and thus potentially far more threatening to "business as usual." This, in fact, may be one reason that they are considerably less apparent in the mainstream than the sugar version, even if they are gaining traction. However, it is also the case that the links between these angles and obesity are more recent and/or relatively less established scientifically.

The role of food additives in obesity, at every stage of production, has been the subject of increasing scrutiny among scientists and researchers. Mounting evidence seems to suggest that various agents utilized in the growing, maintenance, and/or packaging of foods may, like refined sugars, prompt biochemical processes—the same or perhaps different—in the human body that culminate in excess fat. For instance, recent studies suggest a link between obesity and pesticides regularly applied to conventionally grown vegetable and grain crops,[16] findings that are making their way into mainstream news venues, as well: "Endocrine disruptors [including pesticides] are a class of chemicals that mimic hormones and therefore confuse the body. Initially, they provoked concern because of their links to cancers and the malformation of sex organs. Those concerns continue, but the newest area of research is the impact that they have on fat storage."[17]

There has been an uptick in research into the relationship between industrialized livestock farming and obesity as well. Stemming from a number of studies that have linked obesity to general overuse of antibiotics in recent years, emergent research suggests a link between antibiotics routinely administered to livestock to prevent or treat health conditions,[18] and those findings are beginning to appear in the mainstream press, if indirectly or tentatively articulated:

> "The rise of obesity around the world is coincident with widespread antibiotic use," says Blaser. . . . That's one reason farmers add antibiotics to animal feed: The drugs alter the gut bacteria in cattle, pigs, and others, substituting bacteria that are better at extracting maximum calories from feed and thereby making the animals pack on the pounds. . . . Consider buying antibiotic-free meat.[19]

Similarly, in his reporting of the general findings regarding links between "microbiota," or the microbes that constitute a particular community or colony (specifically, the lack thereof), and obesity, food journalist Michael Pollan writes, "prescribed drugs aren't the only antimicrobials finding their way to the microbiota; scientists have found antibiotic residues in meat, milk and surface water as well."[20]

Although few available studies have established a significant link between obesity and the use of hormones to accelerate growth and fertility cycles in livestock,[21] this is another dimension of the food perversion narrative that is beginning to get play in mainstream venues. In lieu of such studies, allusions to the European Union's ban on North American beef, instated in 1999 and consistently upheld in light of confirming studies since (despite North American sanctions and appeals to the World Trade Organization to overturn it) are often made in these mainstream accounts, due to EU findings of general hormonal disruptions in humans attendant to consumption of beef that contained artificial hormones. Also invoked in these reports is the "common sense" perspective: that is, that "consumption of meat from cattle treated with hormones means you are taking them in, too . . . if your cattle has it, your meat has it, and you then have it."[22] Or, in the words of Perrine and Hurlock,

> To bring this all home, imagine you've been in a terrible plane crash in the Andes, like those poor souls depicted in the movie *Alive*. The only way to survive is to pick one of the dead folks to eat. You're given the choice of an obese, grotesquely muscled, man-boob-toting Minnesota Vikings lineman with shrunken testicles who's been injecting himself with hormones for a dozen years, or someone of normal size and body type and hormonal function. (One of the Kardashian sisters, maybe.) Which would you choose? Well, every time you eat conventionally raised beef, you're choosing the Viking.[23]

As noted, this hormonal thread is not as substantiated by obesity studies as are pesticides and antibiotics, at least as yet (or at least in the United States). However, the fact that it is appearing with greater frequency in the mainstream is sufficient to qualify it as a complementary and resonant part of the food perversion discourse.

A fourth and final strand of this (sub)story of food perversion is relevant to additives and preservatives, in the foods themselves or in packaging thereof. Studies have established links between obesity, or "increased adiposity," and a number of food preservatives, including sodium sulphite, sodium benzoate, parabens, "trans fats," and HFCS,[24] and these findings have made their way into the mainstream, primarily as relevant to the last two. HFCS, of course, is a refined sugar, so it is typically engaged via the sugar version of the food perversion variant of obesity as a consequence of environmental factors; but it also has preservative properties, which is one reason why it is added to a vast number of foods, including unexpected ones such as packaged breads, crackers, juice drinks, tonic water, condiments, and salad dressings. Even when its preservative features are superfluous, it is an enormously proliferate additive in the nation's food supply, due primarily to current agricultural policies, which I will discuss as part of the last environmental story. In fact, much was made of HFCS's role in obesity when studies linking the two first came to light,[25] although more recent studies have tempered those early claims,[26] noting that HFCS is not particularly better or worse than any other refined sugar. The Corn Refiners Association lobby has worked extensively to do the same via advertising and public relations campaigns, and mainstream coverage of this "no better, no worse" clarification has followed suit.[27] However, HFCS's role in obesity remains a staple feature of the perverted food story; one of the earliest popular critics of agribusiness and the consequent contemporary US diet of processed foods, Michael Pollan's "repeated condemnation of HFCS as particularly harmful helped damage the sweetener's reputation,"[28] and in light of his status as an erstwhile guru of mainstream food quality consciousness, much mainstream reporting on causes of obesity in the 2000s took their cue from him.[29]

Studies linking trans fats to obesity also have featured prominently in the mainstream, especially in relation to changes voluntarily adopted by schools in food offerings or preparation; the most notorious of these efforts and thus the one that received the greatest coverage was New York City mayor Michael Bloomberg's city-wide ban on the use of trans fats in food preparation, motivated by the studies linking them to obesity as well as heart disease.[30] If specific coverage of the particular relationship between trans fats and obesity are not as regularly or prominently featured in recent years, this is arguably so because that link has attained the level of cultural presumption.

Another variation of the preservative angle is relevant to how foods are packaged, specifically in plastics. Although plastics are, of course, ubiquitous in our contemporary environment and come in myriad forms, those that come in contact with our food, especially at extremely high or low temperatures, have been the subject of considerable concern, on the assumption that our ingestion of problematic agents is both higher and more concentrated. Indeed, extensive research has linked at least certain plastics—specifically, Bisphenol A (BPA) and various phthalates—commonly used in food packaging or preparation with obesity.[31] Those findings have been rather widely publicized in mainstream media contexts, and interestingly, more than any other food product, additive, or preservative—including sugar—plastics are consistently explicitly identified in that coverage as endocrine disruptors in relation to obesity,[32] to a much greater extent than any other factor, despite the fact that all scientific studies that examine any food perverting feature specifically identify its endocrinal disruptive properties.

The food perversion variation of the environmental account of obesity, whether as relevant to refinement, production practices, additives, preservatives, or packaging, heats things up insofar as it prompts a rethinking of how to address the problem. The official story, of course, locates everything—cause and redress—at the feet of the individual. The access version of the environmental narrative implicitly or at least potentially troubles that logic a bit, although it doesn't necessarily unsettle it: after all, individual agency isn't inherently obviated by obstacles to access, and a viable (if remarkably insensitive and impractical) response could be that access-impoverished individuals simply have to work harder or be more creative in light of their lot. The fundamental tenets of the official story that, first, caloric imbalance explains obesity; and second, that the individual ultimately determines how many calories s/he consumes or expends are not inherently unseated in the access narrative. Conversely, the food perversion account does much to unseat both, to varying degrees: it summarily rejects the caloric imbalance model, on the one hand, and further suggests that the individual does not have full control, at least of what happens inside his or her body. More to the point, the responsibility for obesity is shifted substantially in the direction of industry in this account, for it is incontrovertibly the case in this account that industry practices pervert the food. While it could be argued that individuals should simply avoid processed foods entirely, this is a problematic defense in view of the overwhelming degree to which processed food comprises the nation's food supply. Furthermore, that argument, unlike that of access, cannot be shored up against the caloric imbalance model. Thus, the food perversion variation of the environmental story of obesity represents a significant threat to the presumptive neoliberal imaginary of the rationale, autonomous individual and, accordingly, the market and the government in relation to that individual. What fully realizes the threat, however, is the industry corruption variation (or extension) of the environmental story, the last of the three.

## Big Business

If more appropriately characterized as dysfunctional—perhaps corrupted—industry rather than corrupt industry per se, one prong of this narrative variant is relevant to contemporary government food subsidies. The food subsidies provided by the original Farm Bill as part of Roosevelt's New Deal were designed as a temporary measure to secure stability and solvency of farms via a program of loans and price supports in order to protect them from wild price fluctuations due to unpredictable and uncontrollable factors, such as weather conditions and volatility of the economy, especially salient at time on the heels of the Great Depression. This was accomplished via the establishment of grain reserves, a price floor, and conservation set-asides. However, market deregulations and realignments since then have driven agricultural prices so far down that the fraction (as compared to the 1930s) of small farms operational today are utterly reliant on subsidies, and so must overproduce their crops in order to (barely) survive. Moreover, the vast majority of food subsidies today are distributed—in the form of direct payment rather than loans—to "agribusinesses" that, by dint of corporate consolidation and vertical integration patterns prompted by deregulation, have given rise to industrial farming on a massive scale, typically featuring a sophisticated infrastructure of banks, patented seeds and fertilizers, grain trading monopolies, food processing systems, and retail operations. Not only do these entities not require the subsidies they receive to be profitable due to the size and scope of their operations, but their profit margins are substantially enhanced by those subsidies in general, for they can produce and/or purchase and utilize overproduced crops at very little or no cost—indeed, in some cases, at profit.[33]

This is relevant to obesity in the broadest and perhaps most pervasive terms in that, directly due to the subsidy system and concomitant market patterns, the cheapest foods are the most highly processed, making them simultaneously the most economic and obesogenic: in an oft-cited example in the discourse, "Some years ago two nutrition experts went grocery shopping. For a dollar, Adam Drewnowski and S.E. Specter could purchase 1,200 calories of potato chips or cookies or just 250 calories worth of carrots."[34] This is especially relevant to the surplus of corn, in particular, which is the most heavily subsidized of all agricultural crops, to the tune of nearly $5 billion in 2013—nearly $90 billion in the 2000–2010 decade alone.[35] In addition to its proliferation as a cheap refined food in itself—in the form of, for instance, popcorn, corn chips, corn bugles, and corn nuggets—corn's particular relevance to obesity is manifest in two arguably far more significant ways. The incentivized surplus of corn has led to extensive and intensive efforts to ensure consumption of the excess and justify continued production and, thus, subsidization of the crop, effectively securing the vicious cycle. Perhaps most notorious of these has been the refinement of corn into HFCS, which as described earlier has been introduced as a superfluous ingredient to all manner of processed foods and has further been implicated as a key endocrine disruptor, also as noted. In addition, corn has been successfully marketed and adopted as the feed of choice for livestock, perhaps the primary way in which the corn surplus is being consumed. "Animal agriculture" has grown dramatically commensurate with the rise of agribusiness, resulting in the rise of concentrated animal feeding operations (CAFOs), where vast numbers of animals—cows, pigs, chickens, and turkey, most prolifically—are concentrated and managed to the end of meat, dairy, and egg production. But using corn as exclusive (as is typical) or primary feed is inherently problematic because corn has virtually no nutritional value and is difficult or impossible for animals to digest in any case, which inevitably leads to malnourishment, in itself compromising the quality of animals and animal products consumed. These animals are furthermore rendered highly prone to illness—already a high risk due to crowded conditions—requiring medical treatment, primarily antibiotic. In the case of cows, in particular, their stomachs cannot digest corn, so their ill health is essentially guaranteed. This leads many if not most CAFOs to place their livestock on permanent antibiotic regimens as a default preventative measure. Again, as noted in the food perversion discourse described previously, increasing scientific evidence implicates antibiotics as a significant endocrinal disruptor and, thus, cause of obesity. In part due to mass-farmed livestock's shortened and inevitably sickly lives, the administration of growth hormone—yet another endocrinal disruptor, as discussed—to these animals is also standard practice in order to effectively accelerate their life spans and production value before they become too sick.[36]

If the subject and findings are somewhat controversial, specifically with respect to degree of impact, a number of studies have explicitly asserted a link between agricultural subsidies, especially of corn, and obesity, contending that "American farm policy is effectively driving the production and propagation of cheap sugars and oils that lead to widespread weight gain."[37] This perspective achieves narrative weight only to the extent that it is available to and circulated among the broader public, however, and indeed it is: in recent years, food journalists and experts like Michael Pollan, Eric Schlosser, and Marion Nestle have chronicled this link for public audiences in mainstream books, articles, and interviews, and, if in less nuanced ways (in some cases, the argument is predicated on the highly caloric nature of processed subsidized foods), it is being featured in mainstream newspapers and magazines. For instance:

> Agricultural subsidies have helped bring us high-fructose corn syrup, factory farming, fast food, a two-soda-a-day habit and its accompanying obesity . . . [subsidized corn and soy] are the pillars for the typical American diet—featuring an unnaturally large consumption of meat, never-before-seen junk food and a bizarre avoidance of plants—as well as the fortunes of Pepsi, Dunkin' Donuts, KFC and the others that have relied on cheap corn and soy to build their empires of unhealthful food. Over the years, prices of fresh produce have risen, while those of meat, poultry, sweets, fats and oils, and especially soda, have fallen.[38]

Whether specific assertions regarding the link between subsidies and obesity are predicated on a caloric imbalance or endocrinal disruption theory of obesity, this account unequivocally attributes the contemporary obesity crisis to national economic policies, thereby making it incumbent upon government to offer redress, specifically by reining in industry.

In the agricultural subsidies tack of this environmental story of obesity, industry is obviously implicated, but its culpability in the obesity epidemic varies across accounts. While industry is consistently articulated as unscrupulous, this is frequently articulated as amorality: upon appropriate revision of dysfunctional policies, industry will fall into line, this discourse seems to suggest; industry simply follows government's suit. But other accounts ascribe a far more active and nefarious role to industry, which places it in a broader narrative category of aggressive industry. In this genre, the relationship between government and industry is reversed: government either facilitates industry demands or is defeated by industry's superior resources and tactics. Extensive and sophisticated lobbying efforts on the part of food corporations and agribusiness are frequently invoked in this narrative thread: "Calling themselves the Sensible Food Policy Coalition, the nation's biggest foodmakers, fast-food chains, and media companies . . . are trying to derail standards proposed by four federal agencies. The U.S. Chamber of Commerce has also lent its lobbying muscle to the effort."[39] Similar patterns are identified with respect to agricultural subsidies; the "farm lobby" created by agribusiness industry giants is described as enormously effective in not only retaining the Farm Bill, which is up for renewal every five years (and was introduced in the 1930s as a temporary salvo in any case), but staving off proposed cuts or regulations that would benefit the 1% of farms run by individual farmers—including, for instance, by convincing legislators to roll food stamp funding into the bill so that agricultural subsidies could not be cut without similarly curtailing food provision to the poor.[40] The aggressive and extensive actions of lobbies for specific industries implicated in the obesity epidemic, such as corn, sugar, and fast food, are also invoked in this discourse as relevant to efforts to regulate distribution or promotion of their products, for instance via banning vending machines in schools,[41] advertising "unhealthy" foods to children,[42] or limiting the number of fast-food franchises in particular areas.[43] Indeed, the powerful reach and impact of the collective food lobby are described in relation to any food-related effort on the part of the government, even those not directed to regulation or oversight, such as federal nutritional guidelines: one report, describing past influence of the lobby on those guidelines, notes that

> Marion Nestle, a nutrition professor at New York University, says the result [following intensive lobbying by the food industry] was a [food] pyramid that was so watered down it was "useless." The next iteration looks to be as much of a struggle, says Margo Wootan, nutrition policy director for the Center for Science in the Public Interest. "Businesses depend on selling a lot of unhealthy foods."[44]

Indeed, "food lobbies representing large commodities—such as beef and sugar—swarm around the [nutritional guideline development] process, as a prime spot on the pyramid can be a potent marketing tool. And the pyramid is the basis for a host of government food programs, including school lunches."[45]

Some of the discourse in this vein goes further to describe not only industry aggression but deception, especially with respect to downplaying or even denying the unhealthy aspects of manufactured foods, such as packaged cereals and yogurt, which typically feature the same nutritional profile (and obesogens) as candy but are advertised as healthy or diet foods;[46] or, for instance, of HFCS, which was the subject of a massive public relations and advertising campaign by the Corn Refiners Association (the corn lobby) following its excoriation in the mainstream, which "spun" the product as "natural" and "wholesome."[47] A variation of this theme is reflected in coverage that chronicles the new practice of "nutritional enhancement" on the part of the food industry, wherein a designated "healthy" nutrient, like Omega-3, is incorporated into a nutritionally questionable food—for example, a sugary children's cereal—in an effort to redeem the food or at least neutralize that perception.[48] Recently, Michael Moss has contributed substantially to this public narrative by chronicling, in mainstream news and magazine articles as well as a best-selling book, the sophisticated technical, biochemical, and psychological manipulations of "Big Food" to cultivate literal addiction on the part of consumers:

> What I found, over four years of research and reporting, was a conscious effort—taking place in labs and marketing meetings and grocery-store aisles—to get people hooked on foods that are convenient and inexpensive. I talked to more than 300 people in or formerly employed by the processed-food industry, from scientists to marketers to C.E.O.'s. Some were willing whistle-blowers, while others spoke reluctantly when presented with some of the thousands of pages of secret memos that I obtained from inside the food industry's operations.[49]

Moss' exposure of Big Food's "intent on using science not to address the health concerns but to thwart them"[50] effectively puts food industry on a par with Big Tobacco as regards not only its exploitation of but informed, intentional infliction of harm upon consumers. If less concrete simply due to lack of scientific evidence, this account also includes references to the possible role of genetically modified foods in the obesity epidemic. Reports in the regard are generally (necessarily) speculative, and indeed, the fact that little to no research exists to link genetically modified organisms (GMOs) present in GMO foods and obesity, at least in the United States, lends fodder to the speculation, rightly or wrongly, for most of this narrative thread includes references to efforts on the part of powerful GMO industries to prevent or thwart studies or force retraction of findings that purport to identify a link.[51]

Whether describing the contemporary food industry as dysfunctional or corrupt, this variation of the environmental story of obesity squarely and unequivocally locates responsibility for the obesity epidemic on industry and government, if in slightly varying proportions. Irrespective of proportion, however, redress is implicitly or explicitly articulated as a matter of government oversight and regulation, a characterization that dramatically reconfigures—indeed, inverts—presumptive neoliberal logics that posit the autonomous individual consumer-citizen as the premise, catalyst, and justification for free market and laissez-faire government.

## Extenuations

If the caloric imbalance story of obesity retains its dominance, both in terms of cultural presumption and official status, the environmental counternarrative is certainly familiar to the broader public. The fact that it is reactive, drawn diametrically against the official account, may be one reason why it has had difficulty unseating that official version despite the fact that much of it is substantiated by sound, current social and/or medical science. That is, the very fact and degree of its reactivity may foster a perception of the environmental argument as radical and therefore suspect. However, I would argue that if this is relevant, it is a minor reason. More pressing is the fact that attributing obesity to factors other than individual agency and responsibility explicitly calls to account the appropriate roles and responsibilities of agents and entities other than the individual—specifically, the market and the state. Certainly, environmental explanations of obesity constitute a threat to the collective food industry, which has responded variously by limiting public and media access to industry operations and data; funding its own studies to counter and at least raise doubt among the public regarding the validity of independent scientific findings; and creating sophisticated public relations and advertising campaigns that feature its products in a positive light. These actions lend credence to the point that the political economic implications of the environmental account of obesity and consequent industry pushback comprise a significant reason for its relative lack of traction in the mainstream.

But I suggest that a key failure of the environmental account of obesity to resonate with the public is that it, like the official one, fails to account for authenticity, albeit in different ways. As I argued in the last chapter, the failure of the official story of obesity—and, by extension, the neoliberal sensibilities that drive it—is that, in centering rational, individual agency, it fails to account for authenticity, or the "real," lived, embodied experience of obesity. Ironically, despite its diametric reactivity to the official account, the environmental story of obesity does the same; rather than denying authenticity via its predication on the rational individual agent, however, the environmental narrative does so via its predication on an imaginary of an utterly passive, homogeneous populace. While it thus definitively rejects the rationality and autonomy that characterized the neoliberal individual, to the detriment of the caloric imbalance account of obesity, it goes too far in the other direction, attributing agency exclusively to the market and/or the government while denying not only individual agency but in fact the very individual: an egregious and fatal move in a culture so thoroughly steeped in individualism. If the official account of obesity denies authenticity by sterilizing the individual via rationalization and abstraction, the environmental account effectively denies it via homogenization: the individual is rendered nameless, faceless, and entirely passive. Individualism is so deeply entrenched in the culture, politics, and psyche of the United States that any narrative that qualifies the individual, much less negates it, will lack resonance by default. Moreover, in the current Zeitgeist, authenticity, understood as felt, lived experience and desires of unique human beings, is a profoundly resonant concept, inextricably entwined with understandings of the self. Thus, current cultural navigations of who and what the individual is, in obesity stories and otherwise, must account for it. The failure of both the official and environmental stories of obesity, I argue, is essentially that each, in different ways, fails to account for authenticity for a public that is culturally primed to expect and want it. It is this vacuum that the stories of obesity that I chronicle in the following chapters purport to fill. Unlike the official and environmental stories, authenticity is the touchstone for each of these alternative stories, in different ways; identifying and assessing them not only sheds light on how obesity in general and the obesity crisis in particular are apprehended and navigated but also, more broadly, how current exigent tensions around cultural identity—specifically, individualism—are being negotiated.

# 4

# Destiny Obesity

## *The Fatalistic Story of Obesity*

If the official and environmental accounts of obesity represent opposite poles that each fail, for different reasons, to speak to the populace in compelling ways, a number of other stories have stepped into that breach, with considerable cultural resonance and traction. In most cases, each of those narratives draws on tenets of both or either official and environmental accounts, although those tenets are invoked or deployed in distinctive ways. Across the board, however, the touchstone for these alternative cultural stories is authenticity, which, as I have argued, is conspicuously and fatally absent from both the official and the environmental takes. The first of the alternative stories of obesity that I will address is that of fatalism. The reason that I engage it first is that it is clearly predicated on the impasse posed by the respective shortfalls of the official and environmental accounts; indeed, the fatalistic narrative explicitly draws on both of those accounts. But while aspects of one or the other precedent stories are acknowledged in the fatalistic account, neither is championed, culminating in an inevitable stalemate. The bottom line of this account is that, for various reasons, people today are condemned to obesity: it is an inevitable condition due to our contemporary lifestyles, our biology, and/or our natures. Moreover, attempts at structural redress are inappropriate or impractical. Although this account is hardly a hopeful or productive one as relevant to the obesity epidemic, it is a critical one for several reasons: first, it is extremely pervasive, prevalent, and resonant; second, as noted, it exposes the disparities between the official account and the science that inform the environmental narrative; and finally, it implicitly but powerfully centers authenticity in the public conversation about obesity by making its absence in the precedent accounts both conspicuous and salient.

As with all cultural narratives, of obesity and otherwise, the fatalistic narrative features a few variants. The contemporary world is perhaps the most prominent of these; although rife with assumptions regarding the "average" person, this particular tack nonetheless exposes the assumptions and impracticalities that compromise both official and environmental accounts of obesity, respectively. Biology constitutes the second variant of the fatalistic narrative, and it is informed by both studies and conventional wisdom regarding physiological and/or genetic propensities for fat. This variant, too, invokes yet implicitly indicts and rejects both official and environmental explanations for obesity. Finally, the overarching narrative of fatalism is cinched via an articulation of regulatory interventions and measures, real or proposed, as ineffective or inappropriate. While this variation does not inherently or necessarily reject either antecedent account of obesity, it effectively dismisses both as irrelevant.

Although these narrative variants are thus distinct, they converge to the extent that each articulates obesity as inevitable, and each rejects out of hand the redress proposed or implied by both the caloric imbalance and environmental accounts of obesity. Ultimately, the collective fatalistic narrative of obesity surfaces authenticity as the base failing of both the official and environmental accounts by centering the lifestyles, struggles, and thwarted intentions of "real" people, in the case of the contemporary world variant; by acknowledging the bodies we inhabit, individual variations among them, and their relevance to our actions and decisions, in the case of the biological subplot; and, in the case of ineffective regulation, by explicitly invoking principles of varied individual desires and aspirations.

## The Shape of Our Lives

One of the most prevalent characterizations of obesity and the obesity epidemic in the mainstream is that it is an inevitable consequence of the modern world. Even when suggestions and recommendations are offered in tandem with this bleak view, they are typically impractical, at best, and often even acknowledged as such, underscoring the inevitability of obesity. The primary factors identified in this narrative subplot are, broadly, contemporary technologies and the demands of contemporary work, and they are complemented by an additional thread that features nostalgic imaginaries of bygone or distant cultures.

### POWER SURGE

Contemporary technologies comprise the foundation of the "modern world" explanation for obesity, primarily to the extent that our use of and reliance upon them render us sedentary and/or vulnerable to mediated messages or attendant (to media use) practices that promote obesity. Specifically, the proliferation of technologies today in the home and at the workplace, ranging from heavy machinery to push mowers to computers, are cited as replacing physical activity, in terms of both labor and recreation.[1] While this logic clearly draws upon the official caloric imbalance account of obesity, additional mainstream accounts reference studies that identity the "biological impact of mental work" engendered by the use of certain technologies, such as computers and video games, in the form of elevated stress levels that are associated with obesity.[2] Most discourse in this vein, however, focuses upon the effects of media use and consumption on children. The fact that levels of childhood obesity are significantly and directly correlated with the number of hours consuming or engaging any sort of media is widely cited across mainstream formats and genres,[3] with television and internet usage identified as most problematic: "the transformation of American homes into high-def, Web-enabled, TiVo-equipped entertainment centers means that children who come home after a largely sedentary day at a school desk spend an average of three more sedentary hours in front of some kind of screen."[4]

Not only is the very act of media consumption identified as deleterious, but content is indicted as well, primarily as relevant to heavy advertising of "obesogenic" foods targeting children, such as fast food, candy, and sugary cereals, exposure to which is strongly and, again, directly correlated with levels of childhood obesity;[5] elaboration of this (now) commonplace cites the fact that "Big Food" entities devote extensive resources to targeting children because they are especially vulnerable to influence and, if they are secured early in life as a consumer, they will generally develop life-long loyalty to a particular product or brand.[6] Media programming is not immune to charges of fostering obesity, however; some of this discourse implicates popular characters featured in children's programming who serve as questionable role models with respect to their sedentary and/or dietary habits.[7] If these scenarios imply a context of leisure and recreation, which further implicates parents or caregivers, potential redress in the form of limiting computer or screen time is neutralized by complementary accounts that describe nationwide curtailing if not elimination of physical education from school curricula in tandem with heavy, even standard reliance on computer technologies in the contemporary classroom.[8]

In fact, this dilemma is the prototype of the broader fatalistic narrative insofar as it cites both lifestyle—encompassing individual choices as well as cultural trends—and environmental or structural factors, ranging from private industry to school curricula, as contributors to obesity, such that correcting for either alone is insufficient and correcting for both is virtually impossible. Underscoring this futility as relevant to the relationship of technology to obesity in particular, neither contemporary technologies themselves nor their ubiquity are challenged. While the content of media programming represents a qualitatively different scenario to the extent that individual agency (per parental control) is implicitly suggested as redress ("just change the channel," e.g.), it is notable that the fare itself—programming or advertising—is not called to account in this tale; rather, their presence is assumed to be a given. Furthermore, even the limited aspects of contemporary technologies that ostensibly do lend themselves to individual agency and control are qualified in this account, due to the practical and logistical demands of everyday life. To the extent that technologies feature so heavily in contemporary labor and education as well as domestic life, leisure, and relationships—ranging across playing videogames, online shopping, social networks, and texting—individual attempts at redress are presented as extremely inconvenient, at best, if not futile, at worst, especially to the extent that they intersect with structural constraints imposed by industry and/or school curricula.[9]

## HEAVY SCHEDULE

The second way in which obesity is portrayed as a consequence of the modern world is relevant to the nature and demands of work. A primary prong of this variant of the fatalism narrative has to do with time: the average workday, it is often noted in this discourse, has increased substantially relative to years past (in large part due to the fact that wages in the United States have not kept pace with inflation, an ancillary point in this articulation), as has the amount of time people spend commuting to and from work. Not only is this reported as translating into increased sedentariness, to the extent that most people's jobs are not physical and that most people drive or take public transit,[10] but people are also described as having less time available to them to pursue healthful endeavors, such as exercise and preparing healthy meals: "Eating healthily can be expensive and time-consuming—two qualities Americans currently have little appetite for. Hitting up the drive-through is cheap, no-hassle and easy to rationalize."[11] In mainstream deployments of this discourse, experts are often cited or depicted urging people to "make time to exercise as a family" or "take the time to cook with your kids"; but notably, these directives are issued in tandem with explicit acknowledgement of the "time squeeze" that "we all experience" today.[12] As with contemporary technologies, both structural conditions and individual practices relative to work are implicated in obesity in this discourse, but in such a way that addressing one or the other is at least very limited if not ineffective, and addressing both is not possible.

Another way in which contemporary work conditions are implicated relative to obesity in this discourse is hormonal, but specifically and exclusively with respect to stress. That is, news coverage especially as well as other mainstream reports invoke scientific studies that have found high rates of cortisol, also known as the "stress hormone," to be strongly correlated with obesity. Although the details of that relationship continue to be theorized by obesity researchers, it is mobilized in the cultural narrative version as a causal one, wherein high levels of cortisol in the body appear to trigger biochemical processes that lead to the creation and storage of visceral fat, which is "dangerous, and difficult to lose. It's caused by a lot of things, including cortisol, a hormone produced when we're under stress. You can cut calories and exercise religiously, and still have visceral belly fat, and lots of it."[13] Moreover, as reported, a vicious stress-fat cycle ensues that is difficult to disrupt, for the fat cells that are promoted by cortisol appear to themselves generate cortisol.[14] Importantly, higher levels of stress are explicitly linked to either work demands—"longer commutes and more time spent at work and on the computer have made for more sedentary lives [and lead to] greater levels of stress and depression"[15]—or the demands of attempting to attain a work/life balance: "working stress-reduction techniques into your busy days can really help."[16] The stress hormone tack is also taken up in relation to popularly cited studies that have linked obesity to lack of sleep, insofar as sleep correlates inversely with cortisol levels and/or releases hormones that appear to ensure and regulate the body's proper metabolism of fat.[17] In these cases, too, lack of sleep is attributed to our "busy lifestyles" today, a consequence of attempting to both meet and balance the significant demands of work and home, family, or personal life.

Some examples of this narrative raise the possibility of "making life changes," such as scaling back to part-time or flex-time working hours; telecommuting; moving closer to work; changing professions; or alleviating time and stress demands in other ways.[18] However, these suggestions are rare, and when they are extended, they are often explicitly acknowledged as difficult or impractical: "try to carve out time to cook your own meals," exhorts one report[19]; another recommends incorporating 3–4 hours of vigorous activity into every day, even as it acknowledges that, "of course, this isn't possible for most of us."[20] Overwhelmingly, the dimensions and demands of our contemporary lives are presented as inevitable and immutable; moreover, those very features are explicitly identified as contributing if not primary factors in the obesity epidemic.

## LEAN AND SIMPLE

The final way in which the modern-world story of obesity is parlayed in mainstream, to equally fatalistic ends, is nostalgia. That is, just as the world that we inhabit today is depicted as creating inevitable conditions for obesity, worlds removed from us, either by time, distance, or culture, are portrayed as having or having had it right. This is established via two distinct threads, both articulated as superior to contemporary US cultural conditions: historical practices and "old-world" cultural traditions.

Considerable public discourse identifies past behaviors and/or conditions as more appropriate regarding weight management. This is reflected, for instance, in mainstream reports that identify current needs for new obesity-related drugs, technologies, products, services, and procedures for which there had never been a need before, which are typically described in dramatic if not sensational terms. For instance, new ambulance equipment now required to accommodate increasing numbers of obese patients is reported as follows: "a bariatric ambulance that can transport patients weighing up to 1,000 pounds costs $110,000 to build, compared with $70,000 for a standard ambulance . . . . A bariatric cot costs around $4,000, four times the price of a regular cot."[21] The sudden rise in medical products and services for increasingly obese pets at rates never before seen by veterinarians also is presented in the same "what is the world coming to" tone, reinforcing the idealization of the past as relevant to health and fitness.[22] If they represent a different angle, concerns regarding threats to national security per the shrinking pool of viable recruits who are "too fat to fight" are similarly conveyed: "When you get kids today who can't do push-ups, pull-ups or run, this is a fundamental problem not just for the military but for the country."[23]

Explicit reference to habits, practices, and circumstances of prior generations cultivates this perspective; they are invoked as a benchmark against which to measure our wanting contemporary lives. Food features prominently in this discursive variant insofar as "our grandparents'" diets are portrayed uniformly as consisting of natural, whole, pure foods: "We know rather less about our food than our grandparents did because the process of creating food in a lab is less familiar than the process of growing it in a garden."[24] Indeed, labor and food are sometimes romantically conflated in coverage pertinent to "proper" food preparation: one writer reminiscences, "I have lovely memories of my grandmother using a beat-up paring knife . . . for hacking garlic (she did not mince), peeling potatoes and cutting up chicken. She did not own a cutting board, and would probably be as dazzled by a food processor as by an iPhone."[25] This imaginary invokes physical activity of bygone eras in similarly romantic ways, for instance asserting the virtues of physical, usually agrarian work, outdoor recreation, and the benefits of lack of modern transit—the lack of contemporary technologies in general, for that matter. In this vein, one report cited a study that people who live in older neighborhoods—those built prior to the 1950s—tend to be fitter because those areas have sidewalks and large trees, features appreciated in times past by residents who enjoyed evening strolls through the neighborhood.[26]

The majority of this particular story, however, tends to focus on the dramatic and novel problem of childhood obesity, however, especially on the "alarming" and "disturbing" increasing incidence of young children already presenting with diet-related diabetes, high cholesterol, liver disease, and heart disease, conditions associated almost exclusively with aged populations until recently.[27] An oft-quoted finding that underscores the superiority of previous generations on this count is that this generation is the first to have a lower life expectancy than that of their parents.[28] As described previously, this is generally attributed to contemporary habits and practices, for instance media consumption, as compared to days of yore, when children would play physical games outdoors.[29] Some accounts even link reading to greater levels of fitness, implicitly further indicting contemporary behaviors and technologies: "one theory is that though reading is a sedentary activity, it does take time away from less healthful activities, like snacking in front of the TV."[30] Not least of all, this narrative notes that the foods that children consume today—sodas, potato chips, candies, frozen snacks and dinners—were not available to generations past, and furthermore contrasts them sharply with foods that were: the "era of the 64-oz. soda, the 1,200-calorie burger and the 700-calorie Frappuccino, [in which] food companies now produce enough each day for every American to consume a belt-popping 3,800 calories per day" is drawn against a time when

> the prairies ran so dark with buffalo, you could practically net them like cod; the waters swam so thick with cod, you could bag them like slow-moving buffalo. The soil was the kind of rich stuff in which you could bury a brick and grow a house, and the pioneers grew plenty—fruits and vegetables and grains and gourds and legumes and tubers, in a variety and abundance they'd never seen before.[31]

The ambiguity and attendant resignation that coverage in this nostalgic vein imparts are notable. That is, the past is invoked as a benchmark for who we have become rather than what we might do; we cannot return to the past—indeed, it is typically depicted as irrevocably vanished—and the world has changed so dramatically that it is impractical if not impossible to recreate it. Obesity, this particular narrative suggests, is one of the prices we pay for progress.

The nostalgic angle is not limited to the bygone past, however. Discourse in this vein also describes the superior habits and practices of "old world" cultures that persist into the present day. For example, Mediterranean (especially French, Italian, and Greek) and Asian (Japanese, primarily) diets and lifestyles are frequently invoked as very healthful, attributed specifically to such things as a slower pace; whole, fresh foods, often voluptuously rendered; lingering meals; and daily walks in the bucolic countryside.[32] Both implicitly and explicitly, distance from the features of "our" modern world is identified as the most significant predictor of good health. A recent version this narrative was represented in the popular book *Why French Women Don't Get Fat*; according to author Mireille Giuliano, to control one's weight, do as the French do: "Turn off the TV. . . . Go to the market two or three times a week. None of this twice-a-month grocery shopping Americans do. . . . Walk everywhere. . . . Make meals a 2-3 hour affair."[33] Another example of this perspective is evidenced in the invocation of the Amish, where obesity is evidently virtually unheard of despite their location in the heart of the US Midwest, which otherwise features some of the highest rates of obesity in the nation. The lack of obesity among the Amish is specifically attributed to its old-world practices: its members have almost no contact with the contemporary "outside" world, shunning technology of any sort (including cars and machinery) as well as growing and harvesting their own foods.[34]

Perhaps evidently, even though contemporaneous examples of healthy practices are identified as existent today, they are articulated in this narrative as no more available to or feasible for average US citizens than their grandparents' lifestyles. In fact, their literal distance and/or their exotic "otherness" reinforces the inevitability of the circumstances—in this case, obesity—in which we find ourselves today due to social and economic advancement. This perception appears to be secured in accounts that herald the downfall of some of these cultures as they progress economically and socially, and the United States in particular is indicted in this logic, specifically with respect to its highly industrialized economy and similarly industrialized diet: "we created the obesity crisis in America, then exported it. . . . A lot of people used to live in a subsistence world, a more primitive world, and they couldn't afford things like modern vegetable oil. But now we have supermarkets everywhere, and everybody sees the same TV we see and wants the same things we want."[35] The higher incidence of obesity among immigrants to the United States is similarly attributed to contemporary conditions and practices wrought by social "progress": "Interestingly, earlier research found that immigrants tend to be less overweight and obese than people born and raised in the United States. That difference tends to wear off with longer exposure to U.S. culture, including junk food and television."[36] Again, obesity is presented as an inevitable if undesirable byproduct of social progress, as evidenced in this news coverage of old-world traditions. Notably, renouncing or reconfiguring economic and social advances is not presented as a reasonable or viable option, further securing a fatalistic account of obesity.

## The Physiology of Fat

But the shape of our contemporary lives is not the only nail in our metaphoric coffin, accordingly to the fatalistic narrative of obesity. Obesity is also portrayed as inevitable in mainstream discourse that establishes biological predispositions to or determinants of fat. This narrative variant, too, falls out across distinctive threads: the "fat gene"; maternity; neurology; and bacteria.

### BORN TO BE BIG

The presence and role of the so-called "fat gene" comprises the bulk of this subdiscourse of fatalism. Some scientific studies do indeed suggest that some individuals have a greater, apparently genetic propensity to generate and store fat,[37] although other scientists posit that evolutionarily, all people are "programmed" to store fat under certain conditions—specifically, food deprivation—in order to ensure survival as well as fecundity, leading many researchers to refer to it as a "thrifty gene" in order to more accurately represent the phenomenon.[38] While these distinctions are not necessarily drawn in mainstream discourse regarding the subject, what is conveyed is the inevitability of weight gain for at least some if not most people, and the futility of fighting it: whether one's individual DNA programs one to be fat[39] or we have all been endowed with genetic protection courtesy of evolution that now constitutes "a risk factor in an [environment] of caloric abundance,"[40] the overarching message is that very little can be done about it: biology is destiny. Although some popular discourse suggests that hypervigilance and redoubled effort may counteract that destiny, such recommendations are generally impractical or overwhelming, even acknowledged as such; some are even sometimes presented with outright skepticism, for instance when the Amish are invoked as exemplars per a study that was conducted several years ago. Evidently, Amish individuals feature the "fat gene," but they are able to neutralize their predisposition to obesity via the extensive and intensive physical activity that their "rural 19th century lifestyles" require. Accordingly, some mainstream accounts recommended taking their cue to circumvent obesity by performing several hours of vigorous physical activity a day.[41] Other, more general accounts that engage genetic propensity concede that for the "time deprived," the "more intense work needed to improve fitness and lose weight" is less realistic than the "modest amount of exercise that can deliver general health benefits."[42] Moreover, several popular accounts of the fat or thrifty gene describe even extreme efforts as ultimately ineffective precisely due to those efforts: "draconian diets" predicated on caloric restriction and/or elimination of certain foods, such as carbohydrates, are described as creating the very famine conditions that "activate" the fat gene, thus almost always resulting in regaining the lost weight and then some.[43] In addition,

> pushing people to exercise more [could] actually be contributing to our obesity problem . . . [b]ecause exercise depletes not just the body's muscles but the brain's self-control "muscle" as well, [leading] many of us [to] feel greater entitlement to eat a bag of chips during that lazy time after we get back from the gym. This explains why exercise could make you heavier. . . . It's likely that I am more sedentary during my nonexercise hours than I would be if I didn't exercise with such Puritan fury.[44]

The upshot of this discursive thread is, again, futility: obesity is described as biologically predetermined, and efforts to counter or neutralize that propensity are articulated as impractical if not impossible in their extremes—and they may be ineffective or exacerbating if undertaken anyway. A variation of this perspective is apparent in accounts that assert the possibility of being "fat but fit," or "'metabolically healthy.'" That is, despite their excess pounds, many overweight and obese adults have healthy levels of "good" cholesterol, blood pressure, blood glucose and other risks for heart disease."[45] In a similar vein, other accounts note that certain fat ("brown," or subcutaneous), as opposed to visceral ("white") fat is not only not harmful but is actually beneficial.[46] Irrespective of the validity of these fat-but-fit scenarios (and there is some scientific evidence for them), and even if they counter the negative stigma associated with obesity, this tack reinforces the notion that fat and obesity are biologically preordained, and that efforts to resist that—effectively, to resist nature—are futile: "there's just no fighting the natural rhythms or shapes of one's body."[47]

## BIG MAMA

Another way in which the biology thread of the fatalism narrative of obesity is taken up is in relation to women, specifically as regards actual or potential maternity. Consistent with the evolutionary subplot noted earlier, women are broadly portrayed in this variation as genetically predisposed to accrue and retain fat in order to ensure fecundity, especially but not exclusively in times of scarcity, in order to sustain pregnancy and suckle infants. In relation to obesity, that rationale is invoked to explain everything from women's reported relative (to men) inability to control their appetites; greater craving for sweets; propensity to gain weight more quickly and lose it more slowly; and their predisposition to carry their weight in their hips, thighs, and buttocks.[48] Moreover, these predispositions are presented as necessary and functionally beneficial, again as warranted by evolution: "once you store that fat, you don't get rid of it, it pretty much stays there except for extreme circumstance, maybe starvation let's say, or breast feeding."[49] So prevalent are these tenets, irrespective of relatively scant scientific evidence to support them, that they have achieved the level of conventional wisdom in cultural perceptions of obesity. Certainly, this underscores the perception that weight gain, at least for some people (women, in this case), is biologically predetermined and inevitable.

Perhaps not surprisingly, women are identified in terms of causing obesity in their maternal roles, as well. While much of this is relevant to popular depictions of bad nutritional guidance—neglecting to provide healthy meals for their children or pressuring children to clean their plates, for instance, variations on the very familiar cultural trope of the bad mother—it is also apparent in mainstream accounts that cite studies suggesting that what pregnant women eat may determine whether or not their children become obese: "an overweight pregnant woman [may] be creating an environment inside her uterus that predisposes her child to put on fat more quickly than the offspring of normal-weight mothers";[50] pregnancy may be "obesity's ground zero."[51] While this does not suggest universal biological inevitability in the way that the fat or thrifty gene does (ostensibly amped up in women in any case)—it nevertheless supplements the fatalistic perspective that obesity is predetermined insofar as an individual's genetic die are cast before birth:

Perhaps an "obese" environment in the womb alters the wiring of the developing brain so as to interfere with normal appetite control, fat deposition, taste in food, or metabolism. Studies on other animals suggest that parts of the brain that control appetite develop differently under "obese" conditions. And in humans, one study has found that babies born to obese mothers have lower resting metabolic rates than babies whose mothers are of normal weight. . . . If this is right, it raises the alarming possibility that the obesity epidemic has a built-in snow-ball effect. If children born to obese mothers are . . . predisposed to obesity, they may find staying thin especially hard.[52]

While these accounts are arguably a variation on the "bad mother" trope referenced earlier and should be understood as occurring in a gendered cultural context that frequently blames women for social ills, it is notable that bad dietary choices on the part of pregnant women are themselves often articulated in this narrative strand as biologically driven by dint of pregnancy cravings,[53] understood on their own terms as powerful and perhaps even rational—a common belief is that cravings are dictated by the nutritional needs of the fetus. If it is possible to curb one's cravings while pregnant, doing so—like fighting the fat gene—is tantamount to defying nature.

## BRAIN FEEL

Within the fatalistic narrative variant of physiological determinism are mainstream accounts of scientific studies that have identified a link between consumption of foods and the brain's "pleasure centre"—specifically, the brains of individuals who are overweight or obese do not appear to register pleasure upon eating either at all or to the degree that brains of other individuals do.[54] Per the referenced studies, because this pleasure response is genetically and evolutionarily programmed in humans in order to incentivize eating and thus survival, individuals with a compromised response are compelled to eat more, resulting in weight gain and, ultimately, obesity: "The more an individual overeats, the less potent the rewards from eating become and that creates a pattern of overeating."[55] Notably, this theory and attendant mainstream accounts reflect the caloric imbalance account of obesity, but the genetic rationale on which they are founded complements and reinforces other accounts of obesity as preordained and inevitable, and the implied difficulty if not impossibility of overcoming the biological imperatives that lead to it.

## MICROBESITY

Finally, as also engaged via the environmental account of obesity and described in the last chapter, increasing mainstream attention has attended to the role of bacteria in obesity; recent scientific studies have identified certain microbiota that appear to "[help] regulate the calories the body obtains from food and stores as fat."[56] Accounts differ with respect to whether or to what extent "gut flora" may be genetically or environmentally (for instance, via excessive consumption of antibiotics in the industrialized food supply or of GMO foods) determined, and in either scenario, whether and to what extent they can be manipulated remains unclear. In all cases, however, obesity is posited as a consequence of one's biological constitution, thereby reinforcing a fatalistic frame of predetermination and the ambiguity if not futility of efforts to deny that destiny. Even when policy changes, dietary medications, or drug therapies are variously implicated by way of redress, the assertion that obesity is a consequence of biology beyond our direct and immediate control is reinforced.

## Governing Body

The final strand of the culturally resonant fatalism narrative of obesity has to do with government intervention and regulation, which are consistently depicted as either ineffective, deleterious, or both. This subplot clusters around three distinct issues: food provision in schools, as relevant to, for instance, eliminating or reducing vending snack or soda machines in schools, enhancing nutritional profile of school lunches, and rethinking school "bake sales";[57] legislation regarding the sale of certain foods or ingredients, such as trans fats, "Big Gulps," and posting nutritional information at fast food restaurants;[58] and altering access to particular foods in low-income urban neighborhoods, for instance by limiting or denying the establishment of fast-food restaurants or by instating "green carts," mobile produce vendors, in those neighborhoods.[59] Distinctions between these regulatory efforts—including whether they are local, city, or state level—notwithstanding, they are consistently parlayed as problematic in mainstream accounts in two ways: as hurting or violating business; and as curtailing or denying individual agency. Accordingly, those efforts are generally characterized in this narrative as wrongheaded or ineffective; the impasse implied contributes to and enhances the broader fatalistic discourse that describes obesity as inevitable.

### MARKET FARE

Across mainstream genres and formats, regulatory efforts to control, curtail, or eliminate the sale of certain foods are described in negative economic terms. At best, such efforts are described as ineffective, "not really solving the problem,"[60] or misguided: registering skepticism regarding legislation requiring fast-food restaurants to post nutritional information, for instance, CNN medical consultant Sanjay Gupta noted that "since the FDA has required nutrition labels on [packaged] food [17 years ago], obesity has skyrocketed."[61] More forceful objections characterize such regulatory efforts as arbitrary or capricious to the extent that they inappropriately single out and penalize nutritional culprits—such as trans fats, salt, sodas, fast foods, fried foods—with scant or overblown evidence, a "'ridiculous,' 'insane' and wrong-headed approach to solving the national obesity epidemic,"[62] comprising "'backward voodoo economics.'"[63] The "backward" nature of this approach, according to the discourse, includes the anticipated or real negative impact on affected vendors in terms of, for instance, no longer being able to sell certain products, such as "Big Gulps";[64] having to replace less expensive hydrogenated frying oil with single-course vegetable oil;[65] customers driven away upon learning about the questionable nutritional profile of certain products;[66] and no longer being permitted to sell packaged foods and sugary drinks in schools via vending machines.[67]

Moreover, mainstream accounts note the unfair advantages or marked disadvantages to vendors around access to foods. Subsidized "green carts," established in low-income urban areas to correct for the dearth of produce in these "food deserts" threaten to "cannibalize" businesses in the vicinity that, if they do not sell produce, do sell other food products that customers would buy otherwise.[68] Similarly, legislation limiting or preventing the establishment of fast-food restaurant franchises in these areas is characterized as "unfairly blam[ing]" those vendors and the fast-food industry in general, especially as low-income neighborhoods have been historically the most profitable for that industry.[69]

## NANNY CUISINE

Interestingly, although objections to regulation of foods and food access proliferate the mainstream, most do not address their ineffectiveness as relevant to obesity redress on the explicit grounds of individual responsibility—that is, relatively few accounts posit that regulatory efforts will or do fail because people are ultimately responsible for obesity per their habits and practices. On the other hand, the majority of those objections do cite the inappropriateness of regulation on the grounds of "nanny statism," or the denial of individual agency, specifically around self-determination. This begs the question to some extent, but it is certainly in keeping with the cultural, political, and economic sensibilities of the United States. In general, these regulations are characterized as the government "sticking its nose" into private business, implying that obesity is an individual right. More pointedly, in an arguable appropriation of critical cultural sensibilities, several accounts speaking specifically to altering food access in low-income neighborhoods characterize those efforts as "paternalistic," insulting and condescending to disenfranchised communities;[70] or, more broadly, as biased and discriminatory to obese individuals.[71] The inappropriateness of such efforts is even ridiculed in some accounts, for instance with respect to local school boards banning the venerated tradition of annual bake sales in light of rising rates of obesity among its student populations: "there shall be no cupcakes."[72]

Across these articulations, obesity is presented as, if not impervious to regulation, at least morally inappropriate as a subject thereof and thus off the table. As noted, the overarchingly negative mainstream characterizations of regulatory measures do not engage their effectiveness, real or supposed, so much as negative economic impact and denial of individual agency. Deflective though this may be, obesity is thus assumed to be a given, complementing and reinforcing the fatalism identified in other variants of this narrative.

## The Real Deal

The fatalistic narrative of obesity is both prominent and resonant in the mainstream, likely a function of the fact that it explicitly calls out and engages the respective limitations of the competing precedent accounts of obesity: the official caloric imbalance story, on the one hand, and the environmental one, on the other. Notably, rather than identifying possible points of convergence between those accounts or articulating an holistic perspective that encompasses both, this fatalistic story instead presents both as valid but irreconcilably opposed to each other, resulting in a definitive impasse—concretely, as obesity. Specifically, rational individual redress, championed in the official account, is presented as inevitably undermined by the demands of work and limited resources, not to mention genetic determinism; and environmental redress is likewise articulated as ineffective in view of individual rights and/or practices, or of biology. A perhaps cynical interpretation is that this fatalistic narrative appropriates select tenets of the environmental account to the end of either deflecting them or bringing them into alignment with the official, neoliberally informed one, intentionally or not. For instance, representing material or structural constraints implicitly or explicitly as "lifestyle" considerations effectively places responsibility for obesity back in the individual's court, justifying outlandish recommendations in this discourse of herculean individual efforts to combat environmental or even biological constraints.[73] Cynical as it may be, this interpretation is arguably supported by the fact that less malleable environmental tenets, such as the formidable political and economic prowess of Big Agriculture and Big Food, as well as government policies and practices that sustain them, are relatively and conspicuously absent in this narrative. When the roles of industry and/or government are introduced, in the form of (arguably similarly selective and deflective) local, sporadic, or random interventions, they are definitively dismissed as inappropriate, ineffective, or both.

In any event, given that this narrative is formed in the precise breach between the competing, arguably antithetical official and environmental accounts of obesity, it exposes the major narrative failing of both: authenticity. As I have argued in the preceding chapters, the glaring absence of authenticity does much to explain at least the lack of cultural resonance of either precedent narrative, and perhaps their lack of effectiveness, as well. In the case of the official account, authenticity is denied via the rational individual agent; in the environmental narrative, authenticity is denied via the positing of a passive and homogeneous populace. While the fatalistic narrative does not introduce authenticity into this void, it does invoke it by surfacing and centering that void. That is, in the fatalistic narrative, "real," felt, lived experiences of everyday life constitute the precise grounds on which both the official and environmental accounts of obesity are found wanting. In the fatalistic narrative, not only are people endowed with specific, unique, and various bodies, they are also located in the context of time, of space, and of their particular work, relationships, leisure activities, obligations, desires, pleasures, and choices, encompassing everything from how they get to work and the time it takes them to how much sleep they're getting to how they feel when they eat a doughnut to their histories and relationships with bake sales and Big Gulps. The precedent accounts of obesity fail, the fatalistic narrative suggests, to the extent that neither of them even acknowledges the lived experiences, material and personal, inherent in each of these things, much less accounts for them.

While the fatalistic narrative of obesity is arguably the most broadly pervasive of resonant cultural stories of obesity that have formed in response to the failures of the official account, the environmental account, or both, the substantial and increasing cultural traction of those to come in the following chapters is directly attributable to the version of authenticity that each articulates. Feasibly, they could be as appropriately understood as responses to the fatalistic narrative as they are to the official one, insofar as the fatalistic account surfaces and makes poignant the absence of authenticity.

# 5

# Heavy Legacies

*The Cultural Story of Obesity*

In this chapter, I address the first of the unofficial yet highly resonant accounts of obesity that showcase authenticity, which has in this case to do with culture: this account asserts that obesity, as relevant to specific populations at least, is attributable to particular and unique historical cultural practices, traditions, and legacies, including and especially "foodways." Authenticity is engaged in this narrative to the extent that it is conflated with cultural identity. While this conflation is contestable, it is a common one, as a number of scholars have noted.[1] Because authenticity is a notoriously slippery if not illusory concept, perhaps the most effective way to convey what we think it means, or at least what we want it to mean—that is, who we are, at our cores—is by locating it in unique cultural contexts and conditions, and moreover in particularized habits and practices. As I've already noted, my purpose is not to theorize or assert what authenticity "really" is, or even if we can feasibly speak of such thing. Rather, I want to assess how authenticity is invoked, imagined, and mobilized across alternative accounts of obesity, with an eye toward how those stories respectively reflect broader, contemporaneous cultural tensions, in particular with respect to individualism. Certainly, the *idea* of authenticity is enormously salient and powerfully resonant today, which is why it serves as the fulcrum of this project: I believe that authenticity's absence in the prevailing, official account of obesity is significantly responsible for its lack of resonance (and perhaps effectiveness) among the populace, which has prompted competing and relatively more compelling accounts.

The cultural narrative of obesity in the United States is primarily mobilized across contemporary mainstream media in three ways—or more accurately, as relevant to three specific populations: Southern, Midwestern, and immigrant. Already, this pattern suggests important assumptions about what "culture" means as relevant to race, class, nation, and region, assumptions that I will examine in this chapter. While this story is articulated in terms that suggest nuance, thoughtfulness, and compassion, precisely to the extent that (again, "other") cultures and their practices are acknowledged, contextualized, and justified, it also serves to define and configure citizenship in troubling ways, as relevant to obesity—what it is, whom it affects, and what to do about it—as well as more broadly.

## Obesity Cultivated

The relationship between culture and obesity has been examined from a variety of disciplines and perspectives. In the medical literature, culture—independent of genetic or biological considerations—has been assessed as a factor in the incidence of obesity, as relevant for instance to variable access to particular foods; to opportunities of time and space for physical exercise; and to disparate perceptions of obesity, food, or both. These studies variously describe correlations between obesity and class[2] and/or race/ethnicity,[3] especially to the extent that they overlap, and generally find relatively higher rates of obesity among people of color and members of working and poverty classes.

In the social sciences and the humanities, scholars have taken up the matter of obesity and culture in different if not necessarily incommensurate terms. As I have described in an earlier chapter, the varying cultural significance of obesity, both historically[4] and across cultures[5] has been well established; obesity is not only valued differently across contexts, but often defined differently, as well, typically reflective of the broader cultural, political, and economic imperatives of the context in which it occurs. More recently, critics have further engaged the political and practical implications that follow from particular cultural evaluations of obesity, for example assessing the current characterization of the "epidemic" proportions of the problem,[6] ranging from discrimination and ostracization of obese individuals[7] to the economic implications of that characterization.[8] While I am theoretically and philosophically aligned with these cultural perspectives, and in fact have explicitly situated obesity in cultural context for this project, I take a somewhat different approach to the matter here. In this chapter, I assess culture as an explanatory narrative of obesity: I describe the ways in which specific cultures, or the ideas thereof, are implicated as a cause or culprit of obesity. As noted, the primary cultures invoked in this narrative are the US South; the US Midwest; and immigrant (to the US) cultures.

## Places of Reckoning

Perhaps one of the most common metrics employed to demonstrate the prevalence of obesity—indeed, of various public issues, health and otherwise—is geographic distribution. Because of obesity's currently notorious status as a national "epidemic," people are no doubt quite familiar at this point with some version of a map, frequently utilized in media coverage of obesity, that identifies relative proportions of populations that are obese in the United States, often as compared to prior distribution, projected distribution, or both. While populations are assessed on a state-by-state basis, it is visually evident—as well as widely and explicitly acknowledged—that the highest rates of obesity are concentrated in US Southern and Midwestern states.[9]

Although all nations feature cultural variations within their borders, the United States is arguably exceptionally diverse. This is so for a variety of reasons, including but not limited to its history of colonization and slavery; historical and contemporary patterns of immigration; and sheer size, such that subsets of the population, due to varying environmental contexts (urban as opposed to rural, e.g.; mountainous as opposed to plains) and to relative isolation, at least historically, have evolved into highly distinctive subcultures.[10] Thus, discussion of a recognized culture of the United States must attend to its peculiar ethos. Accordingly, I will describe how the US South and Midwest are, respectively, broadly characterized in contemporary culture in order to establish a foundation for my discussion of the cultural narrative of obesity. These characterizations of the US South and Midwest are inevitably selective, superficial, sweeping, and even stereotypical. My intent is not to validate or perpetuate these narrow depictions, but to identify and describe contemporary perceptions of these cultures that continue to resonate among the broader populace. This will allow me to gauge whether and how perceptions of character or behavior associated with those cultures, accurate or not, factor into accounts of obesity that prominently and consistently showcase them as the most obese regions in the most obese nation in the world.[11]

## SOUTHERN SEDITION

Although it's a bit dangerous to venture a claim about which states are included the US South, the US Census Bureau identifies the states of Texas, Oklahoma, Arkansas, Louisiana, Mississippi, Alabama, Florida, Georgia, South Carolina, North Carolina, Kentucky, Tennessee, Virginia, West Virginia, Maryland, Delaware, and the District of Columbia as comprising the region.[12] A host of "Mississippian" Native American tribes first populated the region until the 16th century, when European explorers advanced into the region; by the 17th century, England, France, and Spain had colonized most of the territory, and disease and strife over land virtually decimated the original inhabitants.[13] The predominant immigrant culture in the region at the time was English, comprised of a small number of wealthy, land-owning elite and a large population of indentured laborers; the southern British colonies provided both England and the American colonies to the north with tobacco, corn, wheat, and cotton. As the colonial population and commensurate demand for these resources grew, England began to raid the west

coasts of Africa in order to procure slaves to work the southern territories, a practice that not only continued but escalated in the wake of the American Revolution
in 1776 that secured independence from England.

Although a host of issues contributed to a growing rift between newly established northern and southern states, the primary factor was the issue of slavery
on, variously, moral, economic, and political grounds. Cultural and political distinctions between "free" and "slave" states became more salient and profound,
and as political power became increasingly concentrated in the north, southern
states petitioned unsuccessfully to secede from the Union in order to form their
own confederacy, ultimately culminating in the Civil War. The Union—that is,
the North—prevailed, and slavery was abolished; however, the legacy of the rift
and attendant sentiments continued to resonate, especially in the South. Over
a century later, the Civil Rights movement almost precisely mirrored the same
dynamics and tensions around race, certainly insofar as the South was culturally,
politically, and morally distinguished (by themselves as well as others) as relevant
to its race politics and practices.

Indeed, those distinctions continue to resonate today, reflected in pervasive contemporary perceptions of Southerners by the broader populace as
rebellious; rural; poor; lacking education (typically construed as "ignorant");
uncouth; violent; racist; and white.[14] Most of these qualities are undeniably
negative, some downright unflattering, although notably, some are embraced by
Southerners: rebelliousness, for instance, is valorized in the proud motto of the
"Rebel South," and "redneckedness"—lack of refinement, education, and, perhaps
overridingly, whiteness—is a proudly proclaimed identity of many Southerners
as well.[15] Perhaps in part because Southerners themselves do not entirely reject
the stereotype—"there are Southerners who take pride in everything they consider disparaged, from the Confederate flag to country music"—it is pervasive
and explicit in broader US culture: "A century and a half after the Civil War . . .
[the South] is often pigeonholed as a tobacco-spittin', Bible-thumpin', gun-totin'
(and worse) backwater."[16]

This legacy is, in fact, apparent in contemporary coverage of the relatively high
rates of obesity in the US South. Across mainstream mediated texts, the widely
reported problem of Southern obesity is predominantly and consistently attributed to defiance, impoverishment and race. As noted, the "Rebel South" is a prominent and pervasive cultural imaginary, historically and today—defiance is highly
consistent with prevailing cultural imaginaries of the South. While it is typically
and historically invoked to reference political and ideological divergence, it is
invoked in contemporary coverage of obesity as willfully self-destructive: that
is, Southerners are presented as participating in unhealthy practices despite
being aware of the consequences of their actions: "[the South] embraces fatty,
unhealthy foods and shuns exercise," according to a CBS report.[17] An ABC story
that featured interviews with obese Southerners chronicled particular instances

of the general characterization of Southerners as intentionally electing to engage in harmful behaviors:

> "[I'd] rather have eggs [than oatmeal]. And . . . some good gravy, biscuits, bacon. I can't help it, I love it. I am an eater, I have always been one and I still will be one, but I am trying to watch my sugar, and I am working at it right now, get it on down." Last year,. . . Emmeline died from diabetes complications. [Their brother] Arlen thinks she was in denial about how severe her disease was. "She didn't take care of herself either," he said. "Blind and everything else. Got down so she couldn't walk and stuff. They just don't want to face the facts that stuff is going to happen to them and they let it go until it's too late."[18]

This behavior is depicted as not simply self-destructive but as consciously, even perversely so—indeed, at times, tantamount to Southern identity and pride. One CBS news story reports that public health efforts that placed nutritional experts in community centers and churches throughout the South "found resistance from cooks who say the healthier recipes alter the taste of their dishes. 'Flavor is a big issue—when you modify Southern cooking, then you lose a lot of the flavor,' said Laurita Burley, a clinical nutrition instructor at the Morehouse School of Medicine. 'The reputation of the Southern cook is at risk when you begin to modify it.' "[19] Consumption as well as preparation is depicted as a hallmark of Southern identity: one Southern woman is described as "proudly" reciting her consumption of the quintessentially Southern "Hamdog" sandwich at an Atlanta, GA, eatery: "a hot dog wrapped by a beef patty that's deep fried, covered with chili, cheese and onions and served on a hoagie bun. Oh yeah, it's also topped with a fried egg and two fistfuls of fries."[20]

Perhaps one of the most visible mainstream instances of this defiance was regularly depicted in the first season of *Jamie Oliver's Food Revolution* in 2010, an ABC primetime television series, which featured the efforts of renowned British chef and food/nutrition activist Jamie Oliver to reform the diet of residents of Huntington, West Virginia, at the time notorious as "the fattest city in the fattest nation on earth." Residents' reception to Oliver was consistently presented as belligerent, irrational, and stubborn: "We're not going to sit around and eat lettuce all day," one man asserts. This reaction is consistently contextualized in terms of place, as well, in ways that underscore Southern rebelliousness: "Who are you to come here and tell us what we should do, how we should eat?"[21] CBS reporter (and Southerner) Jordan Covvey, acknowledging the poor diet and lack of exercise among Southerners and, moreover, their irrational allegiance to those practices, writes, "I wish I could rationalize these trends for you. Strangely enough, the research also shows that we know we have problems. More Kentuckians rate themselves in poor general health than any other state."[22]

This attitude of engaging in irrational, self-destructive behavior is character-ized as endemic among Southerners, not merely affecting the general popula-tion but also—even—the very individuals charged with addressing the problem. An NBC story quotes Mississippi State Representative and Chair of the State Public Health Committee Steve Holland as conceding, "We've got a long way to go. We love fried chicken and fried anything and all the grease and fatback we can get in Mississippi."[23] *Jamie Oliver's Food Revolution* similarly chronicles repeated, illogical efforts of myriad school superintendents to stymie his efforts to improve school lunches even as they concede the nutritionally damaging nature of the foods they are providing.[24] At-the-time Mississippi State Superintendent of Education Hank Bounds, cited for his efforts to reform nutrition in state schools, is quoted as saying,

> "We only have students 180 days out of the year for seven hours in a school day. The important thing is that we model what good behavior looks like," he said Monday after finishing a lunch of baked chicken. Bounds ate at a Jackson buffet that's popular with state legislators. The buffet included traditional, stick-to-your-ribs Southern fare: fried chicken, grits, fried okra, turnip greens.[25]

Financial and educational impoverishment, long established as chronic prob-lems in the South in general, are also regularly cited as an explanation for, especially, Southerners' notoriously poor diets as well as for their relative inac-tivity. Often, this rationale is offered in tandem with the characterization of the decadent, rebellious Southerner described earlier, perhaps to offset or balance it: "Income and education have a lot to do with it [the high rates of obesity in the South]—people living in poor communities may not have the money to eat healthier, more expensive foods or may not have access to gyms or safe jogging trails.[26] Similarly, speaking to Mississippi's status as featuring one of the most obese populations in the nation, "while deep-fried Southern cooking is legend-ary, Mississippi also ranks high in poverty statistics and low in education—two factors commonly related to obesity."[27] Noting that about 20% of Southerners live below poverty level, a CBS story reports that "adults who make four times the poverty level are twice as likely to exercise than poor adults. The poverty level for single adults is just under $9,000."[28] Some reports describe concretely the relationship between poverty and the traditional Southern diet: "Poverty and obesity often go hand in hand, doctors say, because poor families stretch their budgets by buying cheaper, processed foods that have higher fat content and lower nutritional value ... [and] poor [Southerners] often fry their foods [because] it's an inexpensive way to increase the calories and feed a family."[29]

Lack of education, often in tandem with financial poverty, is also cited as a primary contributor to the obesity problem in the South, and several reports even note that educational impoverishment, notorious in the South, "trumps" financial. A CNN story cites an expert who asserts that in the South, "education appears to be more closely related to obesity than poverty. 'We do see obesity among people who are in lower socioeconomic levels, but we see it in higher socio-economic levels as well,' he said. 'Being poor does not make you obese, and being rich does not make you thin.'"[30] Another story explicates this link, noting that "a person's education level . . . may be associated with greater access to health infor-mation and the capacity to understand and use health information."[31] If it side-steps the stereotype of the rebellious, defiant Southerner, it plays upon another, not incommensurate one of the unrefined Southerner—poor and uneducated if not ignorant—as described earlier.

Conversely, a third primary pattern to emerge in media coverage of the high rates of obesity in the South departs from conventional, stereotypical percep-tions of Southerners: that is, rather than explicitly or implicitly showcasing the white Southerner, African Americans are invoked and centered in the problem of Southern obesity. This is reflected most obviously in widely reported national statistics that African Americans in the South feature the highest rates of obe-sity: "For every 100 obese whites in the South, there are 151 obese blacks."[32] But in general, *how* statistics are articulated or framed in coverage tell the tale, and this case is no exception.

One way in which the disproportionately high rate of African-American Southerners' obesity is explained in coverage is in tandem with the attribute of poverty, especially rural poverty, in the South: that is, reports note that Southern African Americans are disproportionately poor, and they represent a large demo-graphic in the region: "at the top of the list [of obese individuals] are low-income, mostly African-American communities";[33] "certain ethnic groups, people from rural areas, and people of low socioeconomic status are more likely to be obese than others."[34] Moreover, it is poor Southern Black women who are featured primarily in this coverage, further decentering, if not unseating, the prevalent stereotype of the poor, white ("white trash"), and implicitly male rebel Southerner: Black women are specifically identified as having the very highest obesity rates, in the United States more broadly but especially in the South.[35]

The specter of Black women is further invoked, if implicitly, in another prevalent—and surprising—pattern of coverage: that is, the Southern diet is seamlessly and wholly attributed to Black Southerners. This is rather a novel turn, for while "soul food" has long been understood as emerging from the enslaved South, such that it constitutes a subset of the Southern diet more broadly, that broader Southern diet has not been historically understood as interchangeable with soul food: while similarities are apparent, significant distinctions have been identified.[36] Coverage relevant to obesity in the South, however, summarily erases those distinctions, broadly characterizing the traditional Southern diet as "high in fat and fried food,"[37] typified by "traditional, stick-to-your-ribs Southern fare: fried chicken, grits, fried okra, turnip greens,"[38] and "fried chicken, fried seafood, fried green tomatoes and cornbread slathered in butter."[39] Significantly, however, the Black Southern diet is presented as identical to this: "Fried chicken, greens seasoned with pork fat and buttery cornbread might be a recipe for disaster, but it's a cuisine steeped in tradition. During slavery, blacks made throwaway foods taste good. And, nurse Francis Henderson says tons of calories made sense."[40] Not only the fare but the favored cooking method of the South—deep frying—is attributed to Black Southerners:

> Much of the South's traditional foods date back to the days of slavery. Frying was preferable in the region's hot climate, since it didn't take as long as baking and didn't heat up a house as much. Plus, Burley said, workers didn't have all day to prepare meals; they had to get back into the fields to work. Lard was also plentiful. Today, frying still is popular, especially in poor areas of the South, because it is also inexpensive.[41]

Similarly, a few stories cite a study that attributes fried fish, a widely prevalent Southern offering, to African Americans.[42] The distinction between Southern food and soul food is effectively erased in contemporary coverage of obesity; although this surfaces a historically erased population in contemporary national imaginaries of the South, it appears to do so only to place the high rates of Southern obesity at its feet—to articulate it as "the bane" of health in relation to obesity.[43]

A third pattern apparent in the public discourse of Southern obesity as relevant to Southern Blacks in particular is pertinent to (mis)perceptions of obesity. That is, Black Southerners are presented as compromised or limited in their ability to identify obesity—for example, as misguidedly characterizing heavy individuals as "big boned."[44] They are further characterized as unable to evaluate obesity "properly," that is, negatively—"'Many African-American women view being obese as part of their culture' . . . curvy, overweight women are considered more appealing to black men than normal- or under-weight women[45]—and/or distinguish between healthy and unhealthy practices— "Part of the difficulty comes with the fact many [African Americans] are still eating [fried chicken, greens with bacon and ham, macaroni and cheese] and then sliding into our Mercedes with our ever-widening backsides, wondering what is wrong."[46] As with diet, while some coverage cites this as characteristic of the South in general, it is strongly and consistently linked to Black Southerners, in particular, sometimes implicitly but usually explicitly. One CNN story quotes a biostatistics expert as noting, upon establishing that obesity is highest among "certain ethnic groups," self-reports of obesity in the South may be affected by the fact that "'there's not a social stigma attached to being fat in the South . . . if you ask people how fat they are, they tell you."[47] More explicitly, the story quotes another expert who notes that Black women in the South " 'are more accepting of their body size than white women . . . they are happy with their weight and less likely to try to lose weight.' "[48] In another report, an interviewed (Black) physician shares his own experience of the skewed perceptions of obesity on the part of Black Southerners via a personal anecdote:

> "Once we get there, we have a meal that is absolutely unbelievable," Wyatt said. "I will have—no exaggeration—probably a plate with 4,000 calories on it. And my relatives will say to me, 'Aw, you're not eating much at all today. You should eat more than that.' The culture part of it is if you're not on the big side, folks where I'm from down in Perry County [AL] say you're not healthy. Healthy to them means you're not big enough." By comparison, Wyatt said that a person with a healthy diet should consume no more than 2,000 calories a day.[49]

The stereotype of Southern ignorance, typically associated with white Southerners and frequently in conjunction with racist attitudes, is extended to Black Southerners here, if in terms of naiveté rather than defiance, perversity, and/or immorality. Even if this could be generously construed as a relatively sympathetic or at least contextualized characterization, it is hardly a positive one; moreover, it reinforces deeply entrenched racist imaginaries of people of color as less refined and intelligent than whites.

Notably, the contemporary discourse around obesity in the US South reflects instabilities and tensions that characterize competing accounts of obesity more broadly, including competing individual and environmental explanations of the problem. Acknowledgment of lack of access and resources as well as historical context bespeaks an environmental model, whereas ignorance and defiance invoke a model of personal responsibility. However, I contend that authenticity is the most significant tension addressed in this particular narrative, manifested and mobilized as *culture*. This is efficient to the extent that it handily accommodates both environmental and individual attributions for obesity, for culture is both historically (externally) configured and variously internalized and performed by members of that culture. In this respect, there is an aspect of fatalism to this narrative, as well. But more importantly, and quite unlike the fatalistic account of obesity described in the last chapter, it tenders a resonant narrative of obesity as an intimately felt material and personal experience. Of course, this particular rendering is problematic insofar as structural features are not only elided but entirely without relevance in this articulation. More ominously, obesity is reframed as a problem of an "other" culture(s), thereby drawing hard lines around citizenship, which I will address in the conclusion of this chapter.

## MIDWESTERN SUBSTANCE

The states generally included in most classifications as the US Midwest—Illinois, Indiana, Iowa, Kansas, Michigan, Minnesota, Missouri, Nebraska, North Dakota, Ohio, South Dakota, and Wisconsin ("Census Divisions and Regions," 2012)— are, unlike the South, generally accepted, probably because its history is not as culturally, politically, and morally fraught. As in the South, the Midwest's original human inhabitants included an assortment of Native American tribes until the 17th century, when France, incentivized by the lucrative fur industry, colonized the region as part of a broad swath of land extending from Canada to Louisiana. French control of the region came to an end with the French and Indian War in 1763, and this was followed by westward expansion of established British settlements to the east.[50]

In the wake of the American Revolution, Europeans emigrated to the United States in large numbers, and many made their way to the Midwest, attracted by promising agricultural opportunities and conditions. Indeed, throughout its human history, agriculture has been and remains the major industry of the region, profitable not only in terms of straightforward crop production but export of those crops to other regions, as well: three of the United States' major waterways—the Mississippi, Missouri, and Ohio rivers—run through the Midwest. For those reasons, the Midwest is known as "the nation's breadbasket." This, in conjunction with its geographically central location, made it a natural center for industry and transport in the mid-19th century.[51]

The issue of slavery also features prominently in the history and ethos of the Midwest, albeit in ways very different from, even opposite to, the South. The then-designated "Northwest Ordinance" region, today the heart of the Midwest, was the first US constituency to prohibit slavery. Moreover, the primary routes for the Underground Railroad, which furnished safe passage for escaped slaves to free territories in the north and in Canada prior to the Civil War, were located throughout what is now the Midwest and coordinated by sympathetic, primarily white Midwesterners, particularly in Ohio and Illinois. While escaped slaves certainly entailed the greatest risk in undertaking the endeavor, those who managed the Underground Railroad risked much as well, for at the time, slaves were still legally considered property of their Southern owners, and aiding and abetting their escape carried serious consequences.[52]

Due to its geographic location as well as its "breadbasket" status, the Midwest has been designated as the nation's "heartland," a designation that has symbolic as well as functional significance.[53] Midwesterners are frequently depicted and perceived as hard working (by dint of both the region's farming and industry legacies), dependable, kind, practical, and unsophisticated—not coarse or unrefined, as in the South, but endearingly naïve and old-fashioned.[54] If not consciously or explicitly invoked, the legacy of the Midwest's participation in the Underground

Railroad further endows and enhances this ethos with honesty, authenticity, and moral integrity.[55] Significantly, however, if in quite different ways than apparent in imaginaries of the South, the Midwesterner is also implicitly understood as white.[56]

If the US South is cited as the most obese region in the United States, the Midwest runs a close second: residents of Midwestern cities and states consistently feature significantly higher rates of obesity than any other geographic population save the South, a fact that is widely reported. As with the South, in media coverage of the matter, distinctive and consistent attributions for Midwestern obesity are apparent, and they, too, draw on historical legacies; however, they are quite different than those made regarding the South—specifically, Midwestern obesity is rationalized in relation to geography, abundant food, and diet, all of which are articulated in terms of peculiarly Midwestern culture and "authentic" identity.

While geography is abstractly implicated in coverage of obesity in the South as relevant to the rural poor, it is explicitly and concretely identified as a contributing factor to Midwestern obesity as relevant to suburbia: "Midwestern suburbs [are a] sprawling American landscape of car addiction and epidemic obesity."[57] Indeed, "Midwestern sprawl," or the typical pattern of unplanned, uncontrolled suburban spread outward from large cities in that part of the county, is linked to a higher degree of sedentariness on the part of residents: "In the suburbs, there are environmental risks for obesity because everyone has to drive to get from place to place, so there's much less time or opportunity for physical or leisurely activity."[58] Indeed, most Midwesterners are reported as "arriving and leaving [their destinations] via door-to-door transportation."[59] As reported, the minimal caloric expenditure imposed by the need to navigate geographic distance, for work, school, or shopping, with mechanized transport increases the Midwestern population's propensity for weight gain: "All other factors being equal, each extra degree of sprawl meant extra weight, less walking and a little more high blood pressure, Ewing concluded. Someone living in the most sprawling county—Geauga County outside Cleveland—would weigh 6.3 pounds more than if that same person lived in the most compact area, Manhattan."[60] Moreover, this trajectory is explained as inevitable and even logical, for alternative modes of transit are identified as impractical if not downright dangerous:

> Far worse were Pucher's findings that per trip, American pedestrians are roughly three times more likely to be killed by a passing car than German pedestrians—and over six times more likely than Dutch pedestrians. For bicyclists, Americans are twice as likely to be killed as Germans and over three times as likely as Dutch cyclists.[61]

Interestingly, unlike the South, where geography's role in obesity is implicitly referenced in articulations of the rural poor, explicitly identifying suburbia as playing a causal role in Midwestern obesity depicts it as a problem of the middle class, at least in that region.

Food abundance is also identified as a contributing factor to the prevalence of obesity in the Midwest, drawn especially against its historical agricultural legacy. Copious food is reported as a traditional measure of Midwestern success:

> In the Farm Belt states of the Midwest, said Dr. James L. Watson a professor of anthropology at Harvard, the tradition lingers that a family's success is best embodied by the bounteousness of its table. "If you go to a place like Iowa, where I'm from, you're expected to eat," said Dr. Watson, who studies food and culture. "When you visit somebody's home, they pull out the high-fat cakes and goodies, and if you don't eat, you're not part of the kinship group."[62]

As suggested in the excerpt, the production and presence of abundant food is a measure not only of economic success but of kinship, as well: "hearty" meals and a bounteous table signify strength and vigor of family bonds.[63] Moreover, commensurate consumption—that is, via "hearty" or "healthy" eating or eaters—is reported as traditionally crucial to materializing that symbolic value, to ensure physical health as well as affirm the family: Midwesterners are described as exceptionally "well-fed Americans."[64] Saul reports that Ohio native "John Froman, 50, said he used to spend holidays eating his way from one family dinner to another, putting on weight at each stop. 'You do two Christmases, three Thanksgivings, two New Years; everybody is cooking real big.'"[65] To encourage consumption and, accordingly, secure the significance of food abundance, food is especially conspicuous, visibly so, in the Midwest, according to reports, via what is identified as a typical Midwestern practice: "family style" dinners, where multiple dishes are presented in numerous large, communal platters or bowls distributed across the dinner table from which diners help themselves. "[The town of] Albert Lea [MN] is being encouraged to overhaul its eating routines. . . . Families are adopting new kitchen tips to help cut calories, such as serving food from the stovetop instead of at the table, where second helpings are easy to grab."[66] Abundant food and consumption thereof is portrayed as a fundamentally, even quintessentially Midwestern cultural tradition, a pattern that, notably, complements an articulation of obesity with an imaginary of middle-classness.

However, diet is by far the most prominent causal factor identified in media coverage of Midwestern obesity—specifically, traditional "Midwestern fare," notoriously and interchangeably identified as staunchly "meat-and-potatoes."[67] "Lard still plays a starring role in many kitchens, bacon comes standard in salads, and perhaps the most important event on Kansas City social calendars is a barbecue contest. Even though the region boasts some of the finest farmland in the world, there is a startling lack of fresh produce here."[68] Midwesterners' predilection for "high fat cakes and goodies"[69] and junk food such as "Velveeta or Twinkie[s]"[70] is also frequently cited.[71] Thus, similar to depictions of the Southern diet as culpable in the obesity epidemic, the regional diet of the Midwest is indicted for its nutritionally questionable character, albeit in distinctive ways, as relevant both to the actual fare and, especially, how it—and residents' embracing and indulgence of it—are depicted.

Indeed, campy humor is apparent in nearly all characterizations of the Midwestern diet as relevant to obesity: Midwestern fare is articulated, if playfully and even affectionately, as culinary kitsch. Typical Midwestern restaurant fare, for instance, is described as comprised of "mystery meat and puddles of beans"[72] and "lard-bathed French fries."[73] One article reports the "intrepid" culinary adventures of a woman who dined at a number of school cafeterias throughout the Midwest, "where she ate bagel dogs (yes, that's an entree), yellowish meatloaf and chicken tenders, which she likened to 'squirts of chicken foam.' "[74] Midwesterners themselves are not exempt from this playful mocking; for example, upon asking a server whether the beans were prepared with meat, a vegetarian reporter notes the server's response: " 'There's no meat,' the waitress replied helpfully. 'It's just pinto beans smashed up with lard.' "[75] Considerable coverage further secures this trope of Midwesterners' benign naiveté regarding food, noting that "the mentality of the Midwest is [that] green is garnish";[76] as well as the chronicling the particular challenges confronting vegetarians who dare to traverse the region: Sulzberger cautions that vegetarians in the Midwest must brace themselves for an "inevitable barrage of questions, if not outright mockery" from Midwesterners, who are likely to point out "squandered opportunity (how could someone turn down all that delicious barbecue?) and others hinting at concerns about survival (are you sure you know what you're getting yourself into?)."[77]

In contemporary discourse around obesity, then, Midwesterners are characterized as highly, if charmingly, traditional and conservative, often naively so, but also practical and benevolent, in literal and immediate ways. Moreover, these qualities are depicted as logical products of their agricultural heritage; for instance, Midwesterners' food traditions—fare and practices—are traced back to the farming legacies of the Midwest, as is their conservatism and skepticism regarding—even resistance to—alternative practices, especially around food. As well, their privileging of motor transit in the face of suburban sprawl is consistently depicted as logical and rational rather than irresponsible or lazy. Thus, as with coverage relevant to Southern obesity, a cultural explanation for obesity is tendered, one that arguably rationalizes tensions inhering between environmental and personal responsibility rationales for obesity. Also as with coverage of Southern obesity, however, structural redress is elided. But this cultural accounting of obesity is especially significant and resonant, again, to the extent that it centers authenticity: that is, obesity is directly and intimately linked to identity and experience, both material and psychological; both historical and contemporary. This articulation of authenticity, as predicated on culture, features problematic implications, political and practical, that bear examination, of course; but it is significant to the extent that it ventures and centers authenticity as the crux of the matter of obesity.

## Imposing Figures

If not defined regionally—at least, not in the same, stable ways as the US South and Midwest—immigrants also feature as the third prominent population in the cultural narrative of obesity. While national imaginaries (read: stereotypes) of immigrants abound, they are both more varied and more contested—indeed, frequently diametrically opposed to each other—than broadly familiar characterizations of Southerners and Midwesterners, respectively. This is so because the figure of the immigrant is situated at the center of heated political debates around immigration policy that turn on a plethora of complex ideologies and anxieties relevant to political and economic values, national security, and/or moral obligations. The issue is further complicated insofar as discourse about immigrants can and does vary as relevant to legal versus illegal status, as well as to the extent that it intersects with racial and ethnic stereotypes: that is, general perceptions of Asians inevitably are reflected in perceptions of Asian immigrants, for example, and the same is true with respect to Latinos, Arabs, Europeans, and so forth.[78]

Nevertheless, it is safe to say that most contemporary public discourse about immigrants and immigration focuses on the influx of Latinos into the United States, legal as well as illegal, specifically whether to regulate it; why or why not; and if so, how. Certainly, the greatest proportion of US immigrants today are Latin American, due to the geographic proximity of impoverished and/or politically unstable Latin American countries to the United States: Mexico and the United States share a border, and Mexico is geographically contiguous with Central and South America, making the United States the most proximate developed or relatively economically advantaged nation to those nations.[79] Moreover, many Latin Americans have established ties and/or family members in the United States, ranging from ancestral lineages that in fact predate US appropriation of Mexican lands in 1848 to recent arrivals, legal or illegal.[80] Latino immigrants have been and continue to be variously imagined as, for example, hardworking, noble, stoic, martyred; or as cunning, predatory, dangerous, lazy. These characterizations, contradictory as they are, arguably constitute the currently prevalent cultural perceptions, in fact, respectively mirroring as they do politically liberal and conservative sensibilities, as least as mobilized in the contemporary United States.[81]

Public awareness and conversation regarding obesity rates among immigrants is grounded in three major sets of research findings: first, that immigrants have significantly higher rates of obesity than the rest of the US population, taken as a whole; second, that rates of obesity among immigrants climb the longer that they are in the United States; and finally, that rates of obesity are extremely high—some of the highest in the country—among second-generation immigrants. As with any findings relevant to obesity, particularly telling is how this data is taken up and circulated in the mainstream. In several respects, the resultant account mirrors the broader discourse regarding immigrants in the United States in general. For instance, with few exceptions, a focus on Latino immigrants dominates mainstream accounts. As well, if those accounts do not blatantly replicate the "dueling" prevalent stereotypes, they do reflect broader tensions around both immigration and race/ethnicity/nation. Indeed, especially notable about this particular version of the cultural narrative of obesity is its ambivalent, even disparate articulations. Nonetheless, collectively, the overarching characterization of immigrant obesity draws upon surprisingly consonant commonplaces and assumptions that inform both perspectives, to the extent that they turn on perceived "authentic" Latin natures and practices. These commonplaces, if mobilized in distinctive, typically paradoxical ways, are apparent across three primary axes in coverage of obesity among immigrants: "othered" bodies; displacement; and cultural illiteracy.

One aspect of the cultural account of obesity as relevant to immigrants engages the immigrant body as "different"—a characterization that explicitly turns on race or ethnicity and implicitly normalizes the white body, for white immigrants do not feature in discussion and coverage in the mainstream, even when included in some of the cited original studies that have been conducted on obesity among immigrants.[82] This is actually a minor theme in the narrative, given that scientists as yet have been unable to identify specific genetic propensity for obesity in anyone, much less as relevant to race/ethnicity. Nonetheless, it is indirectly present in the immigrant story of obesity in two—paradoxical—ways. The first of these suggests that immigrants are physically stronger and more resilient than others in an attempt to explain the fact that first-generation and recent immigrants are significantly healthier than the broader population despite their typically impoverished circumstances: the so-called "Hispanic paradox," for, as noted, most of the research and attendant coverage focuses on Latinos. Some coverage attributes this to the self-selected nature of the sample, such that "those who choose to immigrate could be unusually healthy, since uprooting to another country requires strength and vitality":[83]

> You do not see the sick or the weak crossing rugged deserts to get from Mexico into Texas. . . . The first-generation Mexican immigrants who are strong enough to make it into the United States are often hearty and in good health, experts say, making them likely to live long lives and pass along their good genes to their offspring.[84]

A variant of this interpretation is that immigrants who are assessed in studies are healthier—younger, stronger—representatives of the population because

"Hispanic immigrants tend to return home to die."[85] Other reports suggest that Latinos are healthier as a result of greater levels of physical labor: "it is the physically demanding jobs many immigrants have on construction sites and farms that keep them fit, as opposed to sedentary office jobs that lend themselves to expanding waistlines";[86] similarly, "'weeding fields and walking long distances . . . make you burn too many calories.'"[87]

Paradoxically, however, high rates of obesity among second-generation (or later) immigrants and/or first-generation immigrants who have lived in the United States for relatively longer are also regularly attributed to their physical *frailty*. While one study speculating about Latinos' apparently greater propensity to store fat in the pancreas was briefly cited in the mainstream,[88] the majority of coverage in this vein implicitly suggests that immigrant—specifically, Latino—bodies are markedly more vulnerable than others to environmental obesogens. This is relayed in, for instance, the "shockingly" high rates of obesity among this population relative to the rest of the country:

> Nationwide, the rates of obesity and diabetes among Latinos are soaring to record levels, according to the federal Centers for Disease Control and Prevention and other groups. Latinos in the United States live longer than non-Hispanic whites but have higher disease rates. They are almost twice as likely to die from diabetes and have much higher rates of obesity and high blood pressure.[89]

Researchers are consistently reported as being "stunned" by the findings: "We just couldn't believe the fact that we found roughly a threefold increase from the one extreme [first-generation immigrants] . . . to the people on the other side [third generation]."[90] Moreover, these effects are chronicled as dramatic in their onset, as relative to the gravity of the health issues as well as how early they are experienced:

> Clarissa, [Blanca's] 13-year-old daughter, had a darkening ring around her neck that suggested early-onset diabetes from too much sugar. Now Antonio, 9, was sharing dosages of his mother's cholesterol medication. Now Blanca herself was too sick to work, receiving disability payments at age 40 and testing her blood-sugar level twice each day to guard against the stroke doctors warned was forthcoming as a result of her diet.[91]

An impression of the delicate and sensitive constitutions of Latino immigrants is secured by accounts that suggest they may serve as "'canar[ies] in the coal mine' for the rest of the country, giving a concise picture of what the country might look like in 20 years if appropriate behavior changes aren't made."[92]

Obesity among (virtually entirely Latino) immigrants in mainstream coverage is also attributed to drastic cultural changes, particularly as relevant to diet and family, predicated in both cases upon a romantic imaginary of the "old ways." While the "typical" US diet is necessarily implicated and indicted, it is incidental to the theme of loss that thoroughly and overridingly characterizes this discursive thread.

> Authentic Latino dishes include fresh fruits, herbs and beans, all of which are healthy. But with immigration and acculturation to the United States often comes a change in eating behaviors, such as cooking fewer meals at home, eating larger portions, preparing foods differently, and buying more cheap and convenient fast foods loaded with sodium, fat and sugar.[93]

"Sugary cereals and pizza" and "fast-food outlets,"[94] which are characterized across mainstream accounts as comprising the diet of immigrants, are contrasted sharply with traditional foods, often home grown: " 'People here are so poor that we grow a lot of our own food, we buy only what we need.' "[95] And the foods that they do purchase are depicted as similarly wholesome: "Hispanic families shop in aisles stocked with fresh produce and protein: chili-drenched oranges, pineapples and mangos; whole-roasted chickens; tubs of black beans."[96] Accordingly, reinstating access to and consumption of these traditional foods on the part of immigrants is consistently encouraged in mainstream coverage: "immigrants might do well to cling to healthy traditions such as diets rich in fruits, vegetables and fiber";[97] a doctor is quoted as saying, "I tell them to go back to what they ate at home: rice and lentils and fruits. To recover what they have lost."[98] Commensurately, not consuming—even lack of access to—US foods is articulated as beneficial: "Immigrants may be used to a more rural setting overseas where there's no access to soft drinks or they are too expensive, and here they find them all over the place and at a very low cost."[99]

Culturally traditional familial structures and practices are also invoked in a similar, romanticized fashion to account for high rates of obesity among established or latter-generation immigrants. This is parlayed in concrete ways, insofar as

> [o]nce immigrant families arrive here, their lives and routines change dramatically. Parents work around the clock at cleaning and construction jobs, and there may be little time to shop and cook. There is constant physical effort but virtually no beneficial exercise, such as jogging or swimming. Children are kept indoors for safety, often supervised by older siblings and quieted with soda, snacks and microwaved noodles.[100]

This is drawn specifically, both implicitly and explicitly, against "the ways of the old country," wherein Latino mothers cook "rice and beans daily" as well as other whole foods[101] and Latino families "[sit] down at the dinner table" together[102] rather than make "trips to fast-food outlets, including several Central American chicken chains ... weekend family rituals."[103] In accounts that address first-generation Latino immigrants' relative health in relation to that of their children and grandchildren, intact but threatened traditional Latino bonds are cited in abstract, sometimes in mystical ways: it is linked to " '*corazón*,' or 'heart' ... it is the strength of the Hispanic family unit ... 'It's hard to measure, but it's palpable in this culture,' Dr. Cardenas said, 'and it's something that carries you from cradle to grave.' "[104] As with the traditional Latino diet, the traditional family structure is articulated in terms of loss; immigrants' displacement from both is identified as a—often, *the*—primary factor in high rates of obesity, in directly proportionate ways—indeed, as several accounts suggest, the further removed immigrants are from these things, the higher their rates of obesity, which is proffered to explain statistical differences in progressive generations of immigrants.[105] Here, too, conversation around immigrant obesity is overlaid with a fundamental paradox, in this case between abundance and wholesomeness—of food and family, in particular—on the one hand, and impoverishment and lack of those very things on the other, no doubt reflective of the polar political ideologies that inform apprehension of "the immigration question" in general.

A final feature of the public account of immigrant obesity is relative to ignorance on the part of immigrants, which is also variously—again, paradoxically—attributed to either problematic, ingrained traditional beliefs around diet and/or body; or to conscious harmful practices undertaken to the end of assimilation. As relevant to the first scenario, for instance, a Latina notes in one report that "in my country, if you are thin, people think you are not healthy,"[106] an attitude apparently confirmed in other reports that note, "This is the problem within the Hispanic community ... We love our curves, but the line between beautiful and deadly curves is blurred."[107] "Hispanic" women, in particular, are cited as especially ill-informed across reports that cite studies indicating that overweight Latinas are significantly more likely than "non-Latino white women" to perceive their weight as normal.[108] This traditional attitude is articulated relevant to children as well, sometimes characterized as inherently misguided, whether in relation to body—"Latino families tend to think that a fat child is healthy and a thin one is not. It is a big problem," food quantity—"it all starts with our grandparents. We are taught to fill our stomachs"—or food quality "[Marisol Quiroz] thought she was cooking healthy meals, but they were heavy on the white rice she liked from her childhood in the Dominican Republic. The family [had to learn] about proper portion size."[109] But it is typically identified as problematic in conjunction with the high availability in the United States of cheap processed and packaged foods: "Throughout Central America and Mexico, it is widely believed that children should be chubby, and a common term of endearment for a spouse is 'gordo' or 'gordita,' which means 'fatty.' " This attitude, coupled with easy access to and convenience of cheap, fast, and processed food, is represented as a recipe for obesity, if not disaster: "You have acquired the habits of the promised land, and they are slowly killing you."[110] Moreover, (especially new) immigrants, several reports cite, may simply be unaware of the risks of too much junk food or of opportunities for exercise";[111] or they may "come here thinking everything in America must be good for them, whether it is fast food or infant formula. They don't realize the damage all this is doing."[112] "We need to get more educated and think in a different way," an immigrant is quoted as saying. "We are not in Guatemala now."[113]

More recently, ignorance is implicated in the immigrant obesity problem not as lack of awareness but as consciously, perversely bad choices: several mainstream accounts cite studies that indicate that immigrants, especially second-generation immigrants, may "get fat to fit in":[114] that is, strategically "choose [to consume] high-calorie, fatty foods in an attempt to appear more American"[115] precisely in order to assimilate into dominant US culture—"which is to say they *try* to be fat."[116] While "choosing typical American dishes" is attributed primarily to immigrants' desire to "show that they belong and to prove themselves as Americans," it is also cited as especially prevalent among children of immigrants, who, it is speculated, may be embarrassed by consuming food from their home country in front of others."[117] If ignorance is construed differently—once again, even paradoxically—in this accounting, it is nonetheless generally commensurate with other articulations and sediments it as a culturally salient characteristic of immigrants, at least as relevant to the prevalence of obesity among that population.

Although characterizations of the high incidence of obesity among (overwhelmingly Latino) immigrants are sometimes divergent, even paradoxical, they draw upon notably consonant commonplaces and assumptions about "authentic" cultural identity. The first of these is that immigrants are embodied, more so than "real" US Americans. This is reflected both in the centering of the superior strong, laboring immigrant body in this narrative, *and* in articulations of the immigrant body as inferior, frail or more susceptible to the foods and environment of the United States. Of course, the notion that people of color are more embodied—that is, visceral, primitive, sensuous—than white people is a deeply entrenched and highly troubling stereotype; if it is articulated in relatively subtle ways here, perhaps even earnestly proffered in the spirit of offering nuanced, sensitive, and contextualized understanding of the matter of obesity among immigrants, it is no less effective in establishing immigrants as "different" in ways that turn on race and nation and privilege whiteness. Invoking the body to secure this enhances a perception that this difference is "authentic," materially felt, experienced, and therefore "true." A corollary to this, of course, firmly established in both implicit and explicit ways, is that immigrants (specifically, their bodies) do best in their native cultures; whether articulated in terms that indict US dietary culture and practices in ways that valorize those of immigrants or that attribute obesity to immigrant physical or intellectual shortcomings, both accounts converge to the extent that immigration hurts immigrants, if not inevitably and irrevocably, at least to the extent that they assimilate. If physical restoration of immigrants to their "native" lands is not advanced outright in these accounts, cultural restoration very much is; acknowledgment, revival, and maintenance of their "authentic," traditional culture and identities is consistently touted as an appropriate antidote to immigrant obesity. Here, too, as with centering the body in accounts of immigrant obesity, what is significant is not only that difference is underscored—to some extent inevitable, as immigrant status is the very premise for the narrative—but that it is substantially augmented, moreover in markedly regressive ways that reentrench powerful cultural and racist stereotypes, even when ostensibly sensitively rendered. This is accomplished precisely via authenticity: immigrant obesity is articulated as a felt, lived, material experience that is powerfully and inevitably grounded in cultural identity.

## Stock Response

The articulation of obesity with culture or cultural identity is the first mainstream vernacular account of obesity that acknowledges and engages authenticity. In this narrative, authenticity is articulated as interchangeable with cultural identity, which is not a shared assumption among scholars and philosophers, although it is a common enough popular perception. As noted at the start of this chapter, my purpose is not to assert, as relevant to this account of obesity or any other, what (or even whether) authenticity is; rather, my goal is to establish its various salience for and deployments in contemporary public stories of obesity, including as they reflect broader cultural and political tensions. In this particular story, most conspicuous is the fact that authenticity—or cultural identity—is something that "other" people have: rebellious white Southerners; marginalized Black Southerners; quirky, naïve (white) Midwesterners; and (overwhelmingly Latino) immigrants, with the odd Asian immigrant community very rarely featured. Immediately apparent on the heels of this observation is the default conflation of culture and authenticity with, primarily, races and ethnicities other than white, and in the case of relevant white populations, with antiquated practices and personas. In both scenarios, these populations are drawn against a presumed normative contemporary whiteness by virtue of historical distance or racial/ethnic "difference." Figuratively, these "others" are set apart, cordoned off, often under a guise of veneration—for example, via imaginaries of martyred immigrants, descendants of slaves, or misguided benevolent conservatism—or in ways that characterize populations as belligerently "opting out," as with defiant white Southerners. The practical implications of this narrative, significantly, are that these populations are implicitly articulated as ineligible for aid or intervention, at the very least insofar as the chasms that prevent "us" from adequately understanding "them" and how to engage "them" on "their" terms; but also, and perhaps most troublingly, on an implicit moral basis that articulates intervention as inappropriate—insensitive, patronizing, and/or ethnocentric. For instance, a story that intricately connects foodways to historical and contemporary injustices wrought upon marginalized individuals by those more privileged cannot justify a replication of that pattern, to which intervention is, in this narrative, implicitly tantamount—for example, by promoting assimilation or the eradication of cultural practices.

To place these narrative dynamics in broader context, specifically in terms of the current national tensions and negotiations around individualism in the wake of neoliberalism in crisis, what is particularly notable about this cultural narrative is its clear delineation between authenticity and individualism. As I have argued, I believe that the current crisis in neoliberalism prompted a rift between the neoliberal imaginary of the individual as autonomous and rational, and the currently salient and resonant concept of authenticity, understood as uniquely lived, felt, experience. Because obesity is inescapably embodied and because it is similarly inescapably imbricated with consumption, current competing stories of obesity inevitably reflect this broader tension, specifically to the end of reconciling, in various ways, the relationship between philosophical and political ideals of individualism and the current cultural imperative of authenticity. In this cultural narrative of obesity, this tension is negotiated in ways that appropriate select features of authenticity but ultimately reject it. In effect, this narrative could be characterized as restorative of presumptive neoliberal individualism, one that acknowledges and even showcases authenticity but rationalizes it as problematic, unproductive, and unsustainable, drawing it against and ultimately promoting individualism predicated on autonomy, agency, and rationality.

Most obviously, authenticity is generally articulated in this narrative as harmful and dangerous for those "others" who have it, at least in contemporary national context; even in cases where authenticity is touted as beneficial—that is, the old-world foodways of immigrants—that is only the case if and when they are restored, literally or figuratively, to their "native" cultures. In all cases, authenticity is presented as contraindicated with health. Capitalizing on the conflation of authenticity with cultural identity, authenticity is also associated with passivity via a herd mentality, to the extent that members of these identified cultural communities take their cues from those around them. The emergent postulate, then, is that for one to be healthy—literally and figuratively, that is, in terms of success and happiness—one must transcend or renounce one's culture, a rational act of conscious agency. This is an interesting and clever sleight of logic, in that authenticity, which is generally commonly associated with personal identity and material, lived experience, is radically depersonalized, sited instead as communal, abstract, and reactive, associated moreover with unhappiness and failure. By implication, conversely, individualism is predicated on strategic rational choices made to the end of realizing personal needs and desires. Furthermore, by associating individualism with health, the material, embodied experience of self is similarly divorced from authenticity. In this vein, the extent to which "authentic others" are articulated as more in and of their bodies in this narrative is notable: they are described as physically or genetically predisposed to obesity and fat, and/or more prone or unable to resist their bodies' demands or responses. The primitivization of "others," especially people of color, is a very well established trope; as played out in this narrative, just as one is encouraged to renounce one's authentic cultural identity in order to secure health and leanness, one is encouraged to disembody, or to apprehend the body as an object—a move perfectly correlated with the conventional neoliberal imaginary of the rational, autonomous individual (not to mention the official account of obesity). Notably, structural interventions are summarily elided in this narrative—when they are identified, they are consistently presented as ineffective or limited, and they are also, implicitly and sometimes explicitly, presented as morally questionable to the extent that they smack of patronizing assumptions and directives. Of course, the notions that individuals are ultimately, exclusively responsible for their own welfare, and that structural intervention is a categorical impediment to that objective, are foundational tenets of neoliberalism, highly complementary to the imaginary of rational, autonomous individualism on which it turns.

On its own terms, the cultural narrative of obesity advances authenticity, which is conflated with cultural identity, as an explanatory device for obesity, effectively establishing authenticity as harmful and dangerous: a liability, indeed an obstacle to individual health. More broadly, this account can be understood in relation to broader cultural and political navigations of individualism, until recently, under neoliberal logics, imagined as rational and autonomous. In that context, this cultural narrative of obesity can be feasibly apprehended as a rationalization of that imaginary of individualism. In this story, authenticity is centered and acknowledged, but it is ultimately drawn against individualism and found wanting: a burden of legacy, an unbearable weight of tradition.

# 6

# Heavy Heart

## *The Story of Emotional/Spiritual Dysfunction*

The second culturally prevalent account of obesity that showcases authenticity turns on spirituality and emotionality, which, although sometimes invoked in distinctive ways, are generally conflated in this perspective. In this narrative, obesity is not articulated as the problem; rather, it is an embodied symptom of emotional/spiritual dysfunction. Specifically, obesity is presented as a manifestation of repression or management of one's emotions, needs, and/or desires—that is, of the "authentic" self. Again, my goal in this book is not to explore authenticity or establish what it is, or even that there is such a thing. Likewise, my interest in this chapter is not in asserting or defining spirituality: both of these endeavors are beside the point of my aims. However, the ideas—or imaginaries—of authenticity and spirituality that inform and drive this narrative are very much central to it. My interest is in assessing how they are configured and mobilized to the end of making sense of obesity in a broader contemporary context that has surfaced deep tensions around cultural identity, particularly as relevant to the founding political precept of individualism.

Whereas the cultural narrative of obesity discussed in the last chapter situates authenticity in opposition to individualism, the spiritual/emotional narrative configures that relationship quite differently: that is, it proposes individualism as a, indeed *the*, path to authenticity. The conditions that engender the spiritual and/ or emotional pain that ultimately manifest in obesity are consistently traced in this account to prioritizing others over oneself: accordingly, the moral of this story is that privileging the self, by making conscious, strategic, and rational choices to that end, is the only way to realize authenticity. Interestingly if not exactly surprisingly, this story of obesity abounds in the mainstream, albeit virtually exclusively in popular entertainment fare—but it is by far the predominant account in that broad genre. While all of the other stories of obesity that I have recounted thus far are available across genres, this is the first in which this is not the case—with few exceptions, it is virtually absent from news coverage. However, it is everywhere, apparently deeply resonant with the broader populace; in fact, as I will illustrate, some of its tenets have assumed the level of conventional wisdom in contemporary cultural understandings of obesity.

## Manifest Malady

In this narrative, commensurate with the conventional, caloric imbalance model, obesity is linked to overconsumption of (typically "bad") food, but that practice is presented here as incidental, a misguided attempt to repress or manage emotional pain, stress, or confusion. This rationale is captured in catchphrases so familiar that they have reached the level of mantras in contemporary culture: for example, obesity is understood to result from "using food to stuff feelings," "eating to fill an emotional hole," "emotional eating"; the first step to overcoming obesity, in this story, is to understand that "it's not what you're eating, it's what's eating you."

This narrative has been prevalent and pervasive in the broader culture for the last decade, and its entrée into the mainstream can arguably be attributed primarily to Oprah Winfrey, highly popular talk show host of the *The Oprah Winfrey Show*, which ended its successful 25-year run in 2011; and powerful media mogul for the last 15 years: owner of, respectively, her own production company (Harpo), magazine (*O*), radio station (Oprah Radio), and television network (OWN). Winfrey's influence on the public agenda as well as on shaping public opinion and behavior, ranging from political and social issues to recreation, has been widely noted; while that influence was arguably at its zenith when her daily talk show was in active production, she continues to be recognized as a powerfully influential cultural icon.[1] What has certainly persisted is the broader foundation, rationale, and objective for that influence, which is spirituality: that is, that which is seen as "feeding the soul" (a phrase much associated with Winfrey) is endorsed and cultivated. Illouz argues that this credo is rhetorically mobilized in a national "discourse of authentic selfhood," of which, she argues, Winfrey was an early and principal purveyor if it did not necessarily originate with her, and it remains strongly associated with her. However, Illouz and others note, that discourse has essentially obtained "received" status: that is, it is so deeply embedded in and infused throughout the culture that it is no longer reliant upon any single oracle.[2] According to this discourse, success, happiness, and health—in other words, self-actualization—can only be achieved via intensive "work" on, care of, and love for the self. Importantly, while the authentic self that serves as the locus of this discourse is frequently addressed in spiritual terms, it is rarely articulated with religion; indeed, it is often *dis*articulated from it. Rather, the emphasis is on specifically personal, highly individual fulfillment. Distillations of the discourse include slogans such as "live your best life," "be your best self," and "take responsibility for your own future," which has led several critics to note the congruence between this "discourse of authentic selfhood" and neoliberal sensibilities that privatize individual welfare and, moreover, frequently turn on consumption to the end of self-actualization: Illouz has described this phenomenon as "emotional capitalism."[3] The discourse of authentic selfhood writ large, then, has been well established, including as it links to neoliberalism. My aim here is not to reassert that discourse but to examine its particular instantiation and mobilization in relation to obesity—one that narratively establishes obesity as a symptom and consequence of emotional or spiritual pain, a materialization of the unactualized self.

If the discourse of authentic selfhood cannot be directly attributed to (as opposed to popularly associated with) Winfrey, the linking of it to weight, and the resultant understanding of obesity as a symptom of emotional or spiritual pain, arguably can be. This is so because the topic of weight was and remains a regular feature of media content emerging across Winfrey's various outlets; when her talk show was in active production, weight or obesity featured exclusively or primarily in approximately one third of all broadcasts.[4] Those shows continue to be available and easily accessible on Winfrey's popular website, and they remain regular, often primary topics of her magazine, radio program, and television network fare. Moreover, Winfrey herself is notorious for her "weight issues," having visibly lost and (re)gained significant amounts of weight throughout her public career; in fact, this is a frequent, explicit focus of much of her own programming. Winfrey's discussion of her personal "struggle" with weight is consistently and unequivocally framed in terms of spirituality, more precisely in relation to emotional pain or distress.

As with so many topics to which Winfrey has directed her attention and influence, here, too, she has had an impact: the professional "life advisors" that Winfrey regularly includes and consults in relation to weight management—including nutritionists, medical doctors, fitness trainers, psychologists, spiritual advisors—have all achieved significant popular status and attendant success, and in some cases, the attention of the medical community.[5] However, as with (perhaps due to) the precedent and supersedent widespread discourse of authentic selfhood, the emotional/spiritual narrative of obesity has proliferated and infused the culture to the extent that, if Winfrey is its poster child, it is no longer limited to her experience or perspective.

Because obesity is cast in this narrative as a materialized—embodied—symptom of spiritual or emotional dysfunction, it cannot be overcome without confronting and resolving the "real" reasons why one is obese. Repression or denial of painful emotions or experiences perhaps constitute the most salient of these reasons; food, as the story goes, is inappropriately used to "fill a hole" created by unacknowledged emotional needs or "stuff [painful or uncomfortable] feelings." Psychologist Robin Smith, among Winfrey's original cadre of advisors, notes across multiple (Winfrey) venues that "it's not about the food": "there is often a deeper reason for overeating and that we have to get to the root of the void that people are trying to fill with food."[6] Similarly, Winfrey-discovered trainer, nutritionist, "lifestyle guru," and now highly successful author in his own right, Bob Greene, agrees that "weight is symptom of something deep in your life that you need to confront . . . it's not about weight."[7] Medical doctors, too, are cited, noting that "more and more experts believe that severe weight gain is driven by psychological distress of some sort."[8] Dr. Mark Hyman, well known and widely published in the mainstream and author of one of the most popular obesity blogs,[9] notes that "part of why we eat has nothing to do with the food itself, but more our relationship to ourselves and the quality of our lives . . . [we use] food to escape painful emotions or as a means to press the pause button on a life disrupted from its expected trajectory."[10] Weight Watchers, a prominent cultural authority on weight loss and management, likewise acknowledges "the emotions that send you to the fridge: insecurity, sadness, anxiety, boredom, frustration, hurt, loneliness."[11]

In some cases, the emotional pain or damage cited as the "real" problem is profound, rooted in what most would recognize as traumatic events by any measure: Dr. Sharma, another popular obesity blogger, cites a "common association of emotional, physical or sexual trauma with increased emotional eating, binge eating disorder and weight gain."[12] Many accounts invoke highly traumatic events and experiences, such as sexual abuse; David, for instance, featured on an *Oprah* episode, describes how he used food to comfort himself across years of molestation during his childhood, when he had no one to trust or confide in.[13] Extreme and extraordinary traumatic events are especially strongly implicated as well, as when Season 13 *Biggest Loser* contestant Buddy recounts his use of food to cope with grief upon the death of his 5-year-old daughter,[14] or when Carol notes in a *Prevention* magazine article that, "Knowing my child had an incurable disease made me feel helpless. One minute I was sad and the next I was furious, but I could always count on food to make me feel good."[15] This perspective is further validated by findings widely circulated in the popular press of the relationship between obesity and post-traumatic stress disorder (PTSD) experienced by returning war veterans.[16]

Although these examples of emotional pain and distress are extreme, importantly, they are not the only or even most common variants that are justifiable under this rubric; relatively more mundane and common sadness or anxiety likewise prompts spiritual angst and attendant, dysfunctional practices. In the wake of her parents' divorce, Dawn "'turned to food for everything,' she recalls. 'I soothed myself with food. I rewarded myself with food'";[17] "hearing the negative comments and late-night jokes about her weight sent [Star Jones] into an eating spiral. 'The late-night comics [were] crushing,' she says."[18] Similarly, Carnie Wilson,

> daughter of Beach Boy Brian Wilson . . . says she didn't have a typi-
> cal childhood and that she constantly sought attention from him as a
> child. "I didn't have a relationship with him growing up and I believe
> that is a big part of the holes that I have felt in my life," she says. His

battling alcohol, drugs and mental illness made her childhood even more difficult, Carnie says, and she turned to food for comfort. "I used food as a coping mechanism for many, many years, and it was my best friend for a long time."[19]

and simply whenever "food fills a void in your life, like lack of a loving relationship or passion for your job": These instances—indeed, whenever "food fills a void in your life, like lack of a loving relationship or passion for your job"[20]—are all cited as practically on a par with traumatic events, to the extent that food is utilized in every instance to repress or minimize emotional pain. It is this impulse that is narratively centered, not the nature or degree of the pain in question. Indeed, for the same reason, stress is also included in this rubric insofar as it sparks the same practical outcome: "Maybe you had a particularly stressful day, and that sugar rush from a pint of Ben and Jerry's is instant gratification;[21] and "Craving 'comfort foods' is normal when you are feeling anxious—don't feel alone when cravings hit during a big deadline at work."[22] Moral legitimacy of the behavior is established across these instantiations primarily because they resonate; they are framed as not only understandable but relatable, frequently unconscious impulses: note, for instance, how often "you" is utilized in these scenarios, implicating the reader or viewer in the practice. Moral legitimacy is further conferred to the extent that science is invoked to rationalize the impulse, as when Weight Watchers reports research that establishes that "the creation of negative emotional distress sensitizes the reward system in the brain, causing a stronger reaction to appetizing foods. This may help explain why emotional stress can lead to disinhibited eating";[23] and when cardiologist-cum-popular television show host "Dr. Oz" states:

> When you are stressed out, your body is flooded with cortisol, a stress hormone, which makes you crave carbohydrates, sugar and fatty foods. Food is soothing due to the chemical changes it creates in your body. Chocolate is an excellent example. Chocolate boosts the "feel good" neurotransmitters and chemicals in your body that make you more alert and excited.[24]

The narrative logic that describes the (mis)use of food as a means to ameliorate pain or anxiety clearly locates the practice under the rubric of self-medication, which is frequently explicitly acknowledged in this account of obesity: medical doctor Ralph Jones, an author featured on the popular obesity blog Fooducate, acknowledges that "food is used as medication to control and suppress negative feelings such as sadness, anger, depression, anxiety, loneliness or boredom."[25] While some, like Bob Greene, concede that "food is meant to be enjoyed," they caution that "eating is not supposed to be the main source of joy or your main response to stress, boredom, or emptiness in your life."[26] In this vein, but speaking more directly to the point of misuse or abuse of food, another writer notes that

> Sitting down to a yummy sweet along with a cup of tea or coffee is an age old way of self soothing. And a perfectly harmless one if done in moderation. However, when eating becomes what we do to calm down when we're stressed or feel better when we're feeling down or sad or anxious, it can have serious consequences. Food starts to be a "substance" that we use, or rather misuse, to feel better fast.[27]

And of course, the consequence of heavy or consistent abuse of food is articulated with overweight, in general, and especially with obesity: an assumption undergirding this narrative is that the more weight one carries, the more regular or extreme the abuse.

This logic further places the spiritual/emotional story of obesity in conversation with the broader discourse of addiction. That is, consistent with addiction narratives, food is articulated, explicitly and implicitly, as a drug—or at least featuring properties thereof—whose abuse culminates in significantly harmful consequences, physiological as well as psychological. Following this logic, physiologically, obesity is to food what cirrhosis is to alcohol; kidney failure to narcotics; collapsed veins to IV drugs; lung cancer to tobacco. Psychologically, the experiences of shame, isolation, and deprivation are interchangeable. But if a case can be made for food addiction, there are notable gaps in the analogy, the most glaring of which is not, perhaps contrary to popular belief, biochemical. In fact, as noted in some of the passages just cited as well as in the narrative of environmental causes of obesity covered in chapter 3, there is mounting evidence that certain foods or food components indeed prompt biochemical responses that simulate or, in some cases, replicate the effects of powerful drugs and/or alcohol in the brain and body.[28] Psychologically, certainly, the way in which obese individuals "describe their relationship with highly pleasurable food satisfies nearly all of the DSM-IV substance dependence (addiction) criteria of the American Psychiatric Association, and only three out of six criteria are required for establishment of a dependence."[29] Rather, the difference is that, whereas conventionally recognized addictive substances (1) are not required by the body; (2) are understood as if not categorically harmful, at least inherently potentially so if not carefully regulated; and (3) must (according to convention) be entirely eradicated—use or consumption must completely cease—in order to overcome the addiction or manage addictive tendencies, food is diametrically opposite on all counts: (1) it is required in order to sustain life; (2) its consumption is always beneficial, at least in part—if some foods are healthier than others, even "empty" calories provide energy; and (3) it must be regularly, indeed frequently, ingested.

Thus, the incorporation of the concept of addiction into the spiritual/emotional dysfunction account of obesity is modified in two, typically linked ways with respect to redress. The first of these is with regard to how food is framed and engaged—or, more accurately, how it should be *reframed*: a common refrain in the narrative is that "one should develop a healthy relationship with food," specifically one that defines food in purely biological terms, as energy, to the end of a healthy, strong, and efficient body: that is, as "fuel."[30] Indeed, this reframing is often articulated as the most critical or only necessary step in managing "food addiction"—for instance, "the first step [in controlling binge eating or poor food choices] is to remember food is fuel."[31] A second way in which the addiction discourse is modified as relevant to food is rendering food incidental, even irrelevant—erasure of the addictive substance in that case, captured in the familiar mantra "it's not about the food." Accordingly, "work on the self" rather than elimination and avoidance of the offending substance is promoted as the only way to overcome food addiction and its material consequence: obesity.

This is perhaps best reflected in the oft-cited truism in this account of obesity that gastric bypass surgery, an increasingly popular procedure, is not a solution to the "real" problem of emotional pain or dysfunction, and sometimes not even to obesity itself: according to this logic, and supported by numerous cited examples, gastric bypass recipients frequently turn to other addictive substances and behaviors, such as alcoholism, drug addiction, promiscuity, or gambling, once consumption of food as the original drug of choice is constrained.[32] This is so because, again, "it's not about the food" in this narrative, but about emotional and spiritual denial, repression, pain, or dysfunction: food is simply a form of self-medication to manage this distress, and obesity is a consequence of abuse of—addiction to—that medication. In the absence of unrestricted access to food, as with gastric bypass, other substances or practices are inevitably substituted for it, the story goes, because the "real" problem has not been addressed. Moreover, in some reported cases, addiction to food may persist and lead to a regaining of the weight, either by dint of eventual expansion of the minimized stomach or by primary or exclusive consumption of especially "bad" foods. The poster child for this phenomenon—who, ironically, was a poster child for gastric bypass surgery itself when her own surgery was telecast live on the internet in 1990—is Carnie Wilson, who serves as a regularly and highly visible illustration in the mainstream that gastric bypass surgery doesn't "fix" obesity. "How successful are those people going to be if they don't do the [emotional] work?" she has said. In Wilson's case, her "real" issues are identified as rooted in her father's neglect of her during her childhood.[33] Accordingly, the problem of food addiction and, consequently, obesity is only incidentally connected to food, such that the addiction can (only) be "cured" despite necessary consumption of the addictive substance simply by confronting one's emotional demons and given expression to the authentic self: upon doing so, "you will begin to treat your body and your mind and the way in which you intake food so differently . . . you will see food for what it is—it is fuel."[34]

## The Real Deal

As with the official caloric imbalance account of obesity, the individual is clearly centered in this alternative story of obesity as emotional or psychological pain or dysfunction. S/he is similarly situated in both narratives to the extent that obesity is attributed to individual actions and practices; as well, redress can only be accomplished via individual effort and, importantly, rationality. However, the moral dimension of the imaginary of individualism mobilized in the spiritual/emotional dysfunction narrative of obesity is notably distinctive: that is, overcoming obesity is articulated here as a *spiritual opportunity* rather than a moral obligation or expectation. In other words, it is an avenue to personal growth rather than (implicitly social) virtuosity; overcoming obesity is part of a broader project of realizing the authentic self, to "life your best life."[35]

The means by which this is accomplished is, first and foremost, intensive and extensive self-reflection and self-discovery, or "work" on the self: "You can lock up dessert, but you won't lose weight until you find out what your fat wants to tell you."[36] Health and fitness guru Bob Greene, originally one of Winfrey's committee of "life coaches," urges clients to critically assess "the real reason you're eating compulsively; it's a coping mechanism to get you past certain moments that must be painful." Only by doing the "hard work" of rigorous self-examination can one hope to overcome obesity; "our relationship with food is expressing a true need, so unless we learn what it's trying to tell us, permanent weight loss will be impossible. Once we 'get it' and understand the needs that food fulfills, emotional eating, having served its purpose, will stop."[37] Hyman describes what it is entailed in such self-examination and why it works:

> I encourage you to question your appetite for life and increase your curiosity about what you want to get out of it. In what ways do you substitute food for authentic fun, excitement, or satisfaction from living the good life? What really nourishes you and what first step is realistic for you to take to move toward that? If you struggle with emotional eating I propose you accept yourself and all of your emotions first. Sounds easier said than done? By tending to your emotional wellness, perhaps with a trusted professional or friend, you enlighten a piece of yourself that's been left in the dark. By acknowledging your whole being and allowing these emotions to surface, you free yourself from a mental tangle harping on rigidity, judgment, and pain. You'll no longer require food to keep difficult emotions or stress stuffed deep down inside.[38]

Indeed, a host of formerly obese individuals testify to this directive and its effectiveness; Star Jones, for instance, notes that her obesity was a material consequence of the fact that "I was dying," she says. "I now know I was very depressed. I was lonely, and I didn't know how to say, 'I'm lonely.' That's one thing that I have learned in doing a bunch of research and self-analysis."[39] Popular obesity blogger Diane Carbonell confirms, too, that upon "honest" self-examination, she realized that her obesity was a consequence of "us[ing] food as a soother of emotions, and as a way to push down unpleasant feelings and emotions." Once she confronted those emotions, "the weight came off."[40] Similarly, Season 12 *The Biggest Loser* contestant Bernardo notes that the real value of the show was not his weight loss but that "it has given me the emotional strength to understand and deal with why I was fat in the first place; no diet in the world will help you lose weight without that."[41] Indeed, material practices such as "smart" food choices and exercise are endorsed, but only as attendant or complementary to self-reflection; rather than effective measures in themselves, taking "small steps" like "cutting fast food out of your diet or walking everywhere you can . . . will [keep you] motivated to take better care of yourself" as one "get[s] to the root of the void that [you] are trying to fill with food."[42] In fact, exercise in particular is consistently *dis*articulated from weight loss per se, valuable instead to the extent that it fosters self-confidence; "being active" and "moving" are evidence of "a new lease on life,"[43] rather than a means to an end. Like obesity, exercise is simply a material manifestation of one's spiritual state, in this case the decision to actively "take charge" of one's life.[44]

The "hard work" of self-discovery to the end of overcoming obesity entails not only uncovering why one is obese—that is, identifying the experiences and emotions that lie beneath the compulsion to "fill an emotional hole" with food—but also embracing and enacting two principles that counter that repression: self-expression and privileging/prioritizing the self. Self-expression, of course, is the obvious, practical antidote to the repressive tendencies to which obesity is attributed. "Allowing . . . emotions to surface"[45] is crucial to the project of weight loss, this articulation of obesity avers; rather than using food to deny or "stuff" feelings, "listen to [them], express them directly."[46] To this end, if more circuitously, Geneen Roth, author of the popular, bestselling book *Women, Food, and God*—an exemplar of the emotional/spiritual narrative of obesity—recommends writing a "fat dialogue," as she did,

> to learn what [my fat] wanted from me. It rambled on about wanting my attention, then ended up telling me something that forever changed my life: It told me that as long as I was thin, I would be flinging myself at someone who lived across the country, didn't love me, or was otherwise unsuitable. When those words came unsuspectingly out of my pen, I was stunned. I was also nailed. . . . Within a short time after writing that dialogue, I resolved to devote my attention to writing and teaching instead of flinging and convincing. I stopped needing the suffering

of bingeing and extra weight to get my attention and I started losing weight. And buying clothes with real waists.

Roth goes on to recount an analogous anecdote involving a friend who, upon "asking herself how her bingeing was helping her," realized that she was stifling her need to express herself and her desires: " I asked her to name what she would do if she could do anything in the world. 'I would sing,' she said. 'I would get up onstage and belt out some Supremes songs.' . . . Take lessons, I said. Make a home CD. Check out local choirs or clubs or singing groups. I urged her to stop— bingeing—in the name of love and take the direct route to her heart's desire."[47] A *Biggest Loser* contestant echoes this sentiment, noting that her primary motivation for being on the show—weight loss being attendant to it—is that "I don't want to fake my life anymore."[48] The (weight loss) value of giving full and free expressions to one's emotions, desires, and "true" self is similarly described in the proceedings of obesity therapy group wherein the counselor

> didn't nudge Galbo about her binges. She rarely discussed food at all, in fact. . . . instead, she encouraged Galbo to visit and vent her hurts. At first Galbo found this hard to do. Then, one week, Mellin was late for the group meeting, which infuriated the artist.
> "Go ahead," Galbo remembers Mellin saying. "Give it to me. What are you feeling?"
> "I'm feeling angry that you're late," Galbo said.
> "You don't sound angry," Mellin answered.
> Galbo yelled, "I'm feeling angry! I'm angry that you don't care!"
> "What do these feelings remind you of," Mellin asked, "from before you were 5?"
> Galbo burst into tears. "On the first day of kindergarten, my mother took me to the wrong class. Instead of paying attention to me, she was focused on herself."
> "What do you need?"
> "I need the focus to be on me. I need to pay attention to myself."

This exchange, notes the reporter, revealed to Galbo that not only did she use food to repress her desire for attention, but "her bulk provided a safe way to lash out at her mother." Upon learning skills to identify and express her "real" emotions, Galbo was able to shed her excess weight.[49]

"I need the focus to be on me," in fact, captures the bottom line of obesity redress in this narrative: its most prominent and prevalent directive is to "put yourself first." In the words of health guru Bob Greene,

> the number one thing you need to understand [in order to lose weight] is this—you are worthy of a better life. . . . To change, you've got to feel

these three words: 'I deserve this.' You're not going to get anywhere, long term, until you say to yourself, 'Hey, I'm not a bad person, and I really do deserve this.' The people who succeed at losing weight and keeping it off have said to themselves, 'I am worthy of whatever I am seeking.'[50]

Greene, as noted, was "discovered" and brought to mainstream attention by Winfrey more than a decade ago, and while he has become highly successful in his own right, it is perhaps not surprising that his prioritization of the self as relevant to obesity redress aligns with Winfrey's philosophy on the subject, and she is perhaps its most well-known proponent—including in relation to herself. Winfrey's own ongoing "battle" with weight has been the subject of extensive mainstream media coverage over the years; in addressing a significant weight regain a few years ago, she noted. "I didn't follow my own fundamental rule of taking care of self first. . . ."[51] In order to "get a handle on weight," she has consistently asserted, "you have to put *you* on the top of your priority list."[52] This sentiment is by no means exclusive to Winfrey and her disciplines, however; to the contrary, it is widely prevalent in the broader culture, apparent in exhortations that the key to successful weight loss is to "honor yourself," "have reverence for yourself," "and "love yourself," which is frequently manifest as self-indulgence: "take time out for yourself"; "pamper yourself."[53] In this story, overcoming obesity is a project of self-actualization after all, which necessitates privileging the self.

## Bad Company

The project of privileging the self within this narrative is explicitly drawn against other people in ways that clearly render them suspect; that is, the "hard work" of self-actualization specifically relevant to putting oneself first entails resisting the lure of others and/or their needs, which is articulated as a zero-sum game. At the very least, others represent passive potential saboteurs to the extent that one feels an obligation toward them, a compulsion to put their needs first. Chronicling the link between this perceived obligation to others and obesity—the warrant being the "toll on emotional health" brought about by subjugating one's own needs—the popular *Biggest Loser* blog notes:

Some thoughts or beliefs that feed this unhealthy responsibility are ideas such as: "I'm helping others, so it's ok that I neglect myself," others will not like me if I do not say "yes," or I'll take care of me 'next' time. These types of beliefs lead us to take care of others needs before our own, or take on too many responsibilities, which leads to physical, mental, emotional, and spiritual exhaustion.[54]

In her discussion of why she regained a significant amount of weight, Winfrey identifies this same sense of obligation of others as a key culprit in the quest to put self first and, ultimately, lose weight: "Look at falling off the wagon, as I am, not as a weight issue, but a love issue. Like all of you, I'm really good at giving love to other people and my happiness . . . really comes from giving to other people. But we all need to . . . give ourselves at least as much love and support as we give to others, and that means putting ourselves first.[55]

While this dynamic is identified in this narrative as salient to all seeking to overcoming obesity, it is often gendered to the extent that it is frequently described as particularly poignant for women in that they, for reasons variously attributed to social expectations to their natures, are more inclined to suppress their own needs and desires in deference to those of their children, partners, extended family, friends, neighbors, and colleagues. Winfrey has noted this explicitly and frequently, in various venues: women need to "learn that they are more than the roles they play in their lives—wife, mother, sister, daughter, caregiver. 'I know about the grace and kindness you give to everybody else,' Oprah says. 'But there is a greater purpose than your sacrifice to others.'"[56] This greater purpose is their self-actualization, the realization of their "authentic" selves, the repression of which is materialized on their bodies as fat.[57] Indeed, women who fail to lose weight often cite or are framed in terms of their failure to prioritize themselves: Carnie Wilson, for instance, in explaining her inability to lose weight or keep it off, states that she was "trying so hard to be a good mother that I forgot to put myself first."[58] Notably, this gendered articulation spins prioritizing the self, a staple conservative social philosophy, as a socially progressive, implicitly feminist act of resistance.

Subversive others also come in a more active, even if well meaning, form; these are family members and friends, typically, who tempt one "off the wagon" with "bad" foods. In a "Where Are They Now" follow up to Season 8 of *The Biggest Loser*, for instance, contestant Brittany reports having to constantly fend off family members "trying to wear me down";[59] Robin, too, is depicted resisting family members' urgings to "have a piece of pie, girl, you're looking meager."[60] Mac's strategy for dealing with these undermining tactics is to issue an ultimatum, making his visit to his parents' home conditional upon their stocking "lo-cal food" for him.[61] Notably, gender is frequently invoked here, too, albeit in decidedly conventional, even caricaturish ways; that is, mothers are depicted as especially treacherous to one's attempts at weight loss or maintenance, encouraging their children to eat in ways that are presented as self-serving. (The irony of this appears lost in the narrative.) This pattern is frequently described as established in childhood, a fairly straightforward deployment of the "blame it on the mother" trope; for instance, Nancy's mother "used food to show love, so I always associated it with that,"[62] and Jackie realizes, to her chagrin, that she has been doing the same thing with her children: "I thought I was showing them love with the food I was making for them, when I was actually hurting them and setting them up for the same misery and heartache that I had to go through."[63] Even into adulthood, though, mothers remain a threat: Bill reports his difficulty standing his ground when his mother visits and "wants to make the food I loved as a kid";[64] likewise, "Barbara says she knows she's spoiling Billy by letting him eat whatever he wants. 'It's hard saying no to your child when they want something to eat,' she says. 'It gets tiring, but everything I do for him, it's all out of love. It's what mamas do.' Now, Barbara says she understands she's enabling Billy."[65]

In even more specific ways, a similarly troubling dynamic is present as relevant to race/ethnicity. That is, a recurrent theme in this narrative, rarely apparent in coverage of white individuals (the single exception being the rural Deep South), is the explicit depiction of people of color within their "culture" or "communities"—concepts that effectively stand in for race/ethnicity in this account—and the presentation of those very cultures and communities—not simply members of them—as insidious and subversive to individuals' efforts to be healthy and fit. Specifically, the foods associated with those cultures are depicted as decadent in the literal sense of the word: seductive they may be, but they are imminently dangerous, destructive, and sinister. DeJeannette Williams reports her challenges in resisting the tempting bounty at weekly Sunday dinners with her extended family in Georgia;[66] LaToya similarly describes her efforts to "stay strong" at family gatherings where "there's so much temptation" to partake of "the food I grew up eating in my family."[67] People of color who do resist are described as having recognized the error of their communities' ways; Trent, for example, expresses his gratitude for his *Biggest Loser* experience insofar "it's taught me to make better, smarter choices for my family, like baking rather than frying chicken wings, so I can break the cycle."[68] Similarly, Mallory, another contestant on *The Biggest Loser,* reports her revelation that her family's food traditions, which include "fried chicken, collard greens, and sweet potato pie," constitute "bad habits"; she plans to teach her family "the right way to live" upon completion of the show.[69] All of the examples cited feature African Americans (and additional examples abound, as chronicled in the previous chapter); this pattern is not apparent, with one exception, as relevant to white individuals, despite the fact that food is always culturally significant, always tied to and symbolic of identity. The disproportionate, virtually exclusive focus upon the foods and foodways of people of color as "cultural," and, more to the point, the characterization of the consumption of those foods as wrongheaded and even dangerous—that is, eating to identify or connect with one's "community"[70]—is quite troubling, in the same ways that I have chronicled in detail in the last chapter on the cultural narrative of obesity, if it is accomplished quite differently. As taken up in this spiritual/emotional narrative, this particular mobilization seems to suggest that for people of color, specifically and virtually exclusively, "putting themselves first" means rejecting their especially nefarious "cultures" in order to be "better, smarter, [and] healthier."[71]

# Get Real

Like the cultural narrative of obesity described in the prior chapter, the center-piece and rationale of the spiritual/emotional story of obesity is authenticity. Also like the cultural narrative, this one likewise can be feasibly understood as an effort to restore the presumptive neoliberal imaginary of individualism. However, the way in which it narratively accomplishes that is radically different: whereas authenticity is essentially conflated with cultural identity in the cultural narra-tive to the end of distinguishing it from—and drawing it against—individualism, authenticity in the emotional/spiritual narrative is, first, explicitly decoupled from culture; and second, tightly aligned with individualism, to the extent that individualism is posited as the (really, only effective) means to the end of authen-ticity. Effectively, authenticity is posited in this narrative as not only commen-surate with individualism as funded by neoliberal logics but articulated as its organizing, indeed its driving principle.

Within the narrative, as described, obesity is merely a symptom, a material manifestation of emotional, psychological, and/or spiritual distress or dysfunc-tion. Denial or repression of these emotions and experiences—essentially, of the self—is accomplished by eating "for the wrong reasons," for example emotion-ally; to connect with others; to "stuff" feelings; or to "fill a hole," thus resulting in excess weight. Overcoming obesity, then, is a project of self-actualization, a quest for "authentic selfhood," which makes it an opportunity rather than an obligation: obesity is not a source of shame within this narrative, or even something over which one has agency and thus responsibility. This, of course, directly contradicts the official account of obesity, which identifies the obese individual as morally cul-pable for his or her condition due to lack of self-discipline or -control. But rather than reject a conventionally individualist orientation by positing a repressed and passive subject, the competing—and highly resonant—story of obesity as emo-tional or spiritual dysfunction not only sustains but reinforces that orientation by defining it even more stringently and expanding its parameters into a spiritual realm. Specifically, individualism is drawn summarily and categorically against others—in particular, family, friends, community—who are cast as not simply obstacles to but saboteurs of one's quest for authenticity. They are frequently vaguely implicated as the cause of obesity in the first place: the hurt, neglect, or abuse that manifests in obesity is frequently traced to others in this narrative, often originating in childhood, for instance at the hands of parents. Even when it is not, it is typically related to others: a partner or relationship or a stressful work environment, for instance. Moreover, nefarious others are also invoked as contemporary nemeses who can and will—whether passively or actively; inad-vertently or intentionally—subvert requisite efforts to prioritize the self in this project of self-actualization, ranging from felt pressures—internal or external—to "put others first" to others explicitly encouraging "bad" practices. The details are irrelevant; the fact is that others, by definition, hamper one's efforts to "honor" or even "be" oneself.

This characterization of others as obstacles to the authentic self furthermore features notable gendered and raced undertones. Women are depicted as especially vulnerable to the demands, real or perceived, of others. As well, women—especially mothers—are often implicated as particularly prevalent and dangerous saboteurs, in childhood and into adulthood, if inadvertently so, in that they "use food to show love." More abstractly, this is consistent with a depiction of obligation or responsibility—and, materially, fat—as passivity and weakness; accordingly, individualism, articulated with strength and agency—and, materially, leanness—is implicitly correlated with conventionally masculine sensibilities. This is hardly novel, of course, but it is mobilized in this account of obesity in particular ways—for instance, women's resistance to the felt obligations and/or the demands of others is presented as socially progressive. Within this logic, then, rejection of the feminine is a condition of not only weight loss but authenticity. Also as described, "other" (i.e., other than presumed, invisible, normative whiteness) races and ethnicities are explicitly called out as antithetical to the project of self-actualization. In this regard, the conflation of identity and culture is a premise shared across the respective cultural and emotional/spiritual narratives of obesity, as is the correlation of obesity with cultural identity. The difference between the two accounts and their respective logics is that, whereas authenticity is conflated with cultural identity and ultimately drawn against individualism in the cultural narrative, authenticity is drawn against cultural identity in the spiritual/emotional narrative and aligned with individualism: individualism is the only viable path to authenticity in this story. Accordingly, identity and culture—read: racial or ethnic alignments or orientations other than white—are thus exposed as *in*authentic: not only unhealthy but harmful and dangerous, the "downfall"[72] of those seeking realization of the authentic self. Notably, this logic further underscores the white privilege inherent in conventional imaginaries of individualism more broadly, apparent in the cultural narrative as well, albeit in different ways.

The story of obesity as a manifestation of spiritual or emotional dysfunction turns on the prominent, arguably originary point of congruence between authenticity and the neoliberal concept of individualism: self-actualization. As described in the introductory chapter, the current resonance of authenticity has been attributed, at least in part, ironically, to neoliberal logics that justify the privatization of goods and services against an imaginary of a citizen-consumer with unfettered access to market offerings to the end of satisfying his/her needs and desires. As authenticity has gathered steam on other fronts, I have argued, the crisis of neoliberalism mobilized in and by the financial collapse ruptured that imaginary, forcing a tension between authenticity as it is now understood—as felt, lived subjectivity—and self-actualization as sterile, rational, and abstract.

The narrative of obesity as spiritual and emotional dysfunction, however, reconciles these notions by pointing up not only their commensurability but their complementarity: conscious, rational individual practices are redeemed insofar as they are cast in this story as crucial to the project of realizing the authentic self.

Lending fodder to an apprehension of this story of obesity as a salvage project for neoliberal logics and imaginaries are the ways in which the state and the market are construed in relation to the reconfigured authentic individual. The most notable of these is the structural element—that is, government or other oversight or regulatory agencies. These are entirely elided in this account; not even cast as suspect, they simply do not figure in it. But what does happen—and what arguably underwrites this elision—is the invocation of a host of cultural agents who serve as facilitators in the quest for self-actualization: for example, health or lifestyle gurus, therapists, advisors, life coaches, or trainers who can offer health, fitness, nutrition, psychological, and/or spiritual guidance and expertise. Importantly, however, their services are exclusively available at the behest of (and, notably, purchase by) the individual: again, spiritual growth (and attendant, inevitable weight loss, per the narrative) is an opportunity available to the individual, but it can only be achieved via his or her own "hard work" of self-discovery, self-expression, and self-prioritization, or honoring of the self. As definitively established by the characterization of community/others as inherently oppositional to the authentic self, any qualification of self-determination is antithetical to the project. Indeed, the uniform opposition to bariatric surgery in this account can feasibly be understood in these terms: even though one elects that surgery, its purpose is to regulate the body's intake of food, thereby negating agency and autonomy. The cultural agents who stand in—sign in, if you will—for structural intervention deflect attention away from broader or alternative considerations as regards obesity as well as actual regulatory agencies. Moreover, they exemplify the classic neoliberal tenet of the privatization of and consumer-driven regulatory or oversight functions.

If the specter of government or regulation is obfuscated in this narrative via a sort of shell game, the market is the true stealth figure of the trifecta in the reconfigured neoliberalism that informs this account: although not explicitly apparent or referenced, it is pervasive as the amorphous and diffuse backdrop against which the project of authentic selfhood occurs. It is apparent, in the first place, in terms of "resources"—these include the goods and services provided by facilitators described previously, whether in person or via attendant products and materials available for purchase. It is also apparent in a staple tenet of this narrative: that honoring and loving the self entails pampering and indulging that self, which are inherently linked to consumption—for instance, by buying clothes, getting spa treatments, taking a vacation, or getting oneself gifts to both reward oneself for weight loss, but as an important symbolic practice of putting oneself first.[73] If specific products and services are not touted, the market has powerful presumption in that it provides both the means for and warrant of authentic selfhood: consumption is the obvious way by which to accomplish and ensure prioritization of the self. Notably, just as obesity is a material manifestation of emotional and spiritual dysfunction in this story, consumption is subtly but powerfully articulated as a material demonstration of spiritual and emotional balance. Of course, consumption undergoes a makeover in this story, as well, in that lines are drawn between inappropriate consumption—consumption driven by or for others, specifically, to assuage or manage pain or stress wrought by them—and appropriate, even vital consumption, in the interest of the self. But like individualism, consumption is accordingly redrawn and redefined in such a way as to not only sustain but reinforce and expand its reach and significance.

Thus, the emotional/spiritual story of obesity also can be understood as a mobilization of the (re)negotiation of neoliberal logics and imperatives prompted by broader contemporary tensions and anxieties, especially as they circulate around individualism and consumption. In this case, the fundamental imperatives and logics of neoliberalism are not only preserved but powerfully reinforced, specifically by invoking authenticity as its organizing and authorizing principle— self-actualization, a founding neoliberal logic, effectively undergoes a makeover in this story and emerges as authentic selfhood, reconfiguring individualism as a requisite philosophy to that end. Accordingly, the individual is privileged and prioritized, a move accomplished in large part by characterizing society and social welfare—the family and community, in the story proper, and/or their needs—as antithetical to authenticity. The role of the market in the quest for authenticity is secured as presumptive, and structural agents and entities are handily swapped out for privatized cultural versions—lifestyle coaches and advisors of various stripes—designed to facilitate the quest for authenticity, and exclusively at the behest of the individual, at that. The market is thus essentially reinstated as the logical, tangible path to authenticity, for it furnishes the range of goods and services among which the individual may choose on the path to authentic selfhood.

The articulation of obesity as a materialization of spiritual or emotional dysfunction clearly "rings true" among the populace, as evidenced by its sheer pervasiveness in the popular culture and its acceptance as common knowledge. Undoubtedly, the story's acknowledgement of authenticity—in this case, the "real," lived, felt experience of obesity—has much to do with its resonance. I expect that the fact that authenticity is rendered in this narrative as congruent and consistent with the conventional, presumptive imaginary of individualism, however, has a great deal to do with this, as well. A compelling story of authenticity, whether mobilized relative to obesity or anything else, must account for individualism—it is far too fundamental to the national cultural identity to be elided or cursorily acknowledged. Moreover, the neoliberal imaginary of individualism, predicated on autonomy and rationality, is so deeply entrenched today that its presumption cannot be dismissed. For these reasons, this particular story of obesity is a powerful one: it salvages individual rationality and autonomy, articulating them as opportunities rather than obligations, *and* acknowledges felt, lived, embodied experience, lifting the burden of personal moral failure. To be clear, as I have already described, this narrative is troubling on many counts, specifically with regard to how it articulates those against whom the authentic self is drawn. In terms of reconciling currently competing cultural logics, however, it is highly compelling.

# 7

# Fighting Weight

## *Stories of Resistance*

Another resonant if contemporary story of obesity is resistive: that is, resistive to or at least challenging of the very premise of the official account that establishes obesity as undesirable and problematic. That challenge is not new, but it is more typically encountered in academic contexts. Many cultural critics, for instance, assert that current obsession with obesity constitutes a "pathologization of fat"[1] and that the designation of current rates of obesity as "epidemic" or "critical" are even more troubling in their implications. Some, for instance, have observed that that designation literally profits a number of industries and endeavors, ranging from pharmaceutical and surgical interventions; to goods and services directed to weight loss; to products and amenities designed for obese individuals—a constellation that Finkelstein coins "the obesEconomy."[2] Others contend that the current "fat panic" is simply a manifestation of contemporaneous broader social, cultural, and political fears and anxieties—in this case, relative to excess, greed, decadence, and (over)consumption—and as such constitutes a particular variation of irrational moral panics, other examples of which include witch hunts, the Red Scare, and Satanic ritual abuse. These episodes serve to provide material focus and traction for profound, nebulous, and otherwise overwhelming tensions and anxieties characterizing a society in a given historical moment.[3] Feminist critics argue that the culturally gendered dimensions of fat and their role in current concerns about obesity are paramount; chronicling the ways in which fat has long been associated with femininity, they assert that, at base, vilification of fat and material policies and practices around its management or elimination is fundamentally about the discipline, control, and/or subjugation of the feminine.[4] Finally, a number of critics have noted how the cultural vilification of fat is materialized in practices and policies, both formal and informal, that authorize discrimination against overweight and obese individuals.[5]

Dilute or modified versions of some of the preceding critiques can be identified in the mainstream narrative of resistive, but it is mobilized there in two primary ways: fat acceptance and defiant decadence. Although they vary dramatically in terms of imperatives and premises on which they respectively rely, they, like all of the competing stories of obesity currently in circulation, turn on authenticity in confluent ways. In this case, authenticity is *embodied*: the body in its "natural" state serves as both a material and moral narrative touchstone, and self-actualization is attendant to realizing and embracing that natural state. In this way, authenticity is conflated with individualism. Accordingly, attempts to modify or control the body, wherever they originate, are cast as an infringement of individual autonomy and liberty. Although this resistive narrative, like the preceding cultural and spiritual accounts, turns specifically on authenticity in ways that can be said to reflect or engage current instabilities in broader cultural context regarding how the individual is theorized, this one cannot be understood as a restorative project for presumptive neoliberal logics, of individualism or otherwise. On the contrary, its privileging of the natural body renders both market and regulatory entities incidental, at best, and downright malignant, at worst; moreover, rationality, a fundamental precept of the neoliberal imaginary of individualism, is rendered suspect, antithetical to the body and thus, interestingly, to autonomy.

# Big Love

Perhaps the most proliferate version of the resistive narrative of obesity in the mainstream is mobilized as fat acceptance, which troubles the underlying premise of the obesity epidemic that fat is categorically unhealthy or undesirable. The fundamental premise of fat acceptance is that "it's possible to be healthy no matter how fat you are and that weight loss as a goal is futile, unnecessary and counterproductive"[6]—a stance commonly known as "fat but fit" or "healthy at every size." The fat acceptance "movement," even though it is frequently identified as such in the mainstream, is more accurately a ranging set of perspectives and philosophies around fat (a term that is explicitly employed and embraced by those promoting fat acceptance) rather than an organized collectivity. These perspectives are nonetheless unified by an overarching skepticism regarding the current "fat panic" as well as by at least a neutral if not overtly positive take on fat: attitudes on this latter count range from a perception of fat as inevitable and not particularly relevant to health to fat as physiologically beneficial. Lending fodder for these positions is credible research that has established, in some studies, that many overweight (50%) and even obese (33%) individuals have normal biometrics (blood pressure, cholesterol, triglycerides, and blood sugar), and thus are at no greater risk than "normal" weight individuals for diabetes and heart disease; as well as other studies that have identified distinct health benefits to fat as well as, moreover, distinct and significant risks to health associated with chronic dieting.[7]

While not a movement, a Health at Every Size (HAES) "community" has been in existence since the 1960s, prompted by early objections to changing aesthetic mores and social repercussions to overweight and obese individuals, as well as clinical findings noting the futility and/or health detriments of dieting.[8] In 2008, Linda Bacon published a book by the same name chronicling the (at the time) most recent studies that featured these findings,[9] and an HAES website invites visitors to register; take a pledge; read or post blogs; and avail themselves of resources.[10] The premise of fat acceptance is established in the website's fundamental tenet that "the best way to improve your health is to honor your body," and its precepts include

- Accepting and respecting the natural diversity of body sizes and shapes.
- Eating in a flexible manner that values pleasure and honors internal cues of hunger, satiety, and appetite.
- Finding the joy of moving one's body and becoming more physically vital.[11]

Notably, if it defies the demonization of fat, the fat acceptance variation of the resistive story of obesity subscribes to conventional notions of the benefits of physical activity and exercise as regards health and fitness—the difference is that, in the fat acceptance narrative, they are entirely divorced from weight and fat. This precept, too, is funded by widely reported studies that note cardiovascular improvements and decreased health risks resulting from exercise among obese and overweight individuals; thus, fat acceptance advocates "encourage exercise, but for its emotional and physical benefits, not as a way to lose weight."[12] Mainstream accounts often feature success stories like the following:

> [Exercise and no dieting] certainly appears to have worked for Sandy Schaffer, 47. The 5-ft. 5-in., 280-lb. Schaffer began attending the In Fitness & In Health Wellness Center in New York City more than eight years ago, when she weighed an even more prodigious 350 lbs. She credits her workouts there not only with getting her weight down but also with some other impressive numbers. Her total cholesterol has dropped from 220 to 180, her blood pressure is good, and a recent cardiac-stress test showed that her heart is healthy. She now takes four or five fitness classes a week and teaches two or three herself.[13]

Extremely vague and rare directives to "choose nutritious foods" or "make healthy choices" notwithstanding, references to actual foods—good or bad—are conspicuously absent from this narrative; indeed, food in general is articulated as irrelevant to fat or weight. This is likely so because one of the founding assumptions of fat acceptance is that dieting is not simply ineffective—the fact that the vast majority of people who diet not only eventually regain lost weight but gain more on top of that has reached the level of common knowledge—but dangerous, potentially contributing to organ damage, not to mention psychologically damaging: "Food preoccupation" leads to "self-hatred, eating disorders, . . . and poor health."[14] Again, this perception is funded by respected medical findings that indeed have identified the futility of and/or health problems and risks associated with chronic dieting, findings animated in passionate, often bitter accounts in mainstream venues:

> "You relapse, and then you go on a diet again, and this time you're going to do it, it's really going to be it this time," Marianne Kirby, a 30-year-old blogger . . . said in an interview. "And it still doesn't work, not long-term—you end up heavier than before. And you say to yourself: Why did I fall for this again?"[15]

Instead, if no less vague, fat acceptance proponents strongly and explicitly advocate "intuitive eating"[16]—listening to and honoring the body, including when it is hungry and what it craves. As noted, "eating in a flexible manner that values pleasure and honors internal cues" is key tenet of the HAES philosophy.[17] One is encouraged to "be yourself" with respect to food choices: "don't be afraid to order that cheesecake."[18]

If the broader discourse and philosophy of fat acceptance as described earlier is peripherally apparent in the mainstream, it is vastly more familiar and available—and resonant—in that context in specifically gendered terms: as love and acceptance of the overweight female self. That is, acceptance of fat is tantamount to embracing one's "authentic" femaleness in this instantiation. Drawing upon and diffusely reflective of—some critics might say selectively or superficially so—feminist precepts, and referencing as justification the fact that women generally carry proportionately more body fat than men (as well as studies that suggest this is evolutionarily/biologically determined), this perspective boils down to "celebrat[ing] full figures" and encouraging overweight and obese women to "accept their bodies, quit dieting and get on with life."[19] While this variation of the fat acceptance story is apparent in various contexts, in our celebrity-obsessed culture, it is perhaps most visible as relevant to "plus-size" models and celebrities.

Identification and criticism of the enormous cultural pressure on girls and women to be thin is not new, nor is it limited to the realm of feminist scholars; on the contrary, it is a very familiar refrain across mainstream media venues and genres despite the persistence and presumption of the slender ideal. The collective object of critique has perhaps inevitably been extremely thin iconic (due precisely to their visibility and proliferation in the mainstream media) women and girls—specifically, fashion models and popular celebrities. Much of this critique entails the identification of specific women as "too thin," "unrealistic," or "unhealthy role models," and/or critique of "the industry" (the fashion or media industries, e.g.) for endorsing, cultivating, or mandating an extremely slender body ideal for women. Because my interest in this project is in examining cultural

stories of obesity, I am particularly interested in examining mainstream representations of and discourse surrounding iconic women—again, fashion models and
celebrities—who are identified and endorsed as alternatives to the cultural ideal
of thinness in women.

Because thinness, even extreme thinness, has long been and remains a
benchmark of beauty for Western women, at least, women in the public eye
who do not fit that mold constitute something of a spectacle and command
considerable attention in the mainstream. This is frequently apparent in the
form of "fat shaming," or publishing unflattering pictures, images of, and/or
comments about celebrities who do not conform to the slender standard: their
fleshy and dimpled stomachs, thighs, and buttocks are regular, even staple features for entertainment, fashion, and celebrity gossip magazines, tabloids, and
programs. However, sometimes female celebrities who are heavier than their
normative peers are valorized precisely for that reason: that is, for "embracing
their curves."[20] At the time of this writing, "voluptuous" female celebrities frequently (to the point of media saturation, in fact) invoked in this vein include
Kim Kardashian, Christina Hendricks, Kate Winslet, Beyonce, Jennifer Lopez,
Drew Barrymore, Jennifer Lawrence, Sofia Vergara, Kelly Clarkson, and many
others; in the fashion world, models Kate Upton, Crystal Renn, and Robyn
Lawley are similarly celebrated for their "full figures."[21] Across (positive) coverage of these women, their bodies are represented as emblematic of their confidence, independence, and autonomy: "Kim Kardashian says, 'I'm really proud
of my curves, and I hope all you curvy girls out there are embracing yours too!!
Never feel like you have to be the skinniest girl in the room to be the prettiest.
Be confident in yourself and you'll shine!' ";[22] Jennifer Lawrence is quoted as
saying " 'The world has a certain idea—we see this airbrushed perfect model
image. You just have to look past it. You look how you look. And be comfortable. Like, what are you gonna do, be hungry every single day to make other
people happy? That's just dumb.' "[23] Similarly, Valerie Bertinelli is quoted as
saying, "I am between a 6 and an 8. In the business I'm in, that is heavy, but
I am comfortable. . . . I am not going to be told what I have to weigh by society
or a magazine."[24] Moreover, this confidence is articulated with gender, specifically represented as female empowerment, insofar as one realizes and embraces
her natural, authentic womanliness: Scarlett Johansson is reported as saying,
"I would never want to lose my curves, because curves are what make women
look like women. They are what make you sexy"[25]; likewise, Fergie notes that "I
definitely have curves. I think that's what a natural woman should look like";[26]
and Christina Hendricks is quoted in an interview recalling "Back when I was
modeling, the first time I went to Italy, I was having cappuccinos every day, and
I gained 15 pounds. And I felt gorgeous! I would take my clothes off in front of
the mirror and be like 'Oh, I look like a woman.' And I felt beautiful, and I never
tried to lose it, because I loved it."[27]

Further securing the notion that "curves" authenticate femininity are representations that connect them to motherhood: "'I love my curves because they scream, "I'm a mama!"'" Mariska Hargitay is quoted as saying;[28] Jessica Simpson's publicized assertion that she is "so proud" of her "post-baby curves" similarly articulates weight as a warrant for authentic femininity.[29] Extending this logic, women's "curves" are legitimized morally to the extent that they serve as inspiring role models to girls and women: Kate Winslet, for instance, has noted, "'I do feel there's this responsibility in myself to speak steadfast and true, at least be something that a younger generation can look up to and go, "Oh she's alright," "She's got a normal figure." It's important.'"[30] Jennifer Lawrence, too, has noted "I'm never going to starve myself for a part. I don't want little girls to be like, 'Oh I want to look like Katniss [a character played by Lawrence], so I'm going to skip dinner."[31]

Perhaps immediately apparent to those familiar with any of these women, however, is that none are obese; moreover, in at least some if not all cases, even their status as "heavier" or "plus sized" is dubious, an observation apparent occasionally in the mainstream as well. For example, speaking of Christina Hendricks, one reporter observes, "She's very Anna Nicole Smith voluptuous, but we know she can't be more than a size 12 absolute maximum and is definitely not a candidate for the Beth Ditto outsize clothing line."[32] Another story notes, "Model Crystal Renn is hardly fat. At size 12, she is still thinner than the average American woman, who wears a size 14."[33] Yet another reporter asserts that "The reason Jennifer Lawrence is allowed to be a body-positive role model to young girls and 'chubby' women is because she is representative of conventional beauty. Jennifer Lawrence's public image has been built on a foundation of fat girl drag. She can say she's 'obese' by Hollywood standards, but the claim is laughable."[34] In other words, the extra weight that may characterize these women is generally not sufficient to qualify them as overweight by conventional standards, much less obese, and thus the articulation of these women and what they represent as resistive is highly circumscribed.

Interestingly, however, the rhetoric employed in coverage of the celebrities is similar in many respects to that used to characterize those who *are* understood as significantly overweight or obese by conventional standards. Most prominently, as with dubiously "overweight" women, their weight is strongly associated with— evidence of—independence and autonomy. Actor Gabrielle Sidibe, for example, is described as "inspirational" to women for her confident nonconformity to the slender female ideal: "One day I had to sit down with myself and decide I loved myself no matter what my body looked like and what other people thought about my body. I got tired of hating myself";[35] singer Adele is reported as "saying that she doesn't give a rip about what people think about her. She's fine with it and that's all that matters";[36] singer, actor, and talk-show host Queen Latifah has noted that she feels "comfortable—strong, beautiful, talented—in my own skin . . . I've never molded myself to fit other people's ideals."[37] Accordingly, "other people"—fat shamers—who would evaluate obese individuals negatively are presented as vindictive, petty detractors. Film critic Rex Reed epitomized that persona in his characterization of actor Melissa McCarthy as a "hippo" and "tractor-sized" in a 2013 film review. McCarthy's widely circulated response was that " 'I felt really bad for someone who is swimming in so much hate. I just thought, that's someone who's in a really bad spot, and I am in such a happy spot.' "[38] Speaking to the ways in which excess weight is specifically articulated with the actualization of women, McCarthy is reported as

> admit[ting] that 20 years ago the review would have "crushed" her, but now she primarily worries about how such comments might affect younger female readers "that are not in a place in their life where they can say, 'That doesn't reflect on me.'" She told Itzkoff that, for younger women, reading body-shaming rhetoric like Reed's could send the message that "you don't actually look good enough."[39]

Indeed, McCarthy's appearance on the cover of *Elle*, a popular women's fashion magazine, wearing a large coat sparked widespread criticism in the mainstream that she was "covered up" due to her obesity, "a noticeable departure from the usual flash-as-much-skin-as-possible theme" of female celebrities featured on fashion magazine covers.[40] Both *Elle* and McCarthy quickly responded by noting that she had chosen to wear the coat herself; *Elle* released a statement that that "Melissa loved this look, and is gorgeous on our cover."[41]

The positive public discourse surrounding obese female celebrities differs in a notable way from that about celebrities who carry excess weight relative to the ideal but are not understood as obese, however. Specifically, excess weight in substantially obese women is only rarely articulated with gender. It is almost never articulated with motherhood, for instance, with some rare exceptions; and when it is, as in the case of Carnie Wilson, as an explanatory device—motherhood is identified in these women's cases as a contributing cause of excessive and problematic weight gain, rather than as endowing them with a "real" woman's body, as is the case in coverage of less dramatically overweight women. Along these lines, while excess weight in obese women is similarly articulated with self-actualization, it is degendered, relevant to the fully realized spiritual self, conveyed via confidence and love of oneself and one's body, rather than the fulfillment or realization of womanhood or femininity: or, perhaps more accurately, it is gendered to the extent that accepting one's obesity is tantamount to transcending femininity/femaleness. In this vein, obese women are notably desexualized, as well—if they are sometimes described as "voluptuous" or "full figured," this is not typical and, when invoked, an ancillary characterization. Moreover, the coverage never refers coyly to these women's sex lives and/or the approval of their male partners, as it does frequently does with less overweight female celebrities. Rather, obese women's excess weight serves as evidence and expression of spiritual self-actualization, one that perhaps transcends but at least neutralizes gender and sexuality.

An important and very well-known secular variation of the valorization of "plus-size" women is the Dove® Campaign for Real Beauty, an extremely success-ful marketing campaign for Dove® Corporation, which produces skin and hair care products. The Campaign for Real Beauty is described as follows on the web-site for Dove®:

> The campaign started a global conversation about the need for a wider definition of beauty after [a Dove®-commissioned] study proved the hypothesis that the definition of beauty had become limiting and unat-tainable. Among the study's findings was the statistic that only 2% of women around the world would describe themselves as beautiful. Since 2004, Dove® has employed various communications vehicles to challenge beauty stereotypes and invite women to join a discussion about beauty. In 2010, Dove® evolved the campaign and launched an unprecedented effort to make beauty a source of confidence, not anxi-ety, with the Dove® Movement for Self-Esteem.[42]

Across promotional efforts associated with the campaign, including billboards, internet-accessible videos, and magazine and television commercials, Dove® fea-tured "real" women—rather than professional models—of various ages, races, ethnicities, ages, shapes, and sizes. A series of billboards, for instance, each depicted a woman with two "tick boxes" next to her featuring one positive and one negative descriptor, respectively: for instance, a woman with very small breasts appears next to tick boxes that offer the option of "Flat?" or "Flattering?"; and an older woman is depicted with tick boxes that offer either "Wrinkled?" or "Wonderful?" A Dove®-created "educational" video, "Evolution," that went viral and continues to get considerable play on the internet features an "average" woman who, in time-lapse photography over less than a minute and a half, is made up, coiffed, and "photoshopped" to the point that she looks nothing like her origi-nal, un(re)touched self.

Perhaps the most familiar instance of the campaign is a series of Dove® skin-care commercials that feature a number of women, in each case, of various shapes and sizes—most of them overweight to some degree, by current standards—dressed only in their underwear, rendering their bodies, and in particular their fat, con-spicuous. Juxtaposed with legion images of scantily clad "perfect" bodies in the culture historically and today, it was, when first published and broadcast, and argu-ably remains a striking image. Especially remarkable about the campaign is the play and publicity it received in the broader media. It was and sometimes contin-ues to serve, as it evolves, as fodder for talk shows, magazines, and even news cov-erage: an internet search for "Dove Campaign for Real Beauty" reveals scores of "hits" across mainstream media venues and outlets. As suggested by the campaign title itself, authenticity is a key motif of this campaign, such that "real" women, in their "natural," unmodified, and unadorned states are celebrated. "Excess" weight in particular, as with female celebrities and models, is specifically articulated as evidence and expression of realness, the embracing of which is further conflated with female empowerment: coverage of the campaign credits it with offering "an alternative definition of beauty" that inspires girls and women to understand that they, too, are "normal and beautiful."[43] Dove® is lauded for scouting "America for real women . . . with signature curves" for their campaign. "These fearless women may not be size 2 supermodels, but their courage is helping redefine society's opinion of 'real beauty.' 'We've gotten amazing feedback,' Stacy [one of the models] says. 'Women who are saying they use our picture for inspiration who are battling anorexia, and we know we're actually making a difference . . . that's what this is all about.'"[44] Although the Campaign for Real Beauty is not limited to weight or body size, when it is featured it is deployed in exactly the same way as it is for "bigger" female celebrities and actors: that is, as proof and warrant of authenticity and self-actualization. It bears noting that none of the women in any of the ads, however, would be perceived as obese or even significantly overweight, as others have also observed: "Even the most zaftig had relatively flat stomachs and clearly defined waists. These pretty women were not a random sample of the population."[45]

Although it does not qualify as mainstream to the same degree as the noted instantiations of the fat acceptance narrative, at the extreme end of that spectrum lies fat fetishism, which nonetheless makes an occasional appearance on the mainstream stage—perhaps inevitably, as it serves as the definitive, spectacular line in the sand that culturally vindicated fat acceptance may not cross. In other words, it serves a disciplinary function: if embracing one's curves is, in select circumstances, a "Do," fat fetishism is the fat acceptance "Don't," the step too far. Broadly, fat fetishism is exactly what it sounds like: strong sexual attraction to (typically morbidly) obese people—overwhelmingly if not exclusively women, notably, following through on the heavily gendered dimensions of the fat acceptance discourse. A subgenre of pornography, "fat porn," caters to that fetish, featuring nude or nearly nude obese women engaging in sexual activity invariably while eating; or simply eating. Fat fetishism can be mobilized in different ways as relevant to degree or manifestation: for example, as "feederism," where an individual either feeds oneself or is fed by a partner with the goal of extreme weight gain; "squashes," obese women who sit on men (with their consent) for the sexual pleasure of one or both parties; fat admiration, arguably fat fetishism "lite" insofar as it may not be primarily sexual (in mainstream representations, however, that distinction is not drawn); and Big Beautiful Woman (BBW) or Super-Sized Big Beautiful Woman (SSBBW), terms that have their genesis in *BBW Magazine*, a plus-size fashion magazine founded in 1979 but now invoked and utilized sans connection to that magazine. It is the latter—BBW or

SSBBW—that make occasional but impactful appearances on the mainstream stage. Significantly, while the terms are used by and about women in ways and contexts that do not necessarily have anything to do with sex, much less fetishism—as opposed to confidence, for example—when BBWs or SSBBWs do appear in the mainstream, it is consistently in ways that reference and highlight a sexual/fetishistic dimension, quite likely in order to secure spectacular status as well as to establish questionable, prurient morality to the end of their noted disciplinary function.[46]

In nearly all cases, BBW or SSBBW featured in the mainstream have pay-per-view websites, a fact that is emphasized, where people (identified as men, exclusively, in mainstream mediated representations) pay to see the women in poses or activities ranging from coyly flirtatious to pornographic. The women insist that they love their bodies and "feel sexy," attitudes justified by references to or confirmation by (again, exclusively in the mainstream) featured men—identified as "FAs," or "fat admirers," although again, the distinction between fat admiration and fat fetishism is lost in these articulations—who feel the same. The syndicated popular talk shows *The Dr. Oz Show*[47] and *Dr. Phil*,[48] for instance, both have conducted highly rated shows on BBWs and SSBBWs, and they been the subject of numerous lifestyle magazine articles and news coverage as well.[49] Perhaps the most notorious SSBBW who has been introduced to the mainstream is Susanne Eman, a woman whose widely publicized goal was to reach 1800 pounds; other (SS)BBWs who have made mainstream appearances include Pauline Potter, Donna Simpson, and Tammy Jung. All have or had (at the time of their appearances) pay-per-view websites that are sexually fetishistic in nature; select images from the sites are consistently featured in mainstream coverage, featuring the women eating, being fed, or posing provocatively in underwear or swimwear. Indeed, the focus of coverage is largely and predictably visual, as the very reasons for featuring the women are to do with their spectacular and grotesque, per conventional norms, bodies.

As noted, while (SS)BBW is not inherently a sexualized or fetishistic notion, it is consistently featured as such when engaged in the mainstream: Eman, for instance, is introduced as having "a website where men can pay money to watch her eat, weigh and measure herself, and try on clothes that she's outgrown"[50]; Jung is described as "an aspiring Los Angeles fetish model [who] wants to become an Internet sex symbol for men who like large women. She is selling memberships to her adult website, sexysignaturebbw.com, where she shows off her ample frame in teeny bikinis."[51] The women are sexualized in other ways, as well; Potter, for instance, is cited as having lost the "coveted honor" of "Heaviest Woman in the World" after losing 98 pounds upon "having lots and lots of sex with her ex-husband, Alex."[52] The morally questionable character of these women is established not only by dint of their charging money for men's sexual gratification but, implicitly, by the very depravity of sexualizing obesity: "But they're paying to watch you *eat*; doesn't that make you feel exploited?"[53] Featured men—again, FAs—who find these obese women attractive are similarly portrayed as perverse and morally bankrupt; one FA who notes that he has produced a musical tribute to obese women meets Dr. Oz's disapproval: "Do you ever feel guilty that you're making money off of women who are maybe making themselves sick in order to enjoy your admiration, to enjoy your love?"[54] The primary goal of such coverage is intervention: functionally disciplinary cultural agents (in general as well as in this particular instance), Dr. Oz and Dr. Phil are dedicated to revealing to these women the error of their ways; they are chastised for their misguided, foolish, or perverse behaviors. "This woman is on self-destruct in a way you couldn't believe," Dr. Phil noted on his show; similarly, Dr. Oz notes, "as a doctor, I am dumbfounded . . . I've spent my entire career telling people the opposite of what you're doing; I can't pretend that what you're doing makes sense."[55] The women are also told that they are self-delusional: "I can't believe you're really happy at that weight": that "you're hearing what you want to hear [from doctors]"; and that "you have poisoned your ability to see what is really happening in your life."[56]

Feminist critics might well point out that these women are threatening not simply (or not even really) because they upset conventional notions of health and or beauty but because they literally embody the culturally taboo and threatening specter of a voracious, all-consuming, and powerful woman.[57] Coverage of these women certainly fetishizes how much the women eat; that is sort of the point. For instance, Jung's diet is described in lascivious detail:

> I start the day with a huge breakfast of waffles, cream cheese, bacon and sausage then head to McDonalds for a few burgers in the afternoon. I can snack on cheese all day, a couple of blocks is no problem, then for dinner I'll either eat pizzas or make Mexican food. At the end of the day, I make a weight-gain shake from heavy whip cream and a whole tub of ice cream, which Johan feeds me through a funnel. The funnel forces me to drink the shake even when I'm full after a day of eating.[58]

Images of the women eating and/or poised before a table laden with "sinful" foods is a staple feature across these articulations, as well, as is the number of calories the woman consume in a day: "Susanne Eman consumes as much as 20,000 calories a day: that's more than ten times what the average woman should consume!"[59] Other critics have noted further that, if exploitative, fat fetishism and fat pornography— which, again, almost exclusively features obese women—are arguably resistive to the extent that they turn on and endorse the materialization of female carnal pleasure, or at least the perception thereof: women who give full and unfettered reign to their appetites and who furthermore cut imposing figures—literally take up more space—defy crucial cultural tenets of femininity.[60] While these critiques are not explicitly available in mainstream discourse around BBW/SSBBW, it is nonetheless notable that, in the broader, "acceptable" fat acceptance discourse, the few obese women—like Gabrielle Sidibe, Rebel Wilson, and Camryn Manheim—who are included under that rubric are notably desexualized and degendered relative to their less substantially overweight "curvy," "voluptuous," and "full figured" peers. Instead, as noted, their valorization turns on their confidence and self-actualization as human beings, their transcendence of femininity. Thus, it would indeed seem that the fat acceptance line is drawn at the intersection of female obesity and sexuality and all that implies relative to the powerful, visceral female body—at which point, interestingly, it morphs from actualization and authenticity to debasement and deviance.

## Excess Autonomy

In very different ways, gender also drives another prominent and visible variation of the resistive narrative response to the conventional account of obesity: defiant decadence. Unlike the fat acceptance variation, this one is fairly straightforwardly and explicitly reactive: that is, it draws itself diametrically and absolutely against not only normative notions of appropriate body size but, especially, official or conventional ideas, practices, or policies designed to ensure that size. While this variation of the resistive narrative echoes the defiance and rebellious that is attached to white Southerners in the cultural narrative of obesity, here it is not attached to a practice of cultural (read: raced/ethnic) identity as opposed to abstract ideals of nation and masculinity, especially at their intersection. This narrative thread is mobilized in excessive consumption—the right thereto as well as the practice—and unapologetically overweight or obese white male bodies.

Defiant decadence is most commonly available in the mainstream as a principle apparent in reactions to attempts to regulate "obesogenic" foods or practices. Perhaps most notorious among those attempts are former New York City Mayor Michael Bloomberg's various proposals during his tenure—some successful, some not—to promote healthier eating practices in the city, such as banning the use of trans fats by restaurants; requiring restaurants to post nutritional information regarding their fare; and regulating the size of container in which sugary drinks may be sold. While criticism of these efforts included concerns about disproportionate impact on some (especially poor) populations; arbitrariness of application; and economic impact, the vast majority of conversation in the mainstream revolved around charges of "nanny statism," even when that characterization was posed as a point of debate. The obvious counterpoint to that model, of course, is the (often hyper-) assertion of individual rights, which in the United States is frequently conflated with nation: again, the notion of individual liberty has long been and continues to be the conceptual foundation of US cultural identity and attendant political and economic philosophies and practices, and it is taken up narratively in this case in extreme and literal ways. Moreover, as perhaps signaled by the disdainful "nanny" designation to characterize the regulations, reactions are often masculinist in tone, augmenting the already arguably masculinist underpinnings of individualism and autonomy as culturally construed.[61]

As relevant to the regulation and control of food, then—the "governmentality of girth"[62]—resistance is articulated in the form of the endorsement and/or practice of the right to unlimited consumption: "those who want a large soda and are prevented from buying one [are] 'going to display what we call reactance—a rebelliousness, a determination to circumvent this policy, an attitude of "I'll show them." ' "[63] Certainly, this dynamic is apparent in mainstream accounts of Bloomberg's efforts:

> We often hear about how freedom is under attack in the United States—that the government is slowly but surely encroaching on our rights. This may have been true in a gradual sense over the last several decades, but in more recent years we are seeing increased attempts to control, by government decree, our behavior and free will. Since New York City Mayor Bloomberg announced the 20-ounce soda ban last fall, the controversy has garnered national attention. But, this is just the latest example of his attempt to expand the "nanny state" that has become New York City. Emboldened by his mayoral powers, Bloomberg has decided to methodically push his idea of good living by regulatory fiat—a grand social engineering project that presumes he knows what is best for each of us.[64]

This passage highlights the conflation of nation and individual liberties, which consistently comprise the crux of the matter: "People have the right to make choices about what they eat. They shouldn't be told they can't have the large soda or an extra slice of pizza or a third piece of pie just because some politician or unelected bureaucrat thinks it might be bad for them."[65] Other reports confirm that "Even with obesity on the rise, and despite the accompanying toll on health care costs, access to bucket-size sodas was widely seen as a matter of personal choice. 'If you want to drink large drinks and become obese, that's your right.' "[66] While Bloomberg's efforts have far overshadowed other, similar attempts to regulate food access or quantity, such as curtailing the issuing of fast-food franchise licenses in impoverished neighborhoods, reaction to those efforts are highly consistent, chastising either regulatory entities—"the food police, [who are] trying to control what goes into peoples' mouths"[67]—or popular nutritional gurus or experts, like Michael Pollan and Michael Moss, who have become cultural authorities and benchmarks for policy: "If one is looking for good advice on how to eat and cook well, the food elite have a lot to offer. The trouble comes when their pronouncements take the form of dictates and regulation that we all must heed regardless of our tastes."[68] At risk in this characterization is nothing less than

freedom, personal and political; as relevant to food, that means freedom to consume whatever and as much as one pleases.

On that note, a clear mobilization of this sentiment is apparent in displays of
excessive food consumption, which are increasingly available in the mainstream.
Perhaps the classic form of this is competitive eating contests, which are not new
but have garnered significantly more attention in recent years, no doubt commensurate with—as spectacular counterpoint to—the so-named obesity epidemic.
A number of these contests are regularly featured throughout the country and the
world—the food in question ranging from, for example, pizza to pie to cheese curds
to flautas to oysters to sliders—although perhaps the most notorious and spectacular of these is the annual Nathan's Hot Dog Eating Contest, held every July 4 in
New York City: US Independence Day, notably. News coverage of these events is
both national and local, even when the event is not local to the region of the broadcast: they are sufficiently spectacular to serve as "fluff" or "human interest" fare
across broadcast audiences. Moreover, competitive eating has become a popular
cultural genre in its own right in recent years, sufficient to prompt two popular
indie cult film documentaries—*Crazy Legs Conti: Zen and the Art of Competitive
Eating* and *Hungry*—and two books: *Eat This Book: A Year of Gorging and Glory
on the Competitive Eating Circuit*[69] and *Horsemen of the Esophagus: Competitive
Eating and the Big Fat American Dream*.[70]A variation on this theme and very popular
trend currently (if also not new) are restaurant eating contests, which have multi-
plied exponentially in recent years, again likely because they serve as a spectacular
counterpoint to currently salient concerns about obesity: restaurants offer some
incentive—a free meal, a t-shirt, and/or certificate and posted photo—to patrons
who can consume a designated extreme amount of food within a designated amount
of time. The popular cable (Travel Channel) television show *Man v. Food* featured
host Adam Richman doing exactly this: traveling across the country to partake in
restaurant eating contests. Of course, these events provide excellent publicity for
the restaurants, but they—and competitive eating contests as well, which are often
sponsored and/or hosted by restaurants—are engaged in very classic, almost caricaturish terms of sport and athleticism, terms that are also decidedly masculine:

> Elite athletes are carb-loading, protein-gorging, calorie-snorting ani-
> mals who consume massive amounts of food so their bodies can run
> at peak efficiency during competition. But when it comes to gurgitat-
> ing, the stars of the NBA, NFL, MLB and NHL have nothing on the
> competitors at MLE. That's Major League Eating, for those of you not
> in the know.[71]

Ryan Nerz, who spent a year covering the competitive eating circuit in order to
write *Eat This Book*, describes some eaters as "rookies with natural capacity but

mediocre jaw strength, while others were sprinters who might not have the endurance to go the distance." He also recounts witnessing a contest:

> The eaters rip in, dunking the sandwiches in the water cups and cramming them mouthward with no regard for manners or decorum. As performers, they are very Dizzy Gillespie: dimples blowfished, eyes laser-locked on the chow. "Violent" is a word that comes to mind. "Assault" is another.[72]

Accounts, verbal and visual, of the physical consequences of competitive eating are similarly spectacular, specifically grotesque, ranging from distended stomachs and belching at the fairly mild end of the spectrum to vomiting and explosive diarrhea at the other. The masculine underpinnings of discourse around competitive eating is also perhaps obvious; even if the scant few (if highly) successful female competitive eaters who have gained notoriety—really only one in particular: Sonya Thomas—might challenge that perception, they are definitively presented as spectacular exceptions, and spectacular precisely because of their commensurately masculine qualities, sometimes secured via primal references: "The great Sonya Thomas is described as 'a cross between Anna Kournikova, Billie Jean King, and a jackal wild on the Serengeti' . . . [she] eats with no recognizable style. She knows that style bleeds speed. She's a machine. Efficient. Just flat *fast*."[73]

If obesity is not inherently implicated in competitive eating, it serves as an inevitable backdrop for it in light of the contemporary obesity epidemic, and most mainstream accounts engage that irony. Indeed, I would argue that interest in these events has exploded in recent years precisely because of current national fixation on obesity. In general, concerns about obesity tend to be dismissed in these accounts, however, in two ways: first, by dissociating obesity from competitive eating—perhaps rightly so, for individual contestants are (notoriously, in fact) often not obese or even overweight. Other arguments in this vein cite the fact that "Doing it once in a while isn't bad for you, when you do it responsibly," and, as suggested earlier, that "competitive eaters are athletes who train for their sport, working to improve jaw strength and increasing their stomach capacity."[74] Indeed, the health problems that quoted medical experts cite are gastrointestinal in nature.[75] Notably, however, these accounts are dismissive of the issue of obesity more broadly, thereby contributing significantly to the resistive narrative of obesity. This is accomplished visibly by the fact that, again, many competitive eaters are slender: their bodies resist the conventional discourse that excessive food consumption is inherently problematic in general, much less leads to weight gain. More explicitly, when participants, sponsors, or supporters are asked about the ethics of such contests in view of the obesity crisis, they are generally phlegmatic: "While some shudder at the sight of contestants racing to devour food at a time when a third of Americans are obese, competitors just shrug."[76] And if some accounts concede (or report the concessions of others) that obesity may have been a concern for some competitors (but never all, importantly) in the past, they note that "The new generation of eaters is interested in weight-lifting, running. . . . They have more athletic body types than the old generation."[77] This suggests that concerns about obesity are overblown, on the one hand, and easily addressed, on the other; moreover, the appropriate strategies by which to address (resist) it are masculine—to the extent that extreme athleticism is conflated with masculinity—and individual in nature.

Finally, this thread of the resistive narrative is also apparent—really, material-ized—in the defiant overweight or obese (notably, white) male body that revels in and is celebrated for its resistance to conventional masculine physicality, typi-fied by muscularity, strength, and discipline. Contemporary popular actors and celebrities like Jack Black, Will Farrell, Seth Rogan, and Jonah Hill—and before them, Chris Farley and Jim Belushi—have capitalized on their girth, and if they are (primarily) comedic actors, they also feature a significant degree of cultural capital, or "coolness," precisely by dint of their excess weight: their edginess is in large part secured via their fat, sometimes grotesquely displayed bodies, which are read as unconventional at least, and more typically nonconformist or resistive. Another recent example of this is a Southern Comfort (a hard liquor) ad cam-paign that features an unabashedly overweight middle-aged white man, clad only in a "Speedo" bathing suit, strolling confidently down a populated beach to the strains of Odetta's "Whatever's Comfortable"—the featured lyric being "Can't you see/I gotta be me."[78] While under certain, very narrow conditions, some overweight or obese women are valorized in the mainstream, they are celebrated in earnest terms, as valiant and virtuous martyrs, for instance; only overweight and obese men who are celebrated, who are almost always white, can lay claim to being cool, hip, or edgy, a perception secured, I would contend, because the male bodies are understood as embodiments of specifically individual (as opposed to ideological or cultural) resistance, liberty, and autonomy.

Perhaps the most notorious example of this is the Heart Attack Grill, an Arizona-based regional restaurant chain whose "hook" is outrageously and unabashedly unhealthy fare: menu items include a Quadruple Bypass Burger, which comprises 20 patties of beef accompanied by up to 40 undrained (of grease) bacon slices; a Coronary (Hot) Dog ("Dr. Jon's got a HUGE weaner [sic]!"); and Flatliner Fries, which are "deep fried in pure lard."[79] This defiance is also reflected in the restaurant policy that patrons who weigh over 350 pounds may eat free. Not surprisingly—and as intended—the restaurant chain has earned a great deal of publicity, earning national news coverage as well as drawing the fire of various health organizations. Moreover, the specifically masculine nature of individual liberty is undeniable in this example, in every respect. One particular advertisement that received widespread attention features an obese man being served/assisted by an attractive young woman in a skimpy nurse's outfit—part of the restaurant's complementary "nutritional pornography" gimmick: in this variation of a "breastaurant," servers are nurses (all attractive young women clad in scanty nurse's uniforms); managers and supervisors are doctors (apparently always male); and patrons are patients who are administered to by nurses, including being paddled if "patients" do not complete their meals.[80] The ad is a spoof on weight-loss diets; the man notes that he would like to gain a few inches; notably, securing the resistive/anti-state sentiment that is embedded in this discursive thread, the man states that "thanks to our new health care law, I don't even have to pay for my own medical bills." (The website includes, following a list of prices for menu items, "Plus 8.1% tax for our wasteful government to squander.") A (male) "doctor"—noted as the founder of the Heart Attack Grill Diet—appears on the screen to assure medical supervision and guarantee results. The reported side effects include "sudden weight gain, repeated increase in wardrobe size, back pain, male breast growth, loss of sexual partners, lung cancer, tooth decay, liver sclerosis, stroke, and an inability to see your penis. In some cases, mild death may occur."[81] Again, even if these bodies or schticks are understood as amusing and designed to be so, not only their humor but their very cultural value is predicated precisely on their rejection of the norm: in this case, of shame regarding fat bodies and of (especially) attempts to discipline those bodies.

As noted, the gendered dimensions of this particular variation of the resistive narrative of obesity is striking; that is, excessive consumption and/or obesity is tantamount to an assertion—indeed, typically, a spectacular display—of masculinity. This is blatantly apparent in the Heart Attack Grill example, of course, in the restaurant's assumption that patrons are male: the "nurses"/servers are all female—on the website, they are featured provocatively poised over various menu items—and references to the potential development of male breasts and inability to see one's penis in the ad further implies a male patron. As described, competitive eating is articulated in unequivocally hypermasculine terms; and notably, currently "cool" overweight or obese bodies are all (white) male. Given that excess and lack of discipline have been strongly articulated with femininity, leading to—as described earlier in this book—a concomitant popular perception of fat as feminine or feminizing, this may seem counterintuitive or at least paradoxical. But in this case, excess and lack of discipline are, significantly, willful, an assertion of autonomy and independence—classically masculine qualities, as conventionally construed. That is, these men are depicted as actively choosing to consume inordinate amounts of (especially unhealthy) foods and/or to be overweight and obese: rather than lack of *self*-discipline, bespeaking passivity or weakness, their practices and behaviors are evidence of a strategic agenda— certainly so in competitive eating, wherein extreme food consumption is taken up precisely to dominate or control others. Even in those cases that are not explicitly competitive, male excessive eating, overweight, and obesity signal a refusal to comply, to be dominated by others, as is the case in strong negative reactions to "nanny statist" regulations around food—a particular mobilization of these dynamics that further conflates excess, autonomy, and masculinity with nation, as drawn explicitly against the state. The state is cast as feminine/feminizing, as are, accordingly, healthy foods, dietary practices, and body weight in this case. Accordingly, actively resisting those imperatives and impositions via excessive indulgence and/or body weight, frequently drawing upon nationalist tropes of independence and autonomy as warrants for doing so, constitutes material proof and performance of masculinity.

The issue of class is an important variable to assess here as well, specifically as it intersects with masculinity; that is, the foods or, as relevant, bodies in question in all of these cases tend to broadly understood as coarse, cheap, and "trashy"— often, ostentatiously so. Competitive eaters, for instance, do not devour pâté or guinea hens, or even simple, whole fruits or vegetables; featured foods include hot dogs, sliders, pizza, fried chicken, and pie. Foods subject to regulation include sugary drinks, fast food, and vending machine snacks; and the Quadruple Bypass Burger and Southern Comfort liquor are specifically venerated for their lowbrow qualities. Moreover, the obese male bodies that are celebrated in this vein (and their inhabitants) are consistently presented as coarse, unrefined, and unsophisticated—precisely that which endows them with their resistive cultural cachet. Thus, the resistance displayed in excessive food consumption and/ or bodies is also drawn against a perceived elitism—explicitly noted in debates around attempts to regulate foods—such that resistors perceive themselves and/ or are perceived as marginalized. In this context, the glorified nationalist tropes of independence and autonomy on which resistance is often predicated gain greater depth and dimension, especially as they are drawn against the implicitly powerful—notably, feminizing or at least emasculating—state.

In other contexts, such as extreme sports and vigilante films, some critics have identified the "turn to the extreme" as a manifestation of white male backlash, through which white men seek to negotiate feelings of perceived displacement due to political and economic advances of formerly marginalized groups, like women, people of color, and gays and lesbians.[82] Moreover, these endeavors frequently entail an alignment with other culturally abject or inappropriate practices or artifacts: the television show and film franchise *Jackass* is frequently cited as one such example, wherein young men engage in dangerous, ill-advised, or culturally distasteful activities, including unleashing attack dogs on one another, snorting wasabi, excrement catapulting contests, and "butt chugging" alcohol. As Phillipov notes, in so doing, "there is an attempt to reclaim, and positively value, what is perceived to be a culturally abject—and abjected—white masculine subjectivity."[83] The particular variation of the resistive narrative of obesity that I describe here is highly consistent with this imperative; certainly, it brings together and makes sense of the peculiar and consistent constellation of déclassé—culturally

abject—foods and (specifically white, male) bodies; hypermasculinity; and references to and mobilizations of nationalist ideals of autonomy and independence
as drawn explicitly against an imaginary of a powerful, elite, emasculating state.

## Body Politic

The broader resistive narrative of obesity thus features two distinct, in many
ways contradictory threads: fat acceptance and defiant decadence. They both,
however, turn precisely on authenticity articulated in both cases as embodied
and gendered, and both are invested in self-actualization to the end of realizing
the authentic self. As noted, each account mobilizes these aspects differently: fat
acceptance, which is almost exclusively taken up as relevant to the female body,
turns primarily on the full realization of and revelation in femininity, demonstrated by "curves" and a "full figure" on women who carry relatively more weight
than the cultural ideal. Self-actualization is also relevant to obese women, but in
ways that notably desexualize and in some ways even degender them: in those
cases, self-actualization appears to be secured via transcendence of sex and gender. Indeed, the phenomenon of fat fetishism, also made lasciviously available on
occasion in the mainstream, suggests that obese women whose femininity and
(especially) sexuality is foregrounded represent a grotesque, base, and culturally
unacceptable extreme of fat acceptance. In all of these cases, however, the "others"
against whom articulated resistive notions of fat and even obesity are drawn are
normative cultural entities and agents. Conversely, the defiant deviance narrative
thread mobilizes white male masculinity as relevant to absolute individual autonomy, especially as regards (over)consumption—attempts to regulate quality and
quantity of food are equated with constraint, containment, and emasculation.
Accordingly, the authentic self is actualized—materialized—in the demonstrably
unfettered overweight or obese white male body. Contrary to the fat acceptance
variant, then, authenticity is not about aspiring to and occupying an idealized self,
as in the narrative of obesity as spiritual or emotional dysfunction, but excavat-
ing the base "true" self, evidenced by the unrestrained natural body. The "others"
against which the defiantly autonomous self is drawn are regulatory agents and
entities, specifically the state, as well as cultural elites, both of which are construed as emasculating: accordingly, the foods and events that serve as avenues to
authenticity are—like the ideal excavated self—base, crude, and abject.[84]

If the actualized, authentic self looks very different across these narrative
deployments of resistance to the official account of obesity, they are remarkably
confluent when understood within contemporary exigent tensions circulating
around how to (re)imagine the individual. The authentic self is clearly valorized
across these stories, realized and secured to the extent that one's "natural" desires,
compulsions, or essences are given free and full expression (albeit to a point, as

relevant to women): excess weight literally materializes this absolute autonomy. Thus, individualism and authenticity are conflated here insofar as the body is authorized as the appropriate determinant of consumption, rather than one's will or spirit: in the spiritual narrative, authenticity is drawn against the unruly body, which must be regulated. Conversely, regulation and regulatory agents—the state and/or normative cultural agents—are inevitably suspect in the story of resistance; if unconstrained, self-(bodily) determined consumption is critical to the realization of the self, then any entity charged with regulation of consumption is, by definition, antithetical to that end. Interestingly, there is no clear role for the market in this account, either: while consumption is clearly valorized in this account, it is literal, visceral, and exclusively directed toward actualizing the natural body. Modification, artifice, and refinement—staple features of market goods and services—are eschewed in this project, rendering the market incidental, at best, if not, like regulatory agents, antithetical to it.

Thus, in a contemporary context marked by upheaval regarding whether and how to reconceptualize individualism, on its own terms and in consequent relation to the market and the state, this narrative does not attempt to reconcile the imperatives of presumptive neoliberalism, as do (if in different ways) the cultural and spiritual narrative of obesity I have described. Rather, the collective narrative of resistance articulates a novel configuration—actually, conflation—of authenticity, individual autonomy, and the body. Specifically, authenticity is articulated as the unrestrained self, which is further both secured and evidenced via the body—the distinction between individualism and authenticity is dissolved entirely on the body, where those things converge. Indeed, rationality, a key node of presumptive neoliberal individualism, is implicitly cast as suspect in this narrative, as well, rejected in favor of impulsivity. In political economic terms, this certainly challenges neoliberal tenets insofar as it has the potential to reverse the ostensible roles of the state and the market. With a starting point of embodied authenticity and an exclusively literal mobilization of consumption to that end, it is viable to imagine the market as antithetical to that project, invested as it is in the modification or embellishment of the authentic body; and, accordingly, to imagine the state as facilitative of or conducive to the realization (or preservation) of the authentic self—thus implying greater oversight and restraint of the market. Of course, this is not how it plays out in the accounting, just described, as is; indeed, the state in particular is explicitly vilified in one variation. However, the role of the market is so significantly diminished, rendered incidental at best, that it cannot lay claim in any way to the cultivation of authenticity. Moreover, to the extent that it is, collectively, a powerful normativizing agent against which this narrative explicitly draws itself, its tenuous relevance to authenticity is further threatened.

What is clear in this particular narrative deployment of authenticity is a frustration with the monitoring, regulating, disciplining, containment, and denial of the body, for which the state and the market are both articulated as culpable, in implicit and explicit ways—not dissimilar to, if a rather literal version of, what Foucault has identified as biopower. On this point, this narrative also reveals the extent to which cultural sensibilities such as gender, class, and race/ethnicity undergird and drive political economies. The location of authenticity on and in the body in the resistive account is thus instructive insofar as it bespeaks a profound distrust of both market and state apparatuses; rather than libertarian or even anarchist in impulse, then, it reimagines the individual as disarticulated from both, ideally transcendent of either. Again, this dynamic can be identified in a broader contemporary context of disillusionment and distrust of the market and the state, necessitating the very impulse to reconfigure individualism in the first place, specifically in tandem with a felt imperative to acknowledge authenticity, perceived as contraindicated under presumptive neoliberal logics.

Practically, this narrative suggests that obesity campaigns predicated on the official story of obesity that turn on asceticism or denial of the body, whether geared toward public health or profit, inevitably prompt visible, vocal, and resonant resistance, and likely more widespread if less vocal disillusionment. Coupled with the notorious lack of effectiveness of efforts predicated on bodily restraint and discipline that foster at least dissatisfaction if not outright rejection, the resonance of this narrative, in the current context, suggests that campaigns predicated on realizing and cultivating the "authentic" body—in other words, on what to *give* the body rather than what to deny it—may hold significantly greater appeal, resonance, and productive traction than conventional campaigns. More broadly, this story of obesity, in radically reconceptualizing the individual self as the authentic subject, points up distrust and disillusionment that are pervasive in the wake of neoliberalism in crisis; but importantly, it reinforces the cultural primacy of individualism and the need to reimagine it in productive ways.

# 8

# Feeling Fat

*The Story of Disgrace*

The last prominent contemporary story of obesity that I will assess is both pervasive and diffuse: it is the story of disgrace, real or anticipated, as relayed in
the mainstream by people who are or have been obese as well as reflected in the
practices and narratives of people who are not and have not been obese but are
driven—haunted—by its specter. This latter manifestation is apparent in ostensibly dysfunctional practices, like anorexia and bulimia, but also, especially, in
everyday, normative practices of dieting and exercise. In fact, this narrative owes
much to the official obesity narrative of caloric imbalance that turns on personal
responsibility: like that official account, this one subscribes wholly to the notion
that one is entirely personally and moreover morally culpable for his or her obesity.
Whereas authenticity is conspicuously—fatally, as I have argued—absent in that
official discourse, however, authenticity is central and crucial to this variation: it
is deeply felt, specifically as shame. As regards authenticity, this narrative actually
relies upon the same premises that fund the narrative of resistance described in the
last chapter, although it values them in exactly opposite ways and draws commensurately opposite conclusions. That is, the narrative of disgrace similarly identifies authenticity as embodied: as the visceral, impulsive, unfettered, "natural" self.
Also like the narrative of resistance, this story of disgrace is powerfully informed
and driven by gender. However, whereas the authentic embodied self is valorized
and cultivated in the collective resistance narrative, conflated with individualism
in general and individual autonomy in particular, in this story of disgrace, one's
authentic, embodied self is something that must be actively, vigilantly suppressed.
Moreover, the authentic self in this case is thoroughly and consistently feminine,
as construed in conventional, frankly misogynist ways: as passive object as well
as (paradoxically) dangerous and all consuming. As with the cultural account
of obesity, then, authenticity is thus drawn against individualism in the disgrace
narrative, albeit in distinctive ways: here, if individualism is afforded primacy in
ways that are consistent with (even exemplary of) the neoliberal imaginary, it is

defined not against (or, more precisely, with) the market—crucial to neoliberal logics—but exclusively against the authentic self. That is, in this story, the individual is locked in eternal, epic battle with the authentic self, rendering considerations like the market and the state superfluous if not entirely irrelevant.

## Conspicuous Consumption

Perhaps obviously (so to speak), display—in the most literal sense—lies at the core of this narrative of disgrace, mobilized in two very distinct ways: as spectacle and as invisibility. Paradoxical as this may seem, these very different modes are consistent to the extent that both result in social and civic exclusion: social insofar as obesity literally marks one as "different" in distinctly negative ways, and civic insofar as the emphasis on display, however parlayed, strips one of agency—certainly of vitality and validity.

The literally spectacular dimensions of obesity cannot be disputed; in fact, it is staple, even daily fodder for media fare of any stripe (news, entertainment, advertising, self-help) and form (magazines, television, billboards, internet). By definition, the spectacular is set apart from the normative and thus inevitably contains at least a modicum of deviance,[1] but in the case of obesity—perhaps logically—it is taken to an abject extreme. Obese bodies and individuals are articulated as grotesque, degenerate, decadent, and shameful, qualities secured by various techniques of representation. One of these techniques is the routine depiction of "headless" obese bodies or obese individuals whose faces or eyes are blurred or concealed, images that comprise standard, even stock fare for news programs regarding obesity and advertising about obesity, ranging from diet programs or products to plastic surgery. In these cases, bodies are typically displayed in public setting walking laboriously down a street or sitting—taking up a vast amount of space on a bench, for example—and, often, eating: generally decadent foods, like ice cream or fast food. The lingering visual focus is on stomachs, breasts, thighs, and buttocks, which are depicted as straining at clothing and/or as moving pendulously. The fact that heads, faces, and/or eyes are concealed rhetorically underscores the shamefulness of this condition, as does the fact that the individuals depicted are often apparently unaware of being made spectacle, a perception secured by the convention of filming or photographing them from the back. This complements and reinforces the deviant features of spectacle as relevant to obesity by fostering an impression of obese individuals being observed and evaluated as "other" by society at large—and especially cultural authorities, as in the case of news coverage.

Another technique of representation that secures the spectacular obese body entails prurient, virtually pornographic exhibition. Although it is practiced in various venues and programs, it is an especially prevalent practice in popular reality shows available on television and accessible on the internet, like *The Biggest Loser,* *Extreme Makeover: Weight Loss Edition, Ruby,* and *Heavy,* as well as talk shows that devote episodes to obesity, such as *Dr. Oz* and *Dr. Phil.* This technique is at least reminiscent of photographic and filmic conventions of pornography to the extent that obese bodies are fetishized, surveilled, and manipulated in ways that border on or evoke the carnal, albeit in contexts that justify these practices as legitimate, even necessary and beneficial. Obese individuals featured in these shows are frequently (if not constantly) depicted wearing very little clothing, and that which they do wear is typically tight and revealing, such as spandex shorts and bra tops, all the better to reveal masses and mounds of flesh. Gendered sexual conventions are evident in these representations as well, to the extent that women's buttocks and breasts tend to be favored, as are men's protuberant, tumescent bellies that burgeon aggressively over their shorts or underwear. Sometimes, as when they are "weighed in" or assessed for surgical intervention, the near-naked bodies of these men and women are positioned expressly for the purposes of being looked at—in glances and tones of dismay or shock—by authorities (trainers or doctors) and the audience, who may gaze upon them with impunity in capacities of concern and support, or at least in the ostensible interest of enlightenment and understanding. When fat fetishism is the subject of discussion and intervention on the part of professionals such as *Dr. Oz* and *Dr. Phil,* the line between edifying and pornographic representation is especially thin, as the content is directly lifted from the "fat porn" websites of the featured guests. At other times, the participants are depicted vigorously exercising, sweating and laboring in physically compromised or vulnerable positions, sometimes sexually evocative, typically with a trainer looming over, encouraging, or berating them. Prurience is also apparent in depictions of intimate physical manipulations of those bodies in ways not conventionally permitted or apparent—ways that border on the sexual. Medical professionals and trainers touch nearly if not completely nude bodies in exploratory and diagnostic ways, for instance lifting breasts and buttocks to mark surgical incisions or measuring scantily clad breasts, stomachs, hips, and thighs. Trainers also rub, slap, and manipulate laboring obese bodies to the end of encouraging or directing exercise. If these representations are not precisely pornographic, they certainly evoke pornographic tropes and conventions that serve to reinforce and amplify the obese body as spectacle. Moreover, the cultural authorities who oversee and endorse these presentations of the obese body serve to further underscore the spectacular nature of obesity.

The spectacle of obesity is certainly visually apparent, but it is secured discursively, as well, in graphic descriptions of obese individuals—a practice included under the rubric of "fat shaming" that, while nominally frowned upon, remains rampant in contemporary popular culture. Celebrities and public figures are common targets of fat shaming; when relatively heavier, Kim and Khloe Kardashian have been favorite subjects, described variously as "huge," "gross and nasty," and visually compared to a whale[2] (Kim); "huge," a "Yeti," and a "shaved Sasquatch,"[3] (Khloe); ostensibly "plus size" Kate Upton has been described as "a piggy" and "a cow";[4] and Irish opera singer Tara Erraught was described as "a chubby bundle of puppy fat . . . unsightly and unappealing."[5] The line between fat jokes and fat shaming is a fine one, if it in fact exists, as demonstrated in popular coverage of fallout following the former; comedian George Lopez was widely lambasted in 2011 for describing then *Dancing with the Stars* contestant Kirstie Alley as a dancing pig: "She did a nice job, her little hooves tapping away . . . before the show, she went to the market, and then she had roast beef and this is her going all the way home."[6] Joan Rivers, no stranger to controversy regarding her comedic style in general, was routinely called out for her fat jokes about celebrities, for example of singer Adele:

> Rivers first called Adele, 24, "chubby" while visiting *The Late Show* [*with David Letterman*] in February, chatting with host David Letterman about the award-winning singer's appearance at the Academy Awards. "She sang live and said, 'My throat, my throat, I don't know if I can swallow.' And I said, 'Oh, you can swallow,'" Rivers joked.
>
> "What is her song, 'Rolling in the Deep'? She should add 'fried chicken.'" . . . . Rivers didn't back down from her comments, though she revealed Adele confronted her about it
>
> . . . . "She wanted an apology, so I took an ad out on her ass. I said, 'You are not fat.' And then I had room for a lot of other ads."[7]

Fat shaming, whether practiced or reported, is consistently articulated in graphic visual terms, thereby securing the spectacular dimension of fat in general and obesity in particular.

Self-reports of people who are or have been obese, a popular feature of mainstream coverage of obesity, confirm that shameful spectacle is not only a represented or received but a felt experience of obesity, as well. People report feeling like a "freak,"[8] like "everyone is staring,"[9] or that others find them "disgusting" and "repulsive."[10] A number of people report that eating in public while obese is a particularly spectacular event, drawing disparaging glances or comments: one woman reports anticipating the reaction, "Look at the fat woman, being human and hungry for something bad for her! How grotesquely humorous it is when fat people eat!"[11] Another notes, "If I want pretty clothes, I'm sneered at, because only thin people get to wear pretty clothes, since they 'look better on thin people.' If I want to eat a 'bad food' or have a treat, I'm thrown looks of disgust, because that must be what I eat 24/7."[12] "Just last week I was at the swimming pool in my gym when I overheard a woman on her cell tell a friend she was whale watching," another woman reports.[13] In an effort to convey the spectacular experience of being obese, artist Haley Morris-Cafiero, in a photographic series entitled "Wait

Watchers," captured people's responses to her obese body as they observed her engaged in mundane activities in public, such as reading, eating, and walking. Two excerpts illustrate the series:

> I was traveling with students in Barcelona in the summer of 2011, walk-ing through La Rambla, when I noticed two guys making fun of me. I could see them in the reflection of a mirrored building, making ges-tures with their hands to suggest how much bigger I was than the thin girl standing next to me, her small waist accentuated by her crop top and cut-off shorts. They painted her figure in the air like an hourglass. Then they painted my shape like the convex curves of a ball. The guys were saying something, too, but there was only one word I could make out: *Gorda*. Fat woman.
>
> I found a crowded crosswalk farther down La Rambla, used my rangefinder camera to set the exposure and focus of where I would stand, and handed the camera to my assistant. I bought a cup of gelato and began eating it. I've learned I get more successful reactions if I am "doing" something. In my peripheral vision, I saw a teen girl waiting for the signal to cross the street. As I stood there, eating my ice cream, I heard a repetitive "SLAP, SLAP, SLAP" of a hand on skin. I signaled to my assistant to shoot. It was only when I returned home to Memphis and got the film developed that I realized the sound was the girl hit-ting her belly as she watched me eat. She did this over and over. I have five frames of her with various facial expressions. I called the resulting image "Gelato."[14]

The images that Morris-Cafiero captures are especially interesting to the extent that they present her body as a necessary but insufficient condition for spectacle; it is the (re)actions—arguably the "real" spectacular as drawn against Morris-Cafiero's consciously mundane activities—of those who gaze upon that body that fulfill it.

As prevalent and conspicuous as these examples are, obesity as spectacle is possibly most pervasive and profound as a specter that haunts and drives those who are not obese. "Fear of fat," or fat phobia, has been identified by scholars and casual observers alike, and it is widespread—indeed, concerns about obe-sity could not have reached proportions of "epidemic" or "crisis" without it.[15] Arguably, it is most poignant among individuals who are not obese or even over-weight but who are engaged in herculean efforts to prevent it on their persons. The most extreme examples of this are people who suffer from anorexia and buli-mia; while it is commonly held, both among professionals and in the popular cul-ture, that these eating disorders are often if not always "really" about something other than weight, such as control,[16] it is nonetheless true that the specter of fat/

obesity, in particular, mobilizes them. Certainly, it looms large in the self-reports of people who live with these disorders, as apparent in the notorious—and highly popular—"pro-ana" (pro anorexia) and "pro-mia" (pro bulimia) websites, which, while they purport to serve as emotional support for those "in recovery" from the relevant disorder, furnish forums for tips, advice, guidelines, images, and support designed to cultivate and "perfect" the disorders, according to critics.[17] The specter/spectacle of obesity is key, for instance, on the "Motivation" page for the Missanamia website, which includes among its "thinspirational" tips:

1. Bones are clean and pure. Fat is dirty and hangs on your bones like a parasite.
2. If you eat then you'll look like those disgusting, fat, ghetto and trailer-trash hookers on Jerry Springer.
16. Only fat people are attracted to fat people. Do you want pigs to like you because you look like one of them?
20. If you slap a fat person you can see a shockwave ripple over their skin. That's disgusting.
42. Puffy cheeks, double chins, and thick ankles—aren't attractive.
43. Fatty areas stretch and sag as you get older.
44. Ever seen the arms of a fat person wave hello or goodbye?
56. No one wants to see a fat person dance.[18]

Likewise, forum posts on the Myproana website invoke grotesque images of obesity:

"I work at a grocery store and it is truly disgusting to see what people eat. I see these landwhales who buy some lettuce and then 20 bags of crisps, chocolate bars, mayo, fries and what not . . . they smell bad too." (magefix)[19]

"[A disgusting thing I saw today] is the fat, lazy asshole riding the scooter at Walmart. I fucking hate the lazy pieces of shit that ride around on those things." (lol lan)[20]

"[It's repulsive] the ladies who think they can wear a bikini when they are overweight. I work at a bikini boutique and I have to tell them they look great." (mrs. strange catz)[21]

"When I see obese people, it depends on what they are wearing. If they are wearing short shorts and a tank top with their fat rolls hanging out—I just gag. I think, 'What are they wearing?!' It drives me crazy! Because you know they are wearing that because they think they can! I'm all about wearing clothes for your body type! I have friends that are overweight, but they were clothes that fit them and they look stunning! But these girls who 'flaunt their fat' just disgust me! It's people like that that make society believe that 'big' is 'normal', giving us 'skinny' girls a

bad rep! Beacuse [*sic*] apparently I should be 200 pounds and be wearing daisy dukes!" (THEMrsHansmann)[22]

"I'm sorry, but really fat people make me feel so disgusting
When I look at them I feel my food coming up my throath [*sic*]."
(Marie-Leigh-Anna)[23]

Of course, it's hardly surprising that fear of fat, including and especially as
crystallized in the grotesque spectacle of obesity, is powerfully salient for people struggling with anorexia or bulimia. But notably, it is just as salient—*just as*
salient, not diluted—for "normal" people as well who worry about or monitor
their weight (the vast majority of the populace),[24] if it is rendered in less graphic
or potentially offensive terms. On Pinterest, a very popular website that allows
people to create or post favorite things to topical collections ("boards"), for example, the "Diet Inspiration" board features a wealth of images of conventionally
beautiful (i.e., slender) bodies, usually accompanied by inspirational messages,
juxtaposed with fewer but spectacular images of obese bodies as well as visual representations of yellow, globular fat that has been excavated from human bodies.[25]
"Before and After" weight-loss success stories comprise highly popular inspirational fare across media and genres, and they are almost always visually depicted
as well: a "before" photo of the person at his or her highest weight is juxtaposed
with an "after" photo or representation of him or her upon achieving significant
weight loss. These are often accompanied by narratives that underscore the (negatively) spectacular aspects of obesity as relevant to the "before" photos, even if
the subjects themselves were not technically obese: "I saw myself in that picture
and was shocked at how big I was";[26] "before this photo was taken I was in tears
in the hotel room because none of the summer clothes I packed fit me and I was
embarrassed at how I've let myself go. I was smiling but inside I was miserable";[27]
"I didn't recognize the person I saw . . . I looked like I was pregnant."[28] Speaking
to their anxieties about weight, specifically visual concerns are often cited: "My
jeans and shirts had become increasingly snugger [*sic*], but it wasn't until the zip-
per on my favorite dress wouldn't budge that I was forced to confront my new size.
I was mortified, especially when I saw a slab of back fat in the mirror."[29]Other pervasive abject spectacular cues, both visually and discursively conveyed, include
"muffin tops," "bulging thighs," "saddlebags," "bra fat," "batwings," and "cottage
cheese" (thighs or rear end). Again, whether embodied or simply an ominous
specter, cultural fears and disgust regarding obesity are clearly, at least in part,
visual in nature.

Paradoxically, display is also salient to this discourse of disgrace to the extent
that obesity can result in invisibility—the converse of spectacle, to be sure, but
similarly exclusionary. This is commonly evident in accounts of individuals
who are or have been obese: "I was basically ignored by everyone at school,"[30]
one woman states; another woman "noticed that people stopped making eye

contact with her. 'It was like the more visible I became, the more invisible I felt,' she recalled;[31] and Dr. Oz reports that one of his most demoralizing experiences upon donning a "fat suit" over a period of days was being avoided and unacknowledged: "the bigger you are, the more invisible you are."[32] Many explicitly connect this phenomenon to gender, asserting that it is especially germane to obese women; one Jenny Craig member writes "as I gained more and more weight, I became invisible. Men stopped seeing me. I could see them see me, but see right through me. They used to make eye contact or even smile or flirt, but no more."[33] Indeed, a Pinterest board entitled "We're fat, not invisible," is specifically devoted to posting images of "real, fat women" in an effort to counter this social erasure,[34] and in 2011 the indie documentary *The Fat Body (In)Visible*, which examines how two obese women "work to make themselves seen in a world that would rather they remain hidden," was released to critical and popular acclaim.[35] Whether prompted by embarrassment, depression, or real or anticipated ridicule, many obese individuals actively avoid social contexts and interactions, thereby augmenting their invisibility: "I rarely left the house";[36] "didn't attend my kids' school plays";[37] social anxiety about obesity "made me afraid to leave the house ... locked me in a closet with my emotions and a secret stash of food."[38]

Whether manifest as spectacle or invisibility, display figures prominently in this "felt" obesity story of disgrace, and the variations, paradox notwithstanding, are commensurate to the extent that they imply exclusion from social and civic contexts. This is so because the display component inevitably turns on the objectification of obese individuals, thus qualifying if not negating their perception, by themselves or others, as productive or valid cultural members or citizens—they are instead static, passive, and impotent. These dynamics have direct relevance to authenticity: in this discourse, as with the resistive narrative of obesity, authenticity is understood as embodied and natural; but unlike that resistive narrative, it is in this case something to be suppressed and subjugated. This implies a distinction between the individual and the authentic self—also unlike the resistive narrative, which collapses the two—such that the individual serves as a disciplinary agent who must vigilantly control the voracious appetites and impulses of the authentic, embodied self. Moreover, the "split self" rationalizes the apparent paradox between obesity as spectacle and invisibility, such that the spectacular obese body is, literally, the authentic embodied self, while the civic self is repressed and concealed. Although I will elaborate on the gendered dimensions of this discourse later in this chapter, it is relevant to note here that the themes of display (objectification), uncontained bodies, and uncontrolled appetites are highly reflective of long-held cultural tropes and apprehensions of femininity— an observation arguably supported by the relative preponderance of specifically female spectacular obese bodies depicted in the mainstream juxtaposed with the (apparently contradictory but in fact complementary) received knowledge that invisibility is especially "felt" by obese women.

# Management and Labor

Display is one of the nodes of this story of obesity as disgrace; the other is—in part as consequence to display—industry. The passivity attendant to the visual dimensions of obesity, whether manifest as spectacle or erasure, carries over to the extent that inertia is understood as leading inevitably to decay or decadence— apparent, for instance, in descriptions of obese individuals as "letting themselves go," a characterization that further underscores the bifurcation of the authentic and individual selves. Activity, in the form of actual labor, is one prominent rec- ommended corrective, specifically to "laziness," which is a powerful and perva- sive flashpoint of this narrative: it reflects the assumption that obesity is a result of an individual's lack of self-discipline and -regulation, confirming an apprehen- sion of the authentic—natural, embodied—self as dangerous and unacceptable. Of course, this is a direct reflection of the personal responsibility model that com- prises the official account of obesity: that is, that obesity is a function of calories in versus calories out, and one must be vigilant and, literally, active in maintaining the appropriate balance. While the narrative of disgrace is thus obligated to the official narrative, the difference is that the latter is conveyed in the sterile lan- guages of either economics—of caloric "budgets" and "expenditures," for exam- ple; or production—"input versus output" or "fine-tuning" your diet. Moreover and consistent with this impulse, the official story of obesity objectifies the body: it is the object of ministrations by the rational self, but it is not felt or expe- rienced. The narrative of disgrace, on the other hand, is articulated in distinctly moral as well as felt, visceral terms, thereby centering authenticity which is, as I have argued, conspicuously and fatally lacking in the official story of obesity.

Labor is most frequently invoked in this account in literal terms; that is, as physical activity or lack thereof. Despite the fact that it is commonly called out as a stereotype in the mainstream (and indeed, clinical studies consistently suggest that level of physical activity is not significantly correlated with weight), studies consistently confirm that people continue to "believe that we are the greatest gen- eration of lazy, gluttonous, slackers in history—and that's why we're fat";[39] that "Americans are growing fat and lazy."[40] Individuals who are or have been obese report their own experiences of this stereotype: people "see me as a lazy, shift- less person,"[41] writes one woman; another ticks off assumptions that she regularly encounters, including "fat people are lazy. . . . fat people never, ever exercise."[42] So prevalent is this cultural assumption that many obese or formerly obese people internalize this perception: they attribute their obesity to "lack of motivation to exercise,"[43] to "sit[ting] around watching TV,"[44] to "com[ing] up with any and every excuse to get out of a workout. 'The most ridiculous one was that I didn't want to mess up my hair!' "[45]

Certainly, the assumption that laziness is a hallmark of obesity under- girds the plethora of weight-loss fare in popular media. Dozens of weight-loss articles and reports feature the exhortation "Get off the Couch!" in their titles,[46] and the attitude is explicit in the name of Michelle Obama's highly visible national campaign to combat obesity, "Let's Move!" Industry, then—in the form of physical exercise—is touted as not only effective but morally virtuous, symbolizing "important values in our society, values such as discipline, hard work, ambition and willpower."[47] The fact that "workout" is interchangeable with exercise lays the foundation for this conflation, and as relevant to obesity, avoiding it and "keeping the weight off" are attributed overwhelmingly to "combat[ing]" or "fight[ing]" obesity with exercise, not only active but strenuous endeavors.[48] This, too, assumes that the natural inclination or predisposition of the body is to be passive and inert, qualities both conflated with and identified as causes of obesity, as described; the shorthand logic asserts that people are biologically destined to be obese, evoking the fatalistic discourse of obesity. Preventing obesity thus requires vigilance and action, which must be performed in spite of the authentic body's natural proclivities. While the fatalistic account of obesity asserts that efforts to that end are futile, the narrative of disgrace holds out hope and advocates instead the bifurcation of the self, such that the authentic, embodied self is managed and disciplined by the social, civic agent. Indeed, "motivating" oneself to exercise, a concept so common that it is a founding assumption, relies on this bifurcation of the self, which can be mobilized as anything from "tricking" or "fooling" yourself into working out, for example "by tell[ing] yourself 'I have to work out for only seven minutes,' "[49] to coercion—"find[ing] your inner enforcer"[50]—to bribery, specifically by using the authentic self's perceived foibles against it, whether as relevant to food—"sometimes it's food that motivates me. My favorite post-long-run treat is a bagel, and there have definitely been a few runs where I fantasize about that whole-wheat everything bagel for hours"[51]—or to inertia: recommended "post-workout pampering" includes massage, taking a sauna, or a "candlelit soak in the tub."[52] In each case, an apprehension of the self as bifurcated and, moreover, of the authentic self as object and inherently passive is foundational and pervasive assumption; labor, which can be feasibly thought of as productivity, is thus a touchstone of this discourse of disgrace. Notably, this is arguably an animated, visceral mobilization of the "output" dimension of the official story of obesity—mobilized here specifically by and through the critical concept of authenticity.

The counterpart of output, in general and as relevant to the official account of obesity, is input, of course, and it is mobilized in this story of disgrace in similarly (to labor) animated and visceral ways: as literal consumption. This narrative node likewise turns on and cultivates an authentic self that is "othered," castigated, and requiring of vigilant oversight and management. Interestingly, that self is rendered in a way somewhat paradoxical to how it is in relation to labor, insofar as, whereas the natural body is cast in relation to labor as inert and passive, as relevant to consumption it is apprehended as active, specifically as voracious—literally, all consuming, if given half a chance. Paradoxical this may be, but it is not entirely inconsistent with passivity, for this quality is typically described as impulsive, animalistic, and opportunistic. In other words, voraciousness is understood as reflexive rather than deliberate.

Of course, obesity is widely understood, accurately or not, as a consequence of overconsumption, whether described in the dry and clinical terms of the official narrative, like "excess caloric intake"[53] or in more value-laden terms, like gluttony and greed. If popular cultural representations of obese individuals as inherently and incorrigibly gluttonous are available—whether due to moral or character flaws or biologically determined—the vast majority of them articulate the issue in terms of a bifurcated self, as immediately apparent in terms such as self-restraint, self-discipline, and self-control (or lack thereof, in each case) as relevant to the problem of obesity. Again, this is not superficially dissimilar from the official "caloric balance" account of obesity, but it is vitalized in this narrative of disgrace via its predominant focus on the dangerously voracious authentic self. Another way of putting this is that, in the narrative of disgrace, consumption is articulated as a matter of identity negotiation rather than of health or logic.

The stereotype of obese individuals as gluttonous is rampant, of course—references to and speculation regarding how much food, especially, as well as the kinds of decadent foods that obese people are supposed to eat proliferate mainstream popular culture. These articulations vary widely in tone, from fairly clinical ("official discourse" language) assertions that "obesity happens over time when you take in more calories than you use"[54] and that "junk food availability has contributed to the obesity epidemic"[55]—to downright vitriolic: "Hey America, stop eating so damn much. You're really fat and its [sic] gross. Ew. Try a banana or something."[56] Intersecting with the spectacular features of the discourse of disgrace, images of obese individuals eating copious amounts of typically "bad" foods, for example in films such as *The Nutty Professor, Norbit,* and *Wall-E* or television shows like *Saturday Night Live* and *The Daily Show,* abound, as do depictions of tables laden with vast amounts of junk or fast foods that chronicle what an obese person eats in a day, a staple feature of documentary, news, or talk show discussions of obesity.[57] A Google Images search of "obese people eating" conducted at the time of this writing returned 21.8 million results, and although I did not consult all of them, I am confident that most were not flattering.

While the perception of obese individuals as gluttonous is widely identified and decried as a stereotype, it remains persistent, no doubt due to the tenacity of the long-held belief (despite lack of scientific evidence) that caloric imbalance is the cause of obesity, as reflected in the official account. Indeed, so culturally entrenched is it that many obese or formerly obese individuals subscribe to this idea as well, as apparent in their shared narratives and experiences: "I was piling my plate high and finishing every bite—and then some," confesses one woman;[58] "I was greedy and ate too many sausage rolls," states another.[59] Similarly, if in a decidedly different spirit, another woman writes:

The thing that fatties don't let on is that they're deliriously happy most of the time. I certainly am. We get to sink our chops into tureens of whatever takes our fancy and hang the consequences ... Instead of holding back and mumbling "Oh, no, not for me," when skinny waitresses wafts the pudding menu in my direction, I grab it with both hands and sink my lusting eyes into "profiteroles in dark chocolate sauce, vanilla panna cotta with berry coulis, passion fruit pavlova with toffee cream." Yes, yes and yes![60]

The distinction between one's natural, bodily—authentic—inclinations and the disciplinary self is evident in this last passage, and it is apparent across narratives that commonly describe "out of control" appetites: they "can't beat [their] cravings"[61] or are "unable to control" themselves.[62] "After finishing a normal helping of pasta, I have another. And another. Left alone with enough for ten people, I'd eat it all. A trigger goes off in my head or in my body or in my blood sugar—I don't know where it goes off, but I am rendered completely, utterly powerless."[63]

This implicit split between the authentic, embodied self and the rational self is often explained in biological terms: "Our brains are programmed to tell us to go right ahead [and eat whatever is available]"[64] because "humans have an instinctual (even good) fear of hunger . . . Today, most of us know where our next meal is coming from, yet our reaction to hunger has not evolved with our convenience-centered world. . . . If you want to lose weight, however, you must tune in to [and regulate] your body's signal to eat."[65] In not unrelated ways, it is also commonly referenced in terms of addiction, which relies heavily on the bifurcation of the self irrespective of the nature of said addiction, and this is certainly the case with food. Mainstream news, medical, and science accounts of obesity establish that "revolutionary and groundbreaking new studies funded by the National Institutes of Health have shown that the brain scans of food addicts show the same changes and damage as those of a cocaine user,"[66] suggesting that base physiological and psychological impulses must be regulated and restrained; moreover, certain foods, like sugar, salt, and fat, are reported as especially dangerous, wont to trigger "a reptilian brain eating frenzy."[67] Personal accounts corroborate this view; one man reports, "I constantly craved sugar and carbs. I didn't realize that they had hijacked my taste buds, brain chemistry, hormones, and metabolism.[68] A woman reveals that she becomes veritably intoxicated when confronted with tempting foods: "at those times, I am a junkie, a spasm of need and desire, wholly focused on ingesting that bowl of pasta (or doughnuts or ice cream)."[69] The underlying assumption of the split selfcentered on addiction is captured in the inner dialogue recounted by another woman:

It's 4:00 p.m., the hardest hour of my day, and I'm staring down my addiction.
*"Come on,"* says a voice in my head.
"No." I say immediately.

*"Why not?"*

"Because you're bad for me."

*"Only a little. Not that much in the long run. Besides, in 100 years, who'll care?"*

"Not doing it."

*"But you want to. Why shouldn't you do what you want?"*

"Because I'm hurting myself."

*"No you're not, you're making yourself happy. You deserve to be happy. You've been working so hard lately; you deserve a break. Are you one of those pitiful martyrs who thinks [sic] they don't deserve to be happy?"*

"I'm afraid I'll lose control again. What if it all happens all over again?"

*"It won't this time."*

I walk away.

This mental wrestling is familiar, no doubt to anyone who has faced addiction, be it an addiction to drugs, alcohol, sex, shopping, etc.

In my case I was staring at a box of chocolate snack-cakes in the grocery store.[70]

Beating this addiction requires control—often described as herculean—over one's impulses and desires to eat; or, put another way, over one's authentic, "natural," embodied self. Because, unlike most addictive substances, food cannot be avoided, this entails strict oversight and regulation of what and/or how much food one eats. This is typically described as enormously difficult; one woman reports that, to beat her addiction, "I had to plan every morsel of food 24 hours before I ate it, then call a sponsor to report in. Like any addict, I went through withdrawal within 24 hours of giving up my drugs of choice: flour and sugar. I had a severe headache. I had the shakes. And I was furious at the teeny amount of food I was allowed."[71] To "gain control of her food addiction, . . . I was militant. I was my own drill sergeant," reminisces another woman.[72] Food addicts, like addicts to anything, are also advised to avoid triggering situations, acknowledging that control of the (authentic) self might be more difficult in those contexts: "the sight of the bakery where you used to buy brownies might melt your resolve. So shake up your routine. If tortilla chips are your weakness, don't go to Mexican restaurants. If you always have ice cream while watching TV, read a book instead (or knit to keep your hands busy as you watch *CSI: Miami*)."[73]

Notably, however, the assumption of a split self that undergirds this "management" node of the narrative of disgrace is not limited to a food-addiction scenario; on the contrary, it funds virtually all of the mainstream discourse about the control and regulation of food—dieting, in other words. Dieters are told "never get too hungry" because "hunger is a primal urge that's difficult to deny";[74] "next time your mind gets stuck on a certain food, call a friend and redirect your brain by asking how her day's going";[75] and "schedule a cheat day: resist cravings by postponing indulging to a future day when you're free to eat whatever you want."[76] In the same way that people are advised to "trick" themselves into exercising, as just described, a host of "diet tricks" are recommended that encourage people to discipline their base selves by conning them into compliance: for example, dieters are encouraged to drink water before meals "because the water provides a sense of fullness, so not as much food is needed to reach the point of satiety";[77] to eat off of small plates and use smaller utensils (even chopsticks, some sources recommend) to "fool the brain into thinking it's eating more";[78] to eat in a "low-contrast atmosphere" (i.e., ensure that the color of one's plate matches the color of the tablecloth);[79] and to "camouflage" healthy foods they don't like by "sneaking" them into "sauces, chilies, soups, casseroles" or "muffins, breads, and pies."[80]Again, the notion that healthy weight and weight loss are a function of effective management of the natural, embodied self and its urges—and accordingly, that obesity is a function of indulgence thereof—is a founding assumption of this story of disgrace. Obviously, this story is heavily obligated to the official "calories in/calories out," personal responsibility account of obesity, but it is distinctive in very important ways, including to the extent that authenticity is centered and drawn against the rational individual on which the official story is founded.

## Original Sin

Although the story of obesity as disgrace is mobilized in two distinct ways—display and industry—the variations are consistent and coherent to the extent that each (and thus the narrative more broadly) is predicated on authenticity: more specifically, on an apprehension of authenticity as dangerous and destructive. This narrative has its moorings in the official account that characterizes obesity as a straightforward and rational matter of caloric budgeting. As I have argued, the primary failing of that account is that authenticity is entirely absent and thus it does not resonate with the felt experience or understanding of obesity. In the case of the story of disgrace, if it similarly assumes individual responsibility as the cause of and solution to obesity, authenticity is not only featured but drives and subsumes that project. The cultural narrative of obesity similarly imagines the rational individual and authenticity in dialectical relation, but in that case, authenticity is conflated with culture that is characterized as something "others" have, implicitly aligning rational individualism with white privilege and authenticity with primitive, less evolved "other" people and communities. In the case of the story of disgrace, authenticity retains those same troubling primal, decadent features, but it is located in all of us, like a bad seed—an imaginary that does not necessarily offset the raced and privileged dimensions of the cultural notion of authenticity, incidentally, and may in fact fuel fears around it. Finally, the disgrace narrative also reflects, ironically, the narrative of resistance, which I describe in the previous chapter—that account, too, centers authenticity in equally power-ful and primary ways, including its grounding in the body. However, to the great extent to which the narrative of resistance valorizes authenticity, the narrative of disgrace, in equal measure, vilifies it.

The paradoxical aspects within the respective nodes of the story of disgrace—display and industry—at first blush appear incommensurate: in the case of dis-play, disgrace is variously risked by being spectacle or by being invisible; and in the case of industry, by passivity or by voracity. Again, however, these articula-tions cohere around an assumption of the unfettered authentic self whose mate-rialization as an obese body makes one spectacular *and* causes others to shun or discount one; and whose proclivities entail physical passivity *and* rapacious con-sumption. If more subtly, these paradoxes also cohere around gender: certainly, long-held tropes of femininity both objectify women's bodies in spectacular ways and discount them; and characterize women and their bodies as passive and weak as well as dangerously, threateningly consuming, especially of men. Superficially, this may explain why the bulk of cultural attention to (and representations of) obesity and fat focuses upon women's bodies, in particular—and, more abstractly, why fat itself is understood as feminine and feminizing. Indeed, in this narrative, the very concept of the authentic self as a concept—whether as relevant to women or men—is imagined as feminine. Now, this is not necessarily a revelation: scores of feminist critics from various quarters have noted the ways in which nature in general is feminized, positioned as the appropriate subject of domination and control by men or masculinity. Even as relevant to the internal self, scholars have chronicled the ways in which appropriate performance and emulation of masculinity demands repression of emotions, especially, and impulses that are culturally characterized as feminine. What is interesting and perhaps unusually highlighted about authenticity as it is imagined in this story of obesity is that the authentic feminine self is constant and powerful, requiring vigilant and herculean efforts of discipline, monitoring, and control. In these terms, the threat posed by the "obesity crisis" can be understood as one of emasculation and impotence.

Also consistent with gendered convention, governance, control, and con-tainment of the specifically female body (and femininity more broadly) is paramount in this narrative, lending further credence to the imaginary of the authentic body as feminine. This is evident in literal ways per the current slen-der ideal of the female body—slender to an extent that is not easily or health-ily attainable for most women. More abstractly, as reflected in this discourse, everyone is called to be on her or his guard against the insidious feminine within: failure to do so strips one of agency and subjectivity, both of which are accordingly firmly aligned with conventional masculinity. Per display, leaky, soft, excessive bodies must be hidden or tucked away in order to be viable; per industry, the impulses that are perceived to lead to those bodies must be tightly monitored and regulated or contained. This entails, as I have described, an apprehension of the self as split, between the authentic self and what might be understood as the civic self, which is congruent with the neoliberal imaginary of the individual as rational and autonomous and, moreover, logically construed as masculine.

If the gendered sensibilities that inform this narrative reflect our cultural apprehension of fat and obesity more broadly (and are thus reflected in various ways across competing accounts of obesity, for that matter), more recent contestations around cultural identity, specifically relevant to individualism and how it is drawn against state and market, are no less salient. The particular mobilization of authenticity in the disgrace narrative of obesity effectively rejects the state in favor of the individual—individuals are identified as the only appropriate and viable monitor of the authentic self. Furthermore, self-governance is really the *only* role of the individual in this account: other aims, such as self-actualization, happiness, success, are not even acknowledged. This is not because the contained self is equated with the fulfilled self, importantly: in this narrative, the battle to manage the self is ongoing and epic—there is no actualized self at the end. Thus, although the privileging of the individual and the minimization of the role of the state are, on paper, commensurate with neoliberal logics, in practice they are not, specifically because consumption is eliminated as the warrant for those respective roles. That is, the task at hand in this narrative is to restrict and regulate consumption. Perhaps obviously, then, the market is similarly rendered superfluous or irrelevant; very few market offerings are mentioned, much less promoted, in this existential struggle where only monitoring and regulation of the self is relevant. If motivation (to exercise) and denial (of consumption) are the only resources that matter in the fight against obesity, and both are articulated in exclusively moral terms, then the market is obsolete—these resources are internal, not external. In other words, the imaginary of authenticity that drives this narrative inserts itself into the official story of obesity, magnifies the rationality and autonomy that characterize the individual in that account to a caricaturish degree and, perhaps fittingly, swallows them whole.

# 9

# Conclusion

*Getting Real*

What is obesity? What causes it? What can be done about it? These questions occupy the top of the national and, increasingly, global agenda today. As I hope I have demonstrated, these questions defy simple answers, not only or even primarily due to complex and still unfolding science but because fat and, accordingly, obesity can only be understood—indeed, can only mean anything at all—within the historical and cultural context in which they occur. Informed by that context, as with any social issue, a resonant story emerges. The widely accepted contemporary designation of obesity as a national "crisis" or "epidemic," for instance, identified in the early 2000s, is highly reflective of exigent and continuing concerns about national security in the wake of 9/11. Anxieties regarding lack of control, discipline, and regulation that fuel concerns about the obesity epidemic as relevant to the body reflect broader national concerns about security, continence, and preparedness to defend against attack. This is not to say that the fact of excess (however determined, itself specific to particular historical and cultural sensibilities) fat did not exist prior to 9/11; rather, what and how it means, and whether to do anything about it, is inevitably shaped and formed by broader cultural, political, and economic considerations in a given historical moment.

Particularly interesting about obesity in *this* historical moment—more than a decade after its designation as epidemic, which secured its prominence on the public agenda—is the sheer number and contradictory nature of the cultural stories about obesity currently in circulation in the mainstream. Typically, stories about social issues deemed salient in a given context are more coherent, at least in the mainstream. For instance, the War on Cancer, coined by Nixon in 1971 and inevitably informed by national anxieties regarding the failures of the Vietnam Conflict, was and implicitly remains the sanctioned narrative in the mainstream of another health epidemic. Even highly contested social issues, like legalization of drugs, gun control, or gay marriage, tend to coalesce around coherent if oppositional respective narratives in the mainstream. While alternative perspectives may proliferate in each of these instances outside of the mainstream, they are not generally apparent or acknowledged in the broader public discourse.

I contend that the multiple, competing stories of obesity that populate the mainstream today can be traced to the financial crisis of 2008. As with the link between the so-named obesity epidemic and concerns about national security, I am not asserting that the financial crisis created those stories; rather, just as exigent political, economic, and cultural anxieties in a given historical moment always inform our understandings and responses to social issues, the particular anxieties generated and surfaced by the financial crisis inevitably informed the mainstream navigation of the matter of obesity. Moreover, the particular material features of obesity render it remarkably available and ideal for the navigation of those anxieties. Specifically, in addition to the fact that (over)consumption and greed were key features of the financial collapse, it forced a tension between commonly understood or "received" understandings at the time of individualism, the core precept of US cultural identity and political philosophy, and authenticity, a culturally prevalent and powerfully resonant concept today.

In fact, the financial crisis materialized a broader crisis of neoliberalism, the political economy of the United States for the last several decades. Predicated on a particular configuration of an unfettered market, a laissez-faire government, and the individual as consumer citizen, the rationale that mobilizes this trifecta centers upon a rational, autonomous individual whose needs and desires can only be fully realized by goods and services furnished by the market. Accordingly, the role of government is to facilitate rather than regulate the market, to the end of ensuring the individual's access to the full range of market offerings. Consumption is the engine drives neoliberalism; it is articulated as the path to citizenship, which in turn is tantamount to the realization of democracy. The financial crisis—which many economists asserted was inevitable—surfaced the deep flaws of neoliberal principles and practices, especially relevant to corrupt and exploitative practices on the part of unregulated industry. The neoliberal imaginary of individualism also sustained damage as a consequence of the financial crisis: the qualities of rationality and autonomy on which it was predicated were challenged, insofar as consumption under neoliberalism was exposed as frequently, in practice, more appropriately attributable to egregious exploitation of consumers by industry or uninformed or unwise—that is, irrational—personal choices.

Moreover, in the wake of the financial crisis, the public eye turned toward its real, material, lived effects on people, as apparent across news coverage, popular media fare, and the highly visible social movement Occupy Wall Street, comprised of the self-identified "99 percenters," or the real, material bodies who were revealed as conspicuously absent from and furthermore profoundly harmed by neoliberalism in practice. It is precisely at this point that the tension between individualism as culturally presumed under neoliberalism—as rational, autonomous, abstract, and thoroughly defined by or as consumption—and authenticity, or lived, felt, material, and embodied experience, was brought to bear. To place this in broader context, individualism is a nonnegotiable, indeed fundamental basis of US cultural identity; while authenticity does not feature the historical legacy that individualism does in this regard, its contemporary prevalence and resonance (ironically secured in part by the neoliberal imperative of individual self-actualization) are indisputably profound. While authenticity and individualism are not inherently incommensurate concepts, turning as they both do on a conceptualization of the self, the financial crisis forced a culturally exigent rift between them—one that requires resolution, whatever that may look like.

Every social issue, as I have described, inevitably reflects the cultural, political, and economic anxieties particular to the historical moment in which it emerges. Thus, this tension between the presumptive neoliberal imaginary of individualism and authenticity can be identified in current national discourse around issues ranging from unemployment to police violence. Obesity, however, is perhaps an ideal field onto which this particular tension is projected because it materially manifests, by definition, two foundational nodes of that tension: embodied, lived experience and consumption. This is why, I contend, we see so many stories of obesity in circulation today: each story essentially constitutes an alternative negotiation of those currently poignant tensions.

The first, caloric imbalance story of obesity that I assessed—the "official" one, as evidenced in government campaigns and industry articulations—not surprisingly precisely mirrors the neoliberal tenets under which it emerged, including and especially the neoliberal imaginary of the rational, autonomous individual. Obesity is articulated as an exclusive and straightforward matter of inappropriate caloric budgeting by the individual; accordingly, obesity redress entails self-monitoring and -regulation of caloric intake relative to caloric output. While inaccuracy of the base theory of obesity that informs this story has much to do with the lack of effectiveness of obesity campaigns, I contend that the major failure of these initiatives is attributable to a lack of narrative resonance, as evidenced by the fact that so many alternative stories of obesity are available in the mainstream. Specifically, just as the neoliberal imaginary of the individual was found wanting in the financial crisis, it fails in this narrative as well, insofar as it is predicated on unrealistic assumptions of rationality and requires the objectification of the self/body. Our relationships with and practices of food and bodies are not, however, rational, objective, or sterile; on the contrary, they are deeply and intimately felt. In other words, the fatal flaw of the caloric imbalance story of obesity is that it denies authenticity, or at least the imaginary thereof.

Although the environmental story of obesity diametrically opposes the official story—perhaps *because* it does—it, too, fails to account for authenticity, if in very different ways. In that story, by implicating environmental factors and agents as contributors to or causes of obesity, authenticity is denied insofar as individuals are homogenized, genericized, and rendered entirely passive, unwitting victims of larger forces. Indeed, the very notion of individualism itself is vastly undermined, an egregious error in US cultural context. Perhaps predictably the fatalistic story of obesity develops in the gap between the official and environmental accounts: that is, it establishes the inevitability of obesity and the futility of its redress by definitively illustrating how officially prescribed individual efforts are hindered if not obviated by circumstances beyond one's control. In addition, structural interventions invited by the environmental narrative are similarly problematized, articulated as wrongheaded or futile for various reasons. Accordingly, the result is a stalemate; situating rational and autonomous individualism in context inevitably problematizes it, for it can only be sustained as an abstraction, in a vacuum—faced with everyday constraints, the concept quickly erodes. Likewise, positing structural interventions as contradictory to individual autonomy articulates them as ineffective and inappropriate. What the fatalistic story does, then, is implicitly but undeniably surface the failure of each of those narratives to account for authenticity, or the real, lived experience of obesity and its redress.

Stories of obesity that take up and center authenticity do so in various ways, but all draw it in relation to the neoliberal imaginary of the rational, autonomous individual—a tack that is inevitable, given individualism's broader legacy and foundational status to national cultural identity and the presumption (and current crisis) of the neoliberal deployment of the concept. Both the cultural narrative of obesity and the story of obesity as spiritual/emotional dysfunction can be apprehended as attempting to essentially restore at least a modified version of neoliberal individualism by reconciling it against authenticity, albeit in distinctive, even opposite ways. The cultural narrative conflates authenticity with cultural identity and draws it against individualism; authenticity is something that "other" people—especially people of color—have, and it is articulated as harmful and dangerous, not only directly linked to but even the cause of obesity. Health is thus implicitly correlated with conscious disarticulation from one's "culture," making the "right," rational choices, which furthermore secures a perception of appropriate (by contrast) rational, abstract, disembodied individualism—and normative citizenship—as white and privileged. The narrative of obesity as spiritual and emotional dysfunction similarly restores neoliberal logics of individualism, but in entirely different ways: here, authenticity is championed, and individualism is articulated as the requisite path to it. In other words, the relatively sterile and externally oriented neoliberal notion of self-actualization, ensured via unfettered consumption is made over as authentic selfhood; individualism becomes a practice and philosophy of putting oneself first as the means to that end.

The resistive story of obesity and the story of obesity as disgrace are, on the one hand, united in their situation of authenticity squarely in and of the body and its felt experiences and needs. They diverge dramatically, however, with respect to how they apprehend it and how they draw it in relation to individualism. The resistive story privileges embodied authenticity to the extent that it subsumes and actually absorbs individualism, specifically articulated as individual liberty: the two are effectively conflated in this account. Furthermore, any attempt, even by the self, to regulate the body is received as inauthentic and inappropriate. The narrative of disgrace, on the other hand, acknowledges the same voracious embodied authentic self, but deploys the rational individual of the official story of obesity to counter it. Rather than objectify the body as separate from the self, as the official account of caloric imbalance does, by investing authenticity in the body, the story of disgrace effectively splits the self into authentic and individual selves, reinforcing the distinction between the two. While the narrative of disgrace thus mobilizes the official story, it does not replicate it; to the contrary, and ironically, it undermines it. If each of the narratives of obesity feature gendered patterns of articulation, these last two, in particular, in their imaginaries of visceral bodies, are gendered in especially powerful, sometimes paradoxical ways. Neither of these narratives, notably, can be reconciled with neoliberalism—ironic in the case of the story of disgrace in that it is predicated precisely on the official, account of obesity that mobilizes classic neoliberalism. It appears that authenticity that is articulated as embodied—rather than spiritual, as in the case of the story of obesity as spiritual or emotional dysfunction—is impossible shore up against neoliberal tenets.

The fact that these stories of obesity are proliferate in the mainstream and, as evidenced by their prominence, pervasiveness, and traction, clearly resonate with the populace despite the fact that they are so varied and often contradictory is telling. At the very least, it bespeaks a profound dissatisfaction with the official story of obesity, even if it retains cultural presumption even among the populace. That the official account is not rejected out of hand, however— indeed, it arguably has primacy even as vernacular accounts resonate more powerfully—suggests that aspects of it are culturally compelling. These paradoxes and contradictions make sense if these stories are understood as navigations of the currently poignant tension between individualism, or the presumptive neoliberal imaginary thereof, and authenticity. The presence, persistence, and resonance of these stories establish more broadly that authenticity must be acknowledged in this historical moment as the US navigates its cultural identity and political economy in the wake of the financial crisis. Although it does not feature the cultural and philosophical depth and degree that individualism has, authenticity is a powerful concept in its own right that has attained substantial cultural presumption in recent decades and thus cannot be dismissed or underestimated.

# Inside Out

Notably, individualism and authenticity are not incommensurate—on the contrary, they are potentially quite confluent, predicated as they both are on the self. Indeed, the deployment of the concept of self-actualization as a warrant for consumption under neoliberal logics hints at this confluence, although authenticity and self-actualization are not interchangeable, especially per those logics. A predictable response to the forced tension between presumptive neoliberal individualism and authenticity is to draw them in opposition to each other in the interest of containing authenticity and reasserting the neoliberal imaginary—among the stories of obesity, this is essentially what the cultural story attempts to do, in troublingly racialized ways. Another tack, of course, is to attempt to bring them into alignment in ways that ultimately reify presumptive individualism, as the narrative of obesity as spiritual and emotional dysfunction does, by reworking and resituating the neoliberal precept of self-actualization in potentially compelling ways. Locating authenticity in and of the body, however, as the stories of resistance and disgrace respectively do, is categorically untenable for presumptive neoliberalism. The self, it appears, can only be imagined under neoliberal logics as rational, abstract, disembodied. This is so because consumption, on which the current tension between presumptive individualism and authenticity turns, is inevitably radically redefined when invested in the body. The neoliberal imaginary of individualism is thoroughly external, practically as well as philosophically. Practically, consumption of external goods and services is necessarily undertaken to the end of realizing likewise concrete goals and aspirations—this is, in fact, how self-actualization is conceptualized in that imaginary. Philosophically, and no less externally oriented, consumption is the (only) means by which citizenship and, ultimately, democracy can be realized. Authenticity, however, is an inevitably internal experience, understood as deeply intimate, felt subjectivity; accordingly, consumption as imagined under neoliberalism, articulated as it is with things definitively *not* of the self or body, is at least suspect by default if not antithetical to it. This is where the narrative of obesity as spiritual or emotional dysfunction, the most promising in terms of its potential to bring authenticity and individualism into alignment by disembodying authenticity, finds its limit: even in that account, consumption is implicit and ancillary, relevant only to the extent that it might facilitate realization of the authentic spiritual self. In those cases where authenticity is embodied, neoliberal practices and philosophies of consumption are even more difficult to sustain. The cultural story of obesity implicitly acknowledges this by drawing a hard line between authenticity as that which primitivized, embodied "others" have by dint of their cultural allegiances; and individualism, which is accordingly imagined as normative—rational and enlightened. The narratives of resistance and disgrace, which assert authenticity as incorrigibly, undeniably, and universally embodied, mobilize consumption in ways that are impossible to reconcile with neoliberal imperatives, however. Consumption is taken up in those cases in viscerally literal terms, albeit in diametrically opposite ways: as defiance against inauthentic artifice and rationality, in case of resistance, and as harmful and dangerous, in the case of disgrace. Across these stories, the currency of authenticity appears to be expression—of the internal, lived self— rather than consumption; arguably, the inverse of consumption. Certainly, the premium on expression as the cornerstone and pathway to authenticity appears to be confirmed across a host of contemporary and widespread practices, ranging from body art to social media, practices that I would assert are direct evidence of the cultural resonance of authenticity. While conventional—neoliberal—logics of consumption are not necessarily obviated in those practices, they notoriously struggle to make themselves relevant.

But if authenticity isn't going anywhere anytime soon, neither is consumption: the material reality is that consumption—and in particular consumption as operationalized and secured under neoliberal policies over the last several decades—is at least as entrenched as authenticity, arguably more so: it is, at this point, structurally—legally, politically, and even culturally—embedded in the national economy, even the national identity. The tension inherent between received individualism and authenticity as forced by neoliberalism in crisis, then, can feasibly be understood as turning on consumption, at base, and what and how it means—underscoring the suitability, again, of obesity as a field for these navigations. Whether and how these reconciliations can be accomplished on a broader cultural, political, and economic scale is yet to be determined, and certainly beyond the scope of this project: while discourse about obesity serves as an excellent index of those navigations, they remain very much in process, as signified by the continued presence and resonance of multiple, competing obesity stories.

As regards the material "facts" of obesity and the obesity crisis, first, I hope that one of the contributions of this project is to at least prompt a more complex consideration of these designations. This does not necessarily entail rejection of them as opposed to a more thoughtful, reflective apprehension of what it means and what, if anything, to do about it. A feasible analogy may be race/ethnicity: most cultural critics acknowledge that what it is and means is entirely socially constructed, a manifestation of cultural and political sensibilities in a given time. But this does not obviate the fact that it has profound meaning and material implications, as experienced; as culturally accomplished; and as structurally secured. The appropriate response is hardly to proceed as if race doesn't exist or matter; likewise, even if obesity is a cultural construct, it matters.

Unlike the matter of race/ethnicity, however, conventional notions of obesity have engendered alarmist responses and attempts at redress—again, it is the subject of numerous (failed) campaigns and initiatives. To the extent that obesity is correlated with compromised health conditions, this is may be justifiable, even if the blanket vilification of obesity and its contemporary designation as epidemic in proportion warrant critical attention. The primary narrative failure of those campaigns and initiatives, as I have attempted to illustrate, is that they are thoroughly steeped in imaginaries of rationality as relevant to the individual. If the competing vernacular stories of obesity in broad circulation do nothing else, they definitively establish that it is incumbent that whatever redress is proposed must acknowledge and engage the felt, lived experience of obesity rather than objectify and disarticulate the body—and, for that matter, food—from a posited rational individual. It is important to note, however, that mere acknowledgement or incorporation of authenticity into the narrative is insufficient; many of the practices proposed or implied by the various vernacular stories of obesity that do feature authenticity range from dubious to troubling. Practically speaking, in light of the actual science of obesity that links it to endocrinal and hormonal disruption, it appears incontrovertible that structural intervention of at least some kind and degree is necessary in order to realize good health outcomes. Just as I am not a medical doctor or clinician, neither am I a public health administrator or policy maker, so I will refrain from issuing particular recommendations. But perhaps this project illustrates that intervention in cultural or health issues cannot ever be simply about "the facts," whether because those facts are themselves a cultural product or because the facts are bad. The official account of obesity as caloric imbalance, after all, didn't fail because the science on which it is founded is bad (actually nonexistent); in fact, many of the more compelling and resonant vernacular stories of obesity that do feature authenticity likewise draw on "bad" or nonexistent science. Moreover, if lack of evidence were why the official account and attendant efforts of redress have failed, the reactive environmental narrative would earn presumption by default and carry the day. But that "good" science, too, is insufficient to compel adherence; while there are undoubtedly other factors in play, not least pushback from powerful entities who stand to lose should the environmental narrative gain traction, I submit that it, like the official account, ultimately fails because it doesn't "ring true"—that is, it, too, sidesteps authenticity.

## Body Politic

While obesity is an ideal field on which to navigate currently pressing tensions around individualism, authenticity, and consumption, it is no less ideal for navigating more abstract but, at the same time, thoroughly mundane tensions between lived, embodied, material experience and cultural interpretations of those experiences. More to the point, stories about obesity make poignant the distinction between what we, as embodied subjects, experience and how our culture represents and encourages us to perceive that experience. Generally, we reconcile these things in the most efficacious ways at hand, typically either by rejecting one or the other: dismissing or rationalizing our own experience as aberrant or invalid or, more rarely, rejecting the cultural interpretation of it. At the same time, all of us, in very concrete ways—and scholars and philosophers in theoretical ways—have experienced the frustration of not being able to represent or articulate an experience or feeling, adequately or at all; this is especially true in matters of the body. Where the body begins and the world ends—for instance, whether we can understand, experience, or even control our own bodies outside of cultural and ideological perceptions of them—is a complex and complicated matter, one that has engaged scholars from Plato to Rene Descartes to Michel Foucault to Judith Butler.

Most scholarly investigation of the body in relation to society and the symbolic is of a poststructural bent[1], apprehending the body as an "admixture of discourse and matter, one whose inseparability is a critical, though complex attribute."[2] But likely born of an understandable desire to avoid biological determinism, most critical inquiry regarding the body, reflecting Haraway's contention that bodies are "made" rather than born,[3] tends to privilege discursive or symbolic articulations rather than materialities across three primary contexts: actual practices—"body techniques"[4] or "iterations"[5] performed by a subject, for instance; cultural representations of the body[6]; or techniques of regulations, surveillance, disciplining, and monitoring of bodies, by the state and/or the self.[7] In fact, each of the stories of obesity I have examined engages all of these aspects, many of them privileging one or the other tack: for instance, both the official account of obesity and the story of disgrace are prominently predicated on regulation, surveillance, and discipline; and the cultural and resistive stories of obesity respectively, in different ways, turn on bodily techniques, iterations, and practices. But distinctive about the vernacular stories of obesity in particular is that, via authenticity, they commence with and privilege the lived, embodied—that is, material—experience of obesity. As deployed across these stories, authenticity can be understood as a resistance of sorts against privileged discursive articulations of the obese body as a shameful object that must be disciplined, contained, or eradicated. Authenticity represents an attempt to assert and establish material, lived—"real" or "true"— experience not reflected or even acknowledged in sanctioned cultural articulations or representations of a particular (in this case, obese) identity or body: in the current context, articulations and representations that are fueled by the presumptive neoliberal (and decidedly *dis*embodied) imaginary of rational, autonomous individualism. This does not deny the significance of either bodily performances and iterations or the social, political, cultural, and economic context in which they (or lived bodies) are located and made sense of; but it does privilege the lived body—the embodied experience—in ways and to a degree that we haven't seen before on this scale or in such a pervasive, persistent, and available fashion. These stories suggest that discourse about bodies, practical as well as theoretical, must acknowledge, account for, and defer to felt, lived experiences of those bodies.

In these particular stories of obesity, notably, authenticity is conflated with expression—not necessarily surprising, given that authenticity is predicated on a notion of the inner, lived and felt self. This is clear in stories that extol authenticity, such as the story of spiritual and emotional dysfunction and stories of resistance, as well as the fatalistic story, which, if it does not articulate authenticity explicitly, certainly describes the problems inherent in refusing to acknowledge or permit its articulation. Authenticity as expression is apparent even in those stories in which authenticity is suspect or dangerous, such as the cultural story, where authenticity endows certain people and communities with "difference," and the story of disgrace; in these cases, repression of authenticity is advised, but of course this is predicated on an understanding of authenticity as, if not vigilantly controlled, inevitably marked—expressed—on the body. Moreover, in part due to these stories' genesis as responsive to the denial of authenticity in official account of obesity, expression is implicitly drawn against representation in these accounts: that is, felt and lived experience of obesity and expression thereof, however valued, is drawn against received cultural articulations of obesity. Of course, this is a narrow view of representation, for expression itself can only itself be accomplished with representational symbols. But at the very least, by featuring authenticity, these stories—even those that align with conventional sensibilities—collectively suggest, at some level, an awareness of and resistance to what is understood in context as social production, manipulation, and control of representations, at least in some instances. Again, obesity is an ideal, perhaps even inevitable field for these articulations in the first place because it is embodied; when it becomes a site of public discourse, especially in terms of crisis, how it is represented in that discourse inevitably becomes a volatile matter, and in an unusually visible way.

The conflation of authenticity with expression moreover secures the logic across these stories of obesity that authenticity is inherently incommensurate with consumption as imagined and practiced per neoliberal imperatives. The fusion of expression with "the real" is drawn as oppositional to consumption, which is implicitly rendered artificial and superfluous, if not downright antithetical, to the project and aims of authenticity. Again, this is not necessarily evaluated negatively; some stories endorse consumption precisely to the end of stifling the authentic self, and in fact these are the only stories that embrace consumption as underwritten by neoliberalism. Even the story of obesity as spiritual and emotional dysfunction, which valorizes authenticity and aligns it with the neoliberal imaginary of individualism, is vague, circumspect, and selective about the role of consumption: this is, again, where it finds its limit. Because consumption per neoliberal logics is so tightly conflated with citizenship—and, more abstractly, with individualism and even democracy, as described in the first chapter—these competing resonant stories of obesity can and arguably should be understood as contestations about US cultural identity and priorities. In many ways, this is hardly surprising, as these stories formed in the crucible of neoliberalism in crisis as it intersected with extant and acute concerns around obesity, already identified at the time as a national emergency.

I hope to have demonstrated that these stories are not simply differing accounts of what obesity is and what, if anything, to do about it, although they certainly are that. These stories are best understood, I argue, as reflections and mobilizations of broader contemporary cultural tensions and exigent anxieties. But as significant as this alone is, I also hope that this project reveals that these stories are more, even, than this: that is, these stories comprise navigations and blueprints about how to (re)define, understand, and accomplish our personal *and* political identities, and the priorities and practices that follow from them. In telling the tale about fat and obesity, each of these stories tells us, in this moment of crisis, who we "really" are and how and why that matters.

# Notes

Chapter 1

1. Adult obesity facts. (2012). Centers for Disease Control. http://www.cdc.gov/obe-sity/data/adult.html. Accessed October 18, 2012; "Adult obesity rates." (2012). The Robert Wood Johnson Foundation. http://www.rwjf.org/en/about-rwjf/newsroom/newsroom-content/2012/09/adult-obesity-rates-could-exceed-60-percent-in-13-states-by-2030.html. Accessed October 24, 2012; Obesity and overweight. (2012). World Health Organization. http://www.who.int/mediacentre/factsheets/fs311/en/. Accessed October 18, 2012. Obesity update 2012. (2012). Organization for Economic Cooperation and Development. http://www.oecd.org/els/healthpoliciesanddata/49716427.pdf. Accessed October 18, 2012.
2. F as in fat. (2009). Issue Report of the Robert Wood Johnson Foundation. http://healthy-americans.org/reports/obesity2009/Obesity2009Report.pdf. Accessed July 28, 2013; Finkelstein, E. A., Ruhm, C. J., & Kosa, K. M. (2005). Economic causes and consequences of obesity. *Annual Review of Public Health, 26,* 239–257; Hammond, R. A., & Levine, R. (2010).The economic impact of obesity in the United States. *Diabetes, Metabolic Syndrome, and Obesity, 3,* 285–295; Withrow, D., & Alter, D. A. (2010). The economic burden of obe-sity worldwide: A systematic review of the direct costs of obesity. *Obesity Reviews, 12*(2), 131–141.
3. Jaslow, R. (2012, September 25). Retired military leaders say this generation is "too fat to fight." CBS News, Online. http://www.cbsnews.com/8301-504763_162-57520233-10391704/retired-military-leaders-say-this-generation-is-too-fat-to-fight/. Accessed July 27, 2013; Obesity bigger threat than terrorism? (2006, Mar. 1). CBS News Online. http://www.cbsnews.com/stories/2006/03/01/health/main1361849.shtml. Accessed August 10, 2008; Shalikashvili, J. M., & Shelton, H. (April 30, 2010). The latest national security threat: Obesity. *Washington Post.* http://www.washingtonpost.com/wp-dyn/content/article/2010/04/29/AR2010042903669.html. Accessed July 27, 2013.
4. Olshansky, S. J., Passaro, D. J., Hershow, R. C., Layden, J., Carnes, B. A., Brody, J., . . . Ludwig, D. S. (2005). A potential decline in life expectancy in the United States in the 21st century. *New England Journal of Medicine, 352,* 1138–1145.
5. Lustig, R. (2012). *Fat chance: Beating the odds against sugar, processed food, obesity, and disease.* New York: Hudson Street Press; Unger, R. H., & Scherer, P. E. (2010). Gluttony, sloth and the metabolic syndrome: A roadmap to lipotoxicity. *Trends in Endocrinology & Metabolism, 21*(6), 345–352.
6. Finkelstein, E. A., Ruhm, C. J., & Kosa, K. M. (2005). Economic causes and consequences of obesity. *Annual Review of Public Health, 26,* 239–257.
7. Curtis, J. P., Selter, J. G., Wang, Y., Rathore, S. S., Jovin, I. S., Jadbabaie, F., . . . Krumholz, H. M. (2005). The obesity paradox: Body mass index and outcomes in patients with heart failure. *Archives of Internal Medicine, 165*(1), 55–61.

8. Sobal, J., & Maurer, D. (Eds.) (1999). *Weighty issues: Fatness and thinness as social problems*. New York: Aldine de Greuter; Sokolov, R. (1999). Culture and obesity. *Social Research, 66*(1), 31–36.

9. De Garine, I., & Pollock, N. (Eds.). 1995. *Social aspects of obesity*. Amsterdam: Overseas Publishers Association; Cassiday, C. M. (1991). The good body: When big is better. *Medical Anthropology: Cross-Cultural Studies in Health and Illness, 13*(3), 181–213.

10. Swami, V., & Tovee, M. J. (2009). Big beautiful women: The body size preferences of male fat admirers. *Journal of Sex Research, 46*(1), 89–86.

11. Brink, P. J. (1989). The fattening room among the Annang of Nigeria. *Medical anthropology: Cross-cultural studies in health and illness, 12*(1), 131–143; De Garine & Pollock (1995). *Social aspects of obesity*; Tauzin, A. (2007). Women of Mauritania: Cathodic images and presentation of the self. *Visual Anthropology, 20*(1), 3–18.

12. Gilman, S. L. (2010). *Obesity: The biography*. Oxford: Oxford University Press; Levy-Navarro, E. (2008). *The culture of obesity in early and late modernity*. New York: Palgrave Macmillan; Lustig, R. (2012). *Fat chance: Beating the odds against sugar, processed food, obesity, and disease*. New York: Hudson Street Press; Saguy, A. C. (2013). *What's wrong with fat?* New York: Oxford University Press; Schwarz, H. (1986). *Never satisfied: A cultural history of diets, fantasies, and fat*. New York: Free Press.

13. Collingham, L. (2012). *The taste of War: World War II and the battle for food*. London: Penguin. Also Sobal & Maurer (1999). *Weighty issues*. Recently, some researchers have advanced a biological rationale for ostensible selfish behavior associated with obesity in contexts of deprivation; see, e.g., Peters, A. (2011). The selfish brain: Competition for energy resources. *American Journal of Human Biology, 23*(1), 29–34.

14. Bordo, S. (1993). *Unbearable weight: Feminism, western culture, and the body*. Berkeley, CA: University of California Press; Saguy (2013). *What's wrong with fat?*

15. Bordo (1993). *Unbearable weight*; LeBesco, K. (2004). *Revolting bodies? The struggle to redefine fat identity*. Amherst, MA: University of Massachusetts.

16. Bacha, F., Saad, R., Gungor, N., et al. (2003). Obesity, regional fat distribution, and syndrome X in obese black versus white adolescents: Race differential in diabetogenic and atherogenic risk factors. *Journal of Clinical Endocrinology and Metabolism, 88*, 2534–2540; Cossrow, N., & Falkner, B. (2004). Race/ethnic issues in obesity and obesity-related comorbidities. *Journal of Clinical Endocrinology and Metabolism, 89*, 2590–2594; Shugart, H. A. (2013). Weight of tradition: Culture as an explanatory device for obesity in contemporary U.S. news coverage. *Obesity Reviews, 14*, 736–744.

17. De Spiegelaere, M., Hennart, P., & Dramaix, M. (1998). The influence of socioeconomic status on the incidence and evolution of obesity during early adolescence. *International Journal of Obesity, 3*, 268–274; O'Dea, J. A. (2008). Gender, ethnicity, culture and social class influences on childhood obesity among Australian schoolchildren: Implications for treatment, prevention and community education. *Health Social Care in Community, 16*, 282–290; Whitaker, D., Milam, A. J., Graham, C. M., et al. (2013). Neighborhood environment and urban schoolchildren's risk for being overweight. *American Journal of Health Promotion, 27*, 410–416.

18. Gilman, S. L. (2008). *Fat: A cultural history of obesity*. Cambridge, England: Polity Press; Gilman (2010). *Obesity*; Levy-Navarro (2008). *The culture of obesity in early and late modernity*; Saguy (2013). *What's wrong with fat?*

19. Schwarz (1986). *Never satisfied*.

20. Farrell, A. E. (2011). *Fat shame: Stigma and the fat body in American culture*. New York: New York University Press.

21. Knowlton-Le Roux, L. (2007). Reading American fat in France: Obesity and food culture. *European Journal of American Studies, 2*, 2–10.

22. Jutel, A. (2005). Weighing health: The moral burden of obesity. *Social Semiotics, 15*(2), 113–25; Schwarz (1986). *Never satisfied*.

23. Gard, M., & Wright, J. (2005). *The obesity epidemic: Science, morality, and technology.* New York: Routledge.

24. Bouchard, C. (2007). BMI, fat mass, abdominal adiposity, and visceral fat: Where's the beef? *International Journal of Obesity, 13,* 1552–1553.

25. Gard & Wright (2005). *The obesity epidemic;* Oliver, J. E. (2006). *Fat politics: The real story behind America's obesity epidemic.* Oxford: Oxford University Press.

26. De Young, M. (2004). *The day care ritual abuse moral panic.* Jefferson, NC: McFarland.

27. Boero, N. (2012). *Killer fat: Media, medicine, and moral in America's "obesity epidemic."* New Brunswick, NJ: Rutgers; Gard & Wright, J. (2005). *The obesity epidemic;* Levy-Navarro (2008). *The culture of obesity in early and late modernity.*

28. Oliver (2006). *Fat politics.*

29. Finkelstein, E. A., & Zuckerman, L. (2008). *The fattening of America: How the economy makes us fat, if it matters, and what to do about it.* Hoboken, NJ: Wiley & Sons; Shell, E. R. (2002). *The hungry gene: The inside story of the obesity industry.* New York: Grove.

30. LeBesco (2004). *Revolting bodies?;* Saguy (2013). *What's wrong with fat?*

31. Health tidbits. (1999). *Journal of the American Medical Association, 91*(12), 645.

32. Carmona, R. (2003, July 16). The obesity crisis in America. Testimony before the Subcommittee on Education Reform, Committee on Education and the Workforce, United States House of Representatives. http://www.surgeongeneral.gov/news/testimony/obesity07162003.html. Accessed July 28, 2013.

33. Carmona, R. (2003, January 6). Remarks to the 2003 California Childhood Obesity Conference. http://www.surgeongeneral.gov/news/speeches/califobesity.html. Accessed July 28, 2013; Garcia, O. (2010, December 21). Child Nutrition Act: Childhood obesity is a national security threat. *Huffington Post.* http://www.huffingtonpost.com/oz-garcia/child-nutrition-act-childhood-obesity_b_799670.html. Accessed July 28, 2013; Has America reached its tipping point on obesity? (2009, September 9). Stop Obesity Alliance. http://www.stopobesityalliance.org/events/past-events/has-america-reached-its-tipping-point-on-obesity/. Accessed July 28, 2013.

34. E.g., Dworkin, S. L., & Wachs, F. L. (2009). *Body panic: Gender, health, and the selling of fitness* (pp. 65–105). New York: New York University Press; Levy-Navarro (2008). *The culture of obesity in early and late modernity.*

35. The financial collapse of 2008 was not the first, of course, which raises the question of why the notorious Wall Street Collapse of 1929 and ensuing Great Depression did not manifest in the same way regarding fat and/or obesity, already morally suspect at the time. But one of the major (if not *the* major) contributing factors to that earlier collapse, according to most economists, was overproduction, the antithesis of overconsumption—e.g., Devine, J. N. (1983). Underconsumption, overinvestment, and the origins of the Great Depression. *Review of Radical Political Economics, 5*(2), 1–27. Thus, no obvious parallels between the ostensible causes of the collapse and cultural perceptions of fat were apparent during the time of that crisis.

36. Aikins, S. K. (2009). Political economy of government intervention in the free market system. *Administrative Theory and Praxis, 31,* 403–408; Beddoes, Z. M. (2010). Creating financial harmony: What role for government versus the market? *CATO Journal, 30,* 259–64.

37. Barry, A., Osborne, T., & Rose, N. (Eds.). (1996). *Foucault and political reason: Liberalism, neoliberalism and rationalities of government.* Chicago: University of Chicago Press; Giroux, H. A. (2005). The terror of neoliberalism: Rethinking the significance of cultural politics. *College Literature, 32*(1), 1–19; Saad-Filho, A., & Johnston, D. (2004). *Neoliberalism: A critical reader.* London: Pluto.

38. Baldwin, D. A. (Ed.). (1993). *Neorealism and neoliberalism: The contemporary debate.* New York: Columbia University Press; Harvey, D. (2005). *A brief history of neoliberalism.* New York: Oxford University Press.

39. Cob, R. (2014). *The paradox of authenticity in a globalized world*. New York: Palgrave Macmillan; Johnston, J., & Baumann, S. (2010). *Foodies: Democracy and distinction in the gourmet foodscape*. New York: Routledge.

40. Jackson, J. L., (2005). *Real black: Adventures in racial sincerity*. Chicago, IL: University of Chicago Press; Vannini, P., & Williams, J. P. (Eds). (2009). *Authenticity in culture, self, and society*. Surrey, England: Ashgate.

41. Cob (2014). *The paradox of authenticity in a globalized world*; Illouz, E. (2008). *Saving the modern soul: Therapy, emotions, and the culture of self-help*. Berkeley, CA: University of California Press; Jackson (2005). *Real black*; Vannini & Williams.

42. Jhally, S. (1990). *The codes of advertising: Fetishism and the political economy of meaning in the consumer society*. London: Routledge.

43. Cob (2014). *The paradox of authenticity in a globalized world*; Illouz (2008). *Saving the modern soul*; Vannini & Williams (2009). *Authenticity in culture, self, and society*.

44. Illouz, E. (2003). *Oprah Winfrey and the glamour of misery: An essay on popular culture*. New York: Columbia University Press.

45. Sender, K. (2006). Queens for a day: *Queer Eye for the Straight Guy* and the neoliberal project. *Critical Studies in Media Communication, 23*, 131–151.

46. Weber, B. R. (2009). *Makeover TV: Selfhood, citizenship, and celebrity*. Durham, NC: Duke University Press; Shugart, H. A. (2010). Consuming citizen: Neoliberating the obese body. *Communication, Culture, and Critique, 3*(1), 105–126.

47. Curran, J., & Morley, D. (Eds) (2006). *Media and cultural theory*. New York: Routledge; Durham, M. G., & Kellner, D. M. (Eds.) (2006). *Media and cultural studies: Keyworks*. Malden, MA: Blackwell.

48. Jakob, N. G. E. (2010). No alternatives? The relationship between perceived media dependency, use of alternative information sources, and general trust in mass media. *International Journal of Communication, 4*, 589–606; Shapiro, M. A., & Chock, T. M. (2004). Media dependency and perceived reality of fiction and news. *Journal of Broadcast and Electronic Media, 48*, 675–795.

49. Ono, K. A., & Sloop, J. M. (1995). The critique of vernacular discourse. *Communication Monographs, 62*, 19–46.

50. McGee, M. C. (1990). Text, context, and the fragmentation of contemporary culture. *Western Journal of Speech Communication, 54*, 274–289; McKerrow, R. E. (1989). Critical rhetoric: Theory and praxis. *Communication Monographs, 56*(2): 91–111.

51. Furedi, F. (2006). *The culture of fear*. New York: Continuum; Nerlich, B., & Halliday, C. (2007). Avian flu: The creation of expectations in the interplay between science and the media. *Sociology of Health and Illness, 29*(1), 46–65.

## Chapter 2

1. Ogden, C. L., & Carroll, M. D. (2010). Prevalence of overweight, obesity, and extreme obesity among adults: United States, trends 1960–1962 through 2007–2008 (Figure 1). Centers for Disease Control. http://www.cdc.gov/nchs/data/hestat/obesity_adult_07_08/obesity_adult_07_08.pdf. Accessed August 25, 2013; Overweight and obesity: Adult obesity facts. (2013). Centers for Disease Control. http://www.cdc.gov/obesity/data/adult.html. Accessed August 25, 2013.

2. Johnson, T. D. (2012). Hard-hitting public health ad campaigns sparking awareness. *The Nation's Health, 42*(5), 1–10; Walls, H. L., Peeters, A., Proietto, J., & McNeil, J. J. (2011). Public health campaigns and obesity: A critique. *BMC Public Health, 11*, 136–143.

3. E.g., Lustig, R. (2012). *Fat chance: Beating the odds against sugar, processed food, obesity, and disease*. New York: Hudson Street Press.

4. Gard, M., & Wright, J. (2005). *The obesity epidemic: Science, morality, and technology*. New York: Routledge; Lustig (2012). *Fat chance*.

5. Finkelstein, E. A., & Zuckerman, L. (2008). *The fattening of America: How the economy makes us fat, if it matters, and what to do about it*. Hoboken, NJ: Wiley & Sons.

6. Let's move! http://www.letsmove.gov/learn-facts/epidemic-childhood-obesity. Accessed August 1, 2013.

7. We can! http://www.nhlbi.nih.gov/health/public/heart/obesity/wecan/. Accessed August 1, 2013.

8. Childhood obesity prevention. https://webcache.googleusercontent.com/search?q=cache:gLv_sGm7pLkJ:https://www.nhlbi.nih.gov/health/educational/wecan/downloads/opcc-factsheet1.doc+&cd=1&hl=en&ct=clnk&gl=us. Accessed August 1, 2013.

9. Let's move! Get active. http://www.letsmove.gov/get-active. Accessed August 1, 2013.

10. Let's move! Kids take action. http://www.letsmove.gov/kids. Accessed August 1, 2013.

11. We can! http://www.nhlbi.nih.gov/health/public/heart/obesity/wecan/. Accessed August 1, 2013.

12. We can! http://www.nhlbi.nih.gov/health/public/heart/obesity/wecan/. Accessed August 1, 2013.

13. Childhood obesity prevention. https://webcache.googleusercontent.com/search?q=cache:gLv_sGm7pLkJ:https://www.nhlbi.nih.gov/health/educational/wecan/downloads/opcc-factsheet1.doc+&cd=1&hl=en&ct=clnk&gl=us. Accessed August 1, 2013.

14. Let's move! http://www.letsmove.gov/learn-facts/epidemic-childhood-obesity. Accessed August 1, 2013.

15. Let's move! Parents. http://www.letsmove.gov/learn-facts/epidemic-childhood-obesity. Accessed August 1, 2013.

16. Childhood obesity prevention. https://webcache.googleusercontent.com/search?q=cache:gLv_sGm7pLkJ:https://www.nhlbi.nih.gov/health/educational/wecan/downloads/opcc-factsheet1.doc+&cd=1&hl=en&ct=clnk&gl=us. Accessed August 1, 2013.

17. About we can! http://www.nhlbi.nih.gov/health/public/heart/obesity/wecan/about-wecan/index.htm. Accessed August 1, 2013.

18. Let's move! Eat healthy. http://www.letsmove.gov/eat-healthy. Accessed August 1, 2013.

19. We can! Get active. http://www.nhlbi.nih.gov/health/public/heart/obesity/wecan/get-active/index.htm. Accessed August 1, 2013.

20. Let's move! Learn the facts. http://www.letsmove.gov/learn-facts/epidemic-childhood-obesity. Accessed August 1, 2013.

21. Let's move! Organize a school health team. http://www.letsmove.gov/organize-school-health-team. Accessed August 1, 2013.

22. We Can! In your community. http://www.nhlbi.nih.gov/health/public/heart/obesity/wecan/community/index.htm. Accessed August 1, 2013.

23. Barry, C. L., Brescoll, V. L., Brownell, K. D., & Schlesinger, M. (2009). Obesity metaphors: How beliefs about the causes of obesity affect support for public policy. *The Milbank Quarterly, 87*, 7–47; Crawford, R. (1980). Healthism and the medicalisation of everyday life. *International Journal of Health Services: Planning, Administration, Evaluation, 10*(3), 365–388; Lupton, D. (1995). *The imperative of health: Public health and the regulated body*. London: Sage.

24. Shugart, H. A. (2010). Consuming citizen: Neoliberating the obese body. *Communication, Culture, and Critique, 3*(1), 105–26; Zoller, H. M. (2008). Technologies of neoliberal governmentality: The discursive influence of global economic policies in public health. In H. M. Zoller & M. J. Dutta (Eds.), *Emerging perspectives in health communication: Meaning, culture, and power* (pp. 390–410). New York: Routledge.

25. Let's move! Eat healthy. http://www.letsmove.gov/eat-healthy. Accessed August 1, 2013.

26. We can! Partner with us. http://www.nhlbi.nih.gov/health/public/heart/obesity/wecan/partner-with-us/become-partner.htm. Accessed August 1, 2013.

27. Medifast weight loss plan. (2013). Medifast. http://www.medifast1.com/weight_loss_plan/what-you-will-eat.jsp. Accessed August 3, 2013.

28. Jenny Craig: The science. (2013). Jenny Craig. http://www.jennycraig.com/site/how-it-works/science-weight-loss. Accessed August 3, 2013.

29. Weight Watchers how it works. (2013). Weight Watchers. http://www.weightwatchers.com/plan/eat/index.aspx. Accessed August 3, 2013.

30. *Self Magazine* [home page]. *Self*. http://www.self.com. Accessed August 3, 2013.

31. *Men's Health* [home page]. *Men's Health*. http://www.menshealth.com/. Accessed August 3, 2013.

32. Waller, J. (2013, August 2). How to understand fitness supplements and get ripped. *FHM*. http://www.fhm.com/upgrade/mens-style/how-to-understand-fitness-supplements-and-get-ripped-84211. Accessed August 3, 2013.

33. Tools. (2014). Jenny Craig. http://www.jennycraig.com/site/global/tools.jsp. Accessed August 5, 2013.

34. Medifast weight loss plan guides and tools. (2014). Medifast. http://www.medifast1.com/support_tools/plan_guides_and_tools.jsp. Accessed August 5, 2013.

35. Weight Watchers Online. Weight Watchers. http://www.weightwatchers.com/plan/www/online_01.aspx?navid=onlineaag. Accessed August 5, 2013.

36. Duffy, J. (2013, May 22). The best activity trackers for fitness. *PC Magazine*. http://www.pcmag.com/article2/0,2817,2404445,00.asp. Accessed August 5, 2013.

37. Cohen, J. (2013, May 29). 4 new apps you need to achieve real weight loss. *Forbes*. http://www.forbes.com/sites/jennifercohen/2013/05/29/4-new-apps-you-need-to-achieve-real-weight-loss/. Accessed August 5, 2013.

38. Gold's Gym [(home page]. Gold's Gym. http://www.goldsgym.com/. Accessed August 5, 2013.

39. 24Hour Fitness: Press. 24Hour Fitness. http://www.24hourfitness.com/company/press_room/press_releases/2010/20100209.html. Accessed August 5, 2013.

40. Garrard, C. (2009, 27 September). Get a motivation makeover. http://www.self.com/fooddiet/2009/09/motivation-makeover. Accessed August 5, 2013.

41. Lose weight. (2013). *Health*. http://www.health.com/health/lose-weight/. Accessed August 5, 2013.

42. Sinkler, J. (2013, August 4). Push your limits. *Men's Health*. http://www.menshealth.com/fitness/instafit-push-your-limits. Accessed August 5, 2013.

43. Bikini body workout. (2011, June). *Self*. http://www.self.com/fitness/workouts/2011/06/bikini-body-workout-slideshow#slide=1. Accessed August 5, 2013.

44. Douglas, M. (1982). *In the active voice*. London: Routledge & Kegan Paul; Durkheim, E., & Mauss, M. (1963). *Primitive classification*, R. Needham (Trans.). Chicago: University of Chicago Press; Lévi-Strauss, C. (1966). *The culinary triangle*, P. Brooks (Trans.). *Partisan Review*, 33, 586–595; Probyn, E. (2001). *Carnal appetites: FoodSexIdentities*. London: Routledge.

## Chapter 3

1. De Spiegelaere, M., Hennart, P., & Dramaix, M. (1998). The influence of socioeconomic status on the incidence and evolution of obesity during early adolescence. *International Journal of Obesity*, 3, 268–274; Laitinen, J., Power, C., & Järvelin, M. R. (2001). Family social class, maternal body mass index, childhood body mass index, and age at menarche as predictors of adult obesity. *American Journal of Clinical Nutrition*, 74(3), 287–294; Lamerz, A., Kuepper-Nybelen, J., Wehle, C., et al. (2005). Social class, parental education, and obesity prevalence in a study of six-year-old children in Germany. *International Journal of Obesity*, 29, 373–380; Noppa, H., & Bengtsson, C. (1980). Obesity in relation to socioeconomic status: A population study of women in Goteborg, Sweden. *Journal of Epidemiology and Community Health*, 34, 139–142; O'Dea, J. A. (2008). Gender, ethnicity, culture and social class influences on childhood obesity among Australian

schoolchildren: Implications for treatment, prevention and community education. *Health and Social Care in the Community, 16*(3), 282–290.

2. Agne, A., Daubert, R., Munoz, M., et al. (2012). The cultural context of obesity: Exploring perceptions of obesity and weight loss among Latina immigrants. *Journal of Immigrant and Minority Health, 14*(5), 1063–1070; Bacha, F., Saad, R., Gungor, N., et al. (2003). Obesity, regional fat distribution, and syndrome X in obese black versus white adolescents: Race differential in diabetogenic and atherogenic risk factors. *Journal of Clinical Endocrinal Metabolism, 88*(6). 2534–2540; Cossrow, N., & Falkner, B. (2004). Race/ethnic issues in obesity and obesity-related comorbidities. *Journal of Clinical Endocrinal Metabolism, 89*(6): 2590–2594; Long, J. M., Mareno, N., Shabo, R., et al. (2012). Overweight and obesity among white, black, and Mexican American children: Implications for when to intervene. *Journal of Specialists in Pediatric Nursing, 17*(1), 41–50; Melius, J. (2013). Overweight and obesity in minority children and implications for family and community social work. *Social Work and Public Health, 28*(2), 119–128.

3. Hyman, M. (2010, August 14). Why quick, cheap food is actually more expensive. *Huffington Post.* http://www.huffingtonpost.com/dr-mark-hyman/why-quick-cheap-food-is-a_b_681539.html. Accessed September 21, 2013.

4. USDA National Nutrient Database for Standard Reference. http://ndb.nal.usda.gov/. Accessed September 21, 2013.

5. Bittman, M. (2011). Is junk food really cheaper? *New York Times.* http://www.nytimes.com/2011/09/25/opinion/sunday/is-junk-food-really-cheaper.html?pagewanted=all&_r=0. Accessed September 21, 2013; Hyman (2010). Why quick, cheap food is actually more expensive; Nestle, M. (2006). *What to eat: An aisle-by-aisle guide to savvy food choices and good eating.* New York: North Point Press.

6. Nestle (2006). *What to eat*; Parker-Pope, T. (2007, December 5). A high price for healthy food. *New York Times.* http://well.blogs.nytimes.com/2007/12/05/a-high-price-for-healthy-food/. Accessed September 21, 2013. http://www.nytimes.com/2011/09/25/opinion/sunday/is-junk-food-really-cheaper.html?pagewanted=all&_r=0.

7. Parks, S. E., Housemann, R. A., and Brownson, R. C. (2003). Differential correlates of physical activity in urban and rural adults of various socioeconomic backgrounds in the United States. *Journal of Epidemiology and Community Health, 57*(1), 29–35; Powell, L. M., Slater, S., Chaloupka, F. (2004). The relationship between community physical activity settings and race, ethnicity and socioeconomic status. *Evidence-Based Preventive Medicine, 1*(2), 135–144.

8. Gray, S. (2008, September 21). Food justice in inner-city Chicago. *Time 174*(11), 54; Guthman, J. (2011). *Weighing in: Obesity, food justice, and the limits of capitalism.* Berkeley: University of California; Hanc, J. (2011, November 2). World of hunger has a new language. *New York Times.* http://www.nytimes.com/2011/11/02/giving/the-world-of-hunger-has-a-new-language.html. Accessed September 22, 2013; Huber, B. (2011, October 3). Walmart's fresh-food makeover. *Nation, 293*(14), 22–27; Matson, J. (2012). High and dry in a food desert. *Scientific American, 306*(5), 96–96; Stein, J. (2012, May 7). Instant gratification. *Time, 179*(18), 58.

9. Saelens, B., Sallis, J., Frank, L. (2003). Environmental correlates of walking and cycling: Findings from the transportation, urban design, and planning literatures. *Annals of Behavioral Medicine, 25*(2), 80–91. MacMillan, A. (2011, October 20). Moving out of high poverty areas may lower obesity. CNN. http://www.cnn.com/2011/10/20/health/high-poverty-areas-increase-obesity/index.html. Accessed September 21, 2013.

10. Guthman (2011). *Weighing in*; Powell, L. M., Slater, S., & Chaloupka, F. (2004). The relationship between community physical activity settings and race, ethnicity and socioeconomic status. *Evidence-Based Preventive Medicine, 1*(2), 135–144; Rampell, C. (2010, January 15). Rich people exercise more. *New York Times.* http://economix.blogs.nytimes.com/2010/01/15/rich-people-exercise-more/?_r=0. Accessed September 22, 2013.

11. Heavey, S. (2013, January 9). Obesity, lack of insurance cited in U.S. health gap. Reuters http://www.reuters.com/article/2013/01/09/us-usa-health-ranking-idUSBRE9080ZN20130109 9. Accessed September 22, 2013; Katz, D. (2013, September 13). Our severely obese daughters and sons: Of pennies, pounds and sense. *Huffington Post.* http://www.huffingtonpost.com/david-katz-md/childhood-obesity_b_3907198. html. Accessed September 22, 2013; Lustig, R. (2012). *Fat chance: Beating the odds against sugar, processed food, obesity, and disease.* New York: Hudson Street Press; Obesity, lack of insurance take toll on young Americans. (2009, February 19). *U.S. News & World Report,* http://health.usnews.com/health-news/dietfitness/diabetes/articles/2009/02/19/obesity-lack-of-insurance-take-toll-on-young. Accessed September 22, 2013.

12. Lustig (2012). *Fat chance;* Taubes, G. (2007). *Good calories, bad calories: Challenging the conventional wisdom on diet, weight control, and disease.* New York: Knopf; Taubes, G. (2011). *Why we get fat and what to do about it.* New York: Knopf.

13. A heavy burden. (2012, December 15). *Economist, 405*(8815), 7–9; The fat trap. (2012, 22 Jan). *New York Times Magazine,* 8; Lustig, R. (2013, February 12). Still believe "a calorie is a calorie?" *Huffington Post.* http://www.huffingtonpost.com/robert-lustig-md/sugar-toxic_b_2759564.html. Accessed September 29, 2013; Shapiro, E. (2013, January 21). The one I left behind. *People Magazine, 79*(2), 57–58. Taubes, G. (2011, April 17). Is sugar toxic? *New York Times Magazine,* 47; Taubes, G. (2012, May14). New obesity campaigns have it all wrong. *Newsweek, 159*(20), 32–36.

14. Taubes (2012). New obesity campaigns have it all wrong.

15. Lustig, R. (2013). http://www.huffingtonpost.com/robert-lustig-md/sugar-toxic_b_2759564.html. Accessed September 29, 2013.

16. Holtcamp, W. (2013). Obesogens: An environmental link to obesity. *Environmental Health Perspectives, 120*(2), A62–A68; Thayer, K. A., Heindel, J. J., Bucher, J. R., & Gallo, M. A. (2012). Role of environmental chemicals in diabetes and obesity: A national toxicology program workshop review. *Environmental Health Perspectives, 120*(6), 779–789; Wei, Y., Zhu, J., & Nguyen A. (2013, July 8). Urinary concentrations of dichlorophenol pesticides and obesity among adult participants in the US National Health and Nutrition Examination Survey (NHANES) 2005–2008. *International Journal of Hygiene and Environmental Health.* http://www.ncbi.nlm.nih.gov/pubmed/23899931.

17. Kristoff, N. D. (2013, January 20). Warnings from a flabby mouse. *New York Times,* SR11. Also Seidenberg, C. (2012, February 23). All fats are not created equal. *Washington Post,* T13; Szabo, L. (2013, June 6). Genetic link to early puberty found: Mutations could be responsible for a growing trend. *USA Today,* 5D.

18. Cho, I., Yamanishi, S., Cox, L., Methé, B.A., Zavadil, J., Li, K., . . ., Blaser, M. J. (2012). Antibiotics in early life alter the murine colonic microbiome and adiposity. *Nature, 488*(7413), 621–626; Million, M., Lagier, J.-C., Yahav, D., & Paul, M. (2013). Gut bacterial microbiota and obesity. *Clinical Microbiology & Infection, 19*(4), 305–313; Ray, K. (2012). Gut microbiota: Adding weight to the microbiota's role in obesity—exposure to antibiotics early in life can lead to increased adiposity *Nature Reviews Endocrinology, 8*(11), 623.

19. Begley, S. (2013). The war on bugs. *Saturday Evening Post, 285*(2), 58–61.

20. Pollan, M. (2013, May 15). Some of my best friends are germs. *New York Times.* http://www.nytimes.com/2013/05/19/magazine/say-hello-to-the-100-trillion-bacteria-that-make-up-your-microbiome.html?pagewanted=all. Also Chameides, B. (2013, September 5). The obesity plague and antibiotics. *Huffington Post.* http://www.huffingtonpost.com/bill-chameides/the-obesity-plague-and-an_b_3875904.html; Schiffman, R. (2013, September 23). We need to end antibiotics use in meat production now. *Huffington Post.* http://www.huffingtonpost.com/richard-schiffman/we-need-to-end-antibiotics_b_3966755.html.

21. Baillie-Hamilton, P. F. (2002). Chemical toxins: A hypothesis to explain the global obesity epidemic. *Journal of Alternative and Complementary Medicine, 8*(2), 185–192;

Galbraith, H. (2002). Hormones in international meat production: Biological, socio-logical, and consumer issues. *Nutrition Research Reviews, 15*(2), 293–314; Wang, Y., & Beydoun, M. A. (2009). Meat consumption is associated with obesity and central obesity among U.S. adults. *International Journal of Obesity, 33*(6), 621–628.

22. Chemicals in food can make you fat. (2010, February 11). CBS News. http://www.cbsnews.com/2100-500165_162-6197493.html.

23. Perrine, S., & Hurlock, H. (2010, March 8). Fat epidemic linked to chemicals run amok. NBC News. http://www.nbcnews.com/id/35315651/ns/health-diet_and_nutrition/t/fat-epidemic-linked-chemicals-run-amok/#.UkiOIYa9HnM. Accessed September 29, 2013. Also Begley, S. (2009, October). Born to be big. *Newsweek.* http://www.thedaily-beast.com/newsweek/2009/09/10/born-to-be-big.html; Storrs, C. (2011, January 19). Hormones in food: Should you worry? *Health.* http://www.health.com/health/article/0,,20458816,00.html; Tunick, B. (2005, January). Does eating meat make people fat? *Vegetarian Times, 327,* 95.

24. Bray, G. A. (2013). Energy and fructose from beverages sweetened with sugar or high-fructose corn syrup pose a health risk for some people. *Advances in Nutrition, 4*(2), 220–225; Brody, J. E. (2004, March 9). In an obese world, sweet nothings add up. *New York Times,* F:1; Ciardi, C., Jenny, M., Tschoner, A., Ueberall, F., Patsch, J., Pedrini, M., Ebenbichler, C., & Fuchs, D. (2012). Food additives such as sodium sulphite, sodium ben-zoate and curcumin inhibit leptin release in lipopolysaccharide-treated murine adipo-cytes in vitro. *The British Journal of Nutrition, 107*(6), 826–833; Hu, P., Chen, X., Whitener, R. J., Boder, E. T., Jones, J. O., Porollo, A., Chen, J., & Zhao, L. (2013). Effects of para-bens on adipocyte differentiation. *Toxicological Sciences, 131*(1), 56–57; Jaworowska, A., Blackham, T., Davies, I. G., & Stevenson, L. (2013). Nutritional challenges and health implications of takeaway and fast food. *Nutrition Reviews, 71*(5), 310–318; Kavanagh, K., Jones, K. L., Sawyer, J., Kelley, K., Carr, J. J., Wagner, J. D., & Rudel, L. L. (2007). Trans fat diet induces abdominal obesity and changes in insulin sensitivity in monkeys. *Obesity, 15*(7), 1675–1678; Kohli, R., Kirby, M., Xanthakos, S. A., Softic, S., Feldstein, A. E., Saxena, V., . . . Seeley, R. J. (2010). High-fructose, medium chain trans fat diet induces liver fibrosis and elevates plasma coenzyme Q9 in a novel murine model of obesity and nonalcoholic steatohepatitis. *Hepatology 52*(3), 934–944; Vang, A., Singh, P. N., Lee, J., Haddad, E. H. & Brinegar, C. H. (2008). Meats, processed meats, obesity, weight gain and occurrence of diabetes among adults: Findings from Adventist health studies. *Annals of Nutrition & Metabolism, 52*(2), 96–104.

25. Bachman, C. M., Baranowski, T., & Nicklas, T. A. (2006). Is there an association between sweetened beverages and adiposity? *Nutritonal Review 64,* 153–174; Bocarsly, M. E., Powell, E. S., Avena, N. M., Hoebel, B. G. (2010). High-fructose corn syrup causes char-acteristics of obesity in rats: Increased body weight, body fat and triglyceride levels. *Pharmacology, Biochemistry & Behavior, 97*(1), 101–106; Bray, G. A. (2010). Soft drink consumption and obesity: It is all about fructose. *Current Opinion in Lipidology, 21,* 51–57; Olsen, N. J., & Heitmann, B. L. (2008). Intake of calorically sweetened beverages and obesity. *Obesity Reviews, 10,* 68–75.

26. Klurfeld, D. M., Foreyt, J., Angelopoulos, T. J., & Rippe, J. M. (2013). Lack of evidence for high fructose corn syrup as the cause of the obesity epidemic for high fructose corn syrup as the cause of the obesity epidemic. *International Journal of Obesity, 37*(6), 771–773.

27. The checkup: Health in the news and in your life. (2008, December 16). *Washington Post,* HE02; Goldstein, J. (2009). High fructose corn syrup: How dangerous is it? *Prevention 61*(5), 58–61; Weise, E. (2008, December 9). New data not so sour on corn syrup. *USA Today,* 7D.

28. Pollan, M. (2011, October 28). High-fructose corn syrup not necessarily worse than sugar. *Huffington Post.* http://www.huffingtonpost.com/2011/10/28/michael-pollan-high-fructose-corn-syrup-sugar_n_1064246.html. Accessed September 30, 2013.

29. Pollan, M. (2006). *Omnivore's dilemma: A natural history of four meals.* New York: Penguin; Pollan, M. (2008). *In defense of food: An eater's manifesto.* New York: Penguin; Health food imposters. (2009). *Prevention, 61*(10), 72–76; Sweet escape. (2008). *Teen Vogue, 8*(2), 49.

30. Arundel, A. (2003, August 28). A healthful approach to school food: Creative efforts help trim the fat. *Washington Post,* T03; Buckle up—or else: A kinder, gentler paternalism. (2009, September 28). *Newsweek,* 23; Jenkins, Jr., H. W. (2006, December 20). Fat chance. *Wall Street Journal 248*(145), A19; Lueck, T. J., & Severson, K. (2006, December 6). New York bans most trans fats in restaurants. *New York Times,* A1; Neuman, W. (2010, October 14). Group sees food labels spelling out a downside. *New York Times,* B3; Severson, K. (2005, March 9). So much for squeaky clean cookies. *New York Times,* F4; Stoller, G. (2007, July 17). Hotels serve lighter fare for healthy appetites. *USA Today,* D6.

31. Grun, F., Blumberg, B. (2007). Perturbed nuclear receptor signaling by environmental obesogens as emerging factors in the obesity crisis. *Reviews in Endocrine and Metabolic Disorders* 8, 161–171; Hao, C., Cheng, X., Xia, H., Ma, X. (2012). The endocrine disruptor mono-(2-ethylhexyl) phthalate promotes adipocyte differentiation and induces obesity in mice. *Bioscience Reports 32*(6), 619–29; Newbold, R. R., Padilla-Banks, E., Jefferson, W. N., Heindel, J. J. (2008). Effects of endocrine disruptors on obesity. *International Journal of Andrology* 31: 201–208; Rubin, B. S. (2011). Bisphenol A: An endocrine disruptor with widespread exposure and multiple effects. *Journal of Steroid Biochemistry and Molecular Biology 127,* 27–34; Stahlhut, R. W., van Wijngaarden, E., Dye, T. D., Cook, S., & Swan, S. H. (2007). Concentrations of urinary phthalate metabolites are associated with increased waist circumference and insulin resistance in adult U.S. males. *Environmental Health Perspectives 115*(6), 876–88.

32. Begley, S. (2009, September 21). Born to be big: Early exposure to common chemicals may be programming kids to be fat. *Newsweek,* 57; Gillham, C. (2007, November 19). For safer baby bottles. *Newsweek,* 71. Koch, W. (2011, March 7). Study: Most plastics trigger estrogen effect. *USA Today.* http://content.usatoday.com/communities/greenhouse/post/2011/03/bpa-free-plastic-products-estrogen/1#.UknZW4a9HnM; Szabo, L. (2012, September 19). High levels of BPA linked to obesity in kids, teens: Metabolism-changing chemical "obesogens" could be at work. *USA Today,* 4D; Szabo, L, Grossman, C. L., Vegano, D. (2009, October 20). $30M set for study of plastics chemical. *USA Today:* 5D; Weil, E. (2012, March 30). Puberty before age 10: A new normal? *New York Times Magazine.* http://www.nytimes.com/2012/04/01/magazine/puberty-before-age-10-a-new-normal.html?pagewanted=all. Accessed October 15, 2013.

33. Bittman, M. (2011, March 2). Don't end agricultural subsidies. Fix them. *New York Times,* 25; Lavalle, M. (2008, May 19). Fixing the food crisis. *U.S. News & World Report, 144*(14), 36–42; Roll, G. (2005, October 6). Big-farm subsidies versus food stamps. *Christian Science Monitor, 97*(220), 9; Stewart, J. B. (2013, July 20). Richer farmers, bigger subsidies. *New York Times 162*(56203), B1–B5.

34. Fresh fruit, hold the insulin. (2012, April 12). *Scientific American, 306*(5), 12.

35. Ibid.

36. Imhoff, D. (Ed.) (2010). *The CAFO reader: The tragedy of industrial animal factories.* Berkeley: University of California; Pollan (2006). *Omnivore's dilemma;* Schlosser, E. (2001). *Fast food nation.* New York: Houghton-Mifflin.

37. Franck, C., Grandi, S. M., Eisenberg, & M. J. (2013). Agricultural studies and the obesity epidemic. *American Journal of Preventative Medicine, 45*(3), 328; Beghin, H. C., & Jensen, H. H. (2008). Farm policies and added sugars in U.S. diets. *Food Policy, 33,* 480–488; Jackson, R. J., Minfares, R., Naumoff, K. S., Shrimali, B. P., & Martin, L. K. (2009). Agriculture policy is health policy. *Journal of Hunger and Environmental Nutrition 4,* 393–408; Okrent, A. M., & Alston, J. M. (2012). The effects of farm commodity and retail food policies on obesity and economic welfare in the United States. *Agricultural Economics, 94*(3), 611–46; Wallinga, D. (2010). Agricultural policy and childhood obesity. *Health Affairs 29,* 405–410.

38. Bittman (2011) Is junk food really cheaper?, 25; also, Fresh fruit, hold the insulin, (2012); Pollan, M. (2003, October 12). The (agri)cultural contradictions of obesity. *New York Times Magazine, 152* (52634), 41–48; Pollan (2006). *Omnivore's dilemma*; Pollan, M. (2007, November 4). Weed it and reap. *New York Times, 157*(54118), 15; Rosten, E. (2004, June 7). The corn connection. *Time, 163*(23), 83; Schlosser, 2001; Nestle, M. (2002). *Food politics: How the food industry influences nutrition and health.* Berkeley, CA: University of California Press; "The fat of the land." (2009, August 1). *Wall Street Journal, 254*(27), A10; "Why that salad costs more than a Big Mac." (2010, October). *Reader's Digest, 177*(1060), 72.

39. Layton, L., Eggan, D. (2011, July 9). Food, ad industries lobby against nutrition guidelines. *Washington Post.* http://articles.washingtonpost.com/2011-07-09/politics/35267908_1_voluntary-nutrition-guidelines-junk-food-foodmakers; Nestle (2002). *Food politics.*

40. Etter, L., Hitt, G. (2008, March 27). Farm lobby beats back assault on subsidies. *Wall Street Journal 251*(72), A1–12; Imhoff, D. (2011, October 3). Farm Bill 101. *Nation 291*(4), 27–9; Paarlberg, R. L. (2010). *Food politics: What everyone needs to know.* New York: Oxford University Press.

41. Brody, J. (2011, September 13). Attacking the obesity epidemic by first figuring out its cause. *New York Times*, A7; Brower, K. A. (2010, November 22). Duck, sugar! It's a food fight! *Bloomberg Businessweek 4205*, 44; Food for thought. (2012, December 15). *Economist 405*(8815), 9–12; Nixon, R. (2012, January 26). New rules for school meals aim at reducing obesity. *New York Times*: A22; Pear, R., Bennett, K. (2011, April 30). Soft drink industry fights proposed food stamp ban. *New York Times*, A11; Saul, S. (2008, April 3). Menu fight over calories leads doctor to reject post. *New York Times.* A2; Saltmarsh, M. (2010, September 20). Stein, R. (2004, January 16). U.S. says it will contest WHO plan to fight obesity. *Washington Post*, A8; Warner, M. (2006, February 7). Does this good make you groan? *New York Times, 155*(53628), C1–8.

42. Clifford, S. (2008, July 30). Tug of war in food marketing to kids. *New York Times:*,5; Selling candy to kids. (2011, November 19). *New York Times*, 20.

43. Fernandez, M. (2006, September 24). Fast-food restaurants. *New York Times*, A37; Inside the Times. (2008, August 13). *New York Times*, A2; Carlson, T., Maddow, R., Kellerman, M., Geist, W. (2005, August 24). *The Situation*, MSNBC. http://www.lexisnexis.com. ezproxy.lib.utah.edu/lnacui2api/auth/checkbrowser.do;jsessionid=7020692D4B3C2F B788B18FEDB90EDE21.mIchf4wVosSETSf9WtB0lQ?ipcounter=1&cookieState=0&r and=0.11844062457938054&bhcp=1. Accessed October 17, 2013.

44. Brower (2010), Duck, sugar!

45. Heil, E. (2004, September 21). Critics see a food pyramid with lobbyists at the top. *Congress Daily*, 3–5; Layton, 2011.

46. Kuzemchak, S. (2012, June). Sugar shocker. *Parents 87*(7), 54–61; Moss, M. (2013, February 24). (Salt + fat²/satisfying crunch) x pleasing mouth feel = A food designed to addict. *New York Times Magazine*, 34–48; Nestle (2002). Food politics; Neuman, W. (2010, July 24). Ad rules stall, keeping cereal a cartoon staple. *New York Times*, A1; Pollan, M. (2001, May 13). Naturally. *New York Times Magazine.* http://www.nytimes.com/2001/05/13/magazine/naturally.html?pagewanted=all&src=pm. Accessed October 17, 2013; The last course. (2012, December 15). *Economist 405*(8815), 16.

47. Gogoi, P. (2008, September 22). Sweetening a sweetener's rep. *Business Week 4100*, 17; Parker-Pope, T. (2010, September 155). Makers seek new name for syrup. *New York Times*, D1; Vranica, S. (2008, June 23). High fructose corn syrup mixes it up. *Wall Street Journal 251*(146), B7; Warner, M. (2010, May 2). For corn syrup, the sweet talk gets harder. *New York Times.* http://www.nytimes.com/2010/05/02/business/02syrup. html?ref=melaniewarner. Accessed October 17, 2013.

48. Belluz, J. (2010, October 25). The healing power of groceries. *Maclean's 123*(41), 56; Experts say industry food labels deceptive. (2009, October 9). CBS News: www.cbsnews. com/8301-18563_162-5291352.html.

49. Moss, "(Salt and Fat$^2$)," 2013; Moss, M. (2013). *Salt, sugar, fat: How the food giants hooked us*. New York: Random House; Moss, M. (2013, August 28). Wooing us down the aisle. *New York Times, 162*(56242), D1–D5.

50. Moss, "(Salt and fat$^2$)," 2013.

51. Bittman, M. (2013September 9). Late-summer links. *New York Times*. http://bittman. blogs.nytimes.com/2013/09/09/late-summer-links/?_r=0. Accessed October 17, 2013; Greenfield, P. (2013, January/February). Scoop! Weight loss. *Women's Health, 10*(1), 36; Kristof (2013). Warnings from a flabby mouse; Main, E. (2012, August). Are GMOs making you fat? A new reason to be skeptical of Frankenfoods. *Prevention*. http://www. prevention.com/food/healthy-eating-tips/gmo-foods-linked-weight-gain.    Accessed October 17, 2013.

## Chapter 4

1. Carmichael, M. (2008b, December 18). How fat went global. *Newsweek*. http://www. newsweek.com/id/175954. Accessed November 25, 2013; also Bakalar, N. (2008, 15 September). I think, therefore I am fat? *New York Times*. http://www.nytimes.com/2008/ 09/16/health/research/16beha.html?_r=1&scp=88&sq=obesity&st=nyt.    Accessed November 25, 2013; Freeman, D. W. (2011, June 3). Are media to blame for obesity epidemic? CBS News. http://www.cbsnews.com/8301-504763_162-20067704-10391704. html. Accessed November 25, 2013; Manson, J. E. (2007, November). Health answers, please! *Glamour, 105*(11), 130; Rochman, B. (2009, July, 6). First comes love, then comes obesity? *Time*. http://www.time.com/time/magazine/article/0,9171,1907143,00.html. Accessed November 25, 2013; Stengel, R. (2008, June 12). A full plate. *Time*. http:// www.time.com//time/magazine/article/0,9171,1813973,00.html. Accessed November 25, 2013; "Unhealthy boom." (2013, February 9). *New Scientist, 217*(2903), 7.

2. Bakalar (2008). I think, therefore I am fat?; Kantrowitz, B., & Wingert, P. (2008, July 8). What works. *Newsweek*. http://www.newsweek.com/id/144958. Accessed November 25, 2013; Frazier, R. S. (2013, May). So long, stress snacking. *Health, 27*(4), 52; Macqueen, K. (2012, November 19). It's not all in your genes. *Mclean's, 125*(45), 66.

3. St. George, D. (2008, December 2). Media bombardment linked to ill effects during childhood. *Washington Post*. http://www.washingtonpost.com/wp-dyn/content/article/2008/12/01/AR2008120102920.html. Accessed November 25, 2013; also Brody, J. (2010, November 30). Head out for a daily dose of green space. *New York Times*, A7; Cruz, G. (2008, December 4). Why media could be bad for your child's health. *Time*. http:// www.time.com/time/health/article/0,8599,1864141,00.html.    Accessed    November 25, 2013.

4. Kluger, J. (2008, June 12). How America's children packed on the pounds. *Time*. http:// www.time.com/time/health/article/0,8599,1813700,00.html.    Accessed    November 25, 2013; also Lallanilla, M. (2013, February 24). Obesity among kids: A media problem? ABC News. http://abcnews.go.com/Health/Living/story?id=118227. Accessed November 25, 2013; Rich, M. (2008, June). Too much television? *Parents, 83*(7), 40–44; Rosen, M. D. (2011, February). Gaga for gadgets. *Parents, 86*(2), 110–116; Szabo, L. (2008, December 2). Report: TV, internet harm kids. *USA Today*. http://www.usatoday. com/news/health/2008-12-01-media_N.htm?csp=34. Accessed November 25, 2013.

5. Food ads on Nickelodeon slammed in report. (2009, November 24). CBS News. http:// www.cbsnews.com/stories/2009/11/24/health/healthy_living/main5761832.shtml?t ag=contentMain;contentBody. Accessed November 25, 2013; How do you put a nation on a diet? (2012, June 10). *New York Times*, A10; Rabin, R. C. (2009a, December 15). New goal for the obese. *New York Times*, D1.

6. Moss, M. (2013, February 24). (Salt + fat$^2$/satisfying crunch) x pleasing mouth feel = A food designed to addict. *New York Times Magazine*, 34–48; Moss, M. (2013). *Salt, sugar,*

*fat: How the food giants hooked us.* New York: Random House; Moss, M. (2013, August 28). Wooing us down the aisle. *New York Times, 162*(56242), D1–D5; Nestle, M. (2002). *Food politics: How the food industry influences nutrition and health.* Berkeley, CA: University of California Press.

7. E.g., Alderman, L. (2010, February 13). When children are overweight, changes for the whole family. *New York Times,* A5; "Eye catching ads promote junk food to kids." (2008, July 29). CBS news. http://www.cbsnews.com/stories/2008/07/29/business/main4302213.shtml?tag=contentMain;contentBody. Accessed November 25, 2013; Szabo (2008). Report: TV, internet harm kids.

8. Cruz, G. (2008, December 4). Why media could be bad for your child's health. *Time.* http://www.time.com/time/health/article/0,8599,1864141,00.html.          Accessed November 25, 2013; Kluger (2008). How America's children packed on the pounds.

9. Kluger (2008). How America's children packed on the pounds; Rochman (2009). First comes love, then comes obesity?

10. Gardner, A. (2011, May 26). Sedentary jobs helping to drive obesity epidemic. *U.S. News & World Report.*http://health.usnews.com/health-news/diet-fitness/fitness/articles/2011/05/26/sedentary-jobs-helping-to-drive-obesity-epidemic. Accessed November 25, 2013.

11. Summers, N. (2009, April 24). The economics of eating. *Newsweek.* http://search.news-week.com/search?q=obesity+and+summers (¶6). Accessed November 25, 2013; also Gans, K. (2013, April 16). Are people who cook more likely to skip the gym? *Shape.* http://www.shape.com/blogs/weight-loss-coach/are-people-who-cook-more-likely-skip-gym. Accessed November 25, 2013; "Time spent on healthy cooking, exercise are tradeoffs in average American's day, study finds." (2013, April 15). *Huffington Post.* http://www.huffingtonpost.com/2013/04/15/healthy-cooking-exercise-tradeoffs_n_3061276.html. Accessed November 25, 2013.

12. Oliwenstein, L. (2008, June 12). Weighty issues for parents. *Time.* http://www.time.com/time/magazine/article/0,9171,1813953,00.html (¶4). Accessed November 25, 2013; also Hellmich, N. (2009, January 7). Help kids maintain a healthy diet without a hefty cost. *USA Today.* http://www.usatoday.com/news/health/weightloss/2009-01-06-kids-diet_n.htm. Accessed November 25, 2013; Losh, J. (2008, August 8). Dear parents: Your child is fat. *Time.* http://www.time.com/time/health/article/0,8599,1830796,00.html. Accessed November 25, 2013.

13. Start saying goodbye to belly fat. (2008, November 1). *The Early Show,* CBS. http://www.cbsnews.com/stories/2008/11/01/earlyshow/health/main4562801.shtml?tag=contentMain;contentBody. Accessed November 25, 2013; also Health news that makes you go. . . . (2013, July). *Reader's Digest, 182*(1089), 130–139; Is it my hormones? (2011, September). *Self, 33*(9), 94.

14. Raymond, J. (2009, March 26). Big belly, bad memory. *Newsweek.* http://www.newsweek.com/id/129147/page/1. Accessed November 25, 2013; Walsh, B. (2008, June 12). It's not just genetics. *Time.* http://www.time.com/time/magazine/article/0,9171,1813984,00.html. Accessed November 25, 2013.

15. Rabin, R. C. (2009b, June 9). Bad habits asserting themselves. *New York Times,* D5.

16. Grumman, R. (2009, September 18) Why we eat too much. CNN. http://www.cnn.com/2009/HEALTH/09/18/why.overeat.eat.much/index.html?iref=allsearch (¶12). Accessed November 25, 2013.

17. Brownell, K. (2009, February 1). Is it true that lack of sleep might lead to weight gain? ABC News. http://abcnews.go.com/Health/WellnessResource/story?id=6762328. Accessed November 29, 2013; also Bakalar (2008). I think, therefore I am fat?; Irregular sleeping linked to obesity. (2009, May 7). *USA Today.* http://www.usatoday.com/news/health/2008-05-07-sleep-obesity_n.htm. Accessed November 25, 2013; Lack of sleep linked to obesity. (2012, October). *USA Today Magazine, 141*(2809), 14–5; Rubin, C. (2013, November 11). Battling fat? Get more sleep. *U.S. News Digital Report, 5*(41), 20; Savage, L. (2013, June 24). The sleep crisis. *Maclean's, 126*(24), 1.

18. E.g., Gardner (2011). Sedentary jobs helping to drive obesity epidemic; also Raymond (2009). Big belly, bad memory; Start saying goodbye to bellyfat. (2008).

19. Kita, J. (2010, February). Weight loss secrets from around the world. *Reader's Digest*, *176*(1053), 101–105.

20. Heisley, M. (2008, September 8) Got a fat gene? Get active for 3–4 hours a day. *USA Today*. http://www.usatoday.com/news/health/weightloss/2008-09-08-obesity-gene_ n.htm. Accessed November 25, 2013.

21. Zezima, K. (2008, August). Increasing obesity requires new ambulance equipment. *New York Times*. http://www.nytimes.com/2008/health/08ambu.html?r=1&scp= 10&sq=obesity&st=nyt (¶9). Accessed November 25, 2013; also Weaver, C. (2012, September). The plus-size MRI machine. *Wall Street Journal, 256*(44), 11.

22. Pudgy Pet Rescue. (2013). *Shape, 32*(5), 98; Vlahos, J. (2008, July 13). Pill-popping pets. *New York Times*. http://www.nytimes.com/2008/07/13/magazine/13petst.html?_ r=1&scp=101&sq=obesity&st=nyt. Accessed November 25, 2013.

23. Davenport, C., & Brown, E. (2009, November 4). Girding for an uphill battle for recruits. *Washington Post.* http://www.washingtonpost.com/wdyn/content/article/2009/11/04/ AR2009110402899.html (¶11). Accessed November 25, 2013; McClesky, C. M., & Shea, C. (2010). Too fat to fight. *Wall Street Journal, 256*(85), C4.

24. Farris, S. (2012). Eat like an Italian. *Time, 179*(7), 1–4; Klein, E. (2009, July 1). We're getting a bad feeling about our food. *New York Times*, E01. http://www.lexisnexis.com.tproxy01. lib.utah.edu/us/lnacademic/results/docview/docview.do?docLinkInd=true&risb=21_ T8549232329&format=GNBFI&sort=RELEVANCE&startDocNo=1&resultsUrl Key=29_T8549232332&cisb=22_T8549232331&treeMax=true&treeWidth=0&sel RCNodeID=30&nodeStateId=411en_US,1,26&docsInCategory=13&csi=8075&do cNo=5. Accessed November 25, 2013.

25. Bittman, M. (2008, December 14). So your kitchen is tiny. So what? *New York Times*. http://www.lexisnexis.com.tproxy01.lib.utah.edu/us/lnacademic/results/docview/ docview.do?docLinkInd=true&risb=21_T8549463956&format=GNBFI&sort=REL EVANCE&startDocNo=1&resultsUrlKey=29_T8549463959&cisb=22_T85494639 58&treeMax=true&treeWidth=0&selRCNodeID=7&nodeStateId=411en_US,1,6,4& docsInCategory=10&csi=6742&docNo=2. Accessed via Lexis Nexis November 25, 2013.

26. Nagourney, E. (2008a, August 5). Patterns: In older neighborhoods, less weight gain. *New York Times*. http://www.nytimes.com/2008/08/05/health/research/05patt. html?_r=1&scp=44&sq=obesity&st=nyt. Accessed November 25, 2013.

27. E.g., Aleccia, J. (2008, November 12). Obese kids have middle-aged arteries. *Newsweek*. http://www.newsweek.com/id/168702. Accessed November 25, 2013; Bad news. (2013, July 8). *Maclean's, 126*(25), 1; Johnson, L. (2008, August 8). Some teens so heavy they face liver damage, transplants. *USA Today*. http://www.usatoday.com/news/health/ weightloss/2008-09-07-fat-liver-children_n.htm. Accessed November 25, 2013; Park, A. (2008a, July 9). The kiddie cholesterol debate. *Time*. http://www.time.com/time/ health/article/0,8599,1821153,00.html. Accessed November 25, 2013.

28. E.g., Levine, S., & Stein, J. (2008, May 18). Obesity threatens a generation: "Catastrophe" of earlier deaths, higher health costs. *Washington Post*. http://pqasb.pqarchiver.com/ washingtonpost/access/1480441201.html?dids=1480441201:1480441201&FMT=CIT E&FMTS=CITE:FT&date=May+18%2C+2008&author=Susan+Levine%3BRob+Ste in++Washington+Post+Staff+Writers&pub=The+Washington+Post&edition=&startp age=A.1&desc=Obesity+Threatens+a+Generation%3B+%27Catastrophe%27+of+Earl ier+Deaths%2C+Higher+Health+Costs. Accessed November 25, 2013; No longer just 'adult onset.' (2012, May 7). *New York Times*, A22.

29. E.g., Cruz, G. (2008, December 4). Why media could be bad for your child's health. *Time*. http://www.time.com/time/health/article/0,8599,1864141,00.html. Accessed November 25, 2013; Sepkowitz, K. (2013, November 25). This is why your kid is fat. *The*

*Daily Beast.* http://www.thedailybeast.com/articles/2013/11/25/this-is-why-your-kid-is-fat.html. Accessed November 25, 2013.

30. Parker-Pope, T. (2008, October 13). Healthful message, wrapped in fiction. *New York Times.* http://www.nytimes.com/2008/10/14/health/14well.html?scp=42&sq=obesity&st=ny. (11). Accessed November 25, 2013.

31. Kluger (2008). How America's children packed on the pounds, 2.

32. E.g., Belluz, J. (2011). What you need is a beautiful bento lunch. *Maclean's, 123*(3), 64; Brody, J. E. (2009, January 13). New thinking on how to protect the heart. *New York Times.* http://www.lexisnexis.com.tproxy01.lib.utah.edu/us/lnacademic/results/docview/docview.do?docLinkInd=true&risb=21_T8381208004&format=GNBFI&sort=RELEVANCE&startDocNo=1&resultsUrlKey=29_T8381208007&cisb=22_T8381208006&treeMax=true&treeWidth=0&selRCNodeID=24&nodeStateId=411en_US,1,23,12&docsInCategory=4&csi=6742&docNo=1. Accessed via Lexis Nexis November 25, 2013; French tops in eating, drinking (2009, May 5). CNN. http://www.cnn.com/2009/LIVING/worklife/05/05/global.leisure/index.html?iref=allsearch. Accessed November 25, 2013; Kita (2010). Weight loss secrets from around the world; Secrets of the slimmest countries. (2010). *Shape, 29*(5), 100; Squires, S. (2008, July 22). Which diet's best? That's up to you. *Washington Post.* http://www.lexisnexis.com.tproxy01.lib.utah.edu/us/lnacademic/results/docview/docview.do?docLinkInd=true&risb=21_T8381208004&format=GNBFI&sort=RELEVANCE&startDocNo=1&resultsUrlKey=29_T8381208007&cisb=22_T8381208006&treeMax=true&treeWidth=0&selRCNodeID=25&nodeStateId=411en_US,1,23,12&docsInCategory=1&csi=8075&docNo=1. Accessed November 25, 2013.

33. Morales, T. (2009, January 24). Why "French women don't get fat." CBS News. http://www.cbsnews.com/stories/2009/01/12/earlyshow/leisure/books/main666429.shtml. Accessed November 25, 2013.

34. Heisley (2008, September) Got a fat gene?

35. Carmichael (2008a). Is there a surgical cure for diabetes?; also Abend, L. (2009, December 1). In Spain, taking some joy out of the happy meal. *Time.* http://www.time.com/time/world/article/0,8599,1943119,00.html. Accessed November 25, 2013; McLeod, C. (2008, December 20). China wrestles with growing obesity. *USA Today.* http://www.usatoday.com/news/world/2008-12-18-chinaweight_n.htm. Accessed November 25, 2013; Meacham, J. (2010, March 29). It's a global problem. *Newsweek, 155*(13), 37; Rosenthal, E. (2008, September). Fast food hits Mediterranean: A diet succumbs. *New York Times.* http://query.nytimes.com/gst/fullpage.html?res=9E06E6DD1F3DF937A1575AC0A96E9C8B63&scp=4&sq=obesity&st=nyt. Accessed November 25, 2013.

36. Immigrant kids exercise even less than U.S.-born kids. (2008, August 5). *USA Today.* http://www.usatoday.com/news/health/weightloss/2008-08-05-immigrant-exercise_n.htm. Accessed November 25, 2013; also Bahrampour, T. (2009, September 4). Sons of immigrants have high obesity levels, report finds. *Washington Post.* http://www.washingtonpost.com/wp-dyn/content/article/2009/09/03/AR2009090301785.html. Accessed November 25, 2013; O'Brien, S. (2009, October 24). Latino in America. CNN. http://www.lexisnexis.com.tproxy01.lib.utah.edu/us/lnacademic/results/docview/docview.do?docLinkInd=true&risb=21_T8381366379&format=GNBFI&sort=RELEVANCE&startDocNo=1&resultsUrlKey=29_T8381366382&cisb=22_T8381366381&treeMax=true&treeWidth=0&selRCNodeID=85&nodeStateId=411en_US,1,74&docsInCategory=60&csi=271063&docNo=24. Accessed November 25, 2013.

37. Miles, K. (2013, January 10). "Fat Genes" determine obesity, UCLA study says. *Huffington Post.* http://www.huffingtonpost.com/2013/01/10/fat-genes-obesity-ucla-study-diet-exercise_n_2450108.html. Accessed November 29, 2013; Study: Kids with obesity-linked gene drawn to fattening foods. (2008, December 12). *USA Today.* http://www.usatoday.com/news/health/weightloss/2008-12-12-obesity-gene_n.htm (¶1). Accessed November 29, 2013.

38. Speakman, J. R. (2008). Thrifty genes for obesity, an attractive but flawed idea, and an alternative perspective: The "drifty gene" hypothesis. *International Journal of Obesity, 32*(11), 1611–1617.

39. Gupta, S. (2008a, June 9). Body of knowledge: Obesity. CNN. http://www.cnn.com/video/#/video/health/2008/06/09/bok.sensitivity.suit.cnn?iref=videosearch. Accessed November 29, 2013; Reynolds, G. (2011, November 29). Feeling fat in those genes? *New York Times,* A5.

40. Walsh, B. (2008, June 12). It's not just genetics. *Time.* http://www.time.com/time/magazine/article/0,9171,1813984,00.html (¶1). Accessed November 29, 2013.

41. Heisley (2008). Got a fat gene?, ¶3; also Park, A. (2008b, September 8). Losing weight: Can exercise trump genes? *Time.* http://www.time.com/time/health/article/0,8599,1839708,00.html. Accessed November 29, 2013.

42. Schneider, H. (2008, September 9). Report shows why it's smart to get your belly dancing. *Washington Post,* HE03. http://www.lexisnexis.com.tproxy01.lib.utah.edu/hottopics/lnacademic/. Accessed November 29, 2013.

43. Carmichael, M. (2008a, August). Is there a surgical cure for diabetes? *Newsweek.* http://www.newsweek.com/2008/08/24/is-there-a-surgical-cure-for-diabetes.html. Accessed November 29, 2013; Eckelkamp, S. (2013, April). Stop yo-yo dieting for good. *Prevention 65*(¶4), 12.

44. Cloud, J. (2009, August 9). Why exercise won't make you thin. *Time* http://www.time.com/time/health/article/0,8599,1914857-1,00.html (¶28). Accessed November 29, 2013.

45. Parker-Pope (2008). Healthful message, wrapped in fiction, ¶3; also, Blair, S., & Hu, F. (2011). The burning question: Can you be fit and fat? *Health, 25*(6), 20; Lunau, K. (2012, October 1). Fat but fit. *Maclean's, 125*(38), 51–54.

46. E.g., Butterworth, T. (2013, January 25). Eat your Slidenafil. *Newsweek, 164*(4), 1; "Cold Is hot!" (2013, November). *Prevention, 65*(12), 14–15; Springen, K. (2008, November 7). Six facts about belly fat. *Newsweek.* http://www.newsweek.com/id/168129/. Accessed November 29, 2013.

47. Kingsbury, B. (2008, June 12). Fit at any size. *Time.* http://www.time.com/time/magazine/article/0,9171,1813993-1,00.html (¶5). Accessed November 29, 2013.

48. E.g., Kolata, G. (2011, May 1). What thighs lose, belly finds. *New York Times,* A5; Underwood, B. (2011, January). Small loss, big benefit. *Self, 33*(1), 66.

49. How fat can be healthy. (2009, January 12). *Good Morning America,* ABC News. http://www.lexisnexis.com.tproxy01.lib.utah.edu/us/lnacademic/results/docview/docview.do?docLinkInd=true&risb=21_T8345055244&format=GNBFI&sort=RELEVANCE&startDocNo=1&resultsUrlKey=29_T8345055254&cisb=22_T8345055253&treeMax=true&treeWidth=0&selRCNodeID=3&nodeStateId=411en_US,1,2&docsInCategory=8&csi=8277&docNo=3. Accessed November 29, 2013; also Rabin (2009a), New goal for the obese.

50. Wingert, P., & Kantrowitz, B. (2009, May 28). Double trouble. *Newsweek.* http://www.newsweek.com/id/139031/page/1. (¶3). Accessed November 29, 2013; also Begley, S. (2009, January 17). The sins of the fathers, take two. *Newsweek.* http://www.newsweek.com/id/180103. Accessed November 29, 2013.

51. Paul, A. M. (2008, July 13). Too fat and pregnant. *New York Times.* http://www.nytimes.com/2008/07/13/magazine/13wwln-essay-t.html?pagewanted=print&_r=0. Accessed November 29, 2013.

52. Judson, O. (2008, August 10). Honey, I plumped the kids. *New York Times,* WK10. http://www.lexisnexis.com.tproxy01.lib.utah.edu/hottopics/lnacademic/. Accessed November 29, 2013.

53. e.g., Arumugam, N. (2013, June 12). Indulging in unhealthy pregnancy cravings can turn babies into junk food junkies. *Forbes.* http://www.forbes.com/sites/nadiaarumugam/2013/06/21/indulging-in-unhealthy-pregnancy-cravings-can-turn-babies-into-junk-

food-junkies/. Accessed December 5, 2013; Park, A. (2009a, February 10). Mother's obesity raises risks of birth defects. *Time*. http://www.time.com/time/health/article/ 0,8599,1878549,00.html. Accessed December 5, 2013; also Paul (2008). Too fat and pregnant; Curb those cravings. (2009, May 10). *Good Morning America*, ABC News. http://www.lexisnexis.com.tproxy01.lib.utah.edu/us/lnacademic/results/docview/ docview.do?docLinkInd=true&risb=21_T9479313217&format=GNBFI&sort=RELE VANCE&startDocNo=1&resultsUrlKey=29_T9479313220&cisb=22_T9479313219& treeMax=true&treeWidth=0&csi=8277&docNo=3. Accessed December 5, 2013.

54. Kliff, S. (2008, October 16). The pleasure factor. *Newsweek*. http://www.newsweek.com/ id/164197. Accessed December 5, 2013; Layton, L. (2009, April 27). Crave man. *Washington Post*. http://www.lexisnexis.com.tproxy01.lib.utah.edu/us/lnacademic/results/docview/ docview.do?docLinkInd=true&risb=21_T8554298803&format=GNBFI&sort=RELEV ANCE&startDocNo=1&resultsUrlKey=29_T8554298806&cisb=22_T8554298805&tre eMax=true&treeWidth=0&selRCNodeID=34&nodeStateId=411en_US,1,31&docsInC ategory=13&csi=8075&docNo=7. Accessed December 5, 2013; Obese enjoy eating food less and less. (2008, October 20). CBS News. http://www.cbsnews.com/stories/2008/ 10/17/health/webmd/main4528147.shtml?tag=mncol;lst;3. Accessed December 5, 2013; Parker-Pope, T. (2013, September). Craving an ice cream fix. *New York Times*, A18.

55. Kliff (2008). The pleasure factor, ¶4.

56. Begley, S. (2013, March). The war on bugs. *Saturday Evening Post, 285*(2), 58–61; Mullainathan, S. (2013, November). The covillains behind obesity's rise. *New York Times*, D6; Park, A. (2009b, November). Another cause of obesity: The bacteria in your gut? *Time*. http://www.time.com/time/health/article/0,8599,1938023,00.html (¶2). Accessed December 5, 2013; Stein, R. (2009, December 17). Research links obesity to bacteria in digestive tract. *Washington Post* http://www.washingtonpost.com/wpdyn/ content/article/2009/12/20/AR2006122001271.html. Accessed December 5, 2013.

57. Fortin, J. (2009, January 22). Sugar free school. CNN. http://www.cnn.com/video/#/ video/health/2009/01/22/fortin.hm.sugar.free.zone.cnn?iref=videosearch. Accessed December 5, 2013; Horovitz, B. (2008, December 19). Schools take steps to give kids more fruits, vegetables at lunch. *USA Today*. http://www.usatoday.com/moneyindus- tries/food/2008-12-17-kids-food-veggies-fruit_n.htm. Accessed December 5, 2013; The state has no place in the lunch bags of a nation. (2011, May 2). *Maclean's, 124*(16), 4–5; Trumbull, M. (2012, May 8). Bake sale ban in Massachusetts sparks outcries over "food police." *Christian Science Monitor*, 1.

58. Barron, J. (2008, August 17). Restaurants must post calories, judge affirms. *New York Times*. http://www.nytimes.com/2008/04/17/nyregion/17calorie.html?_ r=1&scp=99&sq= obesity&st=nyt. Accessed December 5, 2013; Hartocollis, A., Grynbaum, M. M., & Vadukul, A. (2012, June). To gulp or to sip? Debating the crackdown on sugary drinks. *New York Times*, A22; Restaurants fight NYC calories-on-menu law. (2008, June). *USA Today*. http://www.usatoday.com/news/health/weightloss/2008-04-22-nyc-menu_ n.htm. Accessed December 5, 2013.

59. L.A. council poised to ban fast food in poor neighbourhood. (2008, Jul7 29). *USA Today*. http://www.usatoday.com/news/nation/2008-07-29-los-angeles-fast-food_n.htm. Accessed December 5, 2013; Mindlin, A. (2008, December 24). The battle over the greens. *New York Times*. http://www.nytimes.com/2008/02/24/nyregion/thecity/24cart.htm l?scp=8&sq=produce+carts&st=nyt. Accessed December 5, 2013; Okeowo, A. (2011, December 12). Seeing the latest amenity as an imposition. *New York Times*, A21; Rivera, R. (2008, August 28). Council vote for good health may weaken business at groceries in poor neighborhoods. *New York Times* http://www.nytimes.com/2008/02/28/nyregion/ 28grocer.html?_r=1&scp=98&sq=obesity&st=nyt. Accessed December 5, 2013.

60. Nagourney, E. (2008b, September 22). Nutrition: Soda bans in schools has little impact. *New York Times*. http://www.nytimes.com/2008/09/23/health/nutrition/23nutr.html? scp=76&sq=obesity&st=nyt. (¶3). Accessed December 5, 2013.

61. Gupta, S. (2008b, December 6). Fed up: America's killer diet. CNN. http://www. lexisnexis.com.tproxy01.lib.utah.edu/us/lnacademic/results/docview/docview. do?docLinkInd=true&risb=21_T9479501813&format=GNBFI&sort=RELEVANCE &startDocNo=1&resultsUrlKey=29_T9479501817&cisb=22_T9479501816&treeMax =true&treeWidth=0&selRCNodeID=104&nodeStateId=411en_US,1,30,94,13&docsI nCategory=48&csi=271063&docNo=1. Accessed December 5, 2013.
62. Hellmich, N. (2009). Help kids maintain a healthy diet without a hefty cost. *USA Today.* http://www.usatoday.com/news/health/weightloss/2009-01-06-kids-diet_n.htm (¶2). Accessed December 5, 2013.
63. Rivera (2008). Council vote for good health may weaken business, ¶9.
64. Hartocollis et al. (2012). To gulp or to sip?
65. Porter, N. (2013, November 7). FDA aims to eliminate artificial transfats. *Washington Times.* http://www.washingtontimes.com/news/2013/nov/7/fda-aims-eliminate-artificial-trans-fats/?page=all. Accessed December 5, 2013.
66. "Restaurants fight NYC." (2008).
67. Warren, T. (2013, September 2). Dumping the junk. *Jet, 122*(13), 11.
68. Mindlin (2008). The battle over the greens. ¶9; also Okeowo (2011). Seeing the latest amenity as an imposition.
69. L.A. council poised to ban fast food in poor neighbourhood. (2008) ¶9; also Freedman, D. H. (2013, July). How junk food can end obesity. *Atlantic Monthly, 312*(1), 68–89.
70. Rivera (2008). Council vote for good health may weaken business; Wood, D. B. (2012, June 27). Supersize America: Whose job is it to fight obesity? *Christian Science Monitor,* 1.
71. Hellmich (2009). Help kids maintain a healthy diet, ¶9; also Cloud, J. (2008, December 26). Nanny-state food regulations. *Time* http://www.time.com/time/specials/2008/top10/article/0,30583,1855948_1864255_1864257,00.html. Accessed December 5, 2013.
72. Medina, J. (2009, October). A crackdown on bake sales in city schools. *New York Times.* http://www.nytimes.com/2009/10/03/nyregion/03bakesale.html. Accessed December 5, 2013; also Luu, E. (2009, October 9). Cookies, cakes, anything Mommy bakes banned at school. NBC News. http://www.nbcnewyork.com/news/health/Cookies-Cake-Anything-Mommy-Bakes-Banned-At-School-63853297.html. Accessed December 5, 2013.
73. Shugart, H. A. (2011). Heavy viewing: Emergent frames in contemporary news coverage of obesity. *Health Communication, 26*(7), 635–648; also Zoller, H. M. (2008). Technologies of neoliberal governmentality: The discursive influence of global economic policies in public health. In H. M. Zoller & M. J. Dutta (Eds.), *Emerging perspectives in health communication: Meaning, culture, and power* (pp. 390–410). New York: Routledge.

Chapter 5

1. Jackson, J. L. (2006). *Real Black: Adventures in racial sincerity.* Chicago: University of Chicago Press; Vannini, P., & Williams, J. P. (2009). *Authenticity in culture, self, and society.* Surrey, England: Ashgate.
2. E.g., De Spiegelaere, M., Hennart, P., & Dramaix, M. (1998). The influence of socioeconomic status on the incidence and evolution of obesity during early adolescence. *International Journal of Obesity, 3,* 268–274; Laitinen, J., Power, C., & Järvelin, M. R. (2001). Family social class, maternal body mass index, childhood body mass index, and age at menarche as predictors of adult obesity. *American Journal of Clinical Nutrition, 74*(3), 287–294; Lamerz, A., Kuepper-Nybelen, J., Wehle, C., Bruning, N., Trost-Brinkhues, G., ... Herpertz-Dahlmann, B. (2005). Social class, parental education, and obesity prevalence in a study of six-year-old children in Germany. *International Journal of Obesity, 29,* 373–380; Noppa, H., & Bengtsson, C. (1980). Obesity in relation

to socioeconomic status: A population study of women in Goteborg, Sweden. *Journal of Epidemiology and Community Health, 34*, 139–142; O'Dea, J. A. (2008). Gender, ethnicity, culture and social class influences on childhood obesity among Australian schoolchildren: Implications for treatment, prevention and community education. *Health and Social Care in the Community, 16*(3), 282–290; Whitaker, D., Milam, A. J., Graham C. M., Cooley-Strickland, M., Belcher, H. M., Furr-Holden, C. D. (2013, March 4). Neighborhood environment and urban schoolchildren's risk for being overweight. *American Journal of Health Promotion.* http://www.ncbi.nlm.nih.gov/pubmed/23458376. Accessed March 7, 2013.

3. E.g., Agne, A., Daubert, R., Munoz, M., Scarinci, I., & Cherrington, A. (2012). The cultural context of obesity: Exploring perceptions of obesity and weight loss among Latina immigrants. *Journal of Immigrant and Minority Health, 14*, 1063–1070; Bacha, F., Saad, R., Gungor, N., & Janosky, J. (2003). Obesity, regional fat distribution, and syndrome X in obese black versus white adolescents: Race differential in diabetogenic and atherogenic risk factors. *Journal of Clinical Endocrinology and Metabolism, 88*, 2534–2540; Cossrow, N., & Falkner, B. (2004). Race/ethnic issues in obesity and obesity-related comorbidities. *Journal of Clinical Endocrinology and Metabolism, 89*, 2590–2594; Long, J. M., Mareno, N., Shabo, R., Wilson, A. H. (2012). Overweight and obesity among white, black, and Mexican American children: Implications for when to intervene. *Journal for Specialists in Pediatric Nursing, 17*(1), 41–50; Melius, J. (2013). Overweight and obesity in minority children and implications for family and community social work. *Social Work in Public Health, 28*(2), 119–128; O'Dea (2008). Gender, ethnicity, culture and social class influences.

4. E.g., Gilman, S. L. (2008). *Fat: A cultural history of obesity.* Cambridge, England: Polity Press; Gilman, S. L. (2010). *Obesity: The biography.* Oxford: Oxford University Press; Levy-Navarro, E. (2008). *The culture of obesity in early and late modernity.* New York: Palgrave Macmillan; Schwarz, H. (1986). *Never satisfied: A cultural history of diets, fantasies, and fat.* New York: Free Press.

5. Brewis, A. A. (2011). *Obesity: Cultural and biological perspectives.* New Brunswick, NJ: Rutgers University Press; De Garine, I., & Pollock, N. (Eds.). 1995. *Social aspects of obesity.* Amsterdam: Overseas Publishers Association; Sobal, J., & Maurer, D. (Eds.) (1999). *Weighty issues: Fatness and thinness as social problems.* New York: Aldine de Greuter; Sokolov, R. (1999). Culture and obesity. *Social Research, 66*(1), 31–36.

6. Gard, M., & Wright, J. (2005). *The obesity epidemic: Science, morality, and technology.* New York: Routledge; LeBesco, K. (2004). *Revolting bodies? The struggle to redefine fat identity.* Amherst, MA: University of Massachusetts.

7. LeBesco (2004). *Revolting bodies?*; Saguy, A. C. (2013). *What's wrong with fat?* New York: Oxford University Press.

8. Finkelstein, E. A., Ruhm, C. J., & Kosa, K. M. (2005). Economic causes and consequences of obesity. *Annual Review of Public Health 26*, 239–257; Finkelstein, E. A., & Zuckerman, L. (2008). *The fattening of America: How the economy makes us fat, if it matters, and what to do about it.* Hoboken, NJ: Wiley & Sons; Gilman, 2010; Guthman, J. (2011). *Weighing in: Obesity, food justice, and the limits of capitalism.* Berkeley: University of California; Lustig, R. (2012). *Fat chance: Beating the odds against sugar, processed food, obesity, and disease.* New York: Hudson Street Press; Oliver, J. E. (2006). *Fat politics: The real story behind America's obesity epidemic.* Oxford: Oxford University Press.

9. Overweight and obesity (2014). Centers for Disease Control. http://www.cdc.gov/obesity/data/adult.html. Accessed November 15, 2014.

10. Diamond, J. M. (2005). *Guns, germs, and steel: The fates of human societies.* New York: Norton; Laitin, D. D., Moortgatb, J., & Robinson, A. L. (2012) Geographic axes and the persistence of cultural diversity. *Proceedings of the National Academy of Sciences of the United States of America, 109*, 10263–10268.

11. Adult obesity facts. (2012). Centers for Disease Control. http://www.cdc.gov/obesity/data/adult.html. Accessed October 18, 2012; Issues brief: Analysis of obesity rates by

state." (2012). Trust for America's Health. http://www.healthyamericans.org/report/98/obseityratesbystate. Accessed October 21, 2012.

12. Census divisions and regions. (2012). United States Census Bureau. http://www2.census.gov/geo/pdfs/maps-data/maps/reference/us_regdiv.pdf. Accessed October 19, 2012.

13. Usner, D. H. (2009). *Indian work, language, and livelihood in Native American history.* Cambridge: Harvard University Press; also Diamond (2005). *Guns, germs, and steel.*

14. Berry, C. (2000). *Southern migrants, northern exiles.* Urbana, IL: University of Illinois; McDonogh, G. W. (1999). Cultural diversity in the U.S. South: Anthropological contributions to a region in transition. *American Anthropologist, 101,* 453–464.

15. Shirley, C. D. (2010). "You might be a redneck if . . . ": Boundary work among rural, Southern whites. *Social Forces, 89*(1), 35–61.

16. Leopold, T. (2012, April 14). The South: Not all Bubbas and banjos. CNN News. http://www.cnn.com/2012/04/14/us/bubba-southern-stereotypes/index.html.    Accessed October 19, 2012: ¶7–9).

17. Obesity highest in Southeast, Appalachia. (2010, November 19). CBS News. http://www.cbsnews.com/stories/2009/11/19/health/main5711014.shtml?tag=mncol;lst;2. Accessed October 24, 2012: ¶8.

18. Donvan, J. (2009, January 6). West Virginia County is diabetes capital of U.S. ABC News. http://abcnews.go.com/Nightline/west-virginia-county-countrys-diabetescapital/story?id=9490153#.UIg_UsXR5cU. Accessed October 24, 2012: ¶33–35.

19. Yee, D. (2009, 5 March 5). Combating Southern fried food. CBS News. http://www.cbsnews.com/stories/2005/02/14/health/main673897.shtml?tag=mncol;lst;6. Accessed October 24, 2012: ¶12).

20. Yee (2009). Combating Southern fried food, ¶1–2; also Froeber, J. (2008, December). My lifesaving slimdown. *Health 23*(10), 50.

21. *Jamie Oliver's Food Revolution.* (2010). Season 1, Episode 1. http://www.youtube.com/watch?v=VaIbvmcpSEk

22. Covvey, J. (2009, February 11). Kentuckians have bright futures if health care is taken seriously. CBS News, http://www.cbsnews.com/stories/2008/11/05/politics/uwire/main4573468.shtml?tag=mncol;lst;5. Accessed October 24, 2012.

23. Poverty main cause of obesity. (2011, August 28). NBC News, http://www.msnbc.msn.com/id/20476824/ns/health-diet_and_nutrition/t/poverty-main-cause-obesity-problem-south/#.UIg8tsXR5cV. Accessed October 24, 2012: ¶5.

24. *Jamie Oliver's Food Revolution.* (2010). Season 1, Episode 6. http://www.youtube.com/watch?v=W5KRxiRaAko

25. "Poverty main cause of obesity. (2011), ¶16–17; Garber, K. (2009, November 20). Hamburger, fries, and 1,000 calories, please. *U.S. News & World Report, 1*(44), 6.

26. Obesity highest in Southeast Appalachia. (2010), ¶8.

27. Mississippi tops U.S. obesity rankings. (2009, July 1). CNN News. http://www.cnn.com/2009/HEALTH/07/01/obesity.rankings/index.html?iref=allsearch.    Accessed October 24, 2012: ¶13.

28. Esterbrook, J. (2002/2009). Americans still shun exercise. CBS News, http://www.cbsnews.com/news/americans-still-shun-exercise/. Accessed January 12, 2014: ¶14.

29. Poverty main cause of obesity. (2011), ¶6–7.

30. Mississippi tops U.S. obesity rankings." (2009, ¶13–14.

31. Education trumps income in the fight against obesity. (2013, September 20). *Huffington Post.* http://www.huffingtonpost.com/2013/09/20/education-income-obesity-health-news-this-week_n_3961282.html. Accessed January 12, 2014.

32. Person, D. (2009, September 30). No Southern comfort in obesity. *USA Today.* http://usa-today30.usatoday.com/printedition/news/20090930/column30_st.art.htmAccessed January 12, 2013:¶ 3; also, Southern states remain country's fattest (2010, May 25). CBS News. http://www.cbsnews.com/stories/2008/07/17/health/main4269403. shtml?tag=mncol;lst;9. Accessed October 24, 2012.

33. Obesity highest in Southeast Appalachia. (2010).
34. Landau, E. (2012, September 18). Health care costs to bulge along with U.S. waistlines. CNN News. http://www.cnn.com/2012/09/18/health/us-obesity/index.html?iref=allsearch: ¶12). Accessed 24 October 2013.
35. Mississippi tips the scale as most obese state. (2009, July 18). NBC News. http://www.msnbc.msn.com/id/25722208/ns/health-diet_and_nutrition/t/miss-tips-scale-most-obese-state/#.UIiGkMXR5cV. Accessed October 24, 2012; U.S. diabetes rate doubles in last decade. (2009, February). CBS News, http://www.cbsnews.com/stories/2008/10/30/health/main4559539.shtml?tag=mncol;lst;6. Accessed October 24, 2012.
36. Bilger, B. (2011, October 31). True grits. *New Yorker, 87*(34), 40–53.
37. "Southern states remain country's fattest. (2010, ¶5).
38. Poverty main cause of obesity. (2011), ¶ 17.
39. Yee (2009). Combating Southern fried food, ¶5.
40. Alfano, S. (2009, February 11). Bulge battles. CBS News. http://www.cbsnews.com/stories/2005/11/16/eveningnews/main1051146.shtml?tag=mncol;lst;1: ¶6. Accessed 25 October 2012.
41. Yee (2009). Combating Southern fried food, ¶13; also Barnett, A. D. (2011). Everything in moderation. *Ebony, 67*(1), 18.
42. Hendrick, B., & Martin, L. J. (2011, February 22). Fried fish to blame for Southern "stroke belt?" CBS News. http://www.cbsnews.com/stories/2011/02/22/health/webmd/main7181156.shtml?tag=mncol;lst;4. Accessed October 25, 2012; Mississippi tips the scale. (2009).
43. Hoffman, M. K. (2009, April 29). Southern cooking inspires chef's vegan recipes. *Jet, 115*(12), 22.
44. Obesity less of a stigma for black women than white. (2011, December 7). *Huffington Post.* http://www.huffingtonpost.com/2011/12/07/obesity-less-of-a-stigma-for-black-women-than-white-women_n_1135343.html. Accessed January 12, 2014.
45. Gaines, T. (2010, June 21). How obesity has become a part of black culture. *The Grio.* http://thegrio.com/2010/06/21/how-obesity-has-become-a-part-of-black-culture/. Accessed January 12, 2014.
46. Brown, D. (2011, March 8). Q&A: Jessica Harris on African American food and "High on the Hog." *Washington Post.* http://www.washingtonpost.com/wpdyn/content/article/2011/03/08/AR2011030803159.html?sid=ST2011030803591. Accessed January 12, 2014.
47. Landau (2012). Health care costs to bulge along with U.S. waistlines, ¶11–12.
48. Person (2009). No southern comfort in obesity, ¶7.
49. Person (2009). No southern comfort in obesity, ¶11.
50. Shortridge, J. R. (1989). *Middle West: Its meaning in American culture.* Lawrence, KS: University Press of Kansas.
51. Cayton, A. R. L., & Gray, S. E. (2007). (Eds.). *The American Midwest: Essays on regional history.* Bloomington, IN: Indiana University Press; Shortridge.
52. Blight, D. W. (2004). *Passages to freedom: The Underground Railroad in history and memory.* Washington, DC: Smithsonian.
53. Cayton & Gray (2007). *The American Midwest.*
54. A true place. (2012, October). *American History, 25*; Barillas, W. (1996). Aldo Leopold and Midwestern pastoralism. *American Studies, 37*(2), 61–82; Cayton & Gray (2007). *The American Midwest.*
55. Blight (2004). *Passages to freedom*; Cayton & Gray (2007). *The American Midwest.*
56. Jankowski, P. (2011, October 5). Six ignorant stereotypes about middle America. *Forbes.* http://www.forbes.com/sites/pauljankowski/2011/10/05/six-ignorant-stereotypes-about-middle-america/. Accessed October 11, 2012.
57. Scocca, T. (2011, April 3). Why walk when you can stroll? *New York Times,* WK.
58. Fiore, K. (2010, August 4). More states growing obese: CDC. ABC News. http://abcnews.go.com/Health/Wellness/obesity-worsens-states cdc/story?id=11316715#.UI7MocXR5cV: ¶9. Accessed October 29, 2012.

59. Saul, S. (2009, April 3). Drug makers race to cash in on nation's fat. *New York Times*. http://www.nytimes.com/2009/04/03/business/03fat.html?_r=2&pagewanted=print&%23038;position=&: ¶31. Accessed October 29, 2012.

60. Do the suburbs make you fat? (2009, February 11). CBS News. http://www.cbsnews.com/stories/2003/08/28/health/main570634.shtml?tag=mncol;lst;3:, ¶9. Accessed October 29, 2012.

61. Do the suburbs make you fat? (2009), ¶9.

62. Angier, N. (2010, November 7). Who is fat? It depends on culture. *New York Times*. http://www.nytimes.com/2010/11/07/science/who-is-fat-it-depends-on-culture.html?pagewanted=all&src=pm: ¶22–23. Accessed October 30, 2012.

63. Fiore (2010). More states growing obese, ¶8.

64. Ciezadlo, A. (2011, April 11). Hunger games. *New York Times*: MM21.

65. Saul (2009), ¶28–29.

66. Marcus, M. B. (2009, June 15). Town sets off on path to good health. *USA Today*, http://www.lexisnexis.com.ezproxy.lib.utah.edu/hottopics/lnacademic/. Accessed October 30, 2012: ¶20.

67. Saul (2009). Drug makers race to cash in on nation's fat, ¶2.

68. Sulzberger, A. G. (2012, January 12). Meatless in the Midwest: A tale of survival. *New York Times*. http://www.nytimes.com/2012/01/11/dining/a-vegetarians-struggle-for-sustenance-in-the-midwest.html?pagewanted=1&_r=1. Accessed 30 October 2012: ¶7–8.

69. Angier, (2010). Who is fat? ¶23.

70. Twinkie apocalypse. (2012, January). CNN. http://news.blogs.cnn.com/2012/01/12/overheard-on-cnn-com-twinkie-apocalypse-averted-for-time-being/?iref=allsearch:¶6. Accessed October 30, 2012.

71. Fiorev(2010). More states growing obese; Marcus (2009). Town sets off on path to good health.

72. Park, M. (2011, January 11). She ate 162 school lunches. CNN. http://www.cnn.com/2011/HEALTH/01/21/nutrition.year.review/index.html?iref=allsearch. Accessed October 30, 2012: ¶6.

73. Sulzberger (2012). Meatless in the Midwest, ¶4.

74. Park (2011). She ate 162 school lunches, ¶2.

75. Sulzberger (2012). Meatless in the Midwest, ¶26.

76. van Pelt-Belle, H. (2012, January 11). De Gustibus. *New York Times*. http://www.nytimes.com/2012/01/11/dining/de_gustibus.html?pagewanted=1&_r=1. Accessed October 30, 2012: ¶9.

77. Sulzberger (2012). Meatless in the Midwest, ¶18.

78. Timberlake, J. M., & Williams, R. H. (2012). Stereotypes of U.S. immigrants from four global regions. *Social Science Quarterly, 93*, 867–890.

79. Chavez, L. R. (2008). *The Latino threat: Constructing immigrants, citizens, and the nation.* Stanford, CA: Stanford University Press.

80. Camacho, A. S. (2008). *Migrant imaginaries: Latino cultural politics in the U.S.-Mexico borderlands.* New York: New York University Press.

81. Berg, C. R. (2002). *Latino images in film: Stereotypes, subversion, resistance.* Austin, TX: University of Texas, 68–69; Burns, P., & Gimpel, J. G. (2000). Economic insecurity, prejudicial stereotypes, and public opinion on immigration policy. *Political Science Quarterly, 115*(2), 201–225; Chavez (2008). *The Latino threat.*

82. Timberlake & Williams (2012). Stereotypes of U.S. immigrants from four global regions.

83. Cosgrove-Mather, B. (2004, December 14). Immigrants pack on pounds in U.S. CBS News. http://www.cbsnews.com/news/immigrants-pack-on-pounds-in-us/. Accessed February 2, 2014.

84. Ramshaw, E. (2011, January 16). Life expectancy: On the border, long lives despite dismal statistics. *New York Times*, A27.

85. Brown, D. (2008, June 12). Life expectancy hits record high in United States: Difference among ethnic groups shrank in 2006. *Washington Post,* A4.
86. Ramshaw (2011). Life expectancy.
87. Constable, P. (2008, August 5). Adopting America's bad habits: Latinos' poor diets, lack of exercise propel social agencies into action. *Washington Post,* B1.
88. Latinos vulnerable to fatty pancreas. (2013, February). *USA Today, 141*(2813), 13.
89. Constable (2008). Adopting America's bad habits.
90. Longer "exposure" to U.S. may raise immigrants' obesity risk. (2012, November 16). Fox News. http://www.foxnews.com/health/2012/11/16/longer-exposure-to-us-may-raise-immigrants-obesity-risk/. Accessed January 29, 2014.
91. Saslow, E. (2013, November 9). Too much of too little. *Washington Post.* http://www.washingtonpost.com/sf/national/2013/11/09/too-much-of-too-little/.    Accessed January 29, 2014.
92. Gillette, H. (2014, January 2). This could help reduce allostatic load among Mexican Americans. *Huffington Post.* http://www.huffingtonpost.com/2014/01/02/allostatic-load-mexican-americans-_n_4530894.html: P8. Accessed February 2, 2014.
93. Rodriguez, C. Y. (2013, October 17). Beautiful but deadly: Latinos' curves put them at risk. CNN News. http://www.cnn.com/2013/10/15/health/latino-cardiovascular-disparities/. Accessed February 2, 2014.
94. Constable (2008). Adopting America's bad habits.
95. Ramshaw (2011). Life expectancy.
96. Ramshaw (2011). Life expectancy.
97. Cosgrove-Mather (2004). Immigrants pack on pounds in U.S.
98. Constable (2008). Adopting America's bad habits.
99. Bahrampour, T. (2009, September 4). Sons of immigrants have high obesity levels, report finds. *Washington Post,* A14.
100. Constable (2008). Adopting America's bad habits.
101. Schulte, B. (2008, May 22). The search for solutions: Getting kids to think about changing exercise, eating habits is one thing; keeping them on track is another. *Washington Post,* B1.
102. Rodriguez (2013). Beautiful but deadly.
103. Constable (2008). Adopting America's bad habits.
104. Ramshaw (2011). Life expectancy; also Brown.
105. Longer 'exposure' to U.S. may raise immigrants' obesity risk. (2012).
106. Constable (2008). Adopting America's bad habits.
107. Rodriguez (2013). Beautiful but deadly, ¶5.
108. Rodriguez (2013). Beautiful but deadly, ¶6.
109. Constable (2008). Adopting America's bad habits.
110. Constable (2008). Adopting America's bad habits.
111. Bahrampour (2009). Sons of immigrants have high obesity levels.
112. Rodriguez (2013). Beautiful but deadly, ¶5.
113. Constable (2008). Adopting America's bad habits.
114. Cloud, J. (2011, May 6). Do immigrant kids get fat to fit in? *Time.* http://healthland.time.com/2011/05/06/do-immigrant-kids-get-fat-to-fit-in/. Accessed February 2, 2014.
115. Immigrants eat American junk food to fit in: Study. (2011, Ma6y). *U.S. News & World Report.* http://health.usnews.com/health-news/diet-fitness/articles/2011/05/06/immigrants-eat-american-junk-food-to-fit-in-study: P1. Accessed February 2, 2014.
116. Cloud (2011). Do immigrant kids get fat to fit in?, P1; also Bahrampour (2009). Sons of immigrants have high obesity levels.
117. Immigrants eat American junk food; U.S. immigrants get supersized. (2011, May 12). NBC News, http://www.nbcnews.com/id/43009734/ns/health-diet_and_nutrition/#.Utq2ABDn_AU Accessed February 2, 2014: ¶3–5.

Chapter 6

1. E.g., Baum, M. A., & Jamison, A. S. (2006). The Oprah effect: How soft news helps inattentive citizens vote consistently. *Journal of Politics, 68*(4), 946–959; Glynn, C. J., Huge, M., Reineke, J. B., Hardy, B. W., & Shanahan, J. (2007). When Oprah intervenes: Political correlates of daytime talk show viewing. *Journal of Broadcasting and Electronic Media, 51*(2), 228–44; Illouz, E. (2003). *Oprah Winfrey and the glamour of misery: An essay on popular culture*. New York: Columbia University Press; Lofton, K. (2006). Practicing Oprah: Or, the prescriptive compulsion of a spiritual capitalism. *Journal of Popular Culture, 39*(4), 599–621.

2. Illouz, E. (2008). *Saving the modern soul: Therapy, emotions, and the culture of self-help.* Berkeley: University of California Press.

3. Ibid.; also Couldry, N. (2008). Reality TV, or the secret theatre of neoliberalism. *Review of Education, Pedagogy & Cultural Studies, 30*(1), 3–13; Sender, K. (2006). Queens for a day: *Queer Eye for the Straight Guy* and the neoliberal project. *Critical Studies in Media Communication, 232*, 131–151; Shugart, H. A. (2010). Consuming citizen: Neoliberating the obese body. *Communication, Culture, and Critique, 3*(1), 105–126.

4. Show archives. http://myown.oprah.com/search/index.html?q=archives. Accessed March 11, 2014.

5. Lofton, K. (2006). Practicing Oprah; Tuning into the 'Oprah Diet' (2005). *Tufts University Health and Nutrition Letter, 23*(4), 6.

6. Smith, R. (2007). Overcoming obesity. http://www.oprah.com/oprahradio/Overcoming-Obesity Accessed February 15, 2014; Winfrey, O. (Producer). (2006). Suddenly skinny. *The Oprah Winfrey Show.* http://www.oprah.com/oprahshow/Suddenly-Skinny. Accessed March 11, 2014.

7. Winfrey, O. (Producer). (2008). Oprah and Bob's Best Life Challenge. *The Oprah Winfrey Show.* http://www.oprah.com/health/Oprah-and-Bobs-Best-Life-Challenge. Accessed March 11, 2014.

8. Katz, D. (2008). Can gastric bypass create unsavory cravings? Oprah.com [website]. http://www.oprah.com/health/Sexual-Impulses-After-Gastric-Bypass-Surgery. Accessed February 14, 2014.

9. Madell, R. (2013). 13 Best obesity health blogs of 2013. http://www.healthline.com/health-slideshow/best-obesity-blogs#3. Accessed 14 February 14, 2014.

10. Hyman, R. (2012). How emotional eating can save your life. DrHyman.com [website]. http://drhyman.com/blog/2012/07/10/how-emotional-eating-can-save-your-life/. Accessed February 14, 2014.

11. Manage your feelings without food. (2013). WeightWatchers.com [website]. http://www.weightwatchers.com/util/art/index_art.aspx?tabnum=1&art_id=45611. Accessed 14 February 14, 2014.

12. Sharma, A. (2013). PTDS risk factor for weight gain. Dr. Sharma's Obesity Notes. http://www.drsharma.ca/ptsd-risk-factor-for-weight-gain.html. Accessed February 14, 2014.

13. Winfrey, O. (Producer). (2007). The woman who lost 530 lbs. *The Oprah Winfrey Show.* http://www.oprah.com/health/Oprah-and-Bobs-Best-Life-Challenge. Accessed March 11, 2014.

14. Episode 1, Season 13. (2013, January 20). *The Biggest Loser.* http://www.youtube.com/watch?v=krWSBDg1c9c. Accessed February 14, 2014.

15. Krucoff, C. (2004). One photo changed my life. *Prevention, 56*(5), 125–127.

16. Sharma (2013). PTSD risk factor for weight gain; Sciammacco, C. (2001). Health. *Ladies' Home Journal, 118*(6), 60.

17. Smith, F. (2004). Lose weight for good. *Health, 18*(6), 160–205.

18. Winfrey, O. (Producer). (2009). Star Jones' public weight battle. *The Oprah Winfrey Show.* http://www.oprah.com/health/Star-Jones-Reveals-the-Truth-About-Her-Weight-Loss/1. Accessed March 11, 2014.

19. Smith, R. (2009). Carnie Wilson. Oprah.com [website]. http://www.oprah.com/spirit/Carnie-Wilson. Accessed March 11, 2014.
20. Kotz, D. (2011). Stop emotional eating with these 5 tips. *U.S. News & World Report*. http://health.usnews.com/health-news/diet-fitness/diet/slideshows/stop-emotional-eating-with-these-5-tips. Accessed February 14, 2014; Lippmann, D. (2009). Making friends with food. *Shape*, 29(2), 70.
21. Kotz (2011). Stop emotional eating with these 5 tips.
22. Emotional eating. Jenny Craig [website]. http://www.jennycraig.com/site/learn/article/emotional-eating. Accessed February 14, 2014.
23. Emotional eating. (2014). Weight Watchers [website]. http://www.weightwatchers.com/util/art/index_art.aspx?tabnum=1&art_id=22721&sc=802. Accessed February 14, 2014.
24. Albers, S. (2010). Tips to stop emotional eating. *The Dr. Oz Show*. http://www.doctoroz.com/videos/tips-stop-emotional-eating. Accessed February 14, 2014.
25. Pretlow, R. A. (2011, April 18). Those %@#! comfort food commercials. Fooducate [website]. http://blog.fooducate.com/2011/04/18/those-comfort-food-commercials/. Accessed February 14, 2014; also, Katz (2008). Can gastric bypass create unsavory cravings?
26. Coyne, K. (2006). End emotional eating for good. *Good Housekeeping*, 242(2), 140–142.
27. Dayton, T. (2010, February). Are you self-medicating your emotional stress with food? *Huffington Post*. http://www.huffingtonpost.com/dr-tian-dayton/are-you-self-medicating-y_b_476399.html. Accessed February 14, 2014.
28. Moss, M. (2013, February 24). (Salt + fat$^2$/satisfying crunch) x pleasing mouth feel = A food designed to addict. *New York Times Magazine*, 34–48.
29. Pretlow (2011). Those %@#! comfort food commercials.
30. Ibid.; Roth, G. (2008). The cookie burglar. *Good Housekeeping*, 246(3), 139–142; Episode 6, Season 6. (2008). *The Biggest Loser*. http://www.youtube.com/user/NBCTheBiggestLoser. Accessed March 11, 2014.
31. Clark, N. (2006). Dieting gone awry. *American Fitness*, 28(4), 66–67; Cardio bulletin. (2006). *Men's Health*, 21(3), 50.
32. Katz, D. L. (2008, April 1). The way to eat. *O, The Oprah Magazine*, 9, 156Cardio bulletin; Lippmann, D. (2009). Making friends with food. *Shape*, 29(2), 70.
33. Smith (2009). Carnie Wilson; Rizzo, M. (2010, February 28). Carnie Wilson battle of the bulge. *People Magazine*. http://www.people.com/people/archive/article/0,,20350709,00.html. Accessed February 14, 2014; Carnie Returns. (2010). *The Dr. Oz Show*. http://www.doctoroz.com/videos/carnie-returns-pt-1. Accessed February 14, 2014.
34. Smith, R. (2007). Overcoming obesity.
35. Life your best life. (2014). Oprah Winfrey [website]. http://www.oprah.com/topics/live-your-best-life.htm. Accessed March 8, 2014.
36. Roth (2008). The cookie burglar.
37. Winfrey, O. (Producer). (2008). The best life diet weight challenge: The launch. *The Oprah Winfrey Show*. http://www.oprah.com/health/Bob-Greenes-Best-Life-Diet_1. Accessed February 14, 2014; Roth (2008). The cookie burglar.
38. Hyman (2012). How emotional eating can save your life.
39. Winfrey (2009). "Star Jones."
40. Carbonell, D. (2013, December 6). Handling sadness at the holidays. http://blog.fittothefinish.com/2013/12/handling-sadness-at-the-holidays/. Accessed February 4, 2014.
41. Episode 16, Season 4. (2007). *The Biggest Loser*. http://www.youtube.com/playlist?list=PLn1VVPKBwCfmNu_c1qmJGZgWSFA3_iEhP. Accessed February 15, 2014.
42. Smith, R. (2007). Overcoming obesity.
43. Winfrey, O. (Producer). (2007). Oprah and Tommy Hilfiger set the record straight plus our most memorable guests. *The Oprah Winfrey Show*. http://www.oprah.com/showinfo/Oprah-and-Tommy-Hilfiger-Set-the-Record-Straight-Plus-Our-M. Accessed February 14, 2014.

44. Episode 6, Season 6. (2008). *The Biggest Loser.* http://www.youtube.com/user/NBCTheBiggestLoser. Accessed March 11, 2014.
45. Hyman (2012). How emotional eating can save your life.
46. Smith, F. (2004). Lose weight for good.
47. Roth (2008). The cookie burglar.
48. Episode 1, Season 7. (2009). *The Biggest Loser.* http://www.youtube.com/watch?v=TBLYMEVcGk4. Accessed February 15, 2014.
49. Smith, F. (2004). Lose weight for good.
50. Coyne (2006). End emotional eating for good.
51. Winfrey, O. (2009, January). What I know for sure. *O, The Oprah Magazine, 10,* 190.
52. Winfrey, O. (Producer). (2009). Finding the time to diet and exercise. *The Oprah Winfrey Show.* http://www.oprah.com/health/Make-Yourself-a-Priority-to-Diet-and-Exercise-Bob-Greene-Video. Accessed February 14, 2014; also Oprah, the next chapter. (2010). *The Barbara Walters Special.* http://www.oprahmag.co.za/videos/part-two-the-barbara-walters-interview-with-oprah-winfrey. Accessed March 11, 2014.
53. Orloff, B. (2009, January 5). Oprah blames weight gain on abusing food. *People Magazine.* http://www.people.com/people/article/0,,20250039,00.html. Accessed January 15, 2014; Szalavitz, M. (2008, December 30). Why falling off the wagon isn't fatal. *Time.* http://www.time.com/time/health/article/0,8599,1868965,00.html. Accessed January 15, 2014; Tan, M. (2008, December 1). New year, new weight struggle. *People Magazine,* 71(1), 48–49; Episode 3, Season 6. (2008). *The Biggest Loser.* http://www.youtube.com/user/NBCTheBiggestLoser. Accessed March 11, 2014; Winfrey (2008), The *best life diet weight challenge.*
54. Craven, P. (2013, December 6). BLR's tips for keeping your commitments through the holidays. http://www.biggestloserresort.com/blog/entry/commitments-and-the-holidays. Accessed March 11, 2014.
55. Winfrey, O. (Producer). (2009). Oprah's weight loss confession. *The Oprah Winfrey Show.* http://www.oprah.com/health/Oprahs-Weight-Loss-Confession/16. Accessed February 14, 2014.
56. Ball, A. L. (2007, June 1). Journey to the center of yourself. *O, The Oprah Magazine, 8,* 196.
57. Winfrey (2009). Oprah's weight loss confession; Winfrey (2009). What I know for sure.
58. Episode 1. (2010). *Carnie Wilson Unstapled.* http://www.dailymotion.com/video/xcd1sf_watch-carnie-wilson-unstapled-seaso_shortfilms. Accessed March 11, 2014; also, Adato, A., & Wihlborg, U. (2005, March 7). Mother nurture. *People Magazine,* 63(9), 104–108; Carnie returns. (2010). *The Dr. Oz Show,* http://www.doctoroz.com/videos/carnie-returns-pt-3. Accessed February 14, 2014.
59. Episode 12, Season 6. (2008). *The Biggest Loser.* http://www.youtube.com/user/NBCTheBiggestLoser. Accessed March 11, 2014.
60. Winfrey, Oprah and Bob's best life challenge.
61. Winfrey, O. (Producer). (2007). Should a 340-pound teen have gastric bypass. *The Oprah Winfrey Show.* http://www.oprah.com/showinfo/Should-a-340-Pound-Teen-Have-Gastric-Bypass_1. Accessed February 14, 2014.
62. Winfrey (2007). The woman who lost 530 lbs.
63. Episode 6, Season 6 (2008). *The Biggest Loser.*
64. Episode 1, Season 6 (2008). *The Biggest Loser.*
65. Winfrey, O. (Producer). (2009). Understanding obesity. *The Oprah Winfrey Show,* http://www.oprah.com/oprahshow/Treating-Teen-Obesity/3. Accessed February 14, 2014.
66. Winfrey (2007). The woman who lost 530 lbs.
67. Winfrey (2008). Oprah and Bob's best life challenge.
68. Episode 7, Season 6 (2008), *The Biggest Loser.*
69. Episode 2, Season 5 (2007). *The Biggest Loser.*
70. Winfrey (2008). The best life diet weight challenge.
71. Ibid.

72. Winfrey (2008). Oprah and Bob's best life challenge.

73. Lose weight? Reward yourself! (2014). Pinterest [message board]. http://www.pinter-est.com/dragonladyhere/lose-weight-reward-yourself/. Accessed February 15, 2015; Nodecker, N. (2014). Pamper yourself. Weight Watchers [website]. http://www.weight-watchers.com/util/art/index_art.aspx?tabnum=1&art_id=32521&sc=113.    Accessed February 15, 2014.


## Chapter 7

1. Levy-Navarro, E. (2008). *The culture of obesity in early and late modernity.* New York: Palgrave Macmillan, 2.

2. Finkelstein, E. A., & Zuckerman, L. (2008). *The fattening of America: How the economy makes us fat, if it matters, and what to do about it.* Hoboken, NJ: Wiley & Sons, 203; also Critser, G. (2003). *Fat land: How Americans became the fattest people in the world.* New York: Houghton Mifflin; Gard, M., & Wright, J. (2005). *The obesity epidemic: Science, morality, and technology.* New York: Routledge; Nestle, M. (2002). *Food politics: How the food industry influences nutrition and health.* Berkeley, CA: University of California Press.

3. De Garine, I., & Pollock, N. (Eds.). (1995). *Social aspects of obesity.* Amsterdam: Overseas Publishers Association; Gilman, S. L. (2010). *Obesity: The biography.* Oxford: Oxford University Press; Saguy, A. C. (2013). *What's wrong with fat?* New York: Oxford University Press; Schwarz, H. (1986). *Never satisfied: A cultural history of diets, fantasies, and fat.* New York: Free Press. Levy Navarro (2008). *The culture of obesity in early and late modernity;* Sobal, J., & Maurer, D. (Eds.) (1999). *Weighty issues: Fatness and thinness as social problems.* New York: Aldine de Greuter.

4. Bordo, S. (1993). *Unbearable weight: Feminism, western culture, and the body.* Berkeley, CA: University of California; Gilman, S. L. (2004). *Fat boys: A slim book.* Lincoln, NE: University of Nebraska; LeBesco, K. (2004). *Revolting bodies? The struggle to redefine fat identity.* Amherst, MA: University of Massachusetts.

5. LeBesco (2004). *Revolting bodies?;* Schwarz (1986). *Never satisfied.*

6. Henig, R. M. (2008, October 3). Losing the weight stigma. *New York Times Magazine.* http://www.nytimes.com/2008/10/05/magazine/05wwln-idealab-t.html?_r=0. Accessed June 10, 2014).

7. Bacon, L. (2008). *Health at every size.* Dallas, TX: Banbella; Kluger, J., Aguayo, A. M., August, M., Bower, A., Bowers, P., Cray, D., Dale, S. S., & Locke, L. (2005, June 6). Can you be fat and healthy? *Time,* 165(23), 60–67; Roberts-Grey, G. (2013). Be healthy at every size. *Essence,* 44(3), 84–86.

8. Early critics of the growing fat panic who established the community did go on to create what came to be known as the National Association to Advance Fat Acceptance, which is a bona fade nonprofit "civil rights organization" dedicated to establishing policies and laws to prevent discrimination on the basis of body size. However, while fat acceptance is certainly a mainstream discourse, the organization and its efforts, at least at the time of this writing, remain on the fringes of the broader public consciousness.

9. Bacon (2008). *Health at every size.*

10. Homepage, HAES [website]. http://www.haescommunity.org/. Accessed June 10, 2014.

11. Ibid.

12. Kluger et al. (2005). Can you be fat and healthy?; Bacon (2008). *Health at every size.*

13. Kluger et al. (2005). Can you be fat and healthy?

14. http://www.haescommunity.org. Accessed June 10, 2014.

15. Rabin, R. C. (2008, January 22). In the fatosphere, big is in, or at least accepted. *New York Times.* http://www.nytimes.com/2008/01/22/health/22fblogs.html?_r=0. Accessed June 14, 2014.

16. Henig (2008). Losing the weight stigma.

17. http://www.haescommunity.org/. Accessed June 10, 2014.
18. Rabin (2008). In the fatosphere, big is in, or at least accepted.
19. Ibid.
20. Notably, the logic is obscure: often, the same celebrity is castigated one week for her size and celebrated for it the next, even in the same show, magazine, or website.
21. Adams, R., & Krupnick, E. (2013, December 17). These amazing models shattered body standards in 2013. *Huffington Post*, http://www.huffingtonpost.com/2013/12/17/models-body-image-2013_n_4460732.html. Accessed June 18, 2014; Rice, F. (2013, September 30). 30 inspirational body confidence quotes from women who know what they're talking about. *Marie Claire*, http://www.marieclaire.co.uk/blogs/543637/30-inspirational-celebrity-body-confidence-quotes.html. Accessed June 18, 2014; Schmidt, C. (2014, May 3). Jennifer Lawrence to Lena Dunham. NBC *Today Show*. http://www.today.com/style/jennifer-lawrence-lena-dunham-15-inspiring-celebrity-quotes-about-body-2D79604323. Accessed June 18, 2014; Sy, S., & Hodd, S. (2009, October 1). "'Fat acceptance': Women embrace the F-word." ABC News. http://abcnews.go.com/Nightline/size-model-overweight-women-embraces-curves/story?id=8541567. Accessed June 18, 2014; Wilson, E. (2010, January 13). The triumph of the size 12s. *New York Times*. http://www.nytimes.com/2010/01/14/fashion/14CRYSTAL.html?pagewanted=all&_r=0. Accessed June 18, 2014.
22. Nunez, A. (2011, July 7). Top 10 inspiring quotes from celebrities about working out. *Shape*. http://www.shape.com/celebrities/celebrity-workouts/top-10-inspiring-and-famous-quotes-celebrities-about-working-out. Accessed June 18, 2014.
23. Leyba, C. A. (2013, November 15). 5 fabulous women that embraced their curves. *Marie Claire*. http://www.marieclaire.co.uk/blogs/544919/5-fabulous-women-that-embraced-their-curves.html. Accessed June 18, 2014.
24. Stars' body confidence secrets. (2009, April). *Good Housekeeping, 248*(4), 60.
25. Ibid.
26. Curves rule. (2007, May 7). *People Magazine, 67*(18), 177–182.
27. Rice (2013). 30 inspirational body confidence quotes.
28. Billups, A. (2013, February 8). Mariska Hargitay loves her curves from motherhood. *People Magazine*. http://www.people.com/people/article/0,,20672000,00.html. Accessed June 18, 2014.
29. Jessica Simpson on new baby, weight loss. (2014, January 18). *Good Morning America* [interview], http://gma.yahoo.com/video/jessica-simpson-baby-weight-loss-130250980.html
30. Kate Winslet on 'Titanic 3D' and being a role model. (2011, December 13). *Huffington Post*. http://www.huffingtonpost.com/2011/12/13/kate-winslet-on-titanic-3d_n_1145330.html. Accessed June 18, 2014.
31. Bullock, M. (2012, November). Jennifer Lawrence: Game changer. *Elle*. http://www.elle.com/pop-culture/cover-shoots/jennifer-lawrence-quotes-fashion-photos#slide-1. Accessed June 18, 2014.
32. Amiel, B. (2010, March 22). Confident, truly huge beauties. *Maclean's, 123*(10), 11–12.
33. Sy & Hodd (2009). Fat acceptance.
34. Trout, J. (2014, January 3). Jennifer Lawrence body-shames you more than you might realize. *Huffington Post*. http://www.huffingtonpost.com/jenny-trout/jennifer-lawrence-body-shaming_b_4521379.html. Accessed June 18, 2014.
35. Marcus, S. (2014, May 2). Gabourey Sidibe's speech on confidence is incredibly moving. *Huffington Post*. http://www.huffingtonpost.com/2014/05/02/gabourey-sidibe-confidence-speech_n_5255730.html. Accessed June 18, 2014.
36. Morris, M. (2012, November 12). Why Adele's body image rocks. *Cosmopolitan* http://www.cosmopolitan.com/celebrity/news/adele-body-image. Accessed June 18, 2014.
37. Bertsche, R. (2007, July). Queen Latifah's Aha! moment. *O Magazine*, http://www.oprah.com/spirit/Queen-Latifahs-Aha-Moment. Accessed June 19, 2014.

38. Toomey, A. (2013, June 13). Melissa McCarthy response to Rex Reed's "obese," "hippo" jabs in *Identity Theft* review. *E! News*. http://www.eonline.com/news/429660/melissa-mccarthy-responds-to-rex-reed-s-obese-hippo-jabs-in-identity-theft-review. Accessed June 19, 2014.

39. Melissa McCarthy responds to Rex Reed's cruel comments about her body. (2013, June 13). *Huffington Post*. http://www.huffingtonpost.com/2013/06/13/melissa-mccarthy-rex-reed-response_n_3435596.html. Accessed June 19, 2014.

40. Malkin, M., & Finn, N. (2013, October 21). Melissa McCarthy breaks silence on Elle cover controversy: "I picked the coat!" *E! News*. http://www.eonline.com/news/472687/melissa-mccarthy-breaks-silence-on-elle-cover-controversy-i-picked-the-coat. Accessed June 19, 2014.

41. Toomey, A. (2013, October 18). Covered-up Melissa McCarthy magazine cover draws criticism. *Today Show*. http://www.today.com/entertainment/covered-melissa-mccarthy-magazine-cover-draws-criticism-8C11418627. Accessed June 19, 2014.

42. The Dove® Campaign for Real Beauty. Dove [website]. http://www.dove.us/Social-Mission/campaign-for-real-beauty.aspx. Accessed June 19, 2014.

43. "Dove ads with 'real' women get attention." (2005, August 3). *NBC News*. http://www.nbcnews.com/id/8757597/ns/business-us_business/t/dove-ads-real-women-get-attention/#.U20gNfnwbnM. Accessed June 19, 2014.

44. What's hot. (2005, September 22). *The Oprah Winfrey Show*. http://www.oprah.com/oprahshow/Whats-Hot (5 of 8). Accessed June 19, 2014.

45. Friedman, A. (2013, April 18). Beauty above all else: The problem with Dove's new viral ad. *New York Magazine*. http://nymag.com/thecut/2013/04/beauty-above-all-else-doves-viral-ad-problem.html. Accessed June 19, 2014.

46. Within the broader gay male culture, "bears" constitute a subculture, a community of men who are large and hairy, generally hypermasculine, and vocal about rejecting predominant sensibilities regarding gay male beauty as young, slender, and smooth (hairless). However, because this subculture is not readily available in the mainstream, nor is it centered on obesity or, arguably, overweight (as opposed to large and burly, for instance), it does not feature as part of the fat acceptance discourse of obesity, either as fat fetishism or more broadly.

47. Dying to be the fattest woman. (2011, September 22). *The Dr. Oz Show*, http://www.doctoroz.com/videos/dying-be-fattest-woman-pt-1. Accessed June 19, 2014.

48. I eat 30,000 calories a day!! (2012, May 22). *Dr. Phil*, http://www.youtube.com/watch?v=to7BMBJR9P4. Accessed June 19, 2014.

49. Bering, J. (2013, August 2). Meet the feeders: Getting off by being fat. *Scientific American*. http://scientificamerican.com/bering-in-mind/2013/08/02/meet-the-feeders-getting-off-by-getting-fat/. Accessed June 19, 2014; Moye, D. (2012, May 8). Susanne Eman, 800-pound bride, fitted for world's biggest wedding gown. *Huffington Post*. http://www.huffingtonpost.com/2012/05/07/800-pound-bride-susanne-eman_n_1498377.html. Accessed June 19, 2014; Moye, D. (2013, May 10). Tammy Jung vows to force feed herself to 420 pounds. *Huffington Post*. http://www.huffingtonpost.com/2013/05/10/tammy-jung-force-feeding-_n_3248307.html#slide=1208737. Accessed June 19, 2014.

50. Dying to be the fattest woman. *The Dr. Oz Show*. http://www.doctoroz.com/videos/dying-be-fattest-woman-pt-1. Accessed June 19, 2014.

51. Moye (2013). Tammy Jung vows to force feed herself.

52. Ibid.

53. Dying to be the fattest woman." *The Dr. Oz Show*. http://www.doctoroz.com/videos/dying-be-fattest-woman-pt-2.

54. Ibid., part 3. http://www.doctoroz.com/videos/dying-be-fattest-woman-pt-3.

55. Ibid., part 1. http://www.doctoroz.com/videos/dying-be-fattest-woman-pt-1.

56. Ibid., parts 4/5. http://www.doctoroz.com/videos/dying-be-fattest-woman-pt-4/5.

57. Bordo (1993). *Unbearable weight*; LeBesco (2004). *Revolting bodies*; Shugart, H. A. (2014). Flesh made word: The obese body as cultural matter. *Communication, Culture, and Critique*, 7(1), 55–75.

58. Moye (2013), Tammy Jung vows to force feed herself.
59. "Dying to be the fattest woman." *The Dr. Oz Show.* http://www.doctoroz.com/videos/ dying-be-fattest-woman-pt-1.
60. Bordo (1993). *Unbearable weight*; Hester, J. (2009). Feast of burden. *Bitch Magazine, 44*, 37–53.
61. Sawer, M. (1996). Gender, metaphor and the state. *Feminist Review, 52*, 118–134.
62. Coveney, J. (2011). In praise of hunger: Public health and the problem of excess. In K. Bell, D. McNaughton, & A. Salmon (Eds.), *Alcohol, tobacco and obesity: Morality, mortality and the new public health* (pp. 146–160). London: Routledge.
63. Jaslow, R. (2013, April 11). NYC soda ban would lead customers to consume more sugary drinks, study suggests. *CBS News.* http://www.cbsnews.com/news/nyc-soda-ban-would-lead-customers-to-consume-more-sugary-drinks-study-suggests/. Accessed June 19, 2014.
64. Harned, K. (2013, May 10). The Michael Bloomberg nanny state in New York: A cautionary tale. *Forbes Magazine.* http://www.forbes.com/sites/realspin/2013/05/10/ the-michael-bloomberg-nanny-state-in-new-york-a-cautionary-tale/. Accessed June 19, 2014.
65. Roff, P. (2013, May 3). Bloomberg pizza satire hits too close to home. *U.S. News & World Report.* http://www.usnews.com/opinion/blogs/peter-roff/2013/05/03/bloombergs-food-policing-is-out-of-control. Accessed June 19, 2014.
66. Buckley, C. (2013, March 11). Cheering a setback to the city's drink limits. *New York Times.* http://www.nytimes.com/2013/03/12/nyregion/many-in-ny-say-good-riddance-to-big-soda-ban.html
67. Medina, J. (2011, January 15). In South Los Angeles, new fast-food spots get a "No, thanks." *New York Times.* http://www.nytimes.com/2011/01/16/us/16fastfood.html. Accessed June 19, 2014.
68. Lusk, J. (2013, May 6). Viewpoint: The new food police are out of touch. *Time.* http:// ideas.time.com/2013/05/06/viewpoint-the-new-food-police-are-out-of-touch/. Accessed June 19, 2014.
69. Nerz, R. (2006). *Eat this book.* New York: St. Martin's Press.
70. Fagone, J. (2006, May 1). Horsemen of the esophagus. *The Atlantic.* http://www.theatlantic.com/magazine/archive/2006/05/horsemen-of-the-esophagus/304808/?single_ page=true. Accessed June 19, 2014.
71. Finkel, J. (2009, Jun). All you can eat. *Muscle and Fitness 70*(6), 288.
72. Fagone (2006). Horsemen of the esophagus.
73. Ibid.
74. Some find competitive eating hard to swallow. (2007, November 21). *NBC News.* http:// www.nbcnews.com/id/21915036/ns/health-behavior/t/some-find-competitive-eating-hard-swallow/#.U0rfGfnwbnN. Accessed June 19, 2014.
75. Berl, R. P. (2013, July 5). Joey Chestnut on putting away 69 hot dogs in 10 minutes. *U.S. News & World Report.* http://health.usnews.com/health-news/health-wellness/ articles/2013/07/05/hot-dog-champ-joey-chesnut-and-the-risks-of-competitive-eating. Accessed June 19, 2014.
76. Some find competitive eating hard to swallow. (2007).
77. Park, M. (2009, July 3). Speed eaters gain weight, clog arteries but have few regrets. *CNN News.* http://www.cnn.com/2009/HEALTH/07/03/competitive.eating.stomach/ index.html?eref=ib_us/ Accessed June 19, 2014.
78. Thielman, S. (2012, August 3). Ad of the day: Southern Comfort struts out first work from Weiden + Kennedy. *Adweek,* http://www.adweek.com/news/advertising-branding/ad-day-southern-comfort-142444. Accessed June 19, 2014.
79. Heart Attack Grill (homepage). (n.d.). http://www.heartattackgrill.com/heart-attack-grill.html. Accessed June 19, 2014.
80. Ibid.

81. "Obese model pitches 'Heart Attack Grill.'" (2010, November 15). *ABC News*, http://abcnews.go.com/Health/video/obese-spokesmodel-promotes-heart-attack-grill-12153251. Accessed June 19, 2014.

82. Brayton, S. (2007). MTV's Jackass: Transgression, abjection and the economy of white masculinity. *Journal of Gender Studies, 16,* 57–72; Kusz, K. (2003). BMX, extreme sports, and the white male backlash. In R. E. Rinehart & S. Sydnor (Eds.), *To the extreme: Alternative sports, inside and out* (pp. 153–175). Albany: State University of New York Press; Savran, D. (1996). The sadomasochist in the closet: White masculinity and the culture of victimization. *Differences: A Journal of Feminist Cultural Studies, 8,* 127–152.

83. Phillipov, M. (2013). Resisting health: Extreme food and the culinary abject. *Critical Studies in Media Communication, 30*(5), 385.

84. I had anticipated that the broader resistive discourse would include a third variation, specifically as relevant to race/ethnicity, along the lines apparent in the "obesity as culture" discourse but in valorizing rather than castigating terms. That is, I had expected to find considerable mainstream fare that suggested that women and/or men of color who carry excess weight are resistive to white normative aesthetics and actualize cultural/race/ethnic identity and pride. Although I did find some data that clearly reflects these sentiments, and while a number of off-hand or passing remarks are available in popular media that reference, for instance, the purported predilection of men of color for "thick" women and/or the propensity of women of color to have "junk in the trunk," they were not sufficient, on the whole, to suggest a cohesive or substantial mainstream (sub)discourse.

## Chapter 8

1. Baudrillard, J. (1983a). *Simulations.* New York: Semiotext(e); Best, S. & Kellner, D. (1999). Debord, cybersituations, and the interactive spectacle. *Substance: A Review of Theory and Literary Criticism, 28*(3), 129–156; Debord, G. (1976). *The society of the spectacle.* Detroit: Black and Red.

2. McCrady, R. (2014, 8 April). Kim Kardashian parades her booty around in nude-toned bikini photoshoot. *US Weekly.* http://www.usmagazine.com/celebrity-body/news/kim-kardashian-booty-bikini-photoshoot-pictures-201484. Accessed July 20, 2014; Thompson, E. (2014, February 11). You have to see Kim Kardashian's ass in this photo. *Cosmopolitan.* http://www.cosmopolitan.com/celebrity/news/kim-kardashian-pants. Accessed July 20, 2014; Wilkinson, I. (2013, March 27). Pregnant Kim Kardashian is being fat shamed, and it needs to stop. *Daily Beast.* http://www.thedailybeast.com/articles/2013/03/27/pregnant-kim-kardashian-is-being-fat-shamed-and-it-needs-to-stop.html. Accessed July 20, 2014.

3. Khloe Kardashian sick of being called a sasquatch! She's not fat! 2011, April 27). *Hollywood Life.* http://hollywoodlife.com/2011/04/27/khloe-kardashian-bullied-for-her-weight-and-how-mom-kris-goes-after-her-even-when-cameras-stop-rolling/. Accessed July 20, 2014; Khloe Kardashian on fat shaming. (2013, 1 May). *Examiner.* http://www.examiner.com/article/kourtney-kardashian-on-fat-shaming-i-don-t-think-i-m-prettier-thinner. Accessed July 20, 2014.

4. Fat shaming shockers: How these 10 celebrities fought back" (2014, April 26). *Extra.* http://www.extratv.com/2014/04/26/fat-shaming-celebrities-chrissy-teigen-kim-kardashian-jennifer-lawrence-fought-back/. Accessed July 20, 2014.

5. Critics of opera singer Tara Erraught under fire after fat shaming. (2014, May 28). *Time,* http://time.com/110272/fat-shaming-tara-erraught/. Accessed July 20, 2014.

6. Ekberg, A. (2013, April 1). Adele weight jab. *Yahoo Celebrity.* https://celebrity.yahoo.com/news/adele-weight-jab-joan-rivers-other-celebs-fat-195300132.html.    Accessed July 20, 2014.

7. Monde, C. (2013, April). Joan Rivers sticks to "fat" Adele comments after singer demands apology. *New York Daily News.* commentshttp://www.nydailynews.com/entertainment/gossip/joan-rivers-sticks-fat-adele-comments-article-1.1304702. Accessed July 20, 2014.

8. Tan, M. (2009, June 22). I'm sick of being big. *People Magazine.* http://www.people.com/people/archive/article/0,,20287201,00.html. Accessed July 20, 2014.

9. Bahadur, N. (2013, February 7). Haley Morris-Cafiero, photographer, explores fat stigma in "Wait Watchers" series. *Huffington Post.* http://www.huffingtonpost.com/2013/02/07/haley-morris-cafiero-photographer-wait-watchers-fat-acceptance-weight-stigma_n_2631439.html.

10. Hawksworth, W. (2013, October 18). What it's really like to live as a fat person every day. *Huffington Post.* http://www.huffingtonpost.ca/elizabeth-hawksworth/being-overweight_b_4116510.html. Accessed July 20, 2014.

11. Trout, J. (2014, January 3). Jennifer Lawrence body shames more than you might realize. *Huffington Post.* http://www.huffingtonpost.com/jenny-trout/jennifer-lawrence-body-shaming_b_4521379.html. Accessed July 20, 2014.

12. Hawksworth (2013). What it's really like to live as a fat person.

13. Neporent, L. (2013, January 22). Stigma against fat people the last prejudice, study finds. *Good Morning America.* http://abcnews.go.com/Health/stigma-obese-acceptable-prejudice/story?id=18276788. Accessed July 20, 2014.

14. Morris-Cafiero, H. (2013, April 23). Pictures of people who mock me. *Salon.com.*http://www.salon.com/2013/04/23/pictures_of_people_who_mock_me/. Accessed July 20, 2014.

15. Gilman, S. L. (2008). *Fat: A cultural history of obesity.* Cambridge, UK: Polity; LeBesco, K. (2004). *Revolting bodies? The struggle to redefine fat identity.* Amherst, MA: University of Massachusetts; Levy-Navarro, E. (2008). *The culture of obesity in early and late modernity.* New York: Palgrave Macmillan; Saguy, A. C. (2013). *What's wrong with fat?* New York: Oxford University Press; Schwarz, H. (1986). *Never satisfied: A cultural history of diets, fantasies, and fat.* New York: Free Press.

16. "Anorexia nervosa. (2014). Wikipedia. http://en.wikipedia.org/wiki/Anorexia_nervosa; Accessed July 20, 2014; Eating disorders. (2011). National Institute of Mental Health. http://www.nimh.nih.gov/health/publications/eating-disorders/index.shtml. Accessed July 20, 2014.

17. Anorexia sites draw criticism from psychiatrists. (2009, November 18). *Huffington Post.* http://www.huffingtonpost.com/2009/09/19/anorexia-sites-draw-criti_n_291693.html. Accessed July 20, 2014; Norris, M. L., Boydell, K. M., Pinhas, L., & Katzman, D. K. (2006). Ana and the internet: A review of pro-anorexia websites. *International Journal of Eating Disorders, 39*(6), 443–447.

18. When your body is your cage . . . Ana can be the key to your freedom! Missanamia [website]. http://missanamia.wordpress.com/motivation/. Accessed July 20, 2014.

19. One thing that has disgusted you today. [Forum Thread.] (2013, April 3 [started]). MyProAna [website]. http://www.myproana.com/index.php/topic/5781-one-thing-that-has-disgusted-you-today/. Accessed July 20, 2014.

20. Ibid.

21. Ibid.

22. Opinions on fat people—be honest! [Forum Thread.] (2013, April 3 [started]). MyProAna [website]. http://www.myproana.com/index.php/topic/5746-opinions-on-fat-people-be-honest/. Accessed July 20, 2014.

23. Ibid.

24. Carroll, J. (2005, August 9). Who's worried about their weight? *Gallup,* http://www.gallup.com/poll/17752/whos-worried-about-their-weight.aspx. Accessed July 20, 2014.

25. Diet inspiration. Pinterest [message board]. http://www.pinterest.com/helenhirst/diet-inspiration/. Accessed July 20, 2014.

26. Magno, M. (2011, September). "I did it!" Best before and after weight-loss stories. *Fitness.* http://www.fitnessmagazine.com/weight-loss/success-stories/makeovers/i-did-it-best-before-and-after-weight-loss-stories/#page=3. Accessed July 20, 2014.

27. Before and after fat loss pics. (2014). Tumblr [website], http://beforeandafterfatlosspics.tumblr.com/image/90694163242. Accessed July 20, 2014.

28. Rizzo, M. (2009, April 13). How I let myself go. *People Magazine.* http://www.people.com/people/archive/article/0,,20271043,00.html. Accessed July 20, 2014.

29. I'm fatter than my husband. (2011, October 20). *Marie Claire.* http://www.marieclaire.com/sex-love/relationship-issues/weight-gain-after-marriage. Accessed July 20, 2014.

30. Obese in America. (2014). MSN. http://healthyliving.msn.com/weight-loss/obese-in-america#6. Accessed July 20, 2014.

31. Neporent, L. (2013, September 25). Confessions of a temporarily fat yogi. *ABC News.* http://abcnews.go.com/blogs/health/2013/09/25/confessions-of-a-temporarily-fat-yogi/. Accessed July 20, 2014.

32. Dr. Oz: The bigger you are the more invisible you are. (2014, February 2). *Morning Joe,* MSNBC. http://www.msnbc.com/morning-joe/watch/dr-oz-being-overweight-makes-you-invisible-145565763811. Accessed July 20, 2014.

33. Being invisible [Forum thread]. (2007, July 28 [started]. Jenny Craig [website]. http://community.jennycraig.com/index.php/topic/40921-being-invisible/. Accessed July 20, 2014.

34. We're fat not invisible. (2014). Pinterest [message board]. http://www.pinterest.com/helenhirst/diet-inspiration/. Accessed July 20, 2014.

35. Kristjansson, M. (2014). *The fat body (in)visible* [documentary]. http://www.fatbodyinvisible.com/. Accessed July 20, 2014.

36. Fat, furious, and fed up. (2014, April 4). *Dr. Phil.* http://www.drphil.com/shows/show/2145. Accessed July 20, 2014.

37. Season 2, Episode 7. (2005). *The Biggest Loser,* NBC. http://www.youtube.com/watch?v=SkXd8W5HRTk. Accessed July 20, 2014.

38. Gibbons, B. (2013, February 2). Fat shaming doesn't work—here's why. *Huffington Post.* http://www.huffingtonpost.com/brittany-gibbons/fat-shaming_b_2584298.html. Accessed July 20, 2014.

39. Katz, D. L. (2012, September 13). We're not fat because we're lazy. *U.S. News & World Report.* http://health.usnews.com/health-news/blogs/eat-run/2012/09/13/were-not-fat-because-were-lazy. Accessed July 20, 2014.

40. Jacobs, T. (2014, February 26). America's obesity cure: Laziness? *Salon.com.* http://www.salon.com/2014/02/26/americas_obesity_cure_laziness_partner/. Accessed July 20, 2014; Melnick, M. (2011, March 31). Global spread: More people think "fat people are lazy." *Time.* http://healthland.time.com/2011/03/31/global-spread-more-people-think-fat-people-are-lazy/. Accessed July 20, 2014.

41. Hawksworth (2013). What it's really like to live as a fat person.

42. Cohen, A. (2011, August 8). Big, fat stereotypes play out on the small screen. *NPR Morning Edition.* http://www.npr.org/2011/08/08/138958386/big-fat-stereotypes-play-out-on-the-small-screen. Accessed July 20, 2014.

43. The most inspiring weight-loss success stories of 2013. (2013, December 23). *Shape.* http://www.shape.com/weight-loss/success-stories/most-inspiring-weight-loss-success-stories-2013/slide/4. Accessed July 20, 2014.

44. Paying it forward (success stories). (2014). Weight Watchers [website].http://www.weightwatchers.com/success/art/index.aspx?SuccessStoryId=19961&sc=17. Accessed July 20, 2014.

45. 10 most inspiring success stories. (2013, May 28). *Oxygen.* http://www.oxygenmag.com/slideshow/10-most-inspiring-success-stories/4/. Accessed July 20, 2014.

46. E.g., 5 fitness apps to get you off the couch. (2011, January 3). *Time.* http://healthland.time.com/2011/01/03/5-fitness-apps-to-get-you-off-the-couch. Accessed July 20, 2014;

17 reasons to get off the couch." (2012, December). *Prevention*. http://www.prevention.com/health/healthy-living/17-ways-exercise-sends-health-soaring. Accessed July 20, 2014; Hobson, K. (2009, May 14). 10-week workout. *U.S. News & World Report* http://health.usnews.com/health-news/blogs/on-fitness/2009/05/14/10-week-workout-6-ways-to-motivate-yourself-up-off-the-couch. Accessed July 20, 2014. Joel Harper's get off the sofa workout. (2010, August 19). *The Dr. Oz Show* http://www.doctoroz.com/videos/joel-harpers-get-sofa-workout. Accessed July 20, 2014; Trotter, K. (2012, December 11). Getting off the couch and in workout mode. *Huffington Post*. http://www.huffingtonpost.ca/kathleen-trotter/motivating-yourself-to-exercise_b_2115311.html. Accessed July 20, 2014.

47. Neporent (2013). Stigma against fat people the last prejudice.

48. Dolgoff, S. (2013). What is your weight destiny? *Fitness Magazine*. http://www.fitness-magazine.com/weight-loss/tips/diet-tips/control-weight-destiny/. Accessed July 20, 2014; Exercise helps fight obesity gene. (2011, November 1). *Health*. http://news.health.com/2011/11/01/exercise-obesity-gene/. Accessed July 20, 2014; Reynolds, G. (2012, January 11). Exercise hormone may fight obesity and diabetes. *New York Times*. http://well.blogs.nytimes.com/2012/01/11/exercise-hormone-helps-keep-us-healthy/?_php=true&_type=blogs&_r=0. Accessed July 20, 2014.

49. 12 ways to trick yourself healthy. (2014). *MSN Healthy Living*. http://healthyliving.msn.com/health-wellness/12-ways-to-trick-yourself-healthy. Accessed July 20, 2014; Dreisbach, S. (2014, January 24). Body by *Glamour*: 5 ways to fool yourself into exercising. *Glamour*. http://www.glamour.com/health-fitness/blogs/vitamin-g/2014/01/5-ways-to-fool-yourself-into-e.html; MacMillan, A. (2013, September 29). How to become an exercise addict. ABC News. http://abcnews.go.com/Health/Wellness/exercise-addict/story?id=20397942#11. Accessed July 20, 2014; Pifer, E. (2014, June 29). 5 ways to trick yourself into getting out of bed for a morning workout. *Women's Health*. http://www.womenshealthmag.com/fitness/early-morning-workout-motivation. Accessed July 20, 2014.

50. Soong, J. (2014). 7 habits of highly effective exercisers. *Fitness* .http://www.fitnessmagazine.com/workout/motivation/habits-of-effective-exercisers/. Accessed July 20, 2014; Thore, K. (2013, May 3). How to work out when you totally don't want to. *Women's Health*. http://www.womenshealthmag.com/fitness/gym-motivation-strategies. Accessed July 20, 2014.

51. Turits, M. (2014). How to convince yourself to work out when you so don't want to. *Glamour*. http://www.glamour.com/health-fitness/2012/09/how-to-convince-yourself-to-work-out-when-you-dont-want-to/7. Accessed July 20, 2014.

52. Nodecker, N. (2014). Pamper yourself: 12 post-workout treats. Weight Watchers [website]. http://www.weightwatchers.com/util/art/index_art.aspx?tabnum=1&art_id=32521&sc=113. Accessed July 20, 2014.

53. Healthy weight: It's not a diet, it's a lifestyle! (2014). CDC, http://www.cdc.gov/healthy-weight/calories/. Accessed July 20, 2014.

54. What causes overweight and obesity? (2012). National Institutes of Health. http://www.nhlbi.nih.gov/health/health-topics/topics/obe/causes.html. Accessed July 20, 2014.

55. Datar, A., & Nicosia, N. (2012). Junk food in schools and childhood obesity. *Journal of Policy Analysis and Management, 31*(2), 213–337.

56. Srirachapea. (2012, November 28). (Personal post). Fat is not attractive. Tumblr [website]. http://fatisnotattractive.tumblr.com/. Accessed July 24, 2014.

57. Rovzar, C. (2010, December). Woman eats 30,000 calories for Christmas meal. *New York Magazine*. http://nymag.com/daily/intelligencer/2010/12/woman_eats_30000_for_christmas.html. Accessed July 24, 2014; World's Biggest Bride: Confessions of a Morbidly Obese Woman. (2012, May 22). *Dr Phil*. http://www.drphil.com/shows/show/1857. Accessed July 24, 2014.

58. Gammon, A. (2011, September). Our most inspiring before and after weight-loss photos (Amanda Fulfer). *Shape*. http://www.shape.com/weight-loss/success-stories/our-most-inspiring-after-weight-loss-photos/slide/2. Accessed July 24, 2014.

59. Nelson, S. C. (2013, March 13). Wendy Phillips admits "I'm too fat to work." *Huffington Post*. http://www.huffingtonpost.co.uk/2013/03/13/30st-wendy-phillips-admits-im-too-fat-to-work-wont-lose-weight-nhs-gastric-band_n_2866131.html. Accessed July 24, 2014.

60. Spencer, M. (2003, April 12). I'm fat, I'm greedy, and I'm fabulous. *The Guardian*. http://www.theguardian.com/lifeandstyle/2003/apr/13/foodanddrink.features7. Accessed July 24, 2014.

61. Katrandjian, O. 2011, February 3). Can't beat the fat and sugar cravings? Four steps to help you kick your addiction. *Good Morning America*, ABC News. http://abcnews.go.com/GMA/dr-mehmet-oz-beat-fat-sugar-addiction-detox/story?id=12823912. Accessed July 24, 2014.

62. Kelly, M. (2011). Is your appetite out of control? *Fitness Magazine*. http://www.fitness-magazine.com/weight-loss/eating-help/control-cravings/appetite-out-of-control/. Accessed July 24, 2014.

63. Anonymous. (2005, August). Overeaters anonymous: One food addict's spiritual cure. *O Magazine*. http://www.oprah.com/health/Control-Food-Cravings-How-to-Stop-Overeating. Accessed July 24, 2014.

64. Sole-Smith, V. (2011). Control your cravings for good. *Fitness Magazine*. http://www.fitness-magazine.com/weight-loss/eating-help/control-cravings/how-to-control-cravings/. Accessed July 24, 2014.

65. McIndoo, H. R. (2011, November). 6 ways to stop overeating. *Prevention*. http://www.prevention.com/weight-loss/weight-loss-tips/tips-how-stop-overeating. Accessed July 24, 2014.

66. Peeke, P. M. (2012, October 26). 7 ways to beat your food addiction. Fox News. http://www.foxnews.com/health/2012/10/25/6-ways-to-beat-your-food-addiction/. Accessed July 28, 2014.

67. Hyman, M. (2014, January). Food addiction: Could it explain why 70% of Americans are fat? Dr. Hyman.com [website]. http://drhyman.com/blog/2011/02/04/food-addiction-could-it-explain-why-70-percent-of-america-is-fat/. Accessed July 28 2014; also Moss, M. (2013). *Salt, sugar, fat: How the food giants hooked us*. New York: Random House.

68. Hyman, M. (2014, 1 Apr). Confessions of a food addict. *Huffington Post*. http://www.huffingtonpost.com/dr-mark-hyman/food-addict_b_4679723.html. Accessed July 28, 2014.

69. Anonymous (2005). Overeaters anonymous.

70. Marier, M. (2010, June 11). The fat diaries: Confessions of a food addict. Frum Forum [website]. http://www.frumforum.com/the-fat-diaries-confessions-of-a-food-addict/. Accessed July 28, 2014.

71. Brodesser-Akner, T. (2012, October 18). Confessions of a food addict. *Self*. http://www.self.com/life/health/2012/10/food-addict-confessions/. Accessed July 28, 2014.

72. Angilella, J. (2010, November 8). How I gained control over my food addiction. *Huffington Post*. http://www.huffingtonpost.com/jan-angilella/food-addiction-how-i-rega_b_780080.html. Accessed July 28, 2014.

73. Eller, D. (2011, November). Are you addicted to food? *Prevention*. http://www.prevention.com/weight-loss/weight-loss-tips/how-beat-food-addiction?page=5. Accessed July 28, 2014.

74. Kelly, D. (2013, November). The 25 best diet tips of all time. *Prevention*. http://www.prevention.com/weight-loss/diets/25-best-weight-loss-tips-ever?s=2. Accessed July 30, 2014.

75. Ruderman, Z. (2010, May 24). The 10 best weight loss tips ever. *Cosmopolitan*. http://www.cosmopolitan.com/health-fitness/advice/a3223/10-best-weight-loss-tips-ever-0809/. Accessed July 30, 2014.

76. The 25 best diet tricks of all time. (2014). *Health*. http://www.health.com/health/gallery/0,,20645166_16,00.html. Accessed July 30, 2014.

77. Bedwell, S.-J. (2013, January 9). 3 reasons why you should drink a glass of water before each meal. *Self.* http://www.self.com/flash/health-blog/2013/01/3-reasons-to-drink-water-before-each-meal/. Accessed July 30, 2014.

78. Rossen, J., & Davis, J. (2014, April 22). Experts say you can trick your mind into helping you lose weight. *Today Show*, NBC. http://www.today.com/news/experts-say-you-can-trick-your-mind-helping-you-lose-2D12178338. Accessed July 30, 2014; also Pincott, J. (2013, April 29). Diet strategies: Trick your brain so you actually want to eat less. *Huffington Post* http://www.huffingtonpost.com/2013/04/29/diet-strategies-eat-less-weight-loss-tips_n_3132291.html. Accessed July 30, 2014.

79. Haller, M. (2012, May). 4 simple tricks to eat less. *Prevention*. http://www.prevention.com/food/healthy-eating-tips/trick-yourself-eating-less. Accessed July 30, 2014.

80. Hiatt, K. (2010, November 22). 6 ways to trick yourself into eating fruits and veggies. *U.S. News & World Report*. http://health.usnews.com/health-news/diet-fitness/diet/articles/2010/11/22/6-ways-to-trick-yourself-into-eating-fruits-and-veggies. Accessed July 30, 2014.

## Chapter 9

1. Butler, J. (1990). *Gender trouble: Feminism and the subversion of identity.* New York: Routledge; Butler, J. (1993). *Bodies that matter: On the discursive limits of "sex."* New York: Routledge; Lupton, D. (2012). *Medicine as culture: Illness, disease, and the body.* London: Sage; Foucault, M. (1977). *Discipline and punish: The birth of the prison.* New York: Pantheon; Foucault, M. (1979). *The history of sexuality, volume one: An introduction.* London: Penguin; Turner, B. (1996). The body and society: Explorations in social theory (2nd ed). London: Sage.

2. Rothfield, P. (1992). Backstage in the theatre of representation. *Arena* 99/100: 98–111; Shilling, C. (1991). Educating the body: Physical capital and the production of social inequalities. *Sociology*, 25(4), 653–72.

3. Haraway, D. (1989). The biopolitics of postmodern bodies: Determinations of self in immune system discourse. *Differences*, 1(1), 3–44.

4. Frank, A. (1990). Bringing bodies back in. *Theory, Culture, and Society*, 7(1), 131–62.

5. Butler (1990). *Gender trouble.*

6. Turner (1996). The body and society.

7. Foucault (1979). *The history of sexuality, volume one.*

# References

5 fitness apps to get you off the couch. (2011, January 3). *Time*. http://healthland.time.com/2011/01/03/5-fitness-apps-to-get-you-off-the-couch.

10 most inspiring success stories. (2013, May 28). *Oxygen*. http://www.oxygenmag.com/slideshow/10-most-inspiring-success-stories/4/.

12 ways to trick yourself healthy. (2014). MSN *Healthy Living*. http://healthyliving.msn.com/health-wellness/12-ways-to-trick-yourself-healthy.

17 reasons to get off the couch. (2012, December). *Prevention*. http://www.prevention.com/health/healthy-living/17-ways-exercise-sends-health-soaring.

24Hour Fitness. (2013). http://www.24hourfitness.com/company/press_room/press_releases/2010/20100209.html.

A heavy burden. (2012, December 15). *Economist*, *405*(8815), 7–9.

A true place. (2012, October). *American History*, 25.

Abend, L. (2009, December 1). In Spain, taking some joy out of the happy meal. *Time*. http://www.time.com/time/world/article/0,8599,1943119,00.html.

Adams, R., & Krupnick, E. (2013, December 17). These amazing models shattered body standards in 2013. *Huffington Post*. http://www.huffingtonpost.com/2013/12/17/models-body-image-2013_n_4460732.html.

Adato, A., &Wihlborg, U. (2005, March 7). Mother nurture. *People Magazine*, *63*(9), 104–108.

Adult obesity facts. (2012). Centers for Disease Control. http://www.cdc.gov/obesity/data/adult.html.

Adult obesity rates. (2012).The Robert Wood Johnson Foundation. http://www.rwjf.org/en/about-rwjf/newsroom/newsroom-content/2012/09/adult-obesity-rates-could-exceed-60-percent-in-13-states-by-2030.html.

Agne, A., Daubert, R., Munoz, M., Scarinci, I., & Cherrington, A. L. (2012). The cultural context of obesity: Exploring perceptions of obesity and weight loss among Latina immigrants. *Journal of Immigrant and Minority Health*, *14*(5), 1063–1070.

Aikins, S. K. (2009). Political economy of government intervention in the free market system. *Administrative Theory and Praxis*, *31*(3), 403–408.

Albers, S. (2010). Tips to stop emotional eating. *The Dr. Oz Show* [website]. http://www.doctoroz.com/videos/tips-stop-emotional-eating.

Alderman, L. (2010, February 13). When children are overweight, changes for the whole family. *New York Times*, A5.

Aleccia, J. (2008, November 12). Obese kids have middle-aged arteries. *Newsweek*, http://www.newsweek.com/id/168702.

Alfano, S. (2009, February 11). Bulge battles. CBS News. http://www.cbsnews.com/stories/2005/11/16/eveningnews/main1051146.shtml?tag=mncol;lst;1.

Amiel, B. (2010, March 22). Confident, truly huge beauties. *Maclean's, 123*(10), 11–12.

Angier, N. (2010, November 7). Who is fat? It depends on culture. *New York Times,* http://www.nytimes.com/2010/11/07/science/who-is-fat-it-depends-onculture. html?pagewanted=all&src=pm.

Angilella, J. (2010, November 8). How I gained control over my food addiction. *Huffington Post.* http://www.huffingtonpost.com/jan-angilella/food-addiction-how-i-rega_b_780080. html.

Anonymous. (2005, August). Overeaters anonymous: One food addict's spiritual cure. *O Magazine.* http://www.oprah.com/health/Control-Food-Cravings-How-to-Stop-Overeating.

Anorexia nervosa. (2014). Wikipedia. http://en.wikipedia.org/wiki/Anorexia_nervosa.

Anorexia sites draw criticism from psychiatrists. (2009, November 18). *Huffington Post.* http://www.huffingtonpost.com/2009/09/19/anorexia-sites-draw-criti_n_291693.html.

Arumugam, N. (2013, June 12). Indulging in unhealthy pregnancy cravings can turn babies into junk food junkies. *Forbes.* http://www.forbes.com/sites/nadiaarumugam/2013/06/21/ indulging-in-unhealthy-pregnancy-cravings-can-turn-babies-into-junk-food-junkies/.

Arundel, A. (2003, August 28). A healthful approach to school food: Creative efforts help trim the fat. *Washington Post,* T03.

Bacha, F., Saad, R., Gungor, N., Janosky, J., & Arslanian, S. A. (2003). Obesity, regional fat distribution, and syndrome X in obese black versus white adolescents: Race differential indiabetogenic and artherogenic risk factors. *Journal of Clinical Endocrinology and Metabolism, 88*(6), 2534–2540.

Bachman, C. M., Baranowski, T., & Nicklas, T. A. (2006). Is there an association between sweetened beverages and adiposity? *Nutritional Review,* 64, 153–174.

Bacon, L. (2008). *Health at every size.* Dallas, TX: Banbella.

Bad news. (2013, July 8). *Maclean's, 126*(25), 1.

Bahadur, N. (2013, February 7). Haley Morris-Cafiero, photographer, explores fat stigma in "Wait Watchers" series. *Huffington Post.* http://www.huffingtonpost.com/2013/02/07/ haley-morris-cafiero-photographer-wait-watchers-fat-acceptance-weight-stigma_n_ 2631439.html.

Bahadur, N. (2014, November 5). Haley-Morris' stunning photographs show the strange looks an overweight woman receives in public. *Huffington Post.* http://www.huffingtonpost. com/2014/11/05/haley-morris-cafiero-wait-watchers_n_6108498.html.

Bahrampour, T. (2009, September 4). Sons of immigrants have high obesity levels, report finds. *Washington Post,* A14.

Bailey, F., & Barbato, R. (Producers). (2010). *Carnie Wilson unstapled* [television series]. Los Angeles, CA: World of Wonder Productions.

Baillie-Hamilton, P. F. (2002). Chemical toxins: A hypothesis to explain the global obesity epidemic. *Journal of Alternative and Complementary Medicine, 8*(2), 185–192.

Bakalar, N. (2008, September 15). I think, therefore I am fat? *New York Times.* http://www.nytimes. com/2008/09/16/health/research/16beha.html?_r=1&scp=88&sq=obesity&st=nyt.

Baldwin, D. A. (Ed.). (1993). *Neorealism and neoliberalism: The contemporary debate.* New York: Columbia University Press.

Ball, A. L. (2007, June 1). Journey to the center of yourself. *O, The Oprah Magazine,* 8, 196.

Barillas, W. (1996). Aldo Leopold and midwestern pastoralism. *American Studies, 37*(2), 61–82.

Barnett, A. D. (2011). Everything in moderation. *Ebony, 67*(1), 18.

Barron, J. (2008, August 17). Restaurants must post calories, judge affirms. *New York Times.* http://www.nytimes.com/2008/04/17/nyregion/17calorie.html?_r=1&scp=99&sq= obesity&st=nyt.

Barry, A., Osborne, T., & Rose, N. (Eds.). (1996). *Foucault and political reason: Liberalism, neoliberalism and rationalities of government.* Chicago: University of Chicago Press.

Barry, C. L., Brescoll, V. L., Brownell, K. D., & Schlesinger, M. (2009). Obesity metaphors: How beliefs about the causes of obesity affect support for public policy. *The Milbank Quarterly,* 87, 7–47.

Baudrillard, J. (1983a). *Simulations*. New York: Semiotext(e).

Baum, M. A., & Jamison, A. S. (2006). The Oprah effect: How soft news helps inattentive citizens vote consistently. *Journal of Politics, 68*(4), 946–959.

Beddoes, Z. M. (2010). Creating financial harmony: What role for government versus the market? *CATO Journal, 30*(2), 259–264.

Bedwell, S.-J. (2014). Three reasons why you should drink a glass of water before each meal. *Self*. http://www.self.com/flash/health-blog/2013/01/3-reasons-to-drink-water-before-each-meal/.

Before and after fat loss pics. (2014). *Tumblr* [website]. http://beforeandafterfatlosspics.tumblr.com/image/90694163242.

Beghin, H. C., Jensen, H. H. (2008). Farm policies and added sugars in U.S. diets. *Food Policy, 3*, 480–488.

Begley, S. (2009a, January 17). The sins of the fathers, take two. *Newsweek*. http://www.newsweek.com/id/180103.

Begley, S. (2009b, September 21). Born to be big: Early exposure to common chemicals may be programming kids to be fat. *Newsweek, 57*.

Begley, S. (2013, March). The war on bugs. *Saturday Evening Post, 285*(2), 58–61.

Being invisible [Forum thread]. (2007, July 28 [started]). Jenny Craig. http://community.jennycraig.com/index.php/topic/40921-being-invisible/.

Belluz, J. (2010, October 25). The healing power of groceries. *Maclean's, 123*(41), 56–56.

Belluz, J. (2011). What you need is a beautiful bento lunch. *Maclean's, 123*(3), 64.

Berg, C. R. (2002). *Latino images in film: Stereotypes, subversion, resistance*. Austin, TX: University of Texas.

Bering, J. (2013, August 2). Meet the feeders: Getting off by being fat. *Scientific American*. http://scientificamerican.com/bering-in-mind/2013/08/02/meet-the-feeders-getting-off-by-getting-fat/.

Berl, R. P. (2013, July 5). Joey Chestnut on putting away 69 hot dogs in 10 minutes. *U.S. News & World Report*. http://health.usnews.com/health-news/health-wellness/articles/2013/07/05/hot-dog-champ-joey-chesnut-and-the-risks-of-competitive-eating.

Berry, C. (2000). *Southern migrants, northern exiles*. Urbana, IL: University of Illinois Press.

Bertsche, R. (2007, July). Queen Latifah's aha! moment. *O Magazine*. http://www.oprah.com/spirit/Queen-Latifahs-Aha-Moment.

Best, S., & Kellner, D. (1999). Debord, cybersituations, and the interactive spectacle. *Substance: A Review of Theory and Literary Criticism, 28*(3), 129–156.

Bikini body workout. (2011, June). *Self*. http://www.self.com/fitness/workouts/2011/06/bikini-body-workout-slideshow#slide=1.

Bilger, B. (2011, October 31). True grits. *New Yorker, 87*(34), 40–53.

Billups, A. (2013, February 8). Mariska Hargitay loves her curves from motherhood. *People Magazine*. http://www.people.com/people/article/0,,20672000,00.html.

Bittman, M. (2008, December 14). So your kitchen is tiny. So what? *New York Times*. http://www.lexisnexis.com.tproxy01.lib.utah.edu/us/lnacademic/results/docview/docview.do?docLinkInd=true&risb=21_T8549463956&format=GNBFI&sort=RELEVANCE&st artDocNo=1&resultsUrlKey=29_T8549463959&cisb=22_T8549463958&treeMax=true &treeWidth=0&selRCNodeID=7&nodeStateId=411en_US,1,6,4&docsInCategory=10& csi=6742&docNo=2.

Bittman, M. (2011a, March 2). Don't end agricultural subsidies. Fix them. *New York Times, 25*.

Bittman, M. (2011b). Is junk food really cheaper? *New York Times*. http://www.nytimes.com/2011/09/25/opinion/sunday/is-junk-food-really-cheaper.html?pagewanted=all&_r=0.

Bittman, M. (2013, September 9). Late-summer links. *New York Times*. http://bittman.blogs.nytimes.com/2013/09/09/late-summer-links/?_r=0.

Blair, S., & Hu, F. (2011). The burning question: Can you be fit and fat? *Health, 25*(6), 20.

Blight, D. W. (2004). *Passages to freedom: The Underground Railroad in history and memory*. Washington, DC: Smithsonian.

Bocarsly, M. E., Powell, E. S., Avena, N. M., & Hoebel, B. G. (2010). High-fructose corn syrup causes characteristics of obesity in rats: Increased body weight, body fat, and triglyceride levels. *Pharmacology, Biochemistry &Behavior, 97*(1), 101–106.

Boero, N. (2012). *Killer fat: Media, medicine, and moral in America's "obesity epidemic."* New Brunswick, NJ: Rutgers University Press.

Bordo, S. (1993). *Unbearable weight: Feminism, western culture, and the body.* Berkeley, CA: University of California.

Bouchard, C. (2007). BMI, fat mass, abdominal adiposity, and visceral fat: Where's the beef? *International Journal of Obesity, 13*(10), 1552–1553.

Bray, G. A. (2013). Energy and fructose from beverages sweetened with sugar or high-fructose corn syrup pose a health risk for some people. *Advances in Nutrition, 4*(2), 220–225.

Brayton, S. (2007). MTV's Jackass: Transgression, abjection and the economy of white masculinity. *Journal of Gender Studies, 16*, 57–72.

Brewis, A. A. (2011).*Obesity: Cultural and biological perspectives.* New Brunswick, NJ: Rutgers University Press.

Brink, P. J. (1989). The fattening room among the Annang of Nigeria. *Medical Anthropology: Cross-Cultural Studies in Health and Illness, 12*(1), 131–143.

Brodesser-Akner, T. (2012, October 18). Confessions of a food addict. *Self.* http://www.self.com/life/health/2012/10/food-addict-confessions/.

Brody, J. E. (2004, March 9). In an obese world, sweet nothings add up. *New York Times,* F:1.

Brody, J. E. (2009, January 13). New thinking on how to protect the heart. *New York Times.* http://www.lexisnexis.com.tproxy01.lib.utah.edu/us/lnacademic/results/docview/docview.do?docLinkInd=true&risb=21_T8381208004&format=GNBFI&sort=RELEVANCE&startDocNo=1&resultsUrlKey=29_T8381208007&cisb=22_T8381208006&treeMax=true&treeWidth=0&selRCNodeID=24&nodeStateId=411en_US,1,23,12&docsInCategory=4&csi=6742&docNo=1.

Brody, J. (2010, November 30). Head out for a daily dose of green space. *New York Times,* A7.

Brody, J. (2011, September 13). Attacking the obesity epidemic by first figuring out its cause. *New York Times,* A7.

Broome, D., Koops, M., Silverman, B. (creators).(2004–). *The Biggest Loser* [television series]. Los Angeles, CA: 25/7 Productions.

Brower, K. A. (2010, November 22). Duck, sugar! It's a food fight! *Bloomberg Businessweek, 4205,* 44.

Brown, D. (2008, June 12). Life expectancy hits record high in United States: Difference among ethnic groups shrank in 2006. *Washington Post,* A4.

Brown, D. (2011, March 8). Q&A: Jessica Harris on African American food and "High on the Hog." *Washington Post.* http://www.washingtonpost.com/wpdyn/content/article/2011/03/08/AR2011030803159.html?sid=ST2011030803591.

Brownell, K. (2009, February 1). Is it true that lack of sleep might lead to weight gain? ABC News. http://abcnews.go.com/Health/WellnessResource/story?id=6762328.

"Buckle up—or else: A kinder, gentler paternalism." (2009, September 28). *Newsweek,* 23.

Buckley, C. (2013, March 11). Cheering a setback to the city's drink limits. *New York Times.* http://www.nytimes.com/2013/03/12/nyregion/many-in-ny-say-good-riddance-to-big-soda-ban.html.

Bullock, M. (2012, November 8). Jennifer Lawrence: Game changer. *Elle* http://www.elle.com/pop-culture/cover-shoots/jennifer-lawrence-quotes-fashion-photos#slide-1.

Burns, P., & Gimpel, J. G. (2000). Economic insecurity, prejudicial stereotypes, and public opinion on immigration policy. *Political Science Quarterly, 115*(2), 201–225.

Butler, J. (1990). *Gender trouble: Feminism and the subversion of identity.* New York: Routledge.

Butler, J. (1993). *Bodies that matter: On the discursive limits of "sex."* New York: Routledge.

Butterworth, T. (2013, January 25). Eat your Slidenafil. *Newsweek, 164*(4), 1.

Camacho, A. S. (2008). *Migrant imaginaries: Latino cultural politics in the U.S.-Mexico Borderlands.* New York: New York University Press.

Campbell, B. (Producer). (2009–). *The Dr. Oz show* [television series]. Chicago, IL: Harpo Productions.

Carbonell, D. (2013, December 6). Handling sadness at the holidays. *Fit to the Finish* [website]. http://blog.fittothefinish.com/2013/12/handling-sadness-at-the-holidays/.

Cardio bulletin. (2006). *Men's Health, 21*(3), 50.

Carlson, T., Maddow, R., Kellerman, M., Geist, W. (2005, August 24). *The Situation*, MSNBC. http://www.lexisnexis.com.ezproxy.lib.utah.edu/lnacui2api/auth/checkbrowser.do;jsess ionid=7020692D4B3C2FB788B18FEDB90EDE21.mIchf4wVosSETSf9WtB0lQ?ipcoun ter=1&cookieState=0&rand=0.11844062457938054&bhcp=1.

Carmichael, M. (2008a, August 24). Is there a surgical cure for diabetes? *Newsweek*. http://www.newsweek.com/2008/08/24/is-there-a-surgical-cure-for-diabetes.html.

Carmichael, M. (2008b, December 18). How fat went global. *Newsweek*. http://www.newsweek.com/id/175954.

Carmona, R. (2003a, January 6). Remarks to the 2003 California Childhood Obesity Conference. http://www.surgeongeneral.gov/news/speeches/califobesity.html.

Carmona, R. (2003b, July 16). The obesity crisis in America. Testimony before the Subcommittee on Education Reform, Committee on Education and the Workforce, United States House of Representatives. http://www.surgeongeneral.gov/news/testimony/obesity07162003.html.

Carroll, J. (2005, August 9). Who's worried about their weight? *Gallup*. http://www.gallup.com/poll/17752/whos-worried-about-their-weight.aspx.

Cassiday, C. M. (1991). The good body: When big is better. *Medical Anthropology: Cross Cultural Studies in Health and Illness, 13*(3), 181–213.

Cayton, A. R. L., & Gray, S. E. (2007). (Eds.). *The American midwest: Essays on regional history*. Bloomington, IN: Indiana University Press.

Census divisions and regions. (2012). United States Census Bureau. http://www.census.gov/geo/www/us_regdiv.pdf.

Chameides, B. (2013, September 5). The obesity plague and antibiotics. *Huffington Post*. http://www.huffingtonpost.com/bill-chameides/the-obesity-plague-and-an_b_3875904.html.

Chavez, L. R. (2008). *The Latino threat: Constructing immigrants, citizens, and the nation*. Stanford, CA: Stanford University Press.

Chemicals in food can make you fat. (2010, February 11). CBS News. http://www.cbsnews.com/2100-500165_162-6197493.html.

Childhood Obesity Prevention. (2013). Ad Council. http://www.adcouncil.org/Our-Work/Current-Work/Health/Childhood-Obesity-Prevention.

Cho, I., Yamanishi, S., Cox, L., Methé, B. A., Zavadil, J., Li, K., . . . Blaser, M. J. (2012). Antibiotics in early life alter the murine colonic microbiome and adiposity. *Nature, 488*(7413), 621–626.

Ciardi, C., Jenny, M., Tschoner, A., Ueberall, F., Patsch, J., Pedrini, M., Ebenbichler, C., & Fuchs, D. (2012). Food additives such as sodium sulphite, sodium benzoate and curcumin inhibit leptin release in lipopolysaccharide-treated murine adipocytes in vitro. *British Journal of Nutrition, 107*(6), 826–833.

Ciezadlo, A. (2011, April 3). Hunger games. *New York Times*, MM21.

Clark, N. (2006). Dieting gone awry. *American Fitness 28*(4), 66–67.

Clifford, S. (2008, July 30). Tug of war in food marketing to kids. *New York Times*, 5.

Cloud, J. (2008, December 26). Nanny-state food regulations. *Time*. http://www.time.com/time/specials/2008/top10/article/0,30583,1855948_1864255_1864257,00.html.

Cloud, J. (2009, August 9). Why exercise won't make you thin. *Time*. http://www.time.com/time/health/article/0,8599,1914857-1,00.html.

Cloud, J. (2011, May 6). Health: Do immigrant kids get fat to fit in? *Time*. http://healthland.time.com/2011/05/06/do-immigrant-kids-get-fat-to-fit-in/.

Cob, R. (2014). *The paradox of authenticity in a globalized world*. New York: Palgrave Macmillan.

Cohen, A. (2011, August 8). Big, fat stereotypes play out on the small screen. *NPR morning edition*. http://www.npr.org/2011/08/08/138958386/big-fat-stereotypes-play-out-on-the-small-screen.

Cohen, J. (2013, May 29). 4 new apps you need to achieve real weight loss. *Forbes.* http://www.forbes.com/sites/jennifercohen/2013/05/29/4-new-apps-you-need-to-achieve-real-weight-loss/.

Cold is hot! (2013, November). *Prevention, 65*(12), 14–15.

Collingham, L. (2012). *The taste of war: World War II and the battle for food.* London: Penguin.

Constable, P. (2008, August 5). Adopting America's bad habits: Latinos' poor diets, lack of exercise propel social agencies into action. *Washington Post,* B1.

Cosgrove-Mather, B. (2004, December 14). Immigrants pack on pounds in U.S. CBS News. http://www.cbsnews.com/news/immigrants-pack-on-pounds-in-us/.

Cossrow, N., & Falkner, B. (2004). Race/ethnic issues in obesity and obesity-related comorbidities. *Journal of Clinical Endocrinal Metabolism, 89*(6), 2590–2594.

Couldry, N. (2008). Reality TV, or the secret theatre of neoliberalism. *Review of Education, Pedagogy & Cultural Studies, 30*(1), 3–13.

Coveney, J. (2011). In praise of hunger: Public health and the problem of excess. In K. Bell, D. McNaughton, & A. Salmon (Eds.), *Alcohol, tobacco and obesity: Morality, mortality and the new public health* (pp. 146–160). London: Routledge.

Covvey, J. (2009, February 11). Kentuckians have bright futures if health care is taken seriously. CBS News. http://www.cbsnews.com/stories/2008/11/05/politics/uwire/main4573468.shtml?tag=mncol;lst;5.

Coyne, K. (2006). End emotional eating for good. *Good Housekeeping, 242*(2), 140–142.

Craven, P. (2013, December 6). BLR's tips for keeping your commitments through the holidays. http://www.biggestloserresort.com/blog/entry/commitments-and-the-holidays.

Crawford, R. (1980). Healthism and the medicalisation of everyday life. *International Journal of Health Services: Planning, Administration, Evaluation, 10*(3), 365–388.

Critics of opera singer Tara Erraught under fire after fat shaming (2014, May 28). *Time.* http://time.com/110272/fat-shaming-tara-erraught/.

Critser, G. (2003). *Fat land: How Americans became the fattest people in the world.* New York: Houghton Mifflin.

Cruz, G. (2008, December 4). Why media could be bad for your child's health. *Time.* http://www.time.com/time/health/article/0,8599,1864141,00.html.

Curb those cravings. (2009, May 10). *Good Morning America,* ABC News. http://www.lexisnexis.com.tproxy01.lib.utah.edu/us/lnacademic/results/docview/docview.do?docLinkInd=true&risb=21_T9479313217&format=GNBFI&sort=RELEVANCE&startDocNo=1&resultsUrlKey=29_T9479313220&cisb=22_T9479313219&treeMax=true&treeWidth=0&csi=8277&docNo=3.

Curran, J., & Morley, D. (Eds.). (2006). *Media and cultural theory.* New York: Routledge.

Curtis, J. P., Selter, J. G., Wang, Y., Rathore, S. S., Jovin, I. S., Jadbabaie, F., . . . Krumholz, H. M. (2005).The obesity paradox: Body mass index and outcomes in patients with heart failure. *Archives of Internal Medicine, 165*(1), 55–61.

Curves rule. (2007, May 7). *People Magazine, 67*(18), 177–182.

Datar, A., & Nicosia, N. (2012). Junk food in schools and childhood obesity. *Journal of Policy Analysis and Management 31*(2), 213–337.

Davenport, C., & Brown, E. (2009, November 4). Girding for an uphill battle for recruits. *Washington Post.* http://www.washingtonpost.com/wdyn/content/article/2009/11/04/AR2009110402899.html.

Dayton, T. (2010, February 25). Are you self-medicating your emotional stress with food? *Huffington Post.* http://www.huffingtonpost.com/dr-tian-dayton/are-you-self-medicating-y_b_476399.html.

De Garine, I., & Pollock, N. (Eds.). (1995). *Social aspects of obesity.* Amsterdam: Overseas Publishers Association.

De Spiegelaere, M., Hennart, P., & Dramaix, M. (1998). The influence of socioeconomic status on the incidence and evolution of obesity during early adolescence. *International Journal of Obesity, 3,* 268–274.

De Young, M. (2004). *The day care ritual abuse moral panic.* Jefferson, NC: McFarland.

Debord, G. (1976). *The society of the spectacle.* Detroit: Black and Red.

Diamond, J. M. (2005).*Guns, germs, and steel: The fates of human societies.* New York: Norton.

Diet inspiration. (2014). *Pinterest* [message board]. http://www.pinterest.com/helenhirst/diet-inspiration/.

Do the suburbs make you fat? (2009, February 11). CBS News. http://www.cbsnews.com/stories/2003/08/28/health/main570634.shtml?tag=mncol;lst.

Dr. Oz: The biggeryouarethemoreinvisibleyouare. (2014,February2).*MorningJoe*,MSNBC,http://www.msnbc.com/morning-joe/watch/dr-oz-being-overweight-makes-you-invisible-145565763811.

Dolgoff, S. (2013). What is your weight destiny? *Fitness Magazine.* http://www.fitnessmagazine.com/weight-loss/tips/diet-tips/control-weight-destiny/.

Donvan, J., & Stuart, E. (2009, January 6). West Virginia County is diabetes capital of U.S. ABC News. http://abcnews.go.com/Nightline/west-virginia-county-countrys-diabetescapital/story?id=9490153#.UIg_UsXR5cU.

Douglas, M. (1982). *In the active voice.* London: Routledge & Kegan Paul.

Dove ads with 'real' women get attention. (2005, August 3). NBC News. http://www.nbcnews.com/id/8757597/ns/business-us_business/t/dove-ads-real-women-get-attention/#.U20gNfnwbnM.

Dreisbach, S. (2014, January 24). Body by Glamour: 5 ways to fool yourself into exercising. *Glamour.* http://www.glamour.com/health-fitness/blogs/vitamin-g/2014/01/5-ways-to-fool-yourself-into-e.html.

Duffy, J. (2013, May 22). The best activity trackers for fitness. *PC Magazine.* http://www.pcmag.com/article2/0,2817,2404445,00.asp.

Durham, M. G., & Kellner, D. M. (Eds.). (2006). *Media and cultural studies: Keyworks.* Malden, MA: Blackwell.

Durkheim, E., & Mauss, M. (1963). *Primitive classification* (R Needham, Trans.).Chicago: University of Chicago Press.

Dworkin, S. L., & Wachs, F. L. (2009). *Body panic: Gender, health, and the selling of fitness.* New York: New York University Press.

Eating disorders. (2011). National Institute of Mental Health. http://www.nimh.nih.gov/health/publications/eating-disorders/index.shtml.

Eckelkamp, S. (2013, April). Stop yo-yo dieting for good. *Prevention, 65*(4), 12.

Education trumps income in the fight against obesity. (2013, September 20). *Huffington Post.* http://www.huffingtonpost.com/2013/09/20/education-income-obesity-health-news-this-week_n_3961282.html.

Ekberg, A. (2013, April 1). Adele Weight Jab. *Yahoo Celebrity.* https://celebrity.yahoo.com/news/adele-weight-jab-joan-rivers-other-celebs-fat-195300132.html.

Eller, D. (2011, November). Are you addicted to food? *Prevention.* http://www.prevention.com/weight-loss/weight-loss-tips/how-beat-food-addiction?page=5.

Emotional eating. (2014). *Jenny Craig* [website]. http://www.jennycraig.com/site/learn/article/emotional-eating.

Emotional eating. (2014). *Weight Watchers* [website]. http://www.weightwatchers.com/util/art/index_art.aspx?tabnum=1&art_id=22721&sc=802.

Esterbrook, J. (2002/2009). Americans still shun exercise. CBS News. http://www.cbsnews.com/news/americans-still-shun-exercise/.

Etter, L., & Hitt, G. (2008, March 27). Farm lobby beats back assault on subsidies. *Wall Street Journal, 251*(72), A1–12.

Exercise helps fight obesity gene. (2011, November 1). *Health.* http://news.health.com/2011/11/01/exercise-obesity-gene/.

Experts say industry food labels deceptive. (2009, October 9). CBS News. www.cbsnews.com/8301-18563_162-5291352.html.

Eye catching ads promote junk food to kids. (2008, July 29). CBS News. http://www.cbsnews.com/stories/2008/07/29/business/main4302213.shtml?tag=contentMain;contentBody.

F as in fat. (2009). Issue Report of the Robert Wood Johnson Foundation. http://healthyamericans.org/reports/obesity2009/Obesity2009Report.pdf.

Fagone, J. (2006, May 1). Horsemen of the esophagus. *The Atlantic.* http://www.theatlantic.com/magazine/archive/2006/05/horsemen-of-the-esophagus/304808/?single_page=true.

Farrell, A. E. (2011). *Fat shame: Stigma and the fat body in American culture.* New York: New York University Press.

Farris, S. (2012). Eat like an Italian. *Time, 179*(7), 1–4.

Fat shaming shockers: How these 10 celebrities fought back. (2014, April 26). *Extra.* http://www.extratv.com/2014/04/26/fat-shaming-celebrities-chrissy-teigen-kim-kardashian-jennifer-lawrence-fought-back/.

Fernandez, M. (2006, September 24). Fast-food restaurants. *New York Times,* A37.

Finkel, J. (2009, June). All you can eat. *Muscle and Fitness, 70*(6), 288.

Finkelstein, E. A., Ruhm, C. J., & Kosa, K. M. (2005). Economic causes and consequences of obesity. *Annual Review of Public Health, 26,* 239–257.

Finkelstein, E. A., & Zuckerman, L. (2008). *The fattening of America: How the economy makes us fat, if it matters, and what to do about it.* Hoboken, NJ: Wiley & Sons.

Fiore, K. (2010, August 4). More states growing obese: CDC. ABC News. http://abcnews.go.com/Health/Wellness/obesity-worsens-statescdc/story?id=11316715#.UI7MocXR5cV.

Food ads on Nickelodeon slammed in report. (2009, November 24). CBS News. http://www.cbsnews.com/stories/2009/11/24/health/healthy_living/main5761832.shtml?tag=contentMain;contentBody.

Food for thought. (2012, December 15). *Economist, 405*(8815), 9–12.

Fortin, J. (2009, January 22). Sugar free school. CNN. http://www.cnn.com/video/#/video/health/2009/01/22/fortin.hm.sugar.free.zone.cnn?iref=videosearch.

Foucault, M. (1977). *Discipline and punish: The birth of the prison.* New York: Pantheon.

Foucault, M. (1979). *The history of sexuality, volume one: An introduction.* London: Penguin.

Franck, C., Grandi, S. M., & Eisenberg, M. J. (2013). Agricultural studies and the obesity epidemic. *American Journal of Preventative Medicine, 45*(3), 328.

Frank, A. (1990). Bringing bodies back in. *Theory, Culture, and Society, 7*(1), 131–162.

Frazier, R. S. (2013, May). So long, stress snacking. *Health, 27*(4), 52.

Freedman, D. H. (2013, July). How junk food can end obesity. *Atlantic Monthly, 312*(1), 68–89.

Freeman, D. W. (2011, June 3). Are media to blame for obesity epidemic? CBS News. http://www.cbsnews.com/8301-504763_162-20067704-10391704.html.

French tops in eating, drinking. (2009, May 5). CNN. http://www.cnn.com/2009/LIVING/worklife/05/05/global.leisure/index.html?iref=allsearch.

Fresh fruit, hold the insulin. (2012, April 12). *Scientific American, 306*(5), 12.

Friedman, A. (2013, April 18). Beauty above all else: The problem with Dove's new viral ad. *New York Magazine.* http://nymag.com/thecut/2013/04/beauty-above-all-else-doves-viral-ad-problem.html.

Froeber, J. (2008, December). My lifesaving slimdown. *Health, 23*(10), 50.

Furedi, F. (2006). *The culture of fear.* New York: Continuum.

Gaines, T. (2010, June 21). How obesity has become a part of Black culture. *The Grio.* http://thegrio.com/2010/06/21/how-obesity-has-become-a-part-of-black-culture/.

Galbraith, H. (2002). Hormones in international meat production: Biological, sociological, and consumer issues. *Nutrition Research Reviews 15*(2), 293–314.

Gammon, A. (2011, September 18). Our most inspiring before and after weight-loss photos (Amanda Fulfer). *Shape.* http://www.shape.com/weight-loss/success-stories/our-most-inspiring-after-weight-loss-photos/slide/2.

Gans, K. (2013, April 16). Are people who cook more likely to skip the gym? *Shape.* http://www.shape.com/blogs/weight-loss-coach/are-people-who-cook-more-likely-skip-gym.

Garber, K. (2009, November 20). Hamburger, fries, and 1,000 calories, please. *U.S. News & World Report, 1*(44), 6.

Garcia, O. (2010, December 21). Child Nutrition Act: Childhood obesity is a national security threat. *Huffington Post.* http://www.huffingtonpost.com/oz-garcia/child-nutrition-act-childhood-obesity_b_799670.html.

Gard, M., & Wright, J. (2005). *The obesity epidemic: Science, morality, and technology.* New York: Routledge.

Gardner, A. (2011, May 26). Sedentary jobs helping to drive obesity epidemic. *U.S. News & World Report.* http://health.usnews.com/health-news/diet-fitness/fitness/articles/2011/05/26/sedentary-jobs-helping-to-drive-obesity-epidemic.

Garrard, C. (2009, September 27). Get a motivation makeover. *Self.* http://www.self.com/food-diet/2009/09/motivation-makeover.

Gibbons, B. (2013, February 2). Fat shaming doesn't work—here's why. *Huffington Post.* http://www.huffingtonpost.com/brittany-gibbons/fat-shaming_b_2584298.html.

Gillham, C. (2007, November 19). For safer baby bottles. *Newsweek,* 71.

Gillette, H. (2014, January 2). This could help reduce allostatic load among Mexican Americans. *Huffington Post.* http://www.huffingtonpost.com/2014/01/02/allostatic-load-mexican-americans-_n_4530894.html:P8.

Gilman, S. L. (2008). *Fat: A cultural history of obesity.* Cambridge, UK: Polity Press.

Gilman, S. L. (2010). *Obesity: The biography.* Oxford: Oxford University Press.

Giroux, H. A. (2005). The terror of neoliberalism: Rethinking the significance of cultural politics. *College Literature, 32*(1), 1–19.

Givens, L., & Tenney, M. (Writers). (2002–). *Dr. Phil* [television series]. Harpo Productions: Chicago, IL.

Glynn, C. J., Huge, M., Reineke, J. B., Hardy, B. W., & Shanahan, J. (2007). When Oprah intervenes: Political correlates of daytime talk show viewing. *Journal of Broadcasting and Electronic Media, 51*(2), 228–244.

Gold's Gym [website]. (2013). http://www.goldsgym.com/.

Goldstein, J. (2009). High-fructose corn syrup: How dangerous is it? *Prevention, 61*(5), 58–61.

Gogoi, P. (2008, September 22). Sweetening a sweetener's rep. *Business Week, 4100,* 17.

Gray, S. (2008, September 21). Food justice in inner-city Chicago. *Time, 174*(11), 54.

Greenfield, P. (2013, January/February). Scoop! Weight loss. *Women's Health 10*(1), 36.

Grumman, R. (2009, September 18). Why we eat too much. CNN. http://www.cnn.com/2009/HEALTH/09/18/why.overeat.eat.much/index.html?iref=allsearch.

Grun, F., & Blumberg, B. (2007). Perturbed nuclear receptor signaling by environmental obesogens as emerging factors in the obesity crisis. *Reviews in Endocrine and Metabolic Disorders 8,* 161–171.

Gupta, S. (2008a, June 9). Body of knowledge: Obesity. CNN. http://www.cnn.com/video/#/video/health/2008/06/09/bok.sensitivity.suit.cnn?iref=videosearch.

Gupta, S. (2008b, December 6). Fed up: America's killer diet. CNN. http://www.lexisnexis.com.tproxy01.lib.utah.edu/us/lnacademic/results/docview/docview.do?docLinkInd=true&risb=21_T9479501813&format=GNBFI&sort=RELEVANCE&startDocNo=1&resultsUrlKey=29_T9479501817&cisb=22_T9479501816&treeMax=true&treeWidth=0&selRCNodeID=104&nodeStateId=411en_US,1,30,94,13&docsInCategory=48&csi=271063&docNo=1.

Guthman, J. (2011). *Weighing in: Obesity, food justice, and the limits of capitalism.* Berkeley: University of California Press.

Haller, M. (2012, May). 4 simple tricks to eat less. *Prevention.* http://www.prevention.com/food/healthy-eating-tips/trick-yourself-eating-less.

Hammond, R. A., & Levine, R. (2010). The economic impact of obesity in the United States. *Diabetes, Metabolic Syndrome, and Obesity, 3,* 285–295.

Hao, C., Cheng, X., Xia, H., & Ma, X. (2012). The endocrine disruptor mono-(2-ethylhexyl) phthalate promotes adipocyte differentiation and induces obesity in mice. *Bioscience Reports, 32*(6), 619–629.

Haraway, D. (1989). The biopolitics of postmodern bodies: Determinations of self in immune system discourse. *Differences 1*(1), 3–44.

Hanc, J. (2011, November 2). World of hunger has a new language. *New York Times.* http://www.nytimes.com/2011/11/02/giving/the-world-of-hunger-has-a-new-language.html.

Harned, K. (2013, May 10). The Michael Bloomberg nanny state in New York: A cautionary tale. *Forbes Magazine.* http://www.forbes.com/sites/realspin/2013/05/10/the-michael-bloomberg-nanny-state-in-new-york-a-cautionary-tale/.

Hartocollis, A., Grynbaum, M. M., & Vadukul, A. (2012, June 1). To gulp or to sip? Debating the crackdown on sugary drinks. *New York Times*, A22.

Harvey, D. (2005). *A brief history of neoliberalism.* New York: Oxford University Press.

Has America reached its tipping point on obesity? (2009, September 9). Stop Obesity Alliance. http://www.stopobesityalliance.org/events/past-events/has-america-reached-its-tipping-point-on-obesity/.

Hawksworth, W. (2013, October 18). What it's really like to live as a fat person every day. *Huffington Post.* http://www.huffingtonpost.ca/elizabeth-hawksworth/being-overweight_b_4116510.html.

Health food imposters. (2009). *Prevention, 61*(10), 72–76.

Health news that makes you go. . . . (2013, July). *Reader's Digest, 182*(1089), 130–139.

Health tidbits. (1999). *Journal of the American Medical Association, 91*(12), 645.

Healthy weight: It's not a diet, it's a lifestyle! (2014). CDC. http://www.cdc.gov/healthyweight/calories/.

Heart Attack Grill. (n.d.). Heart Attack Grill [website]. http://www.heartattackgrill.com/heart-attack-grill.html.

Heavey, S. (2013, January 9). Obesity, lack of insurance cited in U.S. health gap. *Reuters.* http://www.reuters.com/article/2013/01/09/us-usa-health-ranking-idUSBRE9080ZN201301099.

Heil, E. (2004, September 21). Critics see a food pyramid with lobbyists at the top. *Congress Daily*, 3–5.

Heisley, M. (2008, September 8). Got a fat gene? Get active for 3–4 hours a day. *USA Today.* http://www.usatoday.com/news/health/weightloss/2008-09-08-obesity-gene_n.htm.

Hellmich, N. (2009, January 7). Help kids maintain a healthy diet without a hefty cost. *USA Today.* http://www.usatoday.com/news/health/weightloss/2009-01-06-kids-diet_n.htm.

Hendrick, B., & Martin, L. J. (2011, February 22). Fried fish to blame for Southern "stroke belt?" *CBS News.* http://www.cbsnews.com/stories/2011/02/22/health/webmd/main7181156.shtml?tag=mncol;lst.

Henig, R. M. (2008, October 3). Losing the weight stigma. *New York Times Magazine.* http://www.nytimes.com/2008/10/05/magazine/05wwln-idealab-t.html?_r=0.

Hester, J. (2009). Feast of burden. *Bitch Magazine, 44*, 37–53.

Hiatt, K. (2010, November 22). 6 ways to trick yourself into eating fruits and veggies. *U.S. News & World Report.* http://health.usnews.com/health-news/diet-fitness/diet/articles/2010/11/22/6-ways-to-trick-yourself-into-eating-fruits-and-veggies.

Hobson, K. (2009, May 14). 10-week workout. *U.S. News & World Report.* http://health.usnews.com/health-news/blogs/on-fitness/2009/05/14/10-week-workout-6-ways-to-motivate-yourself-up-off-the-couch.

Hoffman, M. K. (2009, April 29). Southern cooking inspires chef's vegan recipes. *Jet, 115*(12), 22.

Holtcamp, W. (2013). Obesogens: An environmental link to obesity. *Environmental Health Perspectives, 120*(2), A62–A68.

Horovitz, B. (2008, December 19). Schools take steps to give kids more fruits, vegetables at lunch. *USA Today.* http://www.usatoday.com/moneyindustries/food/2008-12-17-kids-food-veggies-fruit_n.htm.

How do you put a nation on a diet? (2012, June 10). *New York Times*, A10.

How fat can be healthy. (2009, January 12). *Good Morning America*, ABC News. http://www.lexisnexis.com.tproxy01.lib.utah.edu/us/lnacademic/results/docview/docview.do?docLinkInd=true&risb=21_T8345055244&format=GNBFI&sort=RELEVANCE&

startDocNo=1&resultsUrlKey=29_T8345055254&cisb=22_T8345055253&treeMax=t
rue&treeWidth=0&selRCNodeID=3&nodeStateId=411en_US,1,2&docsInCategory=8
&csi=8277&docNo=3.

Hu, P., Chen, X., Whitener, R. J., Boder, E. T., Jones, J. O., Porollo, A., Chen, J., & Zhao, L. (2013). Effects of parabens on adipocyte differentiation. *Toxicological Sciences, 131*(1), 56–57.

Huber, B. (2011, October 3). Walmart's fresh-food makeover. *Nation, 293*(14), 22–27.

Hyman, M. (2010, 1August 14). Why quick, cheap food is actually more expensive. *Huffington Post*. http://www.huffingtonpost.com/dr-mark-hyman/why-quick-cheap-food-is-a_b_681539.html.

Hyman, R. (2012). How emotional eating can save your life. *DrHyman.com* [website]. http://drhyman.com/blog/2012/07/10/how-emotional-eating-can-save-your-life/.

Hyman, M. (2014, April 1). Confessions of a food addict. *Huffington Post*. http://www.huffingtonpost.com/dr-mark-hyman/food-addict_b_4679723.html.

I'm fatter than my husband. (2011, October 27). *Marie Claire*. http://www.marieclaire.com/sex-love/relationship-issues/weight-gain-after-marriage.

Illouz, E. (2003). *Oprah Winfrey and the glamour of misery: An essay on popular culture.* New York: Columbia University Press.

Illouz, E. (2008). *Saving the modern soul: Therapy, emotions, and the culture of self-help.* Berkeley, CA: University of California Press.

Imhoff, D. (2010). (Ed.). *The CAFO reader: The tragedy of industrial animal factories.* Berkeley: University of California.

Imhoff, D. (2011, October 3). Farm Bill 101. *Nation 291*(4), 27–29.

Immigrants eat American junk food to fit in: Study. (2011, May 6). *U.S. News & World Report*. http://health.usnews.com/health-news/diet-fitness/articles/2011/05/06/immigrants-eat-american-junk-food-to-fit-in-study:P1.

Immigrant kids exercise even less than U.S.-born kids. (2008, August 5). *USA Today*. http://www.usatoday.com/news/health/weightloss/2008-08-05-immigrant-exercise_n.htm.

Inside the times. (2008, August 13). *New York Times,* A2.

Irregular sleeping linked to obesity. (2009, May 7). *USA Today*.http://www.usatoday.com/news/health/2008-05-07-sleep-obesity_n.htm.

Is it my hormones? (2011, September). *Self, 33*(9), 94.

Issues brief: Analysis of obesity rates by state. (2012). Trust for America's Health. http://www.healthyamericans.org/report/98/obseityratesbystate.

Jackson, J. L., (2005). *Real Black: Adventures in racial sincerity.* Chicago, IL: University of Chicago Press.

Jackson, R. J., Minfares, R., Naumoff, K. S., Shrimali, B. P., & Martin, L. K. (2009). Agriculture policy is health policy. *Journal of Hunger and Environmental Nutrition, 4*, 393–408.

Jacobs, T. (2014, February 26). America's obesity cure: Laziness? *Salon.com* [website]. http://www.salon.com/2014/02/26/americas_obesity_cure_laziness_partner/.

Jakob, N. G. E. (2009). No alternatives? The relationship between perceived media dependency, use of alternative information sources, and general trust in mass media. *International Journal of Communication, 4*(2010), 589–606.

Jankowski, P. (2011, October 5). Six ignorant stereotypes about middle America. *Forbes*. http://www.forbes.com/sites/pauljankowski/2011/10/05/six-ignorant-stereotypes-about-middle-america/.

Jaslow, R. (2012, September 25). Retired military leaders say this generation is "too fat to fight." CBS News. http://www.cbsnews.com/8301-504763_162-57520233-10391704/retiredmilitary-leaders-say-this-generation-is-too-fat-to-fight/.

Jaslow, R. (2013, April 11). NYC soda ban would lead customers to consume more sugary drinks, study suggests. CBS News. http://www.cbsnews.com/news/nyc-soda-ban-would-lead-customers-to-consume-more-sugary-drinks-study-suggests/.

Jaworowska, A., Blackham, T., Davies, I. G., & Stevenson, L. (2013). Nutritional challenges and health implications of takeaway and fast food. *Nutrition Reviews, 71*(5), 310–318.

Jenkins, H. W.Jr., (2006, December 20). Fat chance. *Wall Street Journal 248*(145), A19.

Jenny Craig [website]. (2013). http://www.jennycraig.com.

Jessica Simpson on new baby, weight loss. (2014, January 18). *Good morning America*, ABC News. http://gma.yahoo.com/video/jessica-simpson-baby-weight-loss-130250980.htm.

Jhally, S. (1990). *The codes of advertising: Fetishism and the political economy of meaning in the consumer society.* London: Routledge.

Johnson, L. (2008, August 8). Some teens so heavy they face liver damage, transplants. *USA Today.* http://www.usatoday.com/news/health/weightloss/2008-09-07-fat-liver-children_n.htm.

Johnson, T. D. (2012). Hard-hitting public health ad campaigns sparking awareness. *The Nation's Health, 42*(5), 1–10.

Johnston, J., & Baumann, S. (2010). *Foodies: Democracy and distinction in the gourmet foodscape.* New York: Routledge.

Judson, O. (2008, August 10). Honey, I plumped the kids. *New York Times,* WK10.

Jutel, A. (2005). Weighing health: The moral burden of obesity. *Social Semiotics, 15*(2), 113–125.

Kantrowitz, B., & Wingert, P. (2008, July 8). What works. *Newsweek.* http://www.newsweek.com/id/144958.

Kate Winslet on 'Titanic 3D' and being a role model. (2011, December 13). *Huffington Post.* http://www.huffingtonpost.com/2011/12/13/kate-winslet-on-titanic-3d_n_1145330.html.

Katrandjian, O. (2011, February 3). Can't beat the fat and sugar cravings? Four steps to help you kick your addiction. ABC *Good Morning America.* http://abcnews.go.com/GMA/dr-mehmet-oz-beat-fat-sugar-addiction-detox/story?id=12823912.

Katz, D. (2008a). Can gastric bypass create unsavory cravings? *Oprah.com* [website]. http://www.oprah.com/health/Sexual-Impulses-After-Gastric-Bypass-Surgery.

Katz, D. (2008b, April 1). The way to eat. *O, The Oprah Magazine, 9,* 156.

Katz, D. (2012, September 13). We're not fat because we're lazy. *U.S. News & World.* http://health.usnews.com/health-news/blogs/eat-run/2012/09/13/were-not-fat-because-were-lazy.

Katz, D. (2013, September 13). Our severely obese daughters and sons: Of pennies, pounds and sense. *Huffington Post.* http://www.huffingtonpost.com/david-katz-md/childhood-obesity_b_3907198.html.

Kavanagh, K., Jones, K. L., Sawyer, J., Kelley, K., Carr, J. J., Wagner, J. D., & Rudel, L. L. (2007).Trans fat diet induces abdominal obesity and changes in insulin sensitivity in monkeys. *Obesity, 15*(7), 1675–1678.

Kelly, D. (2013, November). The 25 best diet tips of all time. *Prevention.* http://www.prevention.com/weight-loss/diets/25-best-weight-loss-tips-ever?s=2.

Kelly, M. (2011). Is your appetite out of control? *Fitness Magazine.* http://www.fitnessmagazine.com/weight-loss/eating-help/control-cravings/appetite-out-of-control/.

Khloe Kardashian sick of being called a sasquatch! She's not fat! (2011, April 27). *Hollywood Life.* http://hollywoodlife.com/2011/04/27/khloe-kardashian-bullied-for-her-weight-and-how-mom-kris-goes-after-her-even-when-cameras-stop-rolling/.

Khloe Kardashian on fat shaming. (2013, May 1). *Examiner.* http://www.examiner.com/article/kourtney-kardashian-on-fat-shaming-i-don-t-think-i-m-prettier-thinner.

Kingsbury, B. (2008, June 12). Fit at any size. *Time.* http://www.time.com/time/magazine/article/0,9171,1813993-1,00.html.

Kita, J. (2010, February). Weight loss secrets from around the world. *Reader's Digest 176*(1053), 101–105.

Klein, E. (2009, July 1). We're getting a bad feeling about our food. *New York Times,* E01.

Kliff, S. (2008, October 16).The pleasure factor. *Newsweek.* http://www.newsweek.com/id/164197.

Kluger, J. (2008, June 12). How America's children packed on the pounds. *Time.* http://www.time.com/time/health/article/0,8599,1813700,00.html.

Kluger, J., Aguayo, A. M., August, M., Bower, A., Bowers, P., Cray, D., Dale, S. S., & Locke, L. (2005, June 6). Can you be fat and healthy? *Time, 165*(23), 60–67.

Klurfeld, D. M., Foreyt, J., Angelopoulos, T. J., & Rippe, J. M. (2013). Lack of evidence for high fructose corn syrup as the cause of the obesity epidemic. *International Journal of Obesity, 37*(6), 771–773.

Koch, W. (2011, March 7). Study: Most plastics trigger estrogen effect. *USA Today.* http://content.usatoday.com/communities/greenhouse/post/2011/03/bpa-free-plastic-products-estrogen/1#.UknZW4a9HnM.

Kohli, R., Kirby, M., Xanthakos, S. A., Softic, S., Feldstein, A. E., Saxena, V., . . . Seeley, R. J. (2010). High fructose, medium chain trans fat diet induces liver fibrosis and elevates plasma coenzyme Q9 in a novel murine model of obesity an nonalcoholic steatohepatitis. *Hepatology, 52*(3), 934–944.

Kotz, D. (2011). Stop emotional eating with these 5 tips. *U.S. News & World Report.* http://health.usnews.com/health-news/diet-fitness/diet/slideshows/stop-emotional-eating-with-these-5-tips.

Knowlton-Le Roux, L. (2007). Reading American fat in France: Obesity and food culture. *European Journal of American Studies, 2*, 2–10.

Kolata, G. (2011, May 1). What thighs lose, belly finds. *New York Times,* A5.

Kristjansson, M. (2014). *The fat body (in)visible* [documentary]. http://www.fatbodyinvisible.com/.

Kristoff, N. D. (2013, January 20). Warnings from a flabby mouse. *New York Times,* SR11.

Krucoff, C. (2004). One photo changed my life. *Prevention, 56*(5), 125–127.

Kusz, K. (2003). BMX, extreme sports, and the white male backlash. In R. E. Rinehart & S. Sydnor (Eds.), *To the extreme: Alternative sports, inside and out* (pp. 153–175). Albany, NY: SUNY Press.

Kuzemchak, S. (2012, June). Sugar shocker. *Parents, 87*(7), 54–61.

Lack of sleep linked to obesity. (2012, October). *USA Today Magazine, 141*(2809), 14–15.

Laitin, D. D., Moortgatb, J., & Robinson, A. L. (2012). Geographic axes and the persistence of cultural diversity. *Proceedings of the National Academy of Sciences of the United States of America, 109*(26), 10263–10268.

Laitinen, J., Power, C., & Järvelin, M. R. (2001). Family social class, maternal body mass index, childhood body mass index, and age at menarche as predictors of adult obesity. *American Journal of Clinical Nutrition, 74*(3), 287–294.

Lallanilla, M. (2013, February 24). Obesity among kids: A media problem? ABC News. http://abcnews.go.com/Health/Living/story?id=118227.

Lamerz, A., Kuepper-Nybelen, J., Wehle, C., Bruning, N., Trost-Brinkhues, G., Brenner, H., Hebebrand, J., & Herpertz-Dahlmann, G. (2005). Social class, parental education, and obesity prevalence in a study of six-year-old children in Germany. *International Journal of Obesity, 29*, 373–380.

Landau, E. (2012, September 18). Health care costs to bulge along with U.S. waistlines. CNN News. http://www.cnn.com/2012/09/18/health/us-obesity/index.html?iref=allsearch.

Lavalle, M. (2008, May 19). Fixing the food crisis. *U.S. News & World Report, 144*(14), 36–42.

Layton, L. (2009, April 27). Crave man. *Washington Post.* http://www.lexisnexis.com.tproxy01.lib.utah.edu/us/lnacademic/results/docview/docview.do?docLinkInd=true&risb=21_T8554298803&format=GNBFI&sort=RELEVANCE&startDocNo=1&resultsUrlKey=29_T8554298806&cisb=22_T8554298805&treeMax=true&treeWidth=0&selRCNodeID=34&nodeStateId=411en_US,1,31&docsInCategory=13&csi=8075&docNo=7.

Layton, L., & Eggan, D. (2011, July 9). Food, ad industries lobby against nutrition guidelines. *Washington Post.* http://articles.washingtonpost.com/2011-07--09/politics/35267908_1_voluntary-nutrition-guidelines-junk-food-foodmakers.

LeBesco, K. (2004). *Revolting bodies? The struggle to redefine fat identity.* Amherst, MA: University of Massachusetts.

Leopold, T. (2012, April 14). The South: Not all bubbas and banjos. CNN News. http://www.cnn.com/2012/04/14/us/bubba-southern-stereotypes/index.html.

Let's Move! [website]. (2013). http://www.letsmove.gov/learn-facts/epidemic-childhood-obesity.

Lévi-Strauss, C. (1966).The culinary triangle (P. Brooks, Trans.). *Partisan Review, 33,* 586–595.

Levine, S., & Stein, J. (2008, May 18). Obesity threatens a generation: "Catastrophe" of earlier deaths, higher health costs. *Washington Post.* http://pqasb.pqarchiver.com/washington-post/access/1480441201.html?dids=1480441201:1480441201&FMT=CITE&FMTS=CITE:FT&date=May+18%2C+2008&author=Susan+Levine%3BRob+Stein++Washington+Post+Staff+Writers&pub=The+Washington+Post&edition=&startpage=A.1&desc=Obesity+Threatens+a+Generation%3B+%27Catastrophe%27+of+Earlier+Deaths%2C+Higher+Health+Costs.

Levy-Navarro, E. (2008). *The culture of obesity in early and late modernity.* New York: Palgrave Macmillan.

Leyba, C. A. (2013, November 15). 5 fabulous women that embraced their curves. *Marie Claire.* http://www.marieclaire.co.uk/blogs/544919/5-fabulous-women-that-embraced-their-curves.html.

Lippmann, D. (2009). Making friends with food. *Shape, 29*(2), 70.

Latinos vulnerable to fatty pancreas. (2013, February). *USA Today, 141*(2813), 13.

Lofton, K. (2006). Practicing Oprah: Or, the prescriptive compulsion of a spiritual capitalism. *Journal of Popular Culture, 39*(4), 599–621.

Long, J. M., Mareno, N., Shabo, R., & Wilson, A. H. (2012). Overweight and obesity among white, black, and Mexican American children: Implications for when to intervene. *Journal for Specialists in Pediatric Nursing, 17*(1), 41–50.

"Longer 'exposure' to U.S. may raise immigrants' obesity risk. (2012, November 16). Fox News. http://www.foxnews.com/health/2012/11/16/longer-exposure-to-us-may-raise-immigrants-obesity-risk/.

L.A. council poised to ban fast food in poor neighbourhood. (2008, July 29). *USA Today.* http://www.usatoday.com/news/nation/2008-07-29-los-angeles-fast-food_n.htm.

Lose weight. (2013). *Health.* http://www.health.com/health/lose-weight/.

Lose weight? Reward yourself! (2014). Pinterest [message board]. http://www.pinterest.com/dragonladyhere/lose-weight-reward-yourself/.

Losh, J. (2008, August 8). Dear parents: Your child is fat. *Time.* http://www.time.com/time/health/article/0,8599,1830796,00.html.

Lueck, T. J., & Severson, K. (2006, December 6). New York bans most trans fats in restaurants. *New York Times,* A1.

Lunau, K. (2012, October 1). Fat but fit. *Maclean's, 125*(38), 51–54.

Lupton, D. (1995). *The imperative of health: Public health and the regulated body.* London: Sage.

Lupton, D. (2012). *Medicine as culture: Illness, disease, and the body.* London: Sage.

Lusk, J. (2013, May 6). Viewpoint: The new food police are out of touch. *Time.* http://ideas.time.com/2013/05/06/viewpoint-the-new-food-police-are-out-of-touch/.

Lustig, R. (2012). *Fat chance: Beating the odds against sugar, processed food, obesity, and disease.* New York: Hudson Street Press.

Lustig, R. (2013, February 27). Still believe "a calorie is a calorie?" *Huffington Post* http://www.huffingtonpost.com/robert-lustig-md/sugar-toxic_b_2759564.html.

Luu, E. (2009, October 9). Cookies, cakes, anything Mommy bakes banned at school. NBC News. http://www.nbcnewyork.com/news/health/Cookies-Cake-Anything-Mommy-Bakes-Banned-At-School-63853297.html.

MacMillan, A. (2011, October 20). Moving out of high poverty areas may lower obesity. CNN. http://www.cnn.com/2011/10/20/health/high-poverty-areas-increase-obesity/index.html.

MacMillan, A. (2013, September 29). How to become an exercise addict. ABC News. http://abcnews.go.com/Health/Wellness/exercise-addict/story?id=20397942#11.

Macqueen, K. (2012, November 19). It's not all in your genes. *Mclean's, 125*(45), 66.

Madell, R. (2013). 13 Best obesity health blogs of 2013. *Healthline.* http://www.healthline.com/health-slideshow/best-obesity-blogs#3.

Magno, M. (2011, September). "I did it!" Best before and after weight-loss stories. *Fitness.* http://www.fitnessmagazine.com/weight-loss/success-stories/makeovers/i-did-it-best-before-and-after-weight-loss-stories/#page=3.

Main, E. (2012, August). Are GMOs making you fat? A new reason to be skeptical of Frankenfoods. *Prevention.* http://www.prevention.com/food/healthy-eating-tips/gmo-foods-linked-weight-gain.

Malkin, M., & Finn, N. (2013, October 21). Melissa McCarthy breaks silence on Elle cover controversy: "I picked the coat!" *E! News.* http://www.eonline.com/news/472687/melissa-mccarthy-breaks-silence-on-elle-cover-controversy-i-picked-the-coat.

Manage your feelings without food. (2013). *Weight Watchers* [website]. http://www.weight-watchers.com/util/art/index_art.aspx?tabnum=1&art_id=45611.

Manson, J. E. (2007, November). Health answers, please! *Glamour, 105*(11), 130.

Marcus, M. B. (2009, June 15). Town sets off on path to good health. *USA Today.,* http://www.lexisnexis.com.ezproxy.lib.utah.edu/hottopics/lnacademic.

Marcus, S. (2014, May 2). Gabourey Sidibe's speech on confidence is incredibly moving. *Huffington Post.* http://www.huffingtonpost.com/2014/05/02/gabourey-sidibe-confidence-speech_n_5255730.html.

Marier, M. (2010, June 11). The fat diaries: Confessions of a food addict. *Frum Forum* [website]. http://www.frumforum.com/the-fat-diaries-confessions-of-a-food-addict/.

Matson, J. (2012). High and dry in a food desert. *Scientific American, 306*(5), 96.

McClesky, C. M., & Shea, C. (2010). Too fat to fight. *Wall Street Journal, 256*(85), C4.

McCrady, R. (2014, April 8). Kim Kardashian parades her booty around in nude-toned bikini photoshoot. *US Weekly.* http://www.usmagazine.com/celebrity-body/news/kim-kardashian-booty-bikini-photoshoot-pictures-201484.

McDonogh, G. W. (1999). Cultural diversity in the U.S. South: Anthropological contributions to a region in transition. *American Anthropologist 101*(2), 453–464.

McGee, M. C. (1990). Text, context, and the fragmentation of contemporary culture. *Western Journal of Speech Communication, 54,* 274–289.

McIndoo, H. R. (2011, November). 6 ways to stop overeating. *Prevention.* http://www.prevention.com/weight-loss/weight-loss-tips/tips-how-stop-overeating.

McKerrow, R. E. (1989). Critical rhetoric: Theory and praxis. *Communication Monographs, 56*(2), 91–111.

McLeod, C. (2008, December 20). China wrestles with growing obesity. *USA Today.* http://www.usatoday.com/news/world/2008-12-18-chinaweight_n.htm.

Meacham, J. (2010, March 29). It's a global problem. *Newsweek 155*(13), 37.

Medifast weight loss plan. (2013). http://www.medifast.com/.

Medina, J. (2009, October 2). A crackdown on bake sales in city schools. *New York Times.* http://www.nytimes.com/2009/10/03/nyregion/03bakesale.html.

Melissa McCarthy responds to Rex Reed's cruel comments about her body. (2013, June 13). *Huffington Post.* http://www.huffingtonpost.com/2013/06/13/melissa-mccarthy-rex-reed- response_n_3435596.html.

Melius, J. (2013). Overweight and obesity in minority children and implications for family and community social work. *Social Work and Public Health, 28*(2), 119–128.

Melnick, M. (2011, March 31). Global spread: More people think "fat people are lazy." *Time.* http://healthland.time.com/2011/03/31/global-spread-more-people-think-fat-people-are-lazy/.

Men's Health [website]. (2013). http://www.menshealth.com/.

Miles, K. (2013, January 10). "Fat genes" determine obesity, UCLA study says. *Huffington Post.* http://www.huffingtonpost.com/2013/01/10/fat-genes-obesity-ucla-study-diet-exercise_n_2450108.html.

Million, M., Lagier, J.-C., Yahav, D., & Paul, M. (2013). Gut bacterial microbiota and obesity. *Clinical Microbiology & Infection, 19*(4), 305–313.

Mindlin, A. (2008, December 24). The battle over the greens. *New York Times.* http://www.nytimes.com/2008/02/24/nyregion/thecity/24cart.html?scp=8&sq=produce+carts&st=nyt.

Mississippi tips the scale as most obese state. (2009, July 18). NBC News. http://www.msnbc. msn.com/id/25722208/ns/health-diet_and_nutrition/t/miss-tips-scale-most-obese-state/#.UIiGkMXR5cV.

Mississippi tops U.S. obesity rankings. (2009, July 1). CNN News. http://www.cnn.com/2009/ HEALTH/07/01/obesity.rankings/index.html?iref=allsearch.

Monde, C. (2013, April 1). Joan Rivers sticks to "fat" Adele comments after singer demands apology. *New York Daily News*, comments. http://www.nydailynews.com/entertainment/ gossip/joan-rivers-sticks-fat-adele-comments-article-1.1304702.

Morales, T. (2009, January 24). Why 'French women don't get fat.' CBS News. http://www. cbsnews.com/stories/2009/01/12/earlyshow/leisure/books/main666429.shtml.

Morris, M. (2012, November 12). Why Adele's body image rocks. *Cosmopolitan*. http://www. cosmopolitan.com/celebrity/news/adele-body-image.

Morris-Cafiero, H. (2013, April 23). Pictures of people who mock me. Salon.com [website]. http://www.salon.com/2013/04/23/pictures_of_people_who_mock_me/.

Moss, M. (2013a, February 24). (Salt + fat$^2$/satisfying crunch) x pleasing mouth feel = A food designed to addict. *New York Times Magazine*, 34–48.

Moss, M. (2013b). *Salt, sugar, fat: how the food giants hooked us*. New York: Random House.

Moss, M. (2013c, August 28). Wooing us down the aisle. *New York Times, 162*(56242), D1-D5.

Moye, D. (2012, May 8). Susanne Eman, 800-pound bride, fitted for world's biggest wedding gown. *Huffington Post*. http://www.huffingtonpost.com/2012/05/07/800-pound-bride-susanne-eman_n_1498377.html.

Moye, D. (2013, May 10). Tammy Jung vows to force feed herself to 420 pounds. *Huffington Post*. http://www.huffingtonpost.com/2013/05/10/tammy-jung-force-feeding-_n_3248307. html#slide=1208737.

Mullainathan, S. (2013, November 10). The co villains behind obesity's rise. *New York Times*, D6.

Nagourney, E. (2008a, August 5). Patterns: In older neighborhoods, less weight gain. *New York Times*. http://www.nytimes.com/2008/08/05/health/research/05patt.html?_ r=1&scp=44&sq=obesity&st=nyt.

Nagourney, E. (2008b, September 22). Nutrition: Soda bans in schools has little impact. *New York Times*. http://www.nytimes.com/2008/09/23/health/nutrition/23nutr.html?s cp=76&sq=obesity&st=nyt.

Nelson, S. C. (2013, March 13). Wendy Phillips admits "I'm too fat to work." *Huffington Post*. http://www.huffingtonpost.co.uk/2013/03/13/30st-wendy-phillips-admits-im-too-fat-to-work-wont-lose-weight-nhs-gastric-band_n_2866131.html.

Neporent, L. (2013a, January 22). Stigma against fat people the last prejudice, study finds. *Good Morning America*, ABC News. http://abcnews.go.com/Health/stigma-obese-acceptable-prejudice/story?id=18276788.

Neporent, L. (2013b, September 25). Confessions of a temporarily fat yogi. ABC News. http:// abcnews.go.com/blogs/health/2013/09/25/confessions-of-a-temporarily-fat-yogi/.

Nerlich, B., & Halliday, C. (2007). Avian flu: The creation of expectations in the interplay between science and the media. *Sociology of Health and Illness, 29*(1), 46–65.

Nerz, R. (2006). *Eat this book*. New York: St. Martin's Press.

Nestle, M. (2002). *Food politics: How the food industry influences nutrition and health*. Berkeley, CA: University of California Press.

Nestle, M. (2006). *What to eat: An aisle-by-aisle guide to savvy food choices and good eating*. New York: North Point Press.

Neuman, W. (2010a, July 24). Ad rules stall, keeping cereal a cartoon staple. *New York Times*, A1.

Neuman, W. (2010b, October 14). Group seeks food labels spelling out a downside. *New York Times*, B3.

Newbold, R. R., Padilla-Banks, E., Jefferson, W. N., & Heindel, J. J. (2008). Effects of endocrine disruptors on obesity. *International Journal of Andrology, 31*, 201–208.

Nixon, R. (2012, January 26). New rules for school meals aim at reducing obesity. *New York Times*, A22.

No longer just 'adult onset.' (2012, May 7). *New York Times*, A22.

Nodecker, N. (2014). Pamper yourself: 12 post-workout treats. *Weight Watchers* [website]. http://www.weightwatchers.com/util/art/index_art.aspx?tabnum=1&art_id=32521&sc=113.

Noppa, H., & Bengtsson, C. (1980). Obesity in relation to socioeconomic status: A population study of women in Goteborg, Sweden. *Journal of Epidemiology and Community Health, 34,* 139–142.

Norris, M. L., Boydell, K. M., Pinhas, L., & Katzman, D. K. (2006). Ana and the internet: A review of pro-anorexia websites. *International Journal of Eating Disorders, 39*(6), 443–447.

Nunez, A. (2011, July 7). Top 10 inspiring quotes from celebrities about working out. *Shape.* http://www.shape.com/celebrities/celebrity-workouts/top-10-inspiring-and-famous-quotes-celebrities-about-working-out.

O'Brien, S. (2009, October 24). Latino in America. CNN. http://www.lexisnexis.com.tproxy01.lib.utah.edu/us/lnacademic/results/docview/docview.do?docLinkInd=true&risb=21_T8381366379&format=GNBFI&sort=RELEVANCE&startDocNo=1&resultsUrlKey=29_T8381366382&cisb=22_T8381366381&treeMax=true&treeWidth=0&selRCNodeID=85&nodeStateId=411en_US,1,74&docsInCategory=60&csi=271063&docNo=24.

O'Dea, J. A. (2008). Gender, ethnicity, culture and social class influences on childhood obesity among Australian schoolchildren: Implications for treatment, prevention and community education. *Health Social Care in Community, 16*(3), 282–290.

Obese enjoy eating food less and less. (2008, October 20). CBS News. http://www.cbsnews.com/stories/2008/10/17/health/webmd/main4528147.shtml?tag=mncol;lst;3.

Obese in America. (2014). MSN. http://healthyliving.msn.com/weight-loss/obese-in-america#6.

Obese model pitches 'Heart Attack Grill.' (2010, November 15). ABC News. http://abcnews.go.com/Health/video/obese-spokesmodel-promotes-heart-attack-grill-12153251.

Obesity and overweight. (2012). World Health Organization. http://www.who.int/mediacentre/factsheets/fs311/en/.

Obesity bigger threat than terrorism? (2006, March 1). CBS News Online. http://www.cbsnews.com/stories/2006/03/01/health/main1361849.shtml.

Obesity highest in Southeast, Appalachia. (2010, November 19). CBS News. http://www.cbsnews.com/stories/2009/11/19/health/main5711014.shtml?tag=mncol;lst;2.

Obesity, lack of insurance take toll on young Americans. (2009, February 19). *U.S. News & World Report.* http://health.usnews.com/health-news/diet/fitness/diabetes/articles/2009/02/19/obesity-lack-of-insurance-take-toll-on-young.

Obesity less of a stigma for black women than white. (2011, December 7). *Huffington Post.* http://www.huffingtonpost.com/2011/12/07/obesity-less-of-a-stigma-for-black-women-than-white-women_n_1135343.html.

Obesity update 2012. (2012). Organization for Economic Cooperation and Development. http://www.oecd.org/els/healthpoliciesanddata/49716427.pdf.

Ogden, C. L., & Carroll, M. D. (2010). Prevalence of overweight, obesity, and extreme obesity among adults: United States, trends 1960–1962 through 2007–2008 (Figure 1). Centers for Disease Control. http://www.cdc.gov/nchs/data/hestat/obesity_adult_07_08/obesity_adult_07_08.pdf.

Okeowo, A. (2011, December 12). Seeing the latest amenity as an imposition. *New York Times*, A21.

Okrent, A. M., & Alston, J. M. (2012). The effects of farm commodity and retail food policies on obesity and economic welfare in the United States. *Agricultural Economics 94*(3), 611–646.

Oliver, J. E. (2006). *Fat politics: The real story behind America's obesity epidemic.* Oxford: Oxford University Press.

Oliwenstein, L. (2008, June 12). Weighty issues for parents. *Time.* http://www.time.com/time/magazine/article/0,9171,1813953,00.html.

Olsen, N. J., & Heitmann, B. L. (2008). Intake of calorically sweetened beverages and obesity. *Obesity Reviews, 10,* 68–75.

Olshansky, S. J., Passaro, D. J., Hershow, R. C., Layden, J., Carnes, B. A., Brody, J., . . .Ludwig, D. S. (2005). A potential decline in life expectancy in the United States in the 21st century. *New England Journal of Medicine, 352*,1138–1145.

One thing that has disgusted you today. [Forum Thread.] (2013, April 3 [started]). *MyProAna*[website]. http://www.myproana.com/index.php/topic/5781-one-thing-that-has-disgusted-you-today/.

Ono, K. A., & Sloop, J. M. (1995). The critique of vernacular discourse. *Communication Monographs, 62*, 19–46.

Opinions on fat people—be honest! [Forum Thread.] (2013, April 3 [started]). *MyProAna* [website]. http://www.myproana.com/index.php/topic/5746-opinions-on-fat-people-be-honest/.

Orloff, B. (2009, January 5). Oprah blames weight gain on abusing food. *People Magazine.* http://www.people.com/people/article/0,,20250039,00.html.

Overweight and obesity. (2014). Centers for Disease Control. http://www.cdc.gov/obesity/data/adult.html.

Overweight and obesity: Adult obesity facts. (2013). Centers for Disease Control. http://www.cdc.gov/obesity/data/adult.html.

Paarlberg, R. L. (2010). *Food politics: What everyone needs to know.* New York: Oxford University Press.

Park, A. (2008a, July 9). The kiddie cholesterol debate. *Time.* http://www.time.com/time/health/article/0,8599,1821153,00.html.

Park, A. (2008b, September 8). Losing weight: Can exercise trump genes? *Time.* http://www.time.com/time/health/article/0,8599,1839708,00.html.

Park, A. (2009a, February 10). Mother's obesity raises risks of birth defects. *Time.* http://www.time.com/time/health/article/0,8599,1878549,00.html.

Park, A. (2009b, November 12). Another cause of obesity: The bacteria in your gut? *Time.* http://www.time.com/time/health/article/0,8599,1938023,00.html.

Park, M. (2009, July 3). Speed eaters gain weight, clog arteries but have few regrets. CNN. http://www.cnn.com/2009/HEALTH/07/03/competitive.eating.stomach/index.html?eref=ib_us/.

Park, M. (2011, January 11). She ate 162 school lunches. CNN. http://www.cnn.com/2011/HEALTH/01/21/nutrition.year.review/index.html?iref=allsearch.

Parker-Pope, T. (2007, December 5). A high price for healthy food. *New York Times.* http://well.blogs.nytimes.com/2007/12/05/a-high-price-for-healthy-food/.

Parker-Pope, T. (2008, October 13). Healthful message, wrapped in fiction. *New York Times.* http://www.nytimes.com/2008/10/14/health/14well.html?scp=42&sq=obesity&st=ny.

Parker-Pope, T. (2010, September 15). Makers seek new name for syrup. *New York Times,* D1.

Parker-Pope, T. (2013, September 23). Craving an ice cream fix. *New York Times,* A18.

Parks, S. E., Housemann, R. A., & Brownson, R. C. (2003). Differential correlates of physical activity in urban and rural adults of various socioeconomic backgrounds in the United States. *Journal of Epidemiology and Community Health, 57*(1), 29–35.

Paul, A. M. (2008, July 13). Too fat and pregnant. *New York Times.* http://www.nytimes.com/2008/07/13/magazine/13wwln-essay-t.html?pagewanted=print&_r=0.

Paying it forward (success stories). (2014). Weight Watchers [website]. http://www.weight-watchers.com/success/art/index.aspx?SuccessStoryId=19961&sc=17.

Pear, R., & Bennett, K. (2011, April 30). Soft drink industry fights proposed food stamp ban. *New York Times,* A11.

Peeke, P. M. (2012, October 26). 7 ways to beat your food addiction. Fox News. http://www.foxnews.com/health/2012/10/25/6-ways-to-beat-your-food-addiction/.

Perrine, S., & Hurlock, H. (2010, March 8). Fat epidemic linked to chemicals run amok. NBC News (Men's Health). http://www.nbcnews.com/id/35315651/ns/health-diet_and_nutrition/t/fat-epidemic-linked-chemicals-run-amok/#.UkiOIYa9HnM.

Person, D. (2009, September 30). No southern comfort in obesity. *USA Today*.http://usato-day30.usatoday.com/printedition/news/20090930/column30_st.art.htm.

Peters, A. (2011). The selfish brain: Competition for energy resources. *American Journal of Human Biology, 23*(1), 29–34.

Phillipov, M. (2013). Resisting health: Extreme food and the culinary abject. *Critical Studies in Media Communication, 30*(5), 385.

Pifer, E. (2014, June 19). 5 ways to trick yourself into getting out of bed for a morning workout. *Women's Health*. http://www.womenshealthmag.com/fitness/early-morning-workout-motivation.

Pincott, J. (2013, April 29). Diet strategies: Trick your brain so you actually want to eat less. *Huffington Post*. http://www.huffingtonpost.com/2013/04/29/diet-strategies-eat-less-weight-loss-tips_n_3132291.html.

Pollan, M. (2001, May 13). Naturally. *New York Times Magazine*. http://www.nytimes.com/2001/05/13/magazine/naturally.html?pagewanted=all&src=pm.

Pollan, M. (2003, October 12).The (agri)cultural contradictions of obesity. *New York Times Magazine, 152*(52634), 41–48.

Pollan, M. (2006). *Omnivore's dilemma: A natural history of four meals*. New York: Penguin.

Pollan, M. (2007, November 4). Weed it and reap. *New York Times, 157*(54118), 15.

Pollan, M. (2008). *In defense of food: An eater's manifesto*. New York: Penguin.

Pollan, M. (2011, October 28). High-fructose corn syrup not necessarily worse than sugar. *Huffington Post*. http://www.huffingtonpost.com/2011/10/28/michael-pollan-high-fructose- corn-syrup-sugar_n_1064246.html.

Pollan, M. (2013, May 15). Some of my best friends are germs. *New York Times*. http://www.nytimes.com/2013/05/19/magazine/say-hello-to-the-100-trillion-bacteria-that-make-up-your-microbiome.html?pagewanted=all.

Porter, N. (2013, November 7). FDA aims to eliminate artificial trans fats. *Washington Times*. http://www.washingtontimes.com/news/2013/nov/7/fda-aims-eliminate-artificial-trans-fats/?page=all.

Poverty main cause of obesity. (2011, August 28). NBC News. http://www.msnbc.msn.com/id/20476824/ns/health-diet_and_nutrition/t/poverty-main-cause-obesity-problem-south/#.UIg8tsXR5cV.

Powell, L. M., Slater, S. & Chaloupka, F. (2004). The relationship between community physical activity settings and race, ethnicity and socioeconomic status. *Evidence-Based Preventive Medicine, 1*(2), 135–144.

Pretlow, R. A. (2011, April 18). Those %@#! comfort food commercials. *Fooducate* [website]. http://blog.fooducate.com/2011/04/18/those-comfort-food-commercials/.

Probyn, E. (2001).*Carnal appetites: FoodSexIdentities*. London: Routledge.

Pudgy Pet Rescue. (2013). *Shape, 32*(5), 98.

Rabin, R. C. (2008, January 22). In the fatosphere, big is in, or at least accepted. *New York Times*. http://www.nytimes.com/2008/01/22/health/22fblogs.html?_r=0.

Rabin, R. C. (2009a, December 15). New goal for the obese. *New York Times*, D1.

Rabin, R. C. (2009b, June 9). Bad habits asserting themselves. *New York Times*, D5.

Rampell, C. (2010,January 15). Rich people exercise more. *New York Times*. http://economix.blogs.nytimes.com/2010/01/15/rich-people-exercise-more/?_r=0.

Ramshaw, E. (2011, January 16). Life expectancy: On the border, long lives despite dismal statistics. *New York Times*, A27.

Ray, K. (2012). Gut microbiota: Adding weight to the microbiota's role in obesity—exposure to antibiotics early in life can lead to increased adiposity. *Nature Reviews Endocrinology, 8*(11), 623.

Raymond, J. (2009, March 26). Big belly, bad memory. *Newsweek*. http://www.newsweek.com/id/129147/page/1.

Restaurants fight NYC calories-on-menu law. (2008, June 22). *USA Today*. http://www.usato-day.com/news/health/weightloss/2008-04-22-nyc-menu_n.htm.

Reynolds, G. (2011, November 29). Feeling fat in those genes? *New York Times,* A5.

Reynolds, G. (2012, January 11). Exercise hormone may fight obesity and diabetes. *New York Times.* http://well.blogs.nytimes.com/2012/01/11/exercise-hormone-helps-keep-us-healthy/?_php=true&_type=blogs&_r=0.

Rice, F. (2013, September 30). 30 inspirational body confidence quotes from women who know what they're talking about. *Marie Claire.* http://www.marieclaire.co.uk/blogs/543637/30-inspirational-celebrity-body-confidence-quotes.html.

Rich, M. (2008, June). Too much television? *Parents, 83*(7), 40–44.

Rivera, R. (2008, August 28). Council vote for good health may weaken business at groceries in poor neighborhoods. *New York Times.* http://www.nytimes.com/2008/02/28/nyregion/28grocer.html?_r=1&scp=98&sq=obesity&st=nyt.

Rizzo, M. (2009, April 13). How I let myself go. *People Magazine.* http://www.people.com/people/archive/article/0,,20271043,00.html.

Rizzo, M. (2010, February 28).Carnie Wilson battle of the bulge. *People Magazine.* http://www.people.com/people/archive/article/0,,20350709,00.html.

Roberts-Grey, G. (2013). Be healthy at every size. *Essence, 44*(3), 84–86.

Rochman, B. (2009, July 6). First comes love, then comes obesity? *Time.* http://www.time.com/time/magazine/article/0,9171,1907143,00.html.

Rodriguez, C. Y. (2013, October 17). Beautiful but deadly: Latinos' curves put them at risk. CNN News. http://www.cnn.com/2013/10/15/health/latino-cardiovascular-disparities/.

Roff, P. (2013, May 3). Bloomberg pizza satire hits too close to home. *U.S. News & World Report.* http://www.usnews.com/opinion/blogs/peter-roff/2013/05/03/bloombergs-food-policing-is-out-of-control.

Roll, G. (2005, October 6). Big-farm subsidies versus food stamps. *Christian Science Monitor, 97*(220), 9.

Rosen, M. D. (2011, February). Gaga for gadgets. *Parents, 86*(2), 110–116.

Rosenthal, E. (2008, September 24). Fast food hits Mediterranean: A diet succumbs. *New York Times.* http://query.nytimes.com/gst/fullpage.html?res=9E06E6DD1F3DF937A1575AC0A96E9C8B63&scp=4&sq=obesity&st=nyt.

Rossen, J., & Davis, J. (2014, April 22). Experts say you can trick your mind into helping you lose weight. NBC *Today Show.* http://www.today.com/news/experts-say-you-can-trick-your-mind-helping-you-lose-2D12178338.

Rosten, E. (2004, June 7). The corn connection. *Time, 163*(23), 83.

Roth, G. (2008). The cookie burglar. *Good Housekeeping, 246*(3), 139–142.

Rothfield, P. (1992). Backstage in the theatre of representation. *Arena, 99/100,* 98–111.

Rovzar, C. (2010, December 27). Woman eats 30,000 calories for Christmas meal. *New York Magazine.* http://nymag.com/daily/intelligencer/2010/12/woman_eats_30000_for_christmas.html.

Rubin, B. S. (2011). Bisphenol A: An endocrine disruptor with widespread exposure and multiple effects. *Journal of Steroid Biochemistry and Molecular Biology, 127,* 27–34.

Rubin, C. (2013, November 11). Battling fat? Get more sleep. *U.S. News Digital Report, 5*(41), 20.

Ruderman, Z. (2010, May 24). The 10 best weight loss tips ever. *Cosmopolitan.* http://www.cosmopolitan.com/health-fitness/advice/a3223/10-best-weight-loss-tips-ever-0809/.

Saad-Filho, A., & Johnston, D. (2004). *Neoliberalism: A critical reader.* London: Pluto.

Saelens, B., J. Sallis, L. Frank. (2003). Environmental correlates of walking and cycling: Findings from the transportation, urban design, and planning literatures. *Annals of Behavioral Medicine, 25*(2), 80–91.

Saguy, A. C. (2013). *What's wrong with fat?* New York: Oxford University Press.

St. George, D. (2008, December 2). Media bombardment linked to ill effects during childhood. *Washington Post.* http://www.washingtonpost.com/wpdyn/content/article/2008/12/01/AR2008120102920.html.

Saslow, E. (2013, November 9). Too much of too little. *Washington Post.* http://www.washingtonpost.com/sf/national/2013/11/09/too-much-of-too-little/.

Saul, S. (2008, April 3). Menu fight over calories leads doctor to reject post. *New York Times*, A2.

Saul, S. (2009, April 3). Drug makers race to cash in on nation's fat. *New York Times*. http://www.nytimes.com/2009/04/03/business/03fat.html?_r=2&pagewanted=print&%23038;position=&.

Savage, L. (2013, June 24). The sleep crisis. *Maclean's, 126*(24), 1.

Savran, D. (1996). The sadomasochist in the closet: White masculinity and the culture of victimization. *Differences: A Journal of Feminist Cultural Studies, 8,* 127–152.

Sawer, M. (1996). Gender, metaphor and the state. *Feminist Review, 52,* 118–134.

Schiffman, R. (2013, September 23). We need to end antibiotics use in meat production now. *Huffington Post.* http://www.huffingtonpost.com/richard-schiffman/we-need-to-end-antibiotics_b_3966755.html.

Schlosser, E. (2001). *Fast food nation.* New York: Houghton-Mifflin.

Schmidt, C. (2014, May 3). Jennifer Lawrence to Lena Dunham. *Today Show,* NBC. http://www.today.com/style/jennifer-lawrence-lena-dunham-15-inspiring-celebrity-quotes-about-body-2D79604323.

Schneider, H. (2008, September 9). Report shows why it's smart to get your belly dancing. *Washington Post,* HE03. http://www.lexisnexis.com.tproxy01.lib.utah.edu/hottopics/lnacademic/.

Schulte, B. (2008, May 22). The search for solutions: Getting kids to think about changing exercise, eating habits is one thing; keeping them on track is another. *Washington Post,* B1.

Schwarz, H. (1986). *Never satisfied: A cultural history of diets, fantasies, and fat.* New York: Free Press.

Sciammacco, C. (2001). Health. *Ladies' Home Journal, 118*(6), 60.

Scocca, T. (2011, April 3). Why walk when you can stroll? *New York Times,* WK.

Seacrest, R. (Producer), & Smith, B. (Director). (2010–2011). *Jamie Oliver's food revolution* [television series]. Los Angeles, CA: Ryan Seacrest Productions.

Secrets of the Slimmest Countries. (2010). *Shape, 29*(5), 100.

Seidenberg, C. (2012, February 23). All fats are not created equal. *Washington Post,* T13.

*Self Magazine* [website]. (2013). http://www.self.com.

Selling candy to kids. (2011, November 19). *New York Times,* 20.

Sender, K. (2006). Queens for a Day: *Queer Eye for the Straight Guy* and the neoliberal project. *Critical Studies in Media Communication, 23*(2), 131–151.

Sepkowitz, K. (2013, November 25). This is why your kid is fat. *The Daily Beast.* http://www.thedailybeast.com/articles/2013/11/25/this-is-why-your-kid-is-fat.html.

Severson, K. (2005, March 9). So much for squeaky clean cookies. *New York Times,* F4.

Shalikashvili, J. M., & Shelton, H. (2010, April 30). The latest national security threat: Obesity. *Washington Post.* http://www.washingtonpost.com/wpdyn/content/article/2010/04/29/AR2010042903669.html.

Shapiro, E. (2013, January 21). The one I left behind. *People Magazine, 79*(2), 57–58.

Shapiro, M. A., & Chock, T. M. (2004). Media dependency and perceived reality of fiction and news. *Journal of Broadcast and Electronic Media, 48*(4), 675–795.

Sharma, A. (2013). PTDS risk factor for weight gain. DrSharma.com [website]. http://www.drsharma.ca/ptsd-risk-factor-for-weight-gain.html.

Shell, E. R. (2002). *The hungry gene: The inside story of the obesity industry.* New York: Grove.

Shilling, C. (1991). Educating the body: Physical capital and the production of social inequalities. *Sociology, 25*(4), 653–672.

Shirley, C. D. (2010). "You might be a redneck if . . ..": Boundary work among rural, southern whites. *Social Forces, 89*(1), 35–61.

Shortridge, J. R. (1989). *Middle West: Its meaning in American culture.* Lawrence, KS: University Press of Kansas.

Shugart, H. A. (2010). Consuming citizen: Neoliberating the obese body. *Communication, Culture, and Critique, 3*(1), 105–126.

Shugart, H. A. (2011). Heavy viewing: Emergent frames in contemporary news coverage of obesity. *Health Communication, 26*(7), 635–648.

Shugart, H. A. (2013). Weight of tradition: Culture as an explanatory device for obesity in contemporary U.S. news coverage. *Obesity Reviews 14*(9), 736–744.

Shugart, H. A. (2014). Flesh made word: The obese body as cultural matter. *Communication, Culture, and Critique,* 7(1), 55–75.

Sinkler, J. (2013, August 4). Push your limits. *Men's Health.* http://www.menshealth.com/fitness/instafit-push-your-limits.

Smith, F. (2004). Lose weight for good. *Health, 18*(6), 160–205.

Smith, R. (2007). Overcoming obesity. Oprah.com [website. http://www.oprah.com/oprahradio/Overcoming-Obesity.

Smith, R. (2009). Carnie Wilson. Oprah.com [website]. http://www.oprah.com/spirit/Carnie-Wilson.

Sobal, J., & Maurer, D. (Eds.) (1999). *Weighty issues: Fatness and thinness as social problems.* New York: Aldine de Greuter.

Sokolov, R. (1999). Culture and obesity. *Social Research, 66*(1), 31–36.

Sole-Smith, V. (2011). Control your cravings for good. *Fitness Magazine.* http://www.fitnessmagazine.com/weight-loss/eating-help/control-cravings/how-to-control-cravings/.

Some find competitive eating hard to swallow. (2007, November 21). NBC News. http://www.nbcnews.com/id/21915036/ns/health-behavior/t/some-find-competitive-eating-hard-swallow/#.U0rfGfnwbnN.

Soong, J. (2014). 7 habits of highly effective exercisers. *Fitness Magazine.* http://www.fitnessmagazine.com/workout/motivation/habits-of-effective-exercisers/.

Southern states remain country's fattest. (2010, May 25). CBS News. http://www.cbsnews.com/stories/2008/07/17/health/main4269403.shtml?tag=mncol;lst;9.

Speakman, J. R. (2008). Thrifty genes for obesity, an attractive but flawed idea, and an alternative perspective: The 'drifty gene' hypothesis. *International Journal of Obesity, 32*(11), 1611–1617.

Spencer, M. (2003, April 12). "I'm fat, I'm greedy, and I'm fabulous. *The Guardian.* http://www.theguardian.com/lifeandstyle/2003/apr/13/foodanddrink.features7.

Springen, K. (2008, November 7). Six facts about belly fat. *Newsweek.* http://www.newsweek.com/id/168129/.

Squires, S. (2008, July 22). Which diet's best? That's up to you. *Washington Post.* http://www.lexisnexis.com.tproxy01.lib.utah.edu/us/lnacademic/results/docview/docview.do?docLinkInd=true&risb=21_T8381208004&format=GNBFI&sort=RELEVANCE&startDocNo=1&resultsUrlKey=29_T8381208007&cisb=22_T8381208006&treeMax=true&treeWidth=0&selRCNodeID=25&nodeStateId=411en_US,1,23,12&docsInCategory=1&csi=8075&docNo=1.

Srirachapea. (2012, November 28). (Personal post). Fat is not attractive. Tumblr [website]. http://fatisnotattractive.tumblr.com/.

Stahlhut, R. W., van Wijngaarden, E., Dye, T. D., Cook, S., & Swan, S. H. (2007). Concentrations of urinary phthalate metabolites are associated with increased waist circumference and insulin resistance in adult U.S. males. *Environmental Health Perspectives, 115*(6), 876–888.

Stars' body confidence secrets. (2009, April).*Good Housekeeping, 248*(4), 60.

Start saying goodbye to belly fat. (2008, November 1). *The Early Show,* CBS. http://www.cbsnews.com/stories/2008/11/01/earlyshow/health/main4562801.shtml?tag=contentMain;contentBody.

Stein, J. (2012, May 7). Instant gratification. *Time, 179*(18), 58.

Stein, R. (2004, January 16). U.S. says it will contest WHO plan to fight obesity. *Washington Post,* A8.

Stein, R. (2009, December 17). Research links obesity to bacteria in digestive tract. *Washington Post.* http://www.washingtonpost.com/wpdyn/content/article/2009/12/20/AR2006122001271.html.

Stengel, R. (2008, June 12). A full plate. *Time.* http://www.time.com//time/magazine/article/0,9171,1813973,00.html.

Stewart, J. B. (2013, July 20). Richer farmers, bigger subsidies. *New York Times, 162*(56203), B1–B5.

Stoller, G. (2007, July 17). Hotels serve lighter fare for healthy appetites. *USA Today,* D6.

Storrs, C. (2011, January 19). Hormones in food: Should you worry? *Health.* http://www.health. com/health/article/0,,20458816,00.html.

Study: Kids with obesity-linked gene drawn to fattening foods. (2008, December 12). *USA Today.* http://www.usatoday.com/news/health/weightloss/2008-12-12-obesity-gene_ n.htm.

Sulzberger, A. G. (2012, January 12). Meatless in the midwest: A tale of survival. *New York Times.* http://www.nytimes.com/2012/01/11/dining/a-vegetarians-struggle-for-sustenance-in-themidwest.html?pagewanted=1&_r=1.

Summers, N. (2009, April 24). The economics of eating. *Newsweek.* http://search.newsweek. com/search?q=obesity+and+summers.

Swami, V., & Tovee, M. J. (2009). Big beautiful women: The body size preferences of male fat admirers. *Journal of Sex Research, 46*(1), 89–96.

Sweet escape. (2008). *Teen Vogue, 8*(2), 49.

Sy, S., & Hodd, S. (2009, October 1). 'Fat acceptance': Women embrace the F-word. ABC News. http://abcnews.go.com/Nightline/size-model-overweight-women-embraces-curves/ story?id=8541567.

Szabo, L. (2008, December 2). Report: TV, internet harm kids. *USA Today* http://www.usato-day.com/news/health/2008-12-01-media_N.htm?csp=34.

Szabo, L. (2012, September 19). High levels of BPA linked to obesity in kids, teens: Metabolism-changing chemical "obesogens" could be at work. *USA Today,* 4D.

Szabo, L. (2013, June 6). Genetic link to early puberty found: Mutations could be responsible for a growing trend. *USA Today,* 5D.

Szabo, L., Grossman, C. L., & Vegano, D. (2009, October 20). $30M set for study of plastics chemical. *USA Today,* 5D.

Szalavitz, M. (2008, December 30). Why falling off the wagon isn't fatal. *Time.* http://www. time.com/time/health/article/0,8599,1868965,00.html.

Tan, M. (2008, December 1). New year, new weight struggle. *People Magazine, 71*(1), 48–49.

Tan, M. (2009, June 22). I'm sick of being big. *People Magazine.* http://www.people.com/peo-ple/archive/article/0,,20287201,00.html.

Taubes, G. (2011, April 17). Is sugar toxic? *New York Times Magazine,* 47.

Taubes, G. (2012, May 14). New obesity campaigns have it all wrong. *Newsweek, 159*(20), 32–36.

Taubes, G. (2007). *Good calories, bad calories: Challenging the conventional wisdom on diet, weight control, and disease.* New York: Knopf.

Taubes, G. (2011). *Why we get fat and what to do about it.* New York: Knopf.

Tauzin, A. (2007). Women of Mauritania: Cathodic images and presentation of the self. *Visual Anthropology, 20*(1), 3–18.

Thayer, K. A., Heindel, J. J., Bucher, J. R., & Gallo, M. A. (2012). Role of environmental chemicals in diabetes and obesity: A national toxicology program workshop review. *Environmental Health Perspectives,*120(6), 779–789.

The 25 best diet tricks of all time. (2014). *Health.* http://www.health.com/health/gallery/ 0,,20645166_16,00.html.

The checkup: Health in the news and in your life. (2008, December 16). *Washington Post,* HE02.

The Dove® campaign for real beauty. Dove.com [website]. http://www.dove.us/Social-Mission/ campaign-for-real-beauty.aspx.

The fat of the land. (2009, August 1). *Wall Street Journal, 254*(27), A10.

The fat trap. (2012, January 22). *New York Times Magazine.* 8.

The last course. (2012, December 15). *Economist, 405*(8815), 16.

The most inspiring weight-loss success stories of 2013. (2013, December 23). *Shape.* http:// www.shape.com/weight-loss/success-stories/most-inspiring-weight-loss-success-stories-2013/slide/4.

The state has no place in the lunch bags of a nation. (2011, May 2). *Maclean's, 124*(16), 4–5.

Thielman, S. (2012, August 3). Ad of the day: Southern Comfort struts out first work from Weiden + Kennedy. *Adweek*. http://www.adweek.com/news/advertising-branding/ad-day-southern-comfort-142444.

Thompson, E. (2014, February 11). You have to see Kim Kardashian's ass in this photo. *Cosmopolitan*. http://www.cosmopolitan.com/celebrity/news/kim-kardashian-pants.

Thore, K. (2013, May 3). How to work out when you totally don't want to. *Women's Health*. http://www.womenshealthmag.com/fitness/gym-motivation-strategies.

Timberlake, J. M., & Williams, R. H. (2012). Stereotypes of U.S. immigrants from four global regions. *Social Science Quarterly, 93*(4), 867–890.

Time spent on healthy cooking, exercise are tradeoffs in average American's day, study finds. (2013, April 15). *Huffington Post*. http://www.huffingtonpost.com/2013/04/15/healthy-cooking-exercise-tradeoffs_n_3061276.html.

Toomey, A. (2013a, June 13). Melissa McCarthy response to Rex Reed's "obese," "hippo" jabs in *Identity Theft* review. *E! News*. http://www.eonline.com/news/429660/melissa-mccarthy-responds-to-rex-reed-s-obese-hippo-jabs-in-identity-theft-review.

Toomey, A. (2013b, October 18). Covered-up Melissa McCarthy magazine cover draws criticism. *Today Show*. http://www.today.com/entertainment/covered-melissa-mccarthy-magazine-cover-draws-criticism-8C11418627.

Trotter, K. (2012, December 11). Getting off the couch and in workout mode. *Huffington Post*. http://www.huffingtonpost.ca/kathleen-trotter/motivating-yourself-to-exercise_b_2115311.html.

Trout, J. (2014, January 3). Jennifer Lawrence body-shames you more than you might realize. *Huffington Post*. http://www.huffingtonpost.com/jenny-trout/jennifer-lawrence-body-shaming_b_4521379.html.

Trumbull, M. (2012, May 8). Bake sale ban in Massachusetts sparks outcries over "food police." *Christian Science Monitor*, 1.

Tunick, B. (2005, January). Does eating meat make people fat? *Vegetarian Times, 327*, 95.

Tuning into the 'Oprah Diet.' (2005). *Tufts University Health and Nutrition Letter 23*(4), 6.

Turits, M. (2014). How to convince yourself to work out when you so don't want to. *Glamour*. http://www.glamour.com/health-fitness/2012/09/how-to-convince-yourself-to-work-out-when-you-dont-want-to/7.

Turner, B. (1996). *The body and society: Explorations in social theory* (2nd ed.). London: Sage.

"Twinkie apocalypse. (2012, January 12). CNN. http://news.blogs.cnn.com/2012/01/12/overheardon-cnn-com-twinkie-apocalypse-averted-for-time-being/?iref=allsearch.

Underwood, B. (2011, January). Small loss, big benefit. *Self, 33*(1), 66.

Unger, R. H., & Scherer, P. E. (2010). Gluttony, sloth and the metabolic syndrome: A roadmap to lipotoxicity. *Trends in Endocrinology & Metabolism, 21*(6), 345–352.

Unhealthy boom. (2013, February 9). *New Scientist, 217*(2903), 7.

U.S. diabetes rate doubles in last decade. (2009, February 11). CBS News. http://www.cbsnews.com/stories/2008/10/30/health/main4559539.shtml?tag=mncol;lst.

U.S. immigrants get supersized. (2011, May 12). NBC News. http://www.nbcnews.com/id/43009734/ns/health-diet_and_nutrition/#.Utq2ABDn_AU.

U.S.D.A National Nutrient Database for Standard Reference. (2013). http://ndb.nal.usda.gov/.

Usner, D. H. (2009). *Indian work, language, and livelihood in Native American history*. Cambridge: Harvard University Press.

van Pelt-Belle, H. (2012, January 11). De gustibus. *New York Times*. http://www.nytimes.com/2012/01/11/dining/de_gustibus.html?pagewanted=1&_r=1.

Vang, A., Singh, P. N., Lee, J., Haddad, E. H. & Brinegar, C. H. (2008). Meats, processed meats, obesity, weight gain and occurrence of diabetes among adults: Findings from Adventist health studies. *Annals of Nutrition & Metabolism, 52*(2), 96–104.

Vannini, P., & Williams, J. P. (Eds). (2009). *Authenticity in culture, self, and society*. Surrey, UK: Ashgate.

Vlahos, J. (2008, July 13). Pill-popping pets. *New York Times*. http://www.nytimes.com/2008/07/13/magazine/13petst.html?_r=1&scp=101&sq=obesity&st=nyt.

Vranica, S. (2008, June 23). High fructose corn syrup mixes it up. *Wall Street Journal, 251*(146), B7.

Waller, J. (2013, August 2). How to understand fitness supplements and get ripped. *FHM*. http://www.fhm.com/upgrade/mens-style/how-to-understand-fitness-supplements-and-get-ripped-84211.

Wallinga, D. (2010). Agricultural policy and childhood obesity. *Health Affairs, 29*, 405–410.

Walls, H. L., Peeters, A., Proietto, J., & McNeil, J. J.(2011). Public health campaigns and obesity: A critique. *BMC Public Health, 11*, 136–143.

Walsh, B. (2008, June 12). It's not just genetics. *Time*. http://www.time.com/time/magazine/article/0,9171,1813984,00.html.

Wang, Y., & Beydoun, M. A. (2009). Meat consumption is associated with obesity and central obesity among U.S. adults. *International Journal of Obesity, 33*(6), 621–628.

Warner, M. (2006, February 7). Does this good make you groan? *New York Times, 155* (53628), C1–8.

Warner, M. (2010, May 2). For corn syrup, the sweet talk gets harder. *New York Times*. http://www.nytimes.com/2010/05/02/business/02syrup.html?ref=melaniewarner.

Warren, T. (2013, September 2). Dumping the junk. *Jet, 122*(13), 11.

We're fat not invisible. Pinterest [message board]. http://www.pinterest.com/helenhirst/diet-inspiration/.

We Can! [website]. (2013). National Institutes of Health. http://www.nhlbi.nih.gov/health/public/heart/obesity/wecan/.

Weaver, C. (2012, September 18). The plus-size MRI machine. *Wall Street Journal, 256*(44), 11.

Weber, B. R. (2009). *Makeover TV: Selfhood, citizenship, and celebrity*. Durham, NC: Duke University Press.

Wei, Y., Zhu, J., & Nguyen, A. (2013, July 8). Urinary concentrations of dichlorophenol pesticides and obesity among adult participants in the U.S. National Health and Nutrition Examination Survey (NHANES) 2005–2008. *International Journal of Hygiene and Environmental Health*. http://www.ncbi.nlm.nih.gov/pubmed/23899931.

Weight Watchers [website]. (2013). http://www.weightwatchers.com/plan/eat/index.aspx.

Weil, E. (2012, March 30). Puberty before age 10: A new normal? *New York Times Magazine*. http://www.nytimes.com/2012/04/01/magazine/puberty-before-age-10-a-new-normal.html?pagewanted=all.

Weise, E. (2008, December 9). New data not so sour on corn syrup. *USA Today*, 7D.

What causes overweight and obesity? (2014). *National Institutes of Health*. http://www.nhlbi.nih.gov/health/health-topics/topics/obe/causes.html.

When your body is your cage . . . Ana can be the key to your freedom! (2014). Missanamia [website]. http://missanamia.wordpress.com/motivation/.

Whitaker, D., Milam, A. J., Graham, C. M., Cooley-Strickland, M., Belcher, H. M., & Furr-Holden, C. D. (2013). Neighbourhood environment and urban schoolchildren's risk for being overweight. *American Journal of Health Promotion, 27*(6), 410–416.

Why that salad costs more than a Big Mac. (2010, October). *Reader's Digest, 177*(1060), 72.

Wilkinson, I. (2013, March 27). Pregnant Kim Kardashian is being fat shamed, and it needs to stop. *Daily Beast*. http://www.thedailybeast.com/articles/2013/03/27/pregnant-kim-kardashian-is-being-fat-shamed-and-it-needs-to-stop.html.

Wilson, E. (2010, January 13).The triumph of the size 12s. *New York Times*. http://www.nytimes.com/2010/01/14/fashion/14CRYSTAL.html?pagewanted=all&_r=0.

Winfrey, O. (Producer). (1986–2011). *The Oprah Winfrey show*. Chicago, IL: Harpo Productions.

Winfrey, O. (2009, January). What I know for sure. *O, The Oprah Magazine, 10*. 190.

Wingert, P., & Kantrowitz, B. (2009, May 28). Double trouble. *Newsweek*. http://www.newsweek.com/id/139031/page/1.

Withrow, D., & Alter, D. A. (2010). The economic burden of obesity worldwide: A systematic review of the direct costs of obesity. *Obesity Reviews, 12*(2), 131–141.

Wood, D. B. (2012, June 27). Supersize America: Whose job is it to fight obesity? *Christian Science Monitor*, 1.

Yee, D. (2009, March 5). Combating Southern fried food. CBS News. http://www.cbsnews.com/stories/2005/02/14/health/main673897.shtml?tag=mncol;lst.

Zezima, K. (2008, August 8). Increasing obesity requires new ambulance equipment. *New York Times*. http://www.nytimes.com/2008/health/08ambu.html?r=1&scp=10&sq=obesity&st=nyt.

Zoller, H. M. (2008). Technologies of neoliberal governmentality: The discursive influence of global economic policies in public health. In H. M. Zoller & M. J. Dutta (Eds.), *Emerging perspectives in health communication: Meaning, culture, and power* (pp. 390–410). New York: Routledge.

# Index

9/11, 7, 17, 143

acquired immune deficiency syndrome (AIDS),
15, 17, 19
agribusiness, 43–47
Big Food, 48, 53, 64
food lobbies, 42, 46–47
agricultural subsidies, 44–47
antibiotics, 9, 20, 41–42, 45, 62
authentic selfhood, 89–90, 101, 103–104, 146

Big Gulp, 9, 62–63, 65
Bloomberg, Michael, 9, 43, 117–118
body mass index (BMI), 2, 5

capitalism, 10, 90
childhood obesity, 1, 7, 22–27, 53, 56
competitive eating, 119–120, 122
concentrated animal feeding operations
(CAFOs), 45
corn, 45–47, 68
Corn Refiners Association, 42, 47
cultural criticism, 1, 3, 13–15, 106, 149

Farm Bill, 44, 47
fat
celebration of, 3, 109–110, 113–114, 121, 123
cultural meanings, 2–5, 18
discrimination, 6, 15, 63, 67, 106
as feminine, 4, 102, 106, 111–112, 116–117,
122–124, 127, 134, 141
fetishism, 114–117, 124, 129
maternal role in, 60–61, 99–100, 102, 111–112
morality of, 3–6, 8–9, 21, 24–25, 28, 64, 92,
101, 105, 111, 127, 137, 150
as spectacle, 6, 110, 128–135, 141
fat gene, 58–59, 61
fat panic, 6, 106–107
financial crisis, 8–9, 11–12, 144–145, 147

food addiction, 93–94, 139
food deserts, 36, 38, 63

gastric bypass, 29, 31, 94
genetically modified organisms (GMOs),
9, 48, 62
green carts, 62–63

Health at Every Size (HAES), 107–109
healthism, 25
high-fructose corn syrup (HFCS), 39,
42–43, 45–47
hormones, 9, 41–42, 55, 138

materiality, 17–18
microbiota, 41, 61–62
moral panic, 6, 106
Moss, Michael, 47–48, 118

nanny statism, 24, 63–64, 117–118, 123. See also
paternalism
Nestle, Marion, 46–47
New Deal, 44
nostalgia, 32, 55–58

Obama, Michelle, 22, 136
obeseconomy, 6, 21, 106
obesity campaigns, 22–23, 126, 145
Childhood Obesity Prevention, 22–24
Let's Move!, 22–26, 136
We Can!, 22–26
Occupy Wall Street, 11–12, 144

paternalism, 22, 24, 26, 63. See also nanny
statism
pesticides, 9, 20, 41–42
plastics, 20, 43

political economy, 9, 11, 14, 25, 144, 147
Pollan, Michael, 41, 43, 46, 118

repression, 88, 90, 94, 96, 99, 101, 141, 152
rhetoric, 15–16, 89, 111–112, 128

Schlosser, Eric, 46
science (of obesity), 1, 20–21, 38–40, 49, 138, 140, 150
self-actualization, 12, 89–90, 98, 101–104, 107, 112–113, 124, 142, 145–146, 148
self-expression, 94, 96–97, 103, 113–114, 124, 149, 152
self-monitoring, 30, 33, 125, 133, 141–142, 145, 151
sexuality, 4, 113, 117, 124

slavery, 68–69, 73, 75
soul food, 72–73
stress, 20, 53–55, 89–95, 101, 104
sugar, 30, 36, 39–43, 46–47, 53, 63, 82, 117, 123, 138

technology, 53, 57
trans fats, 9, 42–43, 62–63, 117

Winfrey, Oprah, 13, 89–91, 95, 98–99
work
    cause of obesity, 52–56, 59, 64–65, 76, 82, 101
    physical labor as exercise, 73, 75, 79, 136
    work on self, 89, 94–96, 98, 103

Underground Railroad, 75–76